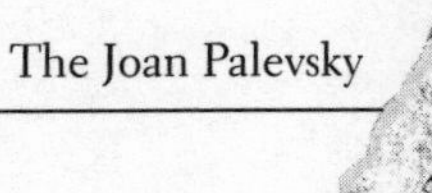

The Joan Palevsky Imprint in Classical Literature

In honor of beloved Virgil—

"O degli altri poeti onore e lume . . ."

—Dante, *Inferno*

The publisher gratefully acknowledges the generous contribution to this book provided by the Classical Literature Endowment Fund of the University of California Press Associates, which is supported by a major gift from Joan Palevsky.

Landscapes, Gender, and Ritual Space

Landscapes, Gender, and Ritual Space

The Ancient Greek Experience

SUSAN GUETTEL COLE

University of California Press
BERKELEY LOS ANGELES LONDON

University of California Press
Berkeley and Los Angeles, California

University of California Press, Ltd.
London, England

Library of Congress Cataloging-in-Publication Data

Cole, Susan Guettel.
Landscapes, gender, and ritual space : the ancient Greek experience / Susan Guettel Cole.
p. cm.
Includes bibliographical references and index.
ISBN 0–520–23544–4 (alk. paper).
1. Greece—Religion. 2. Women—Religious life—Greece—History. 3. Sacred space—Greece—History. 4. Artemis (Greek deity)—Cult. I. Title.

BL795.W65 C65 2004
292.3′5—dc21 2003018995

Manufactured in Canada
13 12 11 10 09 08 07 06 05 04
10 9 8 7 6 5 4 3 2 1

The paper used in this publication is both acid-free and totally chlorine-free (TCF). It meets the minimum requirements of ANSI/NISO Z39.48–1992 (R 1997) *(Permanence of Paper)*. ♾

In memory of Jack Winkler

Contents

Preface

In the very early stages of this project I ran into Jack Winkler at a convention, and he asked me, as he usually did when our paths crossed, what I was working on. I replied, "An article on gender and Greek ritual practice." When I began to describe the collection of epigraphical material in my file drawer, however, he interjected, "That doesn't sound like an article; it sounds like a book!" Our conversation continued as people hurried off to the next sessions and the hall emptied. We sat down at a deserted table, and over a paper plate piled high with French fries, I sketched out the problems. As we dipped fries into ketchup, we talked about developing a context deeper than the one normally provided for discussions of ancient ritual practice. Jack became more and more interested, and while we slowly made our way through the fries, we outlined a book. This was the late 1980s, when Jack was working on *Constraints of Desire* and was himself interested in the extended meaning of "slack" and "taut" in ancient discussions that connect behavior with male body type. For the female body, the contrast between wet and dry seemed, on the face of it, related to issues of pollution, and given that this was the eighties, it should be no surprise that we both positioned these issues in the context of a project about the body; Jack even suggested the title *Watery Bodies*. We imagined a project with two parts. The first half of the book would explore the imagery of female rituals in the context of the broader issues of the body. The second half would target individual divinities and relate their ritual to the life of the city.

I did eventually write the article on the epigraphical material, but by then another file drawer had filled and the individual divinities for the second half of the project had narrowed to two: Artemis and Demeter. In the early nineties, under the influence of survey archaeologists and environmental historians, the ancient landscape had become a special focus of inquiry. Medical theory, archaeological deposits associated with springs, and the systematic placement of sanctuaries of Artemis and Demeter in relation to natural sources of water suggested new connections between the productivity of the landscape, ritual, and female physical function. A National Endowment for the Humanities Summer Seminar on the Greek city in 1990 with Roger Bagnall and twelve energetic colleagues provided the opportunity for sustained and systematic on-site examination of important *poleis* on the Greek mainland, the islands of the Aegean, and in western Turkey as far east as Aphrodisia. As a result, what had begun in the eighties as a book on the body became, in the nineties, a book about landscapes.

I began the real work on the manuscript in 1990–91, with support from the Institute for the Humanities at the University of Illinois at Chicago. Continuing support from the College of Liberal Arts and Sciences and the Baldy Research Group on Gender, Law, and Social Policy at the University of Buffalo kept work going during a decade of teaching and administrative responsibilities. In 1996–97, as an NEH Fellow at the National Humanities Center in North Carolina, I wrote the chapters on landscape, ritual space, and Greek medical theory. By then the project had outgrown the originally planned two parts. Demeter had become too large a subject, and because she deserves it, she will have a book of her own—in many ways a continuation of this one. Artemis seemed the right choice to test the ideas worked out in the first half of the book; hence the chapters on her rituals here.

I have tried out pieces of this manuscript on university audiences in two Londons; in Munich, Paris, Atlanta, Boston, Tallahassee, Chapel Hill; and at meetings of the American Philological Association. The original article on epigraphical evidence for cult regulations appeared in *Helios* (now integrated into chapter 4); Artemis had a trial run with one article in *Classical World* (now with fuller documentation as chapter 6) and another in the volume titled *The Sacred and the Feminine in Ancient Greece,* edited by Sue Blundell and Margaret Williamson (now part of chapter 7). I am, as always, indebted to the interventions of audiences and editors, whose questions and comments helped to focus the issues, and grateful to the publishers who have granted permission to use material that has appeared in other forms elsewhere.

As the project has developed I have been influenced by discussions with many interested critics, in particular Cynthia Patterson, Darice Birge, Helene Foley, Martha Malamud, Chris Faraone, Carolyn Dewald, Seth Schein, Ann Hanson, Dirk Obbink, Sarah Johnston, Jan Bremmer, and Lesley Dean-Jones. Readers will recognize my debts to Michael Jameson, Pauline Schmitt Pantel, and the editors of *Supplementum Epigraphicum Graecum.*

An invitation from Mogens Hansen to participate in the 1994 sessions of the Copenhagen Polis Project provided the opportunity to test my ideas on city gods. I have been challenged by my own students—in particular the ten who braved a seminar on Greek epigraphy at the University of Michigan in 1988, and, at the University of Buffalo, Francesca Behr, Paul Kimball, Almira Poudrier, Michelle Perkins, and Allison Glazebrook. Holly Hamister, Rachel Van Dusen, David Tolcacz, Fiona Crimmins, and Jonathan Strang helped to check the notes and bibliography. Charles Stewart, Carolyn Higbie, and Vance Watrous read with a critical eye large chunks of chapters at formative stages. Barbara Tedlock, Madeline Kaufmann, and Pat Donovan tested the final version for clarity and coherence. At the finish I was saved from many an error by the broad experience—generously shared—of the readers for University of California Press. At the Press itself Kate Toll and Cindy Fulton have offered much, and readers owe a debt of thanks to Carolyn Bond for her sound advice on consistency. The project itself has changed with the times, but I would like to think that Jack Winkler would still recognize the argument, and would be happy to find the book he once helped me to imagine now dedicated to him.

Abbreviations

Abbreviations of the names and works of classical authors follow the *Oxford Classical Dictionary*[3]; periodical titles are abbreviated according to *L'année philologique;* epigraphical references follow *Supplementum Epigraphicum Graecum* (www.let.leidenuniv.nl/history/seg/seg.htm#abbreviations). Other abbreviations are as follows:

Bekker, *Anecdota Graeca*	J. Bekker. *Anecdota Graeca* I–III. 1824–21.
Buck	C. D. Buck. *The Greek Dialects.* Chicago 1955.
Diggle	J. Diggle. *Tragicorum Graecorum Fragmenta Selecta.* Oxford 1998.
FGrH	F. Jacoby. *Die Fragmente der griechischen Historiker.* Leiden 1926–58, reprint 1954–60.
Fouilles de Delphes	*Fouilles de Delphes* III *Inscriptions.* Paris 1910–.
GHI I²	R. Meiggs and D. Lewis. *A Selection of Greek Historical Inscriptions* I²: *To the End of the Fifth Century B.C.* Oxford 1969.
GHI II	M. N. Tod. *A Selection of Greek Historical Inscriptions* II: *From 403 to 323 B.C.* Oxford 1948.
GMP	H. D. Betz. *The Greek Magical Papyri in Translation.* Chicago 1986.
Guarducci Epigrafica	M. Guarducci. *Epigrafia Greca* 1–4. Rome 1978, reprinted 1995.

IMiletos — A. Rehm and P. Herrmann. *Inschriften von Milet* I. Berlin 1997.

IOSPE — B. Latyschev. *Inscriptiones antiquae orae septentrionalis Ponti Euxini Graecae et Latinae* 1–4, 1885–1916.

ICrete — M. Guarducci. *Inscriptiones Creticae* 1–4. Rome 1935–50.

IThessaly — J.-C. Decourt. *Inscriptions de Thessaly* I. Paris 1995.

LIMC — *Lexicon Iconographicum Mythologiae Classicae* 1–9. Zurich 1981–99.

LSAG^{2} — L. H. Jeffery. *The Local Scripts of Archaic Greece.* Oxford 1961 with 1990 supplement.

LSAM — F. Sokolowski. *Lois sacrées de l'Asie mineure.* Paris 1955.

LSCG — ———. *Lois sacrées des cités grecques.* Paris 1969.

LSS — ———. *Lois sacrées des cités grecques. Supplément.* Paris 1962.

Meritt and Traill — B. D. Meritt and J. S. Traill. *The Athenian Councillors.* Vol. 15, *The Athenian Agora.* Princeton 1974.

SEG — *Supplementum Epigraphicum Graecum.*

SIG^{3} — W. Dittenberger. *Sylloge Inscriptionum Graecarum*^{3} 1–4. 1915–24.

Staatsverträge II — H. Bengston. *Die Staatsverträge des Altertums 2: Die Verträge der griechisch römischen Welt von 700 bis 338 vor Chr.*^{2} Munich 1975.

TrGF — Stefan Radt. *Tragicorum Graecorum Fragmenta* 4: Sophocles. Göttingen 1977.

Ziehen — J. de Prott and L. Ziehen. *Leges Graecorum Sacrae.* Leipzig 1906.

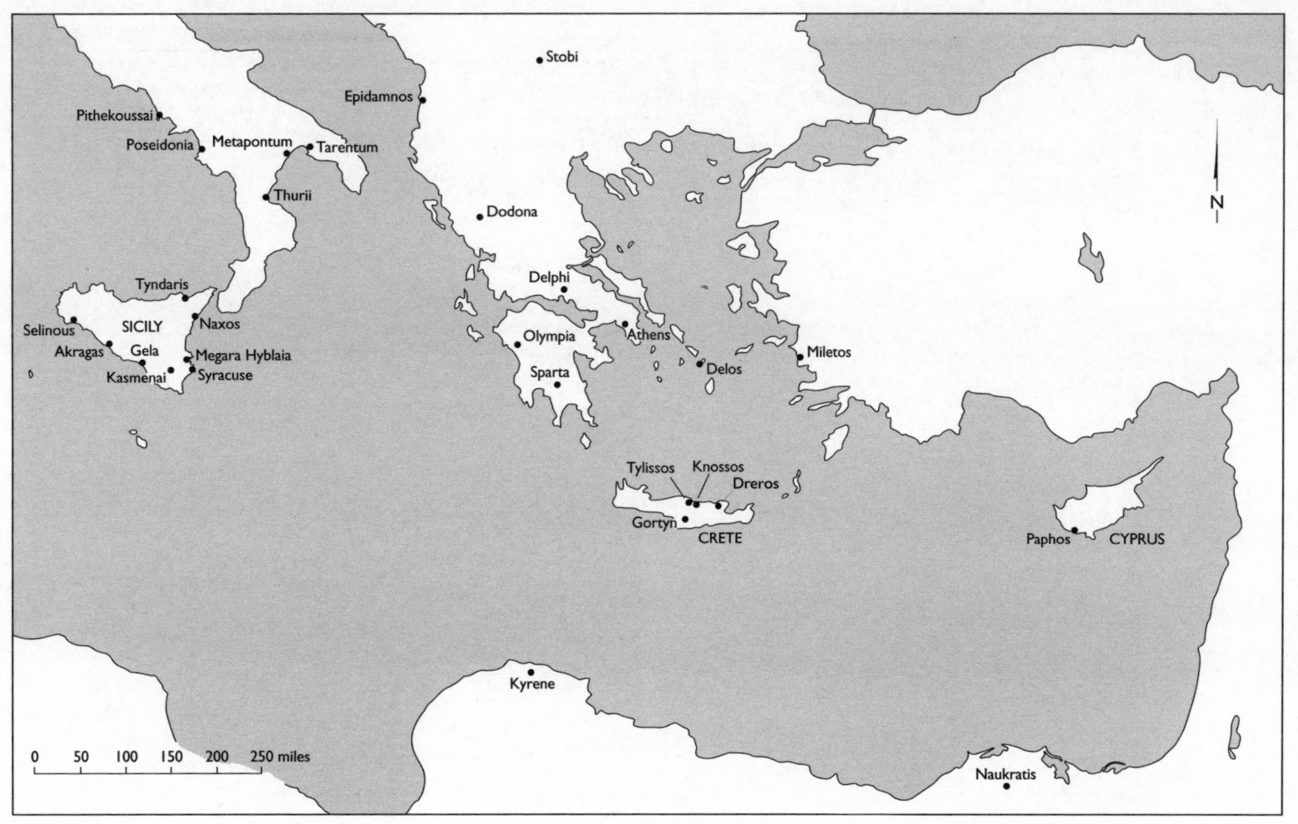

Map 1. The Eastern Mediterranean

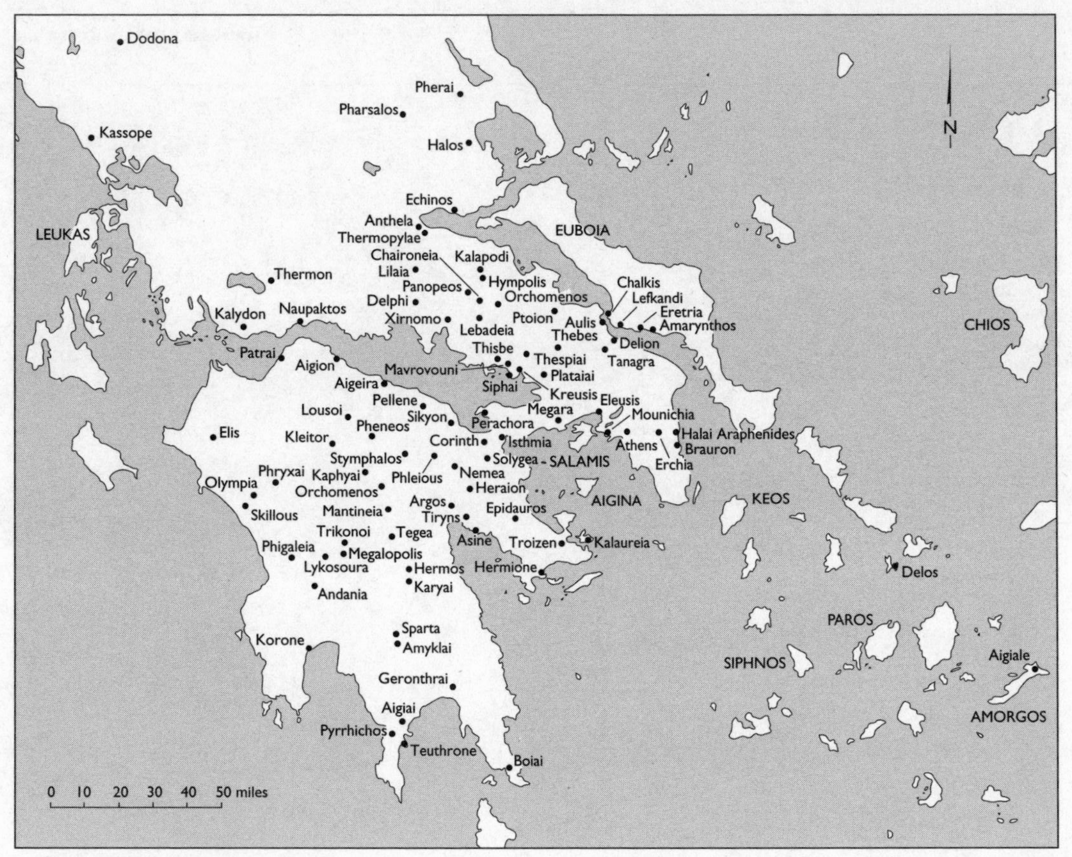

Map 2. Greece and the Western Aegean

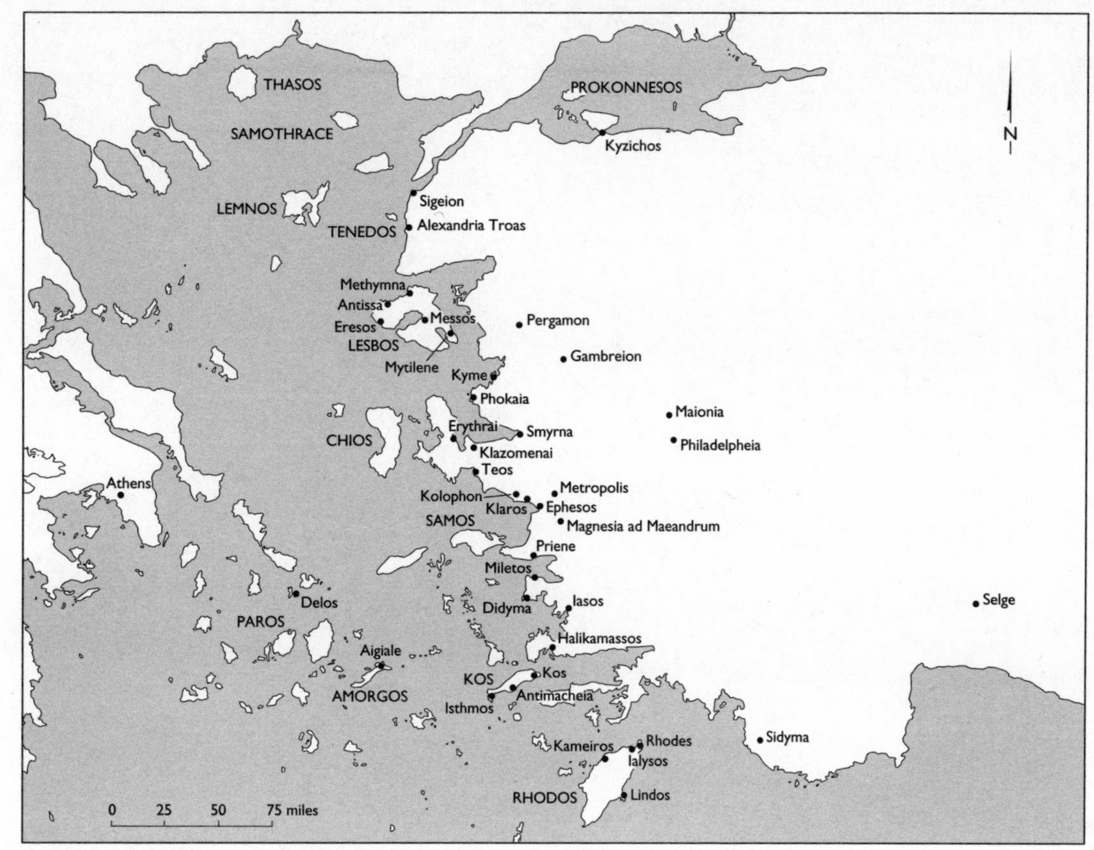

Map 3. Asia Minor and the Eastern Aegean

Introduction

Every individual is nested inside a protective cover of layered identities. Like a colorfully painted Russian *matriuschka* doll containing a whole series of dolls, one inside the other, each person is defined by a combination of relationships. Identities can be taken out, tried on, and displayed one by one to the outside world. Collective and corporate structures work the same way. At different times in the life span of a community, as in the lifetime of an individual, one or another of the layered markers will emerge as dominant, but other markers are never entirely hidden, nor are they effects entirely dormant. Whether a society emphasizes the individual—what we call the self—or chooses to emphasize the collective identity of the group, the issues that divide as well as bind always remain the same: gender, race, ethnicity, political affiliation, citizenship, language, and the habits of everyday life.

Every group has a set of recognizable features or traditional customs by which to differentiate itself from its neighbors and bind its members to a common core. Above all, each identifiable community craves a place to claim as home. Claims are articulated in a variety of ways, but the need for sustenance binds populations very strongly to the land. For the Greeks, the earth (Ge or Gaia) was mother of all—not only feminine in grammatical gender but female in function: source of nourishment and birth mother of the gods. In English it is a short leap from "home" to "homeland," but in Greek, "home" was simply "house," *oikia,* related to *oikos,* "household" or "family." "Homeland," *patris* or *patra,* was a more loaded and challenging idea. *Patris* and *patra* refer to the inherited land claimed by lineages real or imagined and passed down in the male line. Both words were formed with feminine endings on a stem that means not "mother" but "father." The undifferentiated earth was *mother*, but the land bounded by recognizable borders and a territory to be defended was a *father*land.[1]

The imagery of kinship permeated the discourse of public life. In the Archaic period the terminology of family structure defined relationships between old and new cities. A branch settlement—what nineteenth- and twentieth-century historians called a "colony"—the Greeks termed *apoikia*, "a home away from home." The founding city was the "mother-city," *metropolis*. "Mother" cities and "daughter" cities often claimed special ties, but in practice both mothers and daughters were fickle. Cities were "related" to each other by stories of original patterns of foundation but even more by myths of their far-traveling heroes and heroines. Mythical predecessors bred the children required by later descendants in need of ancestors in order to construct fictitious ties of blood with their allies. Claims of consanguinity came naturally to people who accepted descent from local heroes or ancient ancestors born from the earth. At Athens, political differences could not mask the claims of common rituals, and even the disruptions of civil strife could not diminish the rhetorical value attached to shared ancestors.[2]

In the Hellenistic period, when donors were singled out and lavishly praised for their support and concern on behalf of the city, citizens attributed to benefactors the affection of a father for his children.[3] The complexity of political life was ameliorated by stressing the context and security of family relationships. The genealogies that had given shape to the early *polis* in the Archaic period were now adapted to a new political situation. Cities learned to exploit claims of kinship to impart vitality to the diplomatic maneuvers that tied them together. They cemented alliances with the language of common descent and established a tradition of "kinship diplomacy" that lasted into the Roman period.[4]

Claims of consanguinity are only part of the traditional explanation for the common ties between *poleis*, though relationships based on claims of kinship and blood were basic. Herodotus lists four elements that determined what he calls "the Hellenic factor": the same blood, the same tongue, common rituals and shared sanctuaries, and the same habits or way of life.[5] Recent discussions of ethnicity treat these categories as if they

1. L'Homme-Wéry (2000), for the term in Homer, Solon, and early tragedy.
2. Xen. *Hell.* 2.4.20.
3. *IPriene* 108; see also van Bremen (1996) 156–70.
4. Jones (1999).
5. Hdt. 8.144.

were exhaustive, adequate to account for the synergy of nature and culture, the patterns of human interaction with the divine, and the forms of linguistic and symbolic expression that define cultural identity. Another issue, however, largely ignored in such discussions,[6] also requires analysis. That issue—one that intersects with each of Herodotus's four categories in a powerful way—is gender. Herodotus himself does not have a term for the concept, but he is never immune to its effects. In his accounts of the various populations living around the Mediterranean, issues of gender are always just beneath the surface, emerging especially at moments of crisis.

Transactions of gender are a social universal, but every society handles them in its own way and expresses them culturally in its own voice. The ancient Greeks were no different; but when we look for evidence of gender in social interaction, we detect only its consequences. We rarely perceive the actual transaction itself, whether that transaction takes place between individuals or on the larger map of the community. For one thing, gender operates in a context that obscures the process. The experience of dividing and consolidating territory during the early period of the *polis* illustrates the problem. Division of the agricultural territory and allotment of plots to lineages were mirrored in the ritual sphere by the permanent allotment of sacred land to gods. As distinctions deepened between sacred land (reserved for ritual) and agricultural land (restricted to lineages), distinctions between purity and pollution were also sharpened. The process of distinguishing sacred land from productive land resulted in ritual distinctions that recognized real divisions between male and female. We are unable to perceive the division in process. We can notice only the result—in the case of cult practice, expressed in distinctions between purity and pollution. The reproductive capacities that associated females with the agricultural processes of the productive landscape also divided them from sacred space. Not surprisingly, the same ritual system that defined female reproductive processes as polluting placed a high value on female purity in public rituals.

In the Greek *polis,* transactions of gender were played out in a political environment very different from that of other cultural systems around the ancient Mediterranean. For the Greeks, possession of land and house was tied to participation in the political community—an inherited privilege. Because land was originally allotted not to individuals but to lineages, marriage was a locus of anxiety. The same conditions that allotted to the indi-

6. For instance the essays collected in Malkin (2001). The work (on Italy) collected in Cornell and Lomas (1997) constitutes an exception.

vidual male the obligation to cultivate a piece of land also made him responsible for choosing his own wife. These two issues were tied together. Marriage provided the means, and the wife provided the instrument, for securing the allotment *(kleros)* to the lineage for the next generation. Burdens could be heavy. Maintaining minimum levels of agricultural production to sustain a family was always a concern—one complicated by anxiety about female fertility and, for the head of household, anxiety about establishing unchallenged claims to paternity.

In most areas inhabited by Greeks, the unit of political management was the *polis.* Its territory was usually small by modern standards. A central core settlement or town center could contain as few as a couple of hundred adult males. The essential feature was the land, the *chora,* organized around an administrative center and distinguished from neighboring territories by marked boundaries at the frontiers. Stone boundary markers *(horoi)* placed in the soil to mark territory and to distinguish one type of space from another symbolized the various types of space within a divided landscape. These boundary stones were visible on both public and private land, and they designated the limits of different spaces: the edges of a family's holding, the boundaries of a piece of land held as security for a loan on a woman's dowry, the limits of a sacred area restricted for ritual, the borders of a settlement, or the outer limits of a city's territory.

At Athens, the right to share in the government depended on membership in a family claiming descent from local heroes born from the local soil. Perikles in 451 narrowed the definition of citizen by requiring mothers as well as fathers to be by birth *astoi/astai,* "belonging to the city." Women were not participants in the government *(politeia),* nor were they included in the group covered by the expression "the people *(demos)* of the Athenians." Moreover, the term *Athenaios,* "Athenian," was largely restricted to males eligible to take part in political life and was used of females only for priestesses in public cult. Women were included only in the ethnic denominator "Attikoi/Attikai," which associated them with the land of Attika.[7] For females, the relationship to the local homeland was celebrated at the time of marriage by rituals that acknowledged a special tie to the water of a specific local spring.

Males achieved citizenship by birth and service, but a woman's status depended on her father's. Thucydides' Perikles advised obscurity for all women of Athens, and for females in families aspiring to respectability,

7. Patterson (1987).

anonymity was desirable. An Athenian male did all he could to keep his wife's name off other men's lips. When a female had to be mentioned in public, she was therefore more likely to be called by a patronymic than by her husband's name. Reference to a woman as the daughter of a citizen emphasized her legal status and automatically indicated the status of her children. Although a woman's purpose in marrying was to produce children for her husband's family, in name she remained her father's daughter. Consequently, a married woman bridged two identities. She was her husband's wife, but until she died she remained her father's daughter.

The discussion that follows examines how dividing the landscape into ritual space and productive space was related to the social articulation of gender as enacted in ritual. Each chapter pursues a different set of clues. The first three chapters lay out the conceptual issues of landscape and ritual space. The first chapter looks into the rationale for appropriation of territory by the individual *polis*. Chapters 2 and 3 consider the evidence for recognizing sacred space and explore the concept of a centered *polis* nested within the broader networks organized around regional sanctuaries and the institutions of the *prytaneion*.

The fourth and fifth chapters look at the meaning of the female body. Chapter 4 examines distinctions of gender in ritual practice and while demonstrating that women's ritual efforts were focused on reproduction and the health of the family, argues that requirements of purity narrowed the range of female performance. The contradiction inherent in attributing a high category of pollution to childbirth—the only experience where female achievement really counted—reflects the anxieties of a male population concerned about lineage, unpredictable agricultural production, and reproductive failure. Chapter 5 describes how anxieties about reproduction encouraged Hippocratic theorists to account for reproductive success or failure in terms of a relationship between the hydrology of the local landscape and the relative moisture of female bodies. Descriptions of the interior of the female body as a miniature landscape whose moisture content required regulation are consistent with a ritual system that segregated productive and sacred space.

The final two chapters target Artemis as a test case. They examine the location and placement of sanctuaries of Artemis in order to establish the meaning of the rituals so important to individual families and to the larger community of the *polis*. Sanctuaries of Artemis, whether integrated into the landscape or located in the town center, provide a record by which to measure a city's recognition of the contributions of its women.

Like the *matriuschka* doll encapsulated within several layers, every woman was more than she seemed because every woman was imagined to contain within herself a miniature landscape. With her own body, a mother passed on to her children an identity derived from the land—one celebrated at the time of marriage when she bathed with the pure local water that prepared her for the first night of marriage and confirmed her eligibility to become a mother of citizens.

1 Claiming a Homeland

THREE LANDSCAPES

Ancient Greek communities inhabited three landscapes: the natural, the human, and the imagined. The first was the landscape of the physical environment: the mountains, plains, flowing fresh water, and sea that nourished and sustained each community. For the Greeks, the natural world was a unity of land and water—the earth's limits bounded by the streams of the primordial ocean, its surface refreshed by the rivers and springs rising from waters circulating underground.[1]

The human landscape was always segmented, shaped by the needs of agriculture and the conventions of political organization. Agriculture divided the land into fields, which, whether scattered or contiguous, made up the holdings (*kleroi,* "allotments") distributed among families eligible for membership in the political community. Larger territorial units depended on the traditional local boundaries dividing one community from another.[2] In the world of the *polis,* political communities were locally based, and the connection between landholding and political status was replicated in the relationship between the marked fields of the agricultural territory allotted internally to individual lineages and the total externally bounded territory shared by the entire community.

The third landscape was an imagined landscape, joined to the known world but acknowledged to exist beyond the range of normal human experience and impossible for ordinary mortals to reach. This landscape had

1. Rudhardt (1971) 97–101.

2. Alcock (1993) 6, for the variety of meanings in the term "landscape"; 118, for emphasis on local boundaries even in periods of federation.

two parts. One was the imaginary realm belonging to fantastic mythical creatures, such as Amazons or centaurs, who were found beyond the cultivated fields of the civilized landscape—at the outer reaches of the known world[3] near the divine Ocean encircling the edges of the earth.[4] The other realm lay beyond the streams of Ocean and beyond the shadowy transitional space where such sinister creatures as Sirens, Gorgons, Geryon, and Cerberus were said to dwell.[5] This was the world of the dead, a place that could only be imagined, a space beneath the earth, without light, where the dead tried to imitate the living.

These three landscapes coexisted and merged with one another. The realities of the natural environment influenced the shape of political communities, and the resources of local landscapes set limits to agricultural production. Local boundaries, maintained by military contest and the traditions of political negotiation, followed the natural shape of the countryside. The individual *polis* incorporated physical elements of the natural landscape by recognizing shorelines, mountain heights, and watersheds as local boundaries. Political borders, however, were always subject to challenge and change. Stories of threatening creatures at the edges of the earth were inspired by the real tensions associated with maintaining local autonomy and represented the actual risks and anxieties associated with preserving territorial integrity. Similar anxieties emphasized the dangers of crossing cosmic boundaries at the edges of the earth—boundaries that could not be crossed by everyone. Even in myth, only Apollo could visit the land of the Hyperboreans beyond the streams of Ocean, and only privileged heroes could visit the underworld and return again to the land of the living. Human families could not really reinvigorate their own dead, though they tried to reach them by making offerings and pouring libations into the ground at marked grave sites.

The assumption that the earth itself was shared with the gods made it possible to imagine these three landscapes as joined. Stability and continuity required divine approval, represented in myth by negotiation and in experience by ritual. The universe, though considered physically unified, was politically divided. The gods themselves, when they swore their oaths by Earth, Sky, and the River Styx,[6] acknowledged the great natural, cosmic

3. Hall (1997) 50, on myths during the period of colonization.

4. Romm (1992).

5. Rudhardt (1971) 87, for sources. Aesch. *PV* 700–41; 780–806, for a catalogue.

6. Leto swears such an oath when she promises to guarantee Apollo's sanctuary on Delos; *Hymn. Hom. Ap.* 3.83–88.

boundaries; but their triple oath also emphasized the unity between these several spaces. Homer translated natural boundaries into political divisions. He explained that when the sons of Kronos divided the universe among themselves, Zeus was allotted the sky, Poseidon the sea, and their brother Hades the underworld, with the earth to be shared among all three.[7] In practice, however, the earth's gifts were considered controlled by their sister Demeter. Although as goddess of growing plants and patron of agriculture she was a great divinity in her own right, the Homeric division of divine authority assigned her a secondary role. As a result, with space divided between males and process assigned to a female, agricultural fragility was explained in terms of divine conflict. This conflict emphasized a basic tension between Demeter and Zeus and became a template for differences between male and female realms of authority.

Resolution of conflict required negotiation among the great divinities and recognition of a dynamic, three-way relationship between the natural landscape, the cultivated landscape, and the world of the dead. Divine conflict is the central problem of the mythic narrative known as the *Homeric Hymn to Demeter*, the story of the abduction of Demeter's daughter, Kore, by Hades, king of the dead.[8] The poem describes Demeter's search for her lost daughter, her attempt to immortalize a substitute child, her implacable anger when this plan failed, and the consequent disaster she inflicted on human populations. This disaster is described as a "terrible year" sent by the goddess, a single agricultural cycle when no crop grew, people died, and all sacrifice failed. Resolution of divine discord, with restoration of sacrifice in exchange for agriculture, was finally possible only after Zeus and Hades made concessions to Demeter and agreed to allow her daughter, now the bride of Hades, to return from the world of the dead for part of each year.

The story emphasizes the strength of the relationship between mother and daughter, the possible tensions between male and female, and the risks associated with the traditional mobility of women taken in marriage and required to divide their loyalties between parents and husbands. Demeter, goddess of agriculture, and her daughter, queen of the dead, were complementary figures who united the natural landscape, the cultivated landscape, and the realm of the dead.[9] As Persephone and spouse of Hades, the daugh-

7. *Il.* 15.187–93. For division of the universe in Near Eastern myth, see Burkert (1992) 90–91; Bremmer (1994).

8. Richardson (1974); Foley (1994).

9. Clay (1989) 208, 256, recognizes the role of Zeus in the *Homeric Hymn to Demeter* and emphasizes the tripartite division of Olympus, earth, and underworld.

ter represented the realm of the dead. As Kore and unwed virgin, she represented the spontaneous flowering growth of plants. Demeter, as mature female, regulated the growth of the cultivated crops that sustained the agricultural community of the *polis.* Recognizing the unity of mother and daughter, Attic women invoked them simply as "the Two."[10] The communal ritual of the Greek city-state recognized the close relationship between these two goddesses, the close relationship among the landscapes they inhabited, and the cosmic unity their relationship guaranteed.

USING THE LAND

The word used in the Homeric hymn to describe the effect of Demeter's terrible year is *limos,* "hunger" or "famine," the condition that results from crop failure and food shortage. The language of the hymn is consistent with the ecology of the agricultural regions of the Greek Aegean, where fluctuations in rainfall can produce periods of temporary shortfall.[11] Fresh water was always an issue. In a land where perennial rivers are few[12] and alluvial valleys rare,[13] settlement patterns were shaped by access to the groundwater stored in the porous limestone bedrock that often extended from the rugged mountain areas down to the lower plains.[14] The eastern Aegean exhibits a particular type of landscape characteristic of limestone areas, where water collects in underground catchments that Vitruvius describes in the following way:

> The valleys among the mountains receive the rains most abundantly, and on account of the thick woods, the snow stays there longer because of the shade of the trees and the mountains. Later, when it melts, it filters through the cracks in the ground and thereby reaches the foot of the mountains, where gushing springs come belching out.[15]

10. Ar. *Thesm.* 383, 566, etc.

11. Theophr. *Hist. Pl.* 8.7.6; *Caus. Pl.* 3.23.4, for the proverb: *ἔτος φέρει, οὔτι ἄρουρα* ("It is the year that matters, not the land"); see Jameson (1983); Gallant (1991) 46–48.

12. Pausanias, at 8.32.1, makes a point of describing the spring in the theater at Megalopolis as "ever-flowing" (*ἀέναος*). Contrast Plutarch's description of Attika, an area without perennial rivers and few copious springs; Plut. *Sol.* 23.5.

13. Higgins and Higgins (1996) 12–13.

14. Crouch (1993) 63–82; Higgins and Higgins (1996) 13–14.

15. Vitr. *De Arch.* 8.1.7.

City planners situated settlements to take advantage of these perennial springs,[16] which were necessary for the material needs of the community but also valued for ritual.[17]

The Greek Aegean enjoys a climate of dry summers, wet winters, and long growing seasons. Yet within the areas inhabited in antiquity by speakers of the Greek language there was, and still is, considerable environmental diversity[18]—a diversity related directly to the availability of water. On the Greek mainland ecological advantages are distributed unevenly. The eastern half of the mainland combines good harbors with scant resources. Here mild temperatures and a long growing season are compromised by thin soil, steep mountains, and limited rainfall. The western half of the mainland has fewer harbors but is endowed with heavier rainfall, richer soil, and forested mountains.[19] In antiquity, topography influenced development. The eastern sector's geographical orientation, convenient access to the sea, and proximity to a network of islands conveniently located for travel by sea contributed to interchange with western Anatolian and Near Eastern kingdoms. Areas that faced west, although more richly endowed with agricultural resources than those on the eastern side, lacked protected access to the sea and the proximity to the eastern Mediterranean that stimulated the earlier political development and economic competition characteristic of Euboia, the Argolid, the Corinthia, Attika, and the Cyclades.

Successful exploitation of the soil required intense cultivation of all available agricultural lands, whether the broad plains of Messenia, Thessaly, and central Boiotia or the narrow, irregular valleys squeezed between mountain and sea elsewhere.[20] Agriculture was the normal way of life, and most people produced their own food. The land with the best soil and best rainfall was always put to the plow first. Long-term drought and drastic famines were not a real threat, but even minor fluctuations in rainfall could crimp production enough to cause significant scarcity in a particular year.[21] Agriculture was not precarious, but in all periods local resources had to be

16. At Corinth, three perennial springs in close proximity made it easy to choose a site for the city; Salmon (1984) 78–80.

17. Rudhardt (1971) 97–101.

18. Even at a very local level; see Osborne (1987) 29–34, on microclimates.

19. Rackham (1990) 89 fig. 7; Isager and Skydsgaard (1992) 13 fig. 1.2.

20. Rackham (1990) 91–92, 101–5.

21. Osborne (1987) 27–52; Camp (1977), arguing for drought in the eighth century B.C.E., is concerned only with Attika. On crisis and shortfall in general: Garnsey (1988); Gallant (1991).

carefully managed and land carefully used to maintain a constant food supply. Ancient farmers, therefore, usually practiced a mixed production, maximizing resources by matching crops to the local landscape and mixing animal husbandry with agriculture.[22] Barley was the major crop. Flat plains were used for barley and wheat (in that order), and carefully tended hillsides were planted in olive trees, fruit trees, and grapevines.[23]

Shortages in ancient Greece, although often severe, usually lasted only through a single agricultural cycle.[24] Nevertheless, in antiquity the possibility of deprivation was real, practical remedies were few, and even a temporary shortage could have serious effects. Crop disease was always a possibility,[25] and long-term storage of grain—unusual on the communal level[26]—could be impractical for the individual subsistence farmer.[27] Regular production was a goal, and to avoid the threat of shortfall and create the expectation of success, individuals and communities relied on ritual remedies as well as agricultural procedures and political solutions.[28]

SPACE AND COMMUNITY

The individual *polis* was defined by the local landscape, each area's particular geological features shaping the way the territory was divided. Many traditions tied the individual units together, and even divisions wrought by the natural landscape did not completely isolate one political community from another. The Greek language was an important common thread. A shared literature, because it reflected the social and economic systems of exchange, facilitated communication between *poleis*. The epic tradition

22. Hodkinson (1988); Skydsgaard (1988) argues that agriculture and animal husbandry were kept separate. See also Isager and Skydsgaard (1992). The recent discussion about evidence for manuring fields indicates that Hodkinson is right; Alcock, Cherry, and Davis (1994).

23. Van Andel and Runnels (1987).

24. As Jameson points out, (1983) 7, *sitodeia* ("grain shortage") is the common technical term in epigraphical contexts; *limos* is a poetic word.

25. [Xen.] *Ath. Pol.* 2.6, comparing the risks of agriculture with the natural bounty of the sea.

26. Athenians collected donations of 1/600 of the barley crop and 1/1200 of the wheat crop for storage at Eleusis, placed under the care of the sanctuary and used to pay administrative expenses and to pay for expensive public dedications. See *IG* I[3] 78, now covered in detail by Cavanaugh (1996).

27. Jameson (1983) 10–11, 13. But see now Cahill (2000) and Ault (2000).

28. Ritual procedures: at Teos those who interfered with the import of grain were publicly cursed; *GHI* I[2] no. 30, early fifth century. Political solutions: purchase of surplus from abroad for public distribution; *GHI* I[2] no. 196, 330–26 B.C.E.

presented a divine world all Greek communities could respect, no matter how different the local ritual tradition.[29] Beyond the individual community, the great sanctuaries encouraged expressions of regional authority and fostered communication between cities. Although it is no longer possible to observe how this system actually functioned day-to-day, we can identify points of contact between regional sanctuaries and local institutions and thereby reconstruct some of the patterns of operation. There are several ways to read the landscape: first, the physical features of the land; second, the residue of human activity embedded in it; and finally, the language and imagery used to describe and represent it.

One of the languages used to describe the landscape is the language of space. For the ancient Greek community, political identity required a defensible space. The size of a community's territory depended on local topography. On the Greek mainland in the eighth century, the definition of external boundaries was as important for emerging communities as the development of a nucleated town center, and control of agricultural territory was often more important than defense of a central settlement. City walls came late to the Greek mainland, since here, mountains created natural boundaries.[30] Initially, the delineation of political space was expressed more forcibly by military defense of cultivated plains lying between mountains than by control of population centers.

Local topography influenced both settlement patterns and the political division of the landscape. Landlocked regions, protected from aggressors and competitors by distance and mountain ranges, required few artificial defenses. In such areas, populations were scattered in dispersed settlements, as in Lakonia,[31] or in isolated farmsteads, as in some areas of Boiotia.[32] Coastal and island communities faced different problems, and early nucleation was more necessary here than elsewhere. The sea marked a natural boundary, but it also allowed enemies easy access. The earliest fortified communities were built in the ninth and eighth centuries on Aegean islands.[33] However, because these sites did not always remain economically

29. Gould (1994) 104–5.

30. Thucydides, 1.1.2, assumes that the lack of fortification retarded agricultural production, but he does admit that it is difficult to reconstruct the past.

31. Cavanagh and Armstrong (1996), for the Lakonia survey.

32. Snodgrass (1990).

33. Emporio on Chios, Koukounaries on Paros, Dhonoussa-Vathy-Limenari on Naxos, Zagora on Andros, Aghios Andreas on Siphnos, Minoa on Amorgos, Vroulia on Rhodes, and several sites on Crete; Ducrey (1995). For maps, see Snodgrass (1991) 6–10 and fig. 2.

or politically viable, the communities with the earliest fortifications did not always survive as later *poleis.* In spite of frequent claims of local stability, emigration constantly redistributed populations, and sometimes whole communities even moved.[34] City walls and nucleated settlements were more necessary in the complex environments of the Greek communities of Asia Minor and the western Mediterranean than in the emerging *poleis* of the Greek homeland. Greek settlers built walled settlements in the initial phase of settlement on the Ionian coast[35] and later in the diaspora north to the shores of the Black Sea, west to Italy and Sicily, and south to the north coast of Africa. In these areas, fortification signified initial claims to new territory, acted as a barrier to potentially hostile neighbors, and announced the political coherence of the new settlement.

Territorial organization depended on terrain. The local landscape influenced the way the land was divided into governable units: whether organized around a core settlement or dispersed in multiple settlements relatively isolated from one another. The first pattern, that of the *polis,* emphasized political ties. The second, that of the *ethnos,* reflected a communal organization that emphasized descent. In some regions, such as the plains of Thessaly or the mountains of Aitolia, where the landscape encouraged scattered agricultural settlements, conditions were less hospitable to the institutions of the *polis,*[36] and community was defined by broader ethnic affiliations. Organization into *poleis* was characteristic of mainland regions around the Saronic Gulf, the Aegean islands, and the early foundations abroad, whether along the coasts of Asia Minor and the Black Sea or the coastal areas of Sicily and southern Italy. Some areas, like Lakonia, although characterized by a decentralized pattern of local villages, were nevertheless considered single *poleis.* In most areas defined as *poleis,* however, local populations tended to cluster in larger units, and most population centers came to be organized around a fortified citadel *(akropolis)* and a defined administrative center *(agora).*

The demarcation of communal space did not happen without appeals to divine authority. Political identity required the participation of the gods, and political boundaries required the protection of local divinities. Communities defined themselves by ritual, and divine power had to be locally recognized. To the ancient Greek imagination, the landscape was a living

34. Demand (1990).
35. Early fortified sites survived at Smyrna, Iasos, Miletos, and Ephesos; Ducrey (1995).
36. Morgan and Hall (1996).

world, alive with the possibility of divinity. Human activity was structured to avoid angering gods believed to inhabit physical space. Worshippers recognized divine power by allocating sacred space for communication between human and divine. Sanctuaries were often placed in locations appropriate to the function of the divinity, but these functions were always shaped by human requirements.

Sacred space had many forms. On mainland Greece in the Bronze Age, sacred activity had been integrated with political authority, and ritual activity had been concentrated within the ruler's residence. Centralized displays of wealth emphasized the ruler's power. By the tenth century, the new authorities, now decentralized, required different expressions of power, and gods began to be substituted for rulers as guardians of surplus wealth and moderators of human competition. Communal wealth, once collected and displayed in the palace of the Mycenaean leader or deposited in his tomb, was now to be shared with the gods.[37] Divinities needed a place of their own, and sacred space was therefore systematically designated and reserved for divine residence. Sanctuaries of the gods provided clearly marked space for communication with the divine and public space for displays of the gifts that testified to divine support for local political authorities. Space for the gods—which could not belong to individuals—was neutral territory. As early as the tenth century, several salient sites were already accumulating the offerings that marked them as sacred. Altars, gifts, and the debris of sacred meals preceded buildings. In the ninth and eighth centuries, surplus wealth was transferred to the gods in the form of dedications of bronze, exhibited in places associated with divinity to catch the gods' attention and advertise the donors' prestige. By the seventh century, dedications in bronze were giving way to less expensive gifts in ceramic and wood because community investment in ritual had begun to be demonstrated by a new form of public display. Large temples and high altars built in stone would now stand as witnesses to cooperative effort and communal organization.[38]

The gods were allocated their own space as guarantors of community. Their sanctuaries protected public space and preserved neutral territory. The word that defined the piece of land for a divinity was *temenos,* a place "cut off." *Hieron* invested a space with divine presence, and *asylon* filled a space with divine protection. A place that was *hieron* was a sacred place,

37. Rolley (1983).
38. Osborne (1997).

a marked space representing the world of the gods in the human realm. A place that was *asylon* was a place where no person could be seized and no object snatched away.[39] Recognition of divine protection was essential to human cooperation. The first sacred places were simple, open areas, used for communal worship in the form of sacrifices on temporary altars, ritual meals, and deposits of gifts to the gods.[40] Eventually, however, the more significant of these places would be embellished with boundary markers, fences, or walls, permanent altars, and elaborate temple structures.[41] The security of the community, symbolically represented in the Bronze Age by the body of the ruler, alive or dead, was now represented by spaces designated for the gods and maintained in exchange for their protection.

Sanctuaries recognized the gods and protected the landscape. Within the territory of the individual community, border sanctuaries marked boundaries, defined sovereignty,[42] and claimed the gods' protection.[43] In the countryside, sacred spaces protected the agricultural land, served the rural population, and provided points of organization for the villages that participated as constituents of the larger political unit.[44] In a traditional *polis*, sanctuaries within the nucleated center *(asty)* tended to be concentrated in the *agora* and on the heights of the *akropolis*—usually the most secure places. They housed the gods of the city, who supported the activities necessary for local political administration. Divine authority was regarded as prior to political organization, and social relationships and political life were ratified by myths of origin, foundation, and charter. Mythical narratives created allegiance to the local community and its institutions, whether that community claimed foundation by autochthony (birth from the soil),[45] immigration,[46] or colonization from abroad.[47]

39. The inscription at the Corinthian spring sanctuary, reprinted by Guarducci, *Epigrafia* 20, is the first epigraphical occurrence of the term *asylos*. Prohibition against seizing that which belongs to the god is expressed in terms of συλᾶν in the Archaic form of the amphictyonic oath as preserved by Aischines, 3.115. For discussion of the variations, see *CID* I: 103–4. Burkert (1996) makes the point that temples provided protection from seizure.

40. Kron (1988).

41. Rolley (1983).

42. De Polignac (1995a).

43. Sinn (1993).

44. Whether *polis* or *ethnos*, Morgan (1997).

45. E.g., Attika. For the meaning of the term "autochthony," see Rosivach (1987).

46. Kolophon: Migeotte (1992) 214–23 no. 69.

47. Dougherty (1993).

The definition of a political community required divine sanctions. Where defense was important, communities tended to organize rituals and public activities around a central high place, and for that reason, some of the earliest epigraphical evidence for political unity is associated with an *akropolis.* The earliest fortified communities identified the security of these heights with Athena, called Polias not because she was goddess of the city but because she was the goddess of the secured height. Her title had a strictly spatial reference that defined her as guardian of the πόλις in its original meaning as *akropolis.* At Zagora on Andros, the entire community lived close together in a dense, fortified settlement perched on a flat cliff top. Community and fortification occupied the same space, recognized in one of the earliest local inscriptions: "To the goddess of the *akropolis*"[48]—a dedication to the goddess who protected the security of both.

Ritual created community by creating and maintaining protected communal space. The first step in the process required the recognition of communal property, *ta demosia,* defined as whatever belonged to the group. When protected by the gods, such possessions were secure not only from seizure but also from personal or private use. Kept in a place defined as *asylon,* they could be used only by the group acting together and only in activities that acknowledged the gods. A place designated as sacred, *hieron,* belonged to the gods and protected the property necessary for communal ritual. Access to such space and access to its implements defined membership in the community.

An early Argive inscription, located in the temple of Athena Polias on the Larisa, articulates the distinction between individual and group.[49] Here community took precedence over the individual. This text regulates the use of ritual equipment and reserves the equipment dedicated in the temple for collective, public ritual. The collective (δαμόσιον) could use the equipment for sacred rites, but a private person (ϝhεδιέσταs = ἰδιώτηs) could not take them out of the sanctuary and put them to private use. An official, the *damiourgos,* determined the fines if anyone damaged the sacred things. By proscribing private exploitation of communal property, this pronouncement defined public property in terms of public ritual. Like other early Greek regulations, this one made no distinction between the sacred and the political. Participation in public ritual was necessarily a political act; at Argos, participation in the collective rites of Athena was one of the ways a

48. *Πολι*[άδι] inscribed (retrograde) on a bronze bowl; Cambitoglou (1981) 84.
49. *LSAG*^{2} 168 no. 8, described on page 158; *SEG* 11.314; Buck 83 (ca. 575–550).

member of the political community expressed political privilege and acknowledged political obligation.

In much the same way, an even earlier text from Tiryns associated Athena and Zeus with *akropolis,* community, and communal ritual. This inscription was carved directly into the old fortification wall of the Mycenaean citadel. The seventh-century text mentions public institutions and offices defined by important communal acts—officeholders who presided at ceremonies where wine was drunk, guardians of memory responsible for correct performance of sacred acts, the assembly, the community, and communal property or concerns.[50] The fortified citadel, a place of communal ritual, provided the protected space for communal acts. The location was not only appropriate but necessary.[51] Tiryns had been a well-known Bronze Age site, but the new Tiryns was not the same community that once had served a Mycenaean ruler on the same spot. Seventh-century ritual emphasized not a ruler but a group whose identity depended on association with a sacred space. In the new political organization of the early Greek *polis,* distinctions between communal space and space in the possession of individuals made the gods direct participants in the community. *Akropolis, agora,* and public sanctuaries drew the population together, and the major town sanctuaries became magnets for public ceremony, demonstration of wealth, and, with the eventual development of writing, public display of the laws regulating communal behavior.

Sanctuaries placed at or near natural borders indicated the limits of a community's political reach. A clear example of this process can be observed at Eretria on Euboia, settled originally in the eighth century, probably by immigrants from an earlier, abandoned settlement at nearby Lefkandi. Here the two most important divinities were Apollo and Artemis. The major settlement at Eretria has been located near the harbor, centered around a small hairpin-shaped temple of Apollo, with no trace of a city wall until the Archaic period. The earliest wall was probably built about the same time as the first peripteral temple of Apollo, constructed in the late seventh or early sixth century directly above the earlier temple. Artemis,

50. Verdeles, Jameson, and Papachristodoulou (1975) 150–205; Dubois (1980) 25–56; *SEG* 30.380; *LSAG*^{2} 443 no. 9a (late seventh century). The text is inscribed in "Schlangenschrift" on blocks of the wall at the critical passageway leading to the underground water supply for the *akropolis* of Tiryns. Note psilosis. The inscription is important evidence for an embryonic *polis* at Tiryns before the migration of the population to Halieis sometime after 479; see Jameson (1969) 313–15.

51. See Ducrey (1995) for early fortified sites. For temples of Athena at Emporio, Koukounaries, and Zagora, Schilardi (1988) 45–46.

equal in status to her brother, had her temple on one of the frontiers of Eretrian territory. Her sanctuary has been located at the old Mycenaean site of Amarynthos, on the coastal road where the Erasinos River meets the sea.[52] Apollo marked the center of the settlement, his twin sister, Artemis, an external boundary. Eretria recognized both divinities and both sites as fundamental to the *polis*'s existence and durability. Eventually, the major treasury of the city would be stored at the sanctuary of Artemis, and her festival, the Artemisia, would be one of the city's major festivals. Artemis and Apollo, together with their mother, Leto, constituted the divine triad by which the *polis* swore its collective oaths. In the Classical period, Artemis was pictured with Apollo on the reliefs decorating important public regulations.[53] Her sanctuary, located at one of the extremities of the city's territory, represented the security of the *polis*. Eretria appears not to have needed a fortification wall completely encircling the central settlement until the fourth century.

Where there was no clearly defined central settlement the gods provided a ritual focus to create and maintain political organization. Although the Lakedaimonians never had a distinct, centralized residential community, the Spartans nevertheless imposed their authority over the rest of the people of Lakonia. Insulated from their enemies by distance and protected by mountains, the Lakedaimonians did not need a city wall until military pressure in the fourth century forced them to initiate a defensive strategy. In Lakonia, although a large part of the population remained dispersed, clustered in separate villages, common sanctuaries provided the space for recognizable communal activities. Those eligible for participation expressed community and common identity in the organized festivals at the precinct of Ortheia in Limnai, at the Menelaion, or at their sanctuary of Athena Chalkioikos on the Spartan *akropolis*.[54]

Greek cities created themselves by claiming a landscape. De Polignac has explained this phenomenon in terms of the early history of the *polis*,

52. Knoepfler (1988). The site of the sanctuary is identified and described in detail by Sapouna-Sakellaraki (1992), with map, 251. The sanctuary is located near the church of Aghia Kyriaki. Traces of a small, almost square building have been preserved, together with an underground chamber, probably constructed to accommodate a natural spring, 240. Dedications were steady from the end of the Geometric period through the Hellenistic period, declining in quality only in the first century B.C.E., when they finally taper off. There are significant concentrations of ceramic figurines, including kourotrophic females, females with offerings, and male and female children. The sanctuary seems to have served both males and females.

53. Meyer (1989) nos. 5, 6, 17.

54. Hodkinson (1997); (1998).

arguing that local claims to territory were originally made by maintaining control of major border or rural sanctuaries.[55] He describes the developing *polis* as a unified spatial construct, with a major sanctuary in the countryside or near sensitive borders as a formative element and a major structural support of the *polis* itself. Although his model is not equally applicable everywhere, the basic notion of a ritual unity between a core settlement, its land, and its external sanctuaries was fundamental to *polis* identity and necessary for its survival. Details varied with local conditions; the process was dynamic and flexible, responsive to the demands of local history. As long as the *polis* lasted as a local political institution, Greek cities maintained stability by securing external borders as well as by defending a nucleated center. The process required recognition of a whole community of divinities, each with its own space.

Entitlement to territory was claimed by settlement, defined by boundaries, confirmed by ritual, and expressed by myths of foundation. Pausanias recognizes the importance of boundaries by emphasizing the significance of their recognizable signs. In his day, even tiny Panopeus marked its boundaries by placing inscribed stone markers *(horoi)* at the extremities of its territory.[56] The usual Greek word for a marked boundary, *horos,* does not have this meaning until Herodotus and Pindar,[57] but the concept of a bounded landscape as an element of the *polis* is implied by ritual behavior and settlement patterns.[58] Deliberate marking of sensitive boundaries was characteristic of the Geometric period, when communities began to leave gifts to the gods at the outer edges of their territory at watersheds and mountain passes. Dedications in a sacred space at a frontier or natural border obligated the gods to protect these places. In southern Boiotia, a deposit of Geometric dedications recognized the sensitivity of a place of crossing between sites on the coast (later Siphai and Kreusis) and sites on the plain on the other side of the mountain (later Thisbe, Xironomi, and Thespiai).[59] No temple marked the spot until at least the Archaic period, but Artemis was recognized later by dedications in the precinct inscribed with her name.

55. De Polignac (1995a).

56. One of the boundary stones marking the border between Panopeus (spelled "Phanoteus") and Stiris has recently been found; see Rousset and Katzouros (1992) 197–215.

57. The *horoi* that demarcated the Athenian *agora* are dated ca. 500 B.C.E.; Lalonde (1991) 27, H25–27.

58. Snodgrass (1990), for farmsteads clustered around a central core whose territory is defined by patterns of empty space between one community and the next.

59. Tomlinson and Fossey (1970).

Topography influenced the placement of the earliest Greek sanctuaries—at first, simple precincts without permanent structures. In the eighth century, Athena and Apollo were the most frequently recognized gods; Athena was already associated with *polis* centers (Athens, Sparta, Tegea, Ialysos, Kameiros, Lindos, Emporio on Chios, Miletos, Phokaia, and Syracuse), and Apollo (except for Eretria, Corinth, and Dreros) was usually located far from major settlements (Delphi, Thermon, the Boiotian Ptoion, Maleatas at Epidauros, Delos, Phanai on Chios, Didyma).[60] Artemis, like her twin brother, was well established in the countryside (Lousoi, Mavriki in Arkadia, Sparta, Ephesos, Aulis, Pherai, and Brauron, to name a few of her early sites). Zeus, not yet established in core settlements, was found at remote sites, often but not always on mountains (Olympia, Dodona, Pherai, Mt. Hymettos, Mt. Ithome)[61] or in mountain caves (on Mt. Ida and Mt. Dikte on Crete). Hera was geographically focused in the Peloponnese and on Samos, but usually outside the settlement (the Heraia at Prosymna, Tiryns, Solygeia, Perachora, and on Samos).[62] Hermes was associated with caves (Patsos), Demeter with hills and springs (Knossos and Eleusis), and Hephaistos with the island of Lemnos. The association of certain kinds of space with particular divinities allowed new and fragile communities to recognize their landscape as protected by the gods.

GENEALOGY AND GENDERED LANDSCAPES

The earliest Greek literature incorporates a conceptual organization of territory and boundaries in the form of catalogues and foundation myths tied to specific locations. Geographically based narratives, probably as old as the institutions they claim to explain, locate the individual community in its landscape and connect it to mythic representations of the larger universe. Anthropomorphic representations of divinity and personifications of features of the natural world encouraged the belief that the world of the gods and the world of nature were parts of a single continuum. The major divinities, however, did not directly represent natural phenomena. Rain was

60. Coldstream (1977) 328.
61. Langdon (2000).
62. Hall (1995) 13–14, describes how local patterns often emphasize one divinity over another. In the Argolid in the early Iron Age Demeter is more prominent on the eastern half, and Hera, with similar votives, on the western plain. These distinctions correspond to other local differences, e.g., in dialect and foundation myth.

called water "from Zeus,"[63] and any river or stream could be called "Acheloos," the name of the river god considered to be the father of all flowing fresh water,[64] but personifications of the natural world, such as Ge (Earth), Selene (Moon), Helios (Sun), or local mountains, rivers, and springs, although acknowledged by ritual, were rarely considered dominant divinities. The most important gods were those responsible for protecting and fostering human development. Such divinities were Zeus and Poseidon, represented as capable of controlling aspects of nature, or Demeter and Dionysos, who could put nature to work for human benefit.

Hierarchies of divine authority reflected human categories. To the Greek imagination, the landscape was infused with gender. The language classified the earth, continents, most mountains,[65] islands, countries, cities, trees, lakes, and springs as feminine,[66] and sky, ocean, most rivers and streams, winds, and flowers as masculine. The three major continents—Europe, Asia, and Libya—were female; the rivers that formed their boundaries were male.[67] Long-distance movement tended to be associated with male images,[68] a fixed location or minimal movement with female representations.[69] Analogies between grammatical and social categories of gender provided a rich imagery for representing natural events in terms of human experience.

Metaphors of reproduction, embedded in the ritual system and developed in the imagery of early poetry, created relationships between the human and divine realms and provided a powerful vocabulary to sanction claims to land and territory. Such patterns are established in Hesiod's *Theogony*. This poem exploits a traditional form of cosmogonical epic, well known throughout the Near East, to explain the origins of the universe and the gods. Near Eastern cosmogonies were organized to explain and justify divine kingship. Hesiod's purpose is different. He does (briefly) explain the origin of the gods in relation to the evolution of the natural world, but instead of emphasizing the theme of kingship so prominent in the Near East, he emphasizes the principles of communal decision-making and the estab-

63. *IG* I[3] 84, line 34.
64. E.g., Eur. *Bacch.* 625.
65. Langdon (2000), for Mt. Hymettos represented as a bearded, shaggy male.
66. Hdt, 4.86. The Athena worshipped by the Machlyes was said to have been the daughter of Poseidon and the Tritonian lake; 4.180.
67. Hdt. 2.45.
68. For Homeric similes where warriors massing for battle are compared to torrents, see Arnould (1994) 17–18.
69. Ninck (1921) 21–22. Artem. 2.27, for rivers associated with male characteristics, and lakes and springs with female characteristics.

lishment of a Greek moral order. He justifies the rule of Zeus and recognizes this god as responsible for a system based on principles of *dike* (right behavior) and *themis* (law sanctioned by the gods). The *Theogony* belongs to the period of the early *polis* and personifies the natural world in order to explain, define, and control it.

Hesiod's first principal actor is Earth herself. In his narrative, the female earth, Gaia,[70] is the source of all blessings and all nourishment but cannot be trusted to give forth her sustenance. The poet's concern is the delicate balance between scarcity and plenty, regulated by gods capable of both generosity and contempt. The same contrast is represented in the *Homeric Hymn to Demeter* by the need to placate the divinity responsible for the earth's bounty. In Hesiod's *Works and Days,* this tension is represented as a contrast between a lost paradise (where sustenance was once provided without human labor) and the realities of human existence (where livelihood is an achievement of struggle and hard work). In the *Theogony,* conflict develops when equilibrium in the divine realm is challenged by a crisis of procreation and a three-generation struggle for sexual dominance. Here the establishment of the rule of Zeus is a prerequisite to orderly procreation, and interaction between human and divine is possible only when the principles of right judgment *(dike)* are protected by the god's hand. Divine sexual attraction and divine sexual union can be positive forces for human development, but the poem also shows that the energy of divine sexual union must be used to establish order, not to create disorder.

In the *Theogony,* the entire universe belongs to a single family. The physical world and the moral realm are contiguous, both represented by anthropomorphized divinities designed to account for all human experience. In this universe, relationships are defined in terms of the family, time is represented by the succession of generations, and male authority is inevitable. Concerned to demonstrate a political order subject to human decisions rather than a physical order tied to kingship, the poet is nevertheless constrained by his genre to express political development in terms of genealogy. Genealogy provides the structural framework because family relationships allow the kind of flexibility required to organize a vast amount of disparate material into a coherent account. Hesiod's poem breaks off abruptly, and the possible connection between divine and human genealogy is therefore neither established nor explained. Nevertheless, the genealogical structure outlined in the extant text indicates a concern to link hu-

70. Janko (1982) 234–46; Gaia is the name preferred by poets, but in ritual contexts the earth is usually called Ge.

man and divine worlds. Personifications of political and judicial concepts are therefore categorized as female divinities, subordinated to Zeus either as daughters or as sexual partners in order to account for a structured moral order under his patronage where human political life can flourish.[71]

Genealogy is the earliest form of Greek historiography.[72] Characteristic of oral cultures, genealogical narratives personalize history and create a revisable view of the past that always validates the present.[73] Such narratives do not record specific historical events but are designed to demonstrate the inevitability of particular hierarchical relationships. The *Theogony* provides a divine "history" for the rule of Zeus without regional bias and was thus a narrative that all early Greek communities could accept. Other contemporary genealogies—local tales told to validate claims to territory and to establish ethnic identity—had a narrower goal.[74] Three kinds of early genealogical catalogues are preserved in a work known in antiquity as the *Catalogue of Women* or the *Eoiai* ("Just as" stories). In this poem, geography and genealogy were closely entwined in a series of narratives promoted by the need to link the allocation of bounded territories to local, elite families who claimed descent from the gods. This work originally organized the early foundation myths of major regions of the Greek peninsula. West has noticed that the fragments form a composite series of genealogies made up of two kinds of narrative: local genealogies associated with specific regions and shorter genealogies based on a union between a mortal woman and a god. Stylistic analysis of the earliest fragments suggests to him three stages of composition:

1. consolidation of several local genealogies into a single narrative organized by region;
2. a later and more ambitious project subordinating traditional local genealogies to the genealogy of the family of Deukalion (hero of the Greek flood narrative and progenitor of the human race);
3. shorter genealogical "just as" stories tied to the main stem through female links.[75]

71. West (1966), on the end of the *Theogony*.
72. Fornara (1983) 4–5, on the contributions of Eumelos, Akusilaos, and Hekataios.
73. Tonkin (1992).
74. Calame (1987).
75. West (1985) 146–50; 165–68.

This network of narratives reflects different stages in the political organization of geographical space. West dates the first stage, when local myths were consolidated into a single narrative, to the eighth century. This narrative united at least eight local regions: Elis, Lakonia, Aulis-Hyria, Malis, Pisatis, Messene, Argos (all on the mainland), and Lesbos. West's dating may be too early, but his observation that distinctive narrative patterns are associated with specific regions is suggestive. The second group of narratives is organized around the family of Deukalion in order to stake a claim to common origin. In this version, the immediate descendants of Deukalion establish a sequence of genealogies arranged geographically, each keyed to a principal area: the western Peloponnese, Aitolia, central Greece, and Thessaly. Regional genealogies are thus arranged geographically, moving from east to west. Relationship to Deukalion imposes a unified genealogical stem and implies kinship between regions.[76]

In the third and final stage of composition, a series of local genealogies was interpolated. All begin with the Greek expression meaning "just as," a stylistic device not employed in the other stages of composition. Each of the "just as" genealogies belongs to a local family sprung from a union between a mortal woman and a god—the same pattern of sexual union characteristic of the genealogies at the end of Hesiod's *Theogony*. In the *Catalogue*, as in the *Theogony*, the sexual union of a male god with a mortal female bridges the gap between the human and divine realms without jeopardizing male dominance at the level of the gods.[77]

The genealogical mini-epic in the *Catalogue of Women* demonstrates a strong connection between gender and geographic consciousness. The *Catalogue* organizes the continent according to founding families and emphasizes females as links between regions. Marriage is a key to the narrative because, in genealogical history, females are the link to collateral branches of the family stem.[78] Union of a god with a mortal woman is a necessary motif in the third version because increased awareness of foreign cultures required narratives that could recognize foreign populations as subordinate to Zeus. The list of females in the interpolated family genealogies includes

76. West (1985) 61, for a map of the orderly geographical arrangement of the descendants of Aiolos's five daughters.

77. This pattern is probably the same employed in a work well known to Pausanias, the *Great Eoiai*, which he distinguishes from the "epic on women" (9.31.5) and uses as a source for genealogy (4.2.1).

78. Fowler (1998) 5.

the mothers of heroes (Alkmene, Leda, Danaë, "wives" of Zeus) as well as figures like Io, key to the stem from which all Greek heroic genealogy would grow.[79] Hesiod identified Io's father as Peiren, son of Argos; the epic tradition and Attic tragedians knew her as daughter of Inachos. Either way, by birth she is closely tied to her homeland. In Argive tradition, Inachos is both a god and a river. As daughter of Inachos, Io connects the human landscape with the natural world, and by traveling between continents she links both Africa and Asia to the land of Argos. As partner of Zeus and ancestor of Herakles, she connects the imagined world of the gods with the civilized landscape of human endeavor. Io's presence in the *Catalogue*, together with her prominence later in Herodotus's introductory narrative,[80] suggests the existence of an early Argive narrative very different from Thucydides' version of an eastward diaspora originating from Athens, a narrative that claimed not Athens[81] but Argos as the source of movement to the east.[82] Io seems to belong to an early stage of Argive self-promotion, a time when the ethnic form "Argive" could still be used generically for all Greeks.[83] From the *Catalogue* we can reconstruct the outline of a mythical map and observe how early genealogical myth represented the land carved up by local and regional communities. The genealogies of the *Catalogue*, fragmentary as they are, testify to early and vigorous competition. Each community was claiming a territory of its own and attempting to justify that claim with a narrative designed to project and protect a particular history.[84] The organization of geographical space was a necessary component of that history. The *Catalogue* represents an attempt to stabilize fluid local genealogies and create more or less coherent patterns. The circulation of such a text indicates the development of shared institutions and a new, more broadly defined and self-conscious cultural identity.

79. Eventually the canonical version followed by Apollodorus; West (1985) 44–45. For ethnic distinctions between Perseid and Proitid dynasties in the Argolid, see Hall (1995) 14–15.

80. Hdt. 1.1. See also Aesch. *PV* 640–86, etc.

81. As in Thuc. 1.12.

82. Hall (1989) 48, for Io as keystone in the construction of the heroic genealogies to legitimate Greek expansion. For Aischylos, the Ionians were named for Io; *PV* 840.

83. Hall (1997) 46, for the Homeric use of the ethnics "Argives," "Danaoi," and "Achaians" as generic terms of territoriality, used to contrast those from mainland Greece with Anatolians. Konstan (2001) 32 points out that the last two do not occur in the singular in epic, and when "Argive" is so used, it has a strictly local territorial reference to the Argolid.

84. Calame (1987), on Lakonia; Higbie (1997), on Salamis.

This imagined map of interrelated but individually autonomous communities required a corresponding topography that connected distant components. Popular notions of local and regional hydrology reinforced claims to kinship with the land and reflected attempts to explain not only ties to family but also ethnic ties and relationships within and between communities. Before there was any idea of a common Hellenic identity,[85] local claims of kinship were embedded into wider genealogical systems to emphasize networks of exchange and cooperation. Communities, at first identified with natural features of local topography, adapted to changing conditions. As populations emigrated and established outposts abroad, an expanded ideology of kinship compensated for the handicaps of distance and difference.

Local springs, like the soil itself, conferred identity and helped to create from a group of individual families a single community. Bonds of kinship between hero and homeland are often recognized in the poetic formula of homecoming. Returning after a long absence, Odysseus greets Ithaka by kissing the earth, the "grain-giving plowland," and by praying to the nymphs of the local springs and water sources.[86] When Dionysos returns as an adult to Thebes, his very first act is to greet the streams of Dirke and Ismenos, twin rivers of Thebes and waters of his birthplace.[87] Likewise, a Sophoclean hero returning to the land of Pherai greets first of all the local spring, Hyperieia, because he recognizes her water as kin;[88] and Telephos, returning from abroad, greets the land of Pelops, his paternal home.[89] Citizens had a responsibility to defend the soil that gave them birth and nourishment,[90] and therefore every city projected a strong identity not only with its territory but with the earth itself and the local springs and rivers that were its sources of water.[91]

85. Hall (1989) 9, 50, etc.

86. *Od.* 13.352–60.

87. Eur. *Bacch.* 5. In *Hipp.* 555–57 Thebes is identified by its wall and the water of Dirke.

88. Soph. *TrGF* F 911 Radt. Likewise, leaving Lemnos, Philoktetes, in exile, ironically marks his departure by saying farewell to the springs of the island. In Eur. *Bacch.* 619ff., leaving Athens is described as leaving behind the Kallichorian water of the goddess.

89. Eur. *Tel.* F I.1–3 Diggle.

90. Eur. *Her.* 827, for the idea that in return for the birth of the city's population from the land itself, citizens owed protection to the land; cf. Plat. *Men.* 237b–d.

91. Robert (1962) 180–234, 426; (1980) 165–75. For a survey of local spring divinities, see Larson (2001), especially 121–225, for a catalogue of the evidence.

A new community abroad was "a home away from home" *(apoikia)*, and the originating community was the "mother-city" *(metropolis)*, a concept that implies an intimate relationship with the land. Metaphors of kinship kept ties to the homeland alive and created relationships of mutual obligation,[92] invigorated and reinforced by popular notions of geological unity. The need for dependable water resources for support of newly founded communities encouraged settlement of areas that had limestone catchments.[93] The hydrology of the penetrable Mediterranean landscape with its karst substructure inspired belief in an underground water system that mirrored the one visible on the earth's surface. A river that disappeared in one place could be identified somewhere else in another local river or local spring.[94] Such imagery was easily adaptable to changing conditions of emigration because rivers were believed to be connected underground with distant waterways.[95] A unified system, tying water at home with waters across the sea, maintained bonds of kinship and accounted for the family ties between "daughter" cities and the "mother" cities from which populations claimed to be sprung.[96] There are many examples. Herodotus and Thucydides assume a relationship between the river Acheloös in northwestern Greece and the islands offshore at a place where the water carries silt into the sea.[97] Immigrants to the new Sicilian settlements claimed an even closer relationship to the more distant waterways of home. New foundations at Gela, Selinous, and Akragas all named new rivers after old,[98] and although in the *Iliad* Okeanos is source of all seas, rivers, and springs,[99] cities as far apart as Syracuse, Miletos, Paphos, and Kyzikos all claimed the river Acheloos as father of their own newly found waterways. The Syracusans even explained the copious supplies of fresh water rising from the spring they called Arethusa as an extension of the Alpheios River flowing past Olympia and under the sea, carrying the water from their homeland

92. Dougherty (1993).

93. Crouch (1993).

94. Hdt. 6.76, for the source of the Argive Erasinos at Stymphalos and Kleomenes' unfavorable sacrifices to the river.

95. Eur. *Bacch.* 405–8, for the underground connection between the Nile and the waters of Cyprus.

96. Soph. *TrGF* F 270 Radt, for the Inachos as related to Okeanos; see Fr. 271, for the Inachos in Epiros connected to the Inachos in the Argolid.

97. Hdt. 2.10; Thuc. 2.102.3–6.

98. Weiss (1984) 22, pointing out that Thucydides begins with local rivers when describing Sicilian cities. The practice is noticed by Lepore (1977) and Purcell (1996) 202.

99. *Il.* 21.194–97.

to their new city in Sicily.[100] Kinship and political identity were a matter of birth, but they were also products of nurture. The community shared the food of a common soil and the water from a common source. When Demosthenes calls on "all the gods and all the goddesses" who hold the land *(chora)* of Attika,[101] his words encompass not only Earth herself but the waters he invokes with a famous, metrical Attic oath:

> By Earth, by springs, by rivers, by streams.[102]

An oath of the ephebes at Dreros on Crete echoes the words of this invocation. At the time of a major war with a neighboring *polis*, the ephebes swore an oath by all the gods of their *polis*, including, in the midst of a long list, the major features and representatives of their natural environment:

> . . . by Earth and Sky, heroes and heroines, springs and rivers, and all the gods and goddesses. . . .[103]

100. Paus. 5.7.2–3.

101. Dem. 18.141.

102. *Μὰ γῆν, μὰ κρήνας, μὰ ποταμούς, μὰ νάματα*, parodied by Aristophanes, *Av.* 194 (and attributed to Demosthenes: Antiphanes F 296; Timokles F 38; Plut. *Dem.* 9.4). According to Plutarch, *Vit. Dec. Or.* 845b, Demosthenes was hissed in the assembly for his fancy effects. When Aristophanes' Tereus rallies the flocks, although the birds are here represented as dwelling in the sky, he describes precisely the natural habitat of each species, locating the birds in the gardens, hills, meadows, and well-watered regions throughout the countryside.

103. *SIG*^{3} 527.15–16; Chaniotis (1996) 195–201, no. 7.

2 Ritual Space

DRAWING THE BOUNDARIES BETWEEN HUMAN AND DIVINE

Every *polis* inhabited the same landscape as its divinities. The land was full of gods, and any special feature of the landscape could be associated with a divinity: mountain tops with Zeus, springs with nymphs, caves with Pan, the wilderness with Artemis, the sea with Poseidon. Epithets and titles of the gods could stress ties to a specific place or to the type of space associated with a particular god. Plato exploits these conventions in the *Phaedrus,* where the philosophical argument depends on an extended analogy with religious experience, and susceptibility to the attractions of the site of the dialogue is a preliminary to direct experience of the divine. A detailed description of the physical environment of the area sets the stage for the entire dialogue. We can picture the spot, on the banks of the Ilissos just outside the city wall of Athens, shaded by the branches of a plane tree and cooled by the water of the nearby spring.[1] Plato's Sokrates agrees that the place is charming. At the close of the dialogue, as if inspired by the images of his own vivid language, he offers a prayer to Pan and to "as many of the other gods as are in this place" with an invocation that recognizes how evocative such simple precincts could be.

Respect for the landscape reflected respect for the gods. Precise rules for behavior are not clearly spelled out in any single work of literature, but the general principles can be discerned by looking at a variety of sources. One

1. Sokrates avoids offering an opinion on the meaning of a local myth about the personified north wind; Pl. *Phdr.* 230b–c (for the description), 229c–e (for the myth).

of these is Hesiod's didactic poem *Works and Days,* where respect for the landscape is closely tied to respect for the community. In the context of giving advice about work and marriage and setting up a calendar of agricultural activities synchronized with the seasonal rhythms of the year, the poem also includes, without transition, a list of admonitions about care of the body. Delivered in a dense, even enigmatic, style, the list is divided into two parts: the first concerned with proper dealings with other humans,[2] the second with the right relationship to the world of the gods.[3] The collection as a whole conveys the message that the man who does not acknowledge the power of the divine in certain significant areas of the human realm risks retribution *(opis).*[4] The second section, about the gods, reads:

1. Do not ever pour fiery wine in libation to Zeus or the other immortals at dawn with hands unwashed, for they do not heed you, but they spit back (i.e., "reject") your prayers (724–26).
2. Do not urinate standing and facing the sun; but from the time when the sun sets until it rises, being mindful, you will not urinate, either on the road or off the road walking, nor stripped bare, for the nights belong to the blessed (gods); but a man in service to the gods, acquainted with wisdom, (will urinate) either squatting down or drawing near the wall of the well-fenced courtyard (727–32).
3. Do not expose your genitals when you are spattered with sperm within the house near the hearth, but avoid it (733–34).
4. Do not sow offspring when you have returned from an ill-omened tomb, but rather (when you have returned) from a feast of the deathless (735–36).[5]
5. Do not ever urinate in the waters of rivers flowing forth towards the sea, nor at springs, but avoid this especially—and do not shit there—for this is not better (757–59).[6]

2. Hes. *Op.* 707–23.
3. Hes. *Op.* 724–59.
4. *Opis* is a form of divine vengeance; in early poetry the term describes divine reaction (favorable or unfavorable) to human deeds. See West (1978) 329–30 for a summary of the suggestions about the placement of line 706 ("It is well to have guarded against the retribution *[opis]* of the blessed gods").
5. Plutarch, *De Sera* 562a, interprets this to mean that children are influenced by a parent's emotional state at the time of conception.
6. According to Proclus (Plut. F 98, line 5) Plutarch called these lines "cheap and unworthy of a pedagogical Muse."

6. Never go through with your foot the beautifully flowing water of ever-flowing rivers until you have looked into the beautiful streams and pray, having washed your hands with the very pleasing white water. The one who crosses a river unwashed as to hands and wickedness, toward him the gods feel resentment, and to him they give painful things later (737–41).[7]
7. Do not cut the dry from the fresh from the five-branched (i.e., hand) with the flashing iron at the flourishing feast of the gods (742–43).[8]
8. And do not put the wine-pitcher above the *krater* while people are drinking, for destructive *moira* has been produced by this (744–45).[9]
9. If you are making a home, do not leave it unfinished, lest a cawing crow sit on it and croak (746–47).
10. Do not take up and eat or wash from unconsecrated footed cauldrons, since there is retribution for that, too (748–49).[10]
11. Do not sit a twelve-year-old boy on what does not move (i.e., a tomb), a thing that makes a man unmanly, nor a twelve-month-old boy either, for this produces the same result (750–52).
12. A man should not wash his skin with a woman's bathwater, for there is a baneful penalty in that, too, for a time (753–55).
13. When you come upon burning sacrifices, do not criticize what is being made unseen, for the god resents that, too (755–56).

Directed at a male audience, the list of prohibitions and advice emphasizes the importance of segregating human physical processes from the divine. The compressed style, apparent disorder, and lack of coherent transition between the individual items on the list are not the result of later interpolation, as many have assumed,[11] but replicate the terse style and astringent

7. Xen. *An.* 4.3.19, for sacrifice to a river before crossing.

8. Plutarch, *De Is. et Os.* 352e, recognizes the context of a religious festival where the clean should not touch the unclean and comments that Egyptian prohibitions for priests were more onerous because they were permanent.

9. Quoted by Plutarch, *Quomodo Adul.* 28b, as a requirement needing explanation.

10. Plutarch, *Quaest. Conv.* 703d, explains this to mean that one should not eat from a cooking pot without first making an offering from it to the gods.

11. Wilamowitz (1928) 122, 124–25, 130 found the list structurally disorganized and contaminated by superstition; for other criticism, see West (1978) on

asyndeton characteristic of early laws and oracles and also typical of the aphoristic exchange associated with males contesting at a formal drinking party, the *symposion*.[12]

Hesiod's collection of aphorisms is not concerned with ordinary behavior in daily life but rather delineates correct behaviors for a male in the presence of divinity or at specific critical times, for instance, when seeking divine support, returning home from a funeral, competing with equals at communal feasts, conceiving a child, building a house, or serving a god. The thirteen injunctions measure human anxiety about several personal issues, such as manhood, sexuality, paternal responsibility, transitions between age grades, social behavior, personal hygiene, and the boundaries between male and female. Three relationships are especially important: establishing the right relationship with the world of nature (fire, sun, and water), maintaining the right relationship with home and community, and expressing the right relationship to the world of the dead. In each situation, inattention or disregard jeopardizes an important or critical relationship with a god.

The pungent, cryptic style of this list may cloak but does not completely conceal its messages: in certain situations, human physical processes and activities (urination, defecation, and sexual intercourse) can compromise the divine (flowing water, fire, the sun, Zeus); contact with the dead can compromise the living body (e.g., setting a male child on a tomb can make him unmanly); and the boundaries between the male and female body must be respected. Recognized as essential for human life and necessary for sustenance, water and fire are classified with the divine. In the world of the

---

Op. 706. Moulinier (1952) 34–35 connects the beliefs with the "oriental frontier of the Greek world." The scholiast (probably Proclus; see Pertusi [1955] vii = xxxv, 239–30) explains the passage in the following way: "Men should not strip naked together with women, because, besides being shameful, effluents and secretions flow from female bodies, from which there are polluted things to defile men, and for those (men) going into the same air or those (men) going into the same water, it is necessary to experience these. For this reason, he also says that a penalty endures for some time for those who persist in this, in which time the taint attached to them necessarily lasts." Parker (1983) 291–92 accepts the passage as a series of rules for living a good life but has no confidence in an early date; West, however, finds no reason to follow the majority and prints these lines in his text. Plutarch, on the other hand, recognizes the genre and assumes that the intent was to encourage appropriate ritual behavior.

12. West (1978) 56 compares the style of the gnomic pronouncements of Theognis. For contests of riddles in Greek *symposia,* see the passage quoted from Antiphanes in Ath. 10. 448f. Aeschin. 3.121 contrasts riddles *(ainigmata)* with clear instructions about rules for ritual acts.

Greek city-state, fire and water were also symbols of communal life, gifts of nature to be shared with others. The rules were well known. A stranger's request for fire had to be honored,[13] and those who blocked the water flowing from springs, even of enemies in war time, deserved utter destruction.[14] When the Boiotians complained to the Athenians about the desecration of Delion during the Peloponnesian War, they accused the Athenians of transgressing the laws of the Hellenes, citing as an example of the Athenians' gross misconduct the secular use of sacred water, in normal times left untouched except for the ritual sprinkling before sacrifice.[15]

The individual behaviors on this list are closely related to each other. Eating from an unconsecrated pot, washing in a woman's bathwater, letting a crow caw in an unfinished house,[16] and setting a child on a grave share a similar structure. Each demonstrates disruption of an accepted boundary—whether a boundary between life and death, purity and pollution, or male and female. Dirt, fingernail trimmings, feces, urine, female bodies, and the dead do not in themselves belong to negative categories, but each of these items belongs to a category that acquires negative connotations when mixed with social or ritual situations that call for separation or segregation.[17] Hesiod's list assumes that contact with the divine requires care of the body. The requirements are not onerous, but attention is necessary, because carelessness can disrupt a relationship with a god. Dirty hands are not in themselves forbidden, but dirty hands in the service of a god are out of place. Defecating and urinating are not in themselves insulting, but at a time or place belonging to the gods, such activities require observation of certain protocols. Sexual intercourse is not forbidden or even restricted, but for a male, facing the hearth unwashed after intercourse is an insult to the purity of fire. Cutting one's fingernails is not forbidden, but the gods do not approve of separating the dead (nail) from the living (finger) at a communal feast.[18] Respect for the gods therefore required respect for the body, respect for the home, respect for the community, and above all, respect for the world of nature. The person who observed these categories demonstrated the right relationship with the gods and, by main-

13. At Athens, official curses were offered annually against those who refused to offer fire or water; Leutsch and Schneidewin (1958) 1: 388, and also *Βουζύγης*.
14. Quoted by Aeschin. 2.115 (as from the ancient Amphictyonic oath).
15. Thuc. 4.97.
16. Portends death; Plin. *HN* 10.35.
17. Douglas (1966).
18. Xen. *Mem.* 1.5.4 on allowing personal desires or concern for the body to interfere with the collegiality of a communal celebration, in this case a *symposion.*

taining the correct boundary between human and divine, could hope to avoid retribution. Failure to observe these admonitions could result in penalties in the form of unanswered prayers, divine resentment, bad omens, and even punishment.

Two of Hesiod's aphorisms are concerned with maintaining a proper relationship to flowing water. One (no. 5) advises a man to take care not to pollute rivers or springs with urine or excrement. The other (no. 6) advises clean hands and a prayer before stepping into a river to cross it. Both strictures originate in a belief that rivers and springs are alive with a divine presence. Rivers were male, represented as gods, and springs were female, classified as nymphs. Fresh water, flowing water, and water for public use had to be respected. Water from sacred springs or water directed into sanctuaries had to be kept as clean as possible,[19] and both sanctuary officials and civic administrators posted penalties for contamination of a sacred source of water.[20] Flowing water had to be protected because pure water was used for ritual in both domestic and sanctuary settings.[21] Pure water required attention because it was both a medium for interaction with the divine and, as an antidote to pollution, a marker of important ritual boundaries and transitions for humans.[22]

The Greek ideology of pollution recognized three categories of existence: the dead, the living, and the immortal. Basic rules governing contact between these categories were recognized by all.[23] Only gods could move at will between the natural world and the imagined landscape. In order to be available for human ritual, therefore, they required a sacred space in the human realm *(hieron)*, kept pure because only those who were pure

19. Koerner (1973) 180–81.

20. A fifth-century Athenian inscription prohibited soaking hides in the Ilissos above the sanctuary of Herakles; *LSS* 4. A fifth-century Delian text prohibited washing, swimming, or depositing dung in a sacred fountain; *LSS* 50. The special sanctity of the so-called Sacred Spring at Corinth was protected by an early-fifth-century inscription requiring any unqualified person who went down to the spring to pay a fine; Williams (1969) 36–62. An inscription at Kos prohibited the throwing of sacrificial cakes into a fountain; *LSCG* 152; cf. *LSCG* 75, *LSAM* 57. Inscriptions from Keos and Andania protected the water flowing into a sanctuary; *IG* XII (5) 569 and XII suppl. p. 114 (Keos, sanctuary of Demeter), *LSCG* 65.103–6 (Andania, sanctuary of the two goddesses).

21. A third-century Tean inscription provides a rare list of the various uses for protected water: purification preliminary to public sacrifice, ritual bathing, and the bath of a bride before a wedding ceremony; Herrmann (1965) 39, lines 76–83.

22. Pausanias 2.17.1 describes the stream flowing along the road at the Argive Heraion as the source for the water that female worshippers used for purification.

23. Moulinier (1952); Rudhardt (1958); Parker (1983).

(hagnos) or were made pure (*katharos,* "purified," "clean") could entertain divinity. For humans, communication with the gods required observance of routine rules for purity, and a worshipper who was not purified (*ou katharos,* "not clean") could compromise sacred space and spoil any ritual act in progress. Untroubled themselves by death, the gods avoided death itself. The dead, defined as polluted (*miaroi,* "filthy," and therefore not able to be made clean), were a potential source of pollution for the entire community. Contact with the dead compromised human interaction with the gods because the gods were beings without death *(athanatoi).* In order to create space in the human realm pure enough for communication with the divine, humans therefore had to reserve space free from contamination by death. Indeed, any distinctly human activity (birth, sex, eating food, defecation) could be a source of pollution and therefore a barrier to the gods. Acts that illustrated or demonstrated an individual's claim to have temporarily separated the body from its natural functions—for instance, by sprinkling pure water, avoiding certain foods, or waiting a short time after sexual intercourse—prepared a person to approach the gods. The vocabulary of purity overlapped the vocabulary of cleanliness, but the two states, cleanliness and purity, were not the same.[24]

The same system that recognized special areas as marked off for communication with the gods also required removal of the dead to a place outside the boundaries of the community's inhabited area. The cemetery therefore became a necessary corollary to the city, a shadow community located outside the population center. Except for the tombs of the heroized dead, usually located in the *agora,* graves were normally kept out of nucleated settlements. Consequently, they are often found along main loads leading out of town.[25]

Division of the community's territory recognized the gods' claim to space within the human realm. Boundary stones *(horoi),* fenced enclosures *(periboloi),* and basins of water *(perirrhanteria)* placed at the entrance to a sacred enclosure were visible indicators of the presence of divinity. These physical objects were reminders that any negotiation or interaction with a god required a ritual gesture of purification as acknowledgment of divine status. There is no ancient description of a formally articulated system, but concerns about pollution are already an issue in Homer,[26] and Hesiod's list

24. Neumann (1992) for the meaning of *katharos* in early texts.

25. Carter (1998) 1.25–56, for the clear evidence at Metapontum.

26. For the vocabulary: καθαίρειν, *Od.* 20.152; λύματα, *Il.* 1.314, 14.171; λύθρον, *Il.* 11.169, 20.503; *Od.* 22.402; μιαρός, *Il.* 24.420.

of admonitions includes several categories of activities considered polluting.[27] By the seventh century, however, it is the widespread presence of water basins at sanctuary entrances that indicates how much the demonstration of personal purity already affected relations with the gods.[28] Ritual acts had become social events, and eligibility for participation had to be readily evident. Neither Homer nor Hesiod provides the detail that would help to reconstruct the complete system, but the material evidence makes it clear that a working pollution code had already begun to take shape.

DISCOVERING SACRED SPACE AND CREATING RITUAL SPACE

The gods belonged to the natural world and were therefore considered necessarily prior to the *polis,* even when new cities were founded in new territories. The assumption that the gods predated the community is made clear in the *Homeric Hymn to Apollo,* where Leto stakes out Apollo's claim to the island of Delos before his birth and promises the island a steady stream of worshippers bringing gifts and making sacrifice.[29] Solon describes how he brought those once enslaved in foreign territories and led them back to Attika, "their fatherland, founded by the gods."[30] A fourth-century decree from the Ionian *polis* of Kolophon acknowledges the same idea, recognizing that any change in the city's boundaries required the approval of the city's gods because they had inhabited the place first. Before extending the fourth-century city wall to encompass the original site of old Kolophon, the citizens recalled the history of the city's foundation and decided

> to enclose the old city within the same wall as the existing city—the old city that the gods handed over to our ancestors and that our ancestors settled by building temples and altars, thereby becoming famous among all Greeks. That this might be accomplished quickly, on the fourth day of the coming month, the priest of Apollo and the other priests and priestesses and the *prytanis,* together with the *boule* and those appointed in this decree, are to go down to the old *agora,* and at the altars of the gods left behind for us by our ancestors, they are to

27. Hes. *Op.* 724–59.

28. Water basins appear at entrances to Greek sanctuaries late in the seventh century, an indication that purity was already a prerequisite for contact with a sacred space. For the earliest evidence, see Pimpl (1997).

29. *Hymn. Hom. Ap.* 51–61.

30. Sol. 36.8 (πάτριδ᾽ ἐς θεόκτιτον).

> pray to Zeus Soter, Poseidon who brings security, Apollo of Klaros, Mother Antaia, Athena Polias, and to all the other gods and heroes who dwell in our city *(polis)* and land *(chora)*; and when benefits are bestowed, they are to hold a procession and sacrifice, just as the *demos* decides.[31]

In the course of the procedure, the priests and priestesses of Kolophon visited the altars in the old *agora* to recognize formally the unity between the current site and the original site of the city. The decision to extend the wall was ratified by sacrifices to the gods and heroes who inhabited the walled city (called here *polis*) and its territory *(chora)*. Finally, the decree justified the city's claim to its territory by asserting that the people received the city as a gift from the gods who dwelled in the land itself. According to such claims, a sanctuary was located in the natural home of the deity, whether in the city itself or out in the landscape of the city's territory.

Each *polis* had its own constellation of divinities. Citizens of fourth-century Kolophon knew from experience which of their gods "dwelled" in the town and which in the countryside, and it was natural for them to consider all of these as belonging to the *polis*, just as they considered both the walled town and the surrounding countryside to be their own. The Kolophonians found reassurance and derived a sense of stability from the belief that just as Leto had "discovered" Delos for Apollo,[32] and Apollo himself had "discovered" Delphi for his oracle,[33] their gods had "discovered" their city for them. According to this view, founding a new city required building temples and altars in recognition of the gods' gift. The real history of city foundation, urban planning, and community development was of course far more complex,[34] but cities, competing for status, inspired foundation myths that recognized the gods' direct participation. Divine support justified claims to territory, and evidence of divine approval was a requirement for *polis* identity.

31. Migeotte (1992) 214–23 no. 69; between 311 and 306. Kolophon had a complex history and probably had good reason to rely on the gods for claims to continuity. The old city was more or less abandoned at the time of the Persian advance in about 545, when at least part of the population moved to Italy. The independence of fourth-century Kolophon was short-lived; Lysimachos destroyed the city in 294 and moved most of its population to Ephesos (Paus. 1.9.7).

32. *Hymn. Hom. Ap.* 49.

33. *Hymn. Hom. Ap.* 244–45.

34. Malkin (1987), on *Od.* 6.9–10, the earliest reference to "choosing" a sacred space for a sanctuary. Malkin points out that ἱδρύειν here means "consecrate" as well as "found."

The decree from Kolophon shows that the gods of the *polis* could be anchored anywhere: on the *akropolis*, in the *agora*, or in the surrounding *chora*. The decree assumes the priority of the gods and recognizes that the land belonged to its divine residents long before the time of any human occupation. According to this view, the gods were the first inhabitants of Kolophon and, when the first settlers arrived, space for divine rituals had to be discovered.[35] The people of Kolophon recognized a convention whereby they had to obtain approval from the gods associated with the land if they wanted to introduce changes in the organization of their own civic space. In practice, because there had to be flexibility between competing claims of the gods and the actual needs of any city, the requirements of ritual were satisfied by procedures subject to public discussion and legislative decision. The Kolophonians knew what they had to do because, like other *poleis*,[36] they had administrative procedures for regulating the space allotted to the gods. As a result, ritual space did not have to be discovered; it could also be created.

There were three occasions for creating ritual space: 1) when establishing a new community, 2) when introducing a new ritual, and 3) when a normally secular space was to be used for a temporary ritual event. When a new city was founded or an old city moved, space had to be formally allocated for sacred precincts, altars, and temples of the gods, both within local settlements and out in the countryside. Sacred objects, portable representations of divinity, equipment for special rituals, and fire for sacrifice had to be replicated and transported from the home city to a new site.[37] Conversely, when a new god was imported from elsewhere, convention required that space for sacrifice and divine residence be found. Fifth-century examples at Athens include the cult of Pan, introduced on the north slope of the *akropolis* after Marathon; the healing ritual of Asklepios, brought from Epidauros in the 420s; and the Thracian cult of Bendis, introduced in the Peiraieus after the Peloponnesian War.[38] In a similar fashion, when an

35. As Leto "discovers" Delos (*Hymn. Hom. Ap.* 49) and Apollo "discovers" Delphi (*Hymn. Hom. Ap.* 244–53).

36. The Athenians had a law about sanctuary precincts and the procedures for maintaining the boundaries of ritual space; *IG* I^3 84.25: κατὰ τὸν νόμον ὅσπερ κεῖται τôν τεμενôν.

37. Malkin (1987, 1994). Setting off to found their new city in the sky, Aristophanes' Peisetairos and Euelpides carry a basket (*kanoun*) for sacred equipment and a pot (*chytra*) for sacred fire; Ar. *Av.* 43. See also Ar. *Lys.* 291–98 and Xen. *Hell.* 4.5.4 for sacred fire in pots.

38. Garland (1990).

established sanctuary needed to be enlarged, space already subject to human habitation might have to be appropriated.[39] Ritual space could also be created on a temporary basis by converting a normally secular space to sacred so that an ephemeral ritual, such as a procession, sacrifice, or festival, might take place within a protected area recognized by the gods.

The terminology for ritual space was never sharply defined. *Hieron* (sacred space) and *temenos* (a place cut off, marked off) are the common terms used to describe a sanctuary. *Hieron* emphasized that the space was ready for divine occupation, *temenos,* in this context, that the area was distinguished from areas of human settlement; but even these distinctions were not always maintained in practice. *Peribolos,* whose use extended to any marked space, emphasized the outer perimeter. *Sekos* described an enclosed area, usually a walled precinct.[40] A temple, *naos,* usually housed the cult statue of the god. Separate areas within a temple or precinct, called *abaton* or *adyton,* were often subject to special restriction. Terms like *oikos* (house) and *oikema* (building) were also used for structures in sanctuaries, and the general term for sanctuary, *hieron* (in the sense of "sacred area"), could refer to a sacred building, even the temple itself. Consequently, when one of our ancient informants mentions a *hieron,* we often have no way of confirming whether the term refers to a sacred precinct or a sacred building unless the author actually describes a building or states that the sanctuary did not have one.

To avoid inadvertent pollution, a sacred area needed to be easily identifiable. Large, well-established sanctuaries would have been recognizable from their conventional architecture, elaborate entrances, and, in some cases, a specially designated sacred road or procession route leading directly to the sanctuary. Many sacred plots, however, were not so obviously marked. In the countryside, any grove, spring, modest rock ledge, or cave could belong to a deity. Visitors were expected to understand that such places might be sacred and to realize that they should modify their behavior in a way appropriate to divine requirements.[41]

Sophokles' *Oidipous at Kolonos* defines three kinds of sacred space. The poet assumes his Athenian audience recognizes that the grove of the Semnai Theai—goddesses so holy they could only be feared—at Kolonos was

39. Bergquist (1992) 130–31, 136 for the appropriation of private property to enlarge sanctuaries at Syracuse, Kasmeni, and Megara Hyblaia; and 132 for desacralization, the reverse procedure, at Naxos.

40. In Homer, *sekos* means "sheep-fold"; the idea of a small enclosure open to the sky extends to ritual contexts as well.

41. Pl. *Phd.* 279c.

not to be violated and that Oidipous's intrusion was unacceptable. Verbal clues in Antigone's description of the special features of the precinct supply a familiar image for her listeners. She herself recognizes the sanctity of the grove by its appearance, as she describes a place rich with laurel, olive, and vines. Her description of the foliage, however, could apply to any well-watered rural sanctuary. Such a place might have been identifiable by inscription or a cluster of dedications indicating to visitors that a god held the title. For example, a privately endowed cave sanctuary near Pharsalus in Thessaly had posted at the entrance a long list of those invited to enter, but the status of the place would probably have been obvious to anyone who noticed the "very sacred plants, plaques, votive statues, and many gifts" that were scattered around as well as itemized in the inscribed text.[42]

The natural clues at Kolonos indicate a sacred space, but even Antigone does not recognize the force of the restrictions here. Oidipous, blind and indifferent to whether he is "set down by places where a man can tread or by groves of the gods,"[43] is not shaken, even when a local inhabitant rushes up to warn the two that the ground where he sits is "not right to tread,"[44] "not to be touched,"[45] and "not to be occupied."[46] He interprets his trespass of the grove as a consequence of a prophecy of Apollo[47] and by doing so also complicates the situation, for now he must be recognized as both suppliant to the people of Attika and penitent to the Feared Goddesses themselves.[48] When Antigone offers rites of expiation for her father's violation of their sacred grove, these daughters of Earth and Dark will have to accept not only his compensatory ritual of purification but Oidipous himself.[49]

Oidipous's situation is abnormal and his action flagrantly transgressive, but the conventions for recognizing sacred space conveyed by the scene are not. The action of the play is anchored in a deep respect for the demands of divinity. The text recognizes three types of sacred space: the untrodden precinct of the goddesses, a sanctuary and altar of Poseidon, and, by the end

42. The cave is located on a small plateau, 25 m. in length, accessible by a crude stairway; *IThessaly* I 73, fourth century B.C.E.

43. And therefore restricted; see Soph. *OC* 10: *ἢ πρὸς βεβήλοις ἢ πρὸς ἄλσεσιν θεῶν*.

44. Soph. *OC* 37: *χῶρον οὐχ ἁγνὸν πατεῖν*. Cf. Eur. *Erechtheus* F IV. 87 Diggle, for an *ἄβατον τέμενος* for the Hyakinthidai.

45. Soph. *OC* 39: *ἄθικτος*.

46. Soph. *OC* 39: *οὐδ' οἰκητός*. Cf. *ἀστιβὲς ἄλσος*, 125.

47. Soph. *OC* 97–98.

48. Soph. *OC* 44.

49. Soph. *OC* 466–506.

of the play, the tomb of Oidipous himself. Requirements of space are calibrated to match the character of the god in charge. The action takes place on the hill of Kolonos, from which the sweep of the Attic plain below can easily be seen. The local sanctuary of Poseidon Hippios defines the whole hill as sacred,[50] and here, just out of view of the grove, the god has his altar. Those who meet the qualifications for sacrifice can enter without restriction. In the vicinity is the "Bronze-Footed Threshhold," entryway to the world of the dead, as ominous as the grove of the Dread Goddesses. The grove is very near but separate, a space that cannot be entered. The name of the goddesses is too terrible to speak; one can pass only with eye and face averted and worship only with voiceless prayer.[51]

When Oidipous asks how he can provide the purification these divinities require, he is told to fetch water from an ever-flowing spring; to touch it only with hands properly cleaned; to wreathe the brim of his *krater*s with the flock of a newly shorn, newly born ewe lamb; to stand facing the dawn; to pour out in three streams the pure water laced with honey but no wine; and laying three times nine olive branches on the spot moistened by these libations, to pray without sound and leave without turning around. The rigorous requirements of the ritual match the high sanctity of the spot and define the extreme danger of arousing the anger of the Unnamed Goddesses.[52] Unappeased, they embody the power of a hideous curse, and the passion for revenge drives them to relentless and deadly pursuit.

The grove at Kolonos was exceptional, but the concerns here about recognizing sacred space were real. Official and permanent markers and signs were part of the apparatus of worship. These could include boundary stones *(horoi)*, inscribed[53] or uninscribed; an enclosing wall *(peribolos)*; or a sign on wood or stone at the entrance stating the regulations for entry or use.[54] Rules for entry varied with the nature of the deity, the character of the rites performed, the identity of the worshippers, and even the special characteristics of the place.[55] In the early fifth century, inscribed *horoi* placed at the

50. Soph. *OC* 54.
51. Soph. *OC* 125–32.
52. Soph. *OC* 469–92.
53. Guarducci, *Epigrafia* 4:48, for a boundary stone marking a sanctuary of Cheiron at Poseidonia; and 49–50, for another for Zeus Aglaios at Metapontum, both early examples—sixth century B.C.E.
54. Paus. 8.37.2 describes such an inscription at Lykosoura. For the one actually found there, *IG* V.2 514 (*LSCG* 68).
55. Athenian *horoi* are collected in *IG* II^2 2505–641, supplemented now by Lalonde (1991). For rock-cut *horoi* marking divisions between one deme and another, see Lohmann (1992) 33–34, with fig. 5 (a rock-cut *horos* text on Mt. Megali

entrances to the Athenian *agora* defined a central communal space.[56] The marked-off area at the center of the city included both sacred space *(hieron)*, set aside to recognize the gods, and civic space *(hosion)*, set aside for activities on behalf of the city.[57] Both were protected by conventions that excluded anyone who might compromise the community's relation to its gods. The *horoi* at the corners of the Athenian *agora* marked the external boundaries of the total area; other individual *horoi* within that area indicated individual sanctuaries.[58] Each of the *horoi* at an external corner was inscribed with the first-person address, "I am the *horos* of the *agora.*"[59] Archaic convention represented the boundary stone itself as speaker[60] and emphasized its active role as guardian.[61]

A special water basin, *perirrhanterion*[62] or *hagisterion*,[63] placed at an entrance, was also an indication of a sacred precinct. In form, a *perirrhanterion* was a wide, shallow basin at about hand height upon a narrow column. *Perirrhanteria* were made of stone, sometimes marble or even a precious metal, less often of ceramic. Early examples date from the middle of the seventh century, with the earliest from Samos and Isthmia.[64] Within a few decades, they were to be found throughout the Aegean, the mainland, and as far west as Sicily.[65] By the sixth century such basins were widely dispersed, and it is clear from the decorations that some types were the result of eastern influence.[66] High concentrations clustered at major

---

Baphi defining the border of the deme Atene). Guarducci collects public *horoi* marking civic space in *Epigrafia* 2:430–40, private *horoi* marking possession of land or land held in security for debt in *Epigrafia* 3:227–45, and *horoi* marking sacred space in *Epigrafia* 4:46–73.

56. Lalonde (1991) 10; H25–27. Lalonde points out that these had become necessary because of the exclusion of those considered *atimoi.* Aristophanes parodies the communal bond when Dikaiopolis sets up *horoi* for his own private *agora;* Ar. *Ach.* 719.

57. Connor (1987) 173, with n. 41.

58. For example, the fifth-century boundary marker from the *agora* inscribed simply: *τô hιερô*, "of the sanctuary"; Lalonde (1991).

59. Three, dating to about 500, have been found; Lalonde (1991) 27, H25–27.

60. Ober (1995) for the boundary stone performing a speech act.

61. Engelmann and Merkelbach (1971).

62. Hdt. 1.51; *IG* II^2 1641.38 (Athens); *IG* XI.2 287 A.93 (Delos); *SIG*^{3} 253 II.10 (Delphi); *IG* XII.8 365 (Thasos); *LSS* 91 (Lindos).

63. *LSAM* 12.9 (Pergamon).

64. The most recent survey is found in Pimpl (1997) 14–16.

65. From Samos to Selinous, from Delphi to Sparta; for the early dispersal, see Pimpl (1997) 2, etc.

66. Ginouvés (1962) 306–7, Ducat (1964) for early basins on stands depicting three *korai;* Handorf (1974) for a summary of the earliest examples. The geographic

sanctuaries,[67] where they were often dedicated by ritual attendants to publicize and commemorate personal service. *Perirrhanteria* were located at entrances to sanctuaries to mark the transition between human and divine. A *perirrhanterion* conveyed a warning that entry to a sacred area was impossible for anyone who could not demonstrate the necessary ritual purity. The early diffusion and widespread use of a vessel associated with regulating ritual purity indicates an early and generally accepted concern to represent the sacred *temenos* as separate from secular life.[68]

Where a *perirrhanterion* marked a boundary, a ritual sprinkling was enough to attest to the ritual purity of the worshipper. The verb *perirrhainesthai* (middle voice: "to sprinkle all around oneself") describes a personal act that established eligibility to join in a collective sacrifice. The act is described by the Hippocratic author of *On the Sacred Disease* in the following way:

> We mark out the boundaries of the sanctuaries and precincts of the gods so that no one crosses them unless pure, and when we do enter, we sprinkle all around ourselves, not because we are actually in a state of being polluted, *but because, if we have any possible prior taint, we might purify ourselves of it.*[69]

No author has described the gesture of "sprinkling around," but the one quoted here comes closer than anyone else.[70] This very abbreviated description of the ritual gesture is embedded in a double analogy between, on the one hand, unauthorized healers and purifiers, and on the other, doctors and ritual specialists. The author disapproves of the incantations of freelance purifiers just as he disapproves of the improvised purifications of freelance healers, but the traditional purification rites required for entry to

---

area is widespread: Samos, Rhodes, the Boiotian Ptoion, Corinth, Sparta, Delphi, Aigina, Lindos, Chios, Perachora, Isthmia, and Olympia. For an extensive catalogue and detailed typology, see Pimpl (1997).

67. At Olympia, one cluster of dedications is associated with the temple of Hera and another with the ash altar of Zeus; Pimpl (1997) 24.

68. Rolley (1983) 113. In addition to the *perirrhanteria* at the entrances to sanctuaries, other water basins of various kinds appear in representations of Greek sacrifice, where the sprinkling of water in preliminary rites provided a temporal boundary between ordinary experience and the act of sacrifice. See Eitrem (1915) 78–79; Ginouvés (1962) 311–17; *LSCG* 139.15 (for ritual sprinkling after sexual intercourse before entering a sanctuary).

69. [Hippoc.] *Morb. Sacr.* 1.110–12. The italicized text appears in only one ms.

70. The same verb for sprinkling is used by Theophrastus, *Char.* 16.1, 12, in contexts describing excessive attention to ritual.

a recognized sanctuary and performed on behalf of a divinity, like the medical cures based on a rational *techne,* he accepts as legitimate.

The ritual of the *perirrhanterion* demonstrated purity by an allopathic process that employed pure water to expel any trace of pollution. The water had to come from a pure spring[71] because it had to counteract any residual impurity connected with any person about to enter a sacred space. Some early *perirrhanteria,* take the form of a basin for water set on a column made up of three female figures, *korai.*[72] *Hydrophoroi,* young, unmarried female water-carriers, were frequent components of festival processions. Their own sexual purity testified to the purity of the water they carried,[73] and the triple karyatids who supported the pure water of the *perirrhanterion* imply a similar standard. Not for washing, but sprinkled in small amounts,[74] the water of the *perirrhanterion* signified that all ritual requirements were met. The claim that a sprinkling of water could eradicate "any possible prior taint" meant that the sprinkling could remedy even a taint of which the worshipper was unaware.[75]

The Hippocratic author's use of the middle voice for the verb of sprinkling (*περιρραίνεσθαι*) indicates that the act was self-reflexive and that the worshipper sprinkled the water around her or his own body.[76] Lucian claimed that murderers could not even touch the basins,[77] and Demosthenes says that anyone not clean of hand did wrong to enter the *agora,* referring to an area that in his day was marked off by *perirrhanteria.*[78] The emphasis on hands and touching suggests that when approaching the

71. Cf. the water for the *chernips,* handwashing prior to sacrifice, Thuc. 4.97: (*ὕδωρ . . . ἄψαυστον*).

72. Comments by Pimpl (1997) 56–58.

73. The requirement of virginity for *hydrophoroi* meant that a candidate had to have a spotless reputation. The requirement of virginity for *kanephoroi* at the Panathenaia explains the insult to Harmodios, when the invitation to be a *kanephoros* extended to his sister was withdrawn on the grounds that she was "unworthy;" Thuc. 6.56.

74. Parker (1983) 227.

75. Pl. *Crat.* 405a–b, for purity of body and soul as the goal of ritual bathing and "sprinklings" (*περιρράνσεις*). Such analogies tend to be post-Classical; see Chaniotis (1997).

76. For the same use of the middle voice, cf. Theophr. *Char.* 16; Plut. *Arist.* 20.

77. Lucian *Sacr.* 13.2. For hands polluted by murder, schol. Aesch. *Cho.* 1056; Rhod. 4.702.

78. Dem. 24.60. Theophrastus's *deisidaimon* washed his hands before sprinkling himself; *Char.* 16.1. See Pimpl (1997) 104, for the dedication of a hand and a *perirrhanterion* at Thasos.

perirrhanterion, a worshipper extended a hand, most likely the right,[79] to dip into the pure water. To indicate purity one could then either turn around in place to inscribe a circle of droplets all around the body[80] or simply sprinkle drops of water round about one's clothing.[81] Either action would have defined a temporary boundary around a piece of personal sacred space, creating an invisible envelope that separated the worshipper from even the incidental defilements of ordinary life. The gesture was important because it would have signalled to other participants that anyone pure enough to touch the *perirrhanterion* was eligible to take part in a ceremony honoring the gods and would therefore not jeopardize either the ritual or other participants.[82]

By the middle of the fourth century, then, there were *perirrhanteria* marking a special area within the *agora,* a marked-out area perhaps considered more restricted than the larger area within the *horoi* of the Archaic period.[83] Both *horos* and *perirrhanterion* served to guard and protect, and to remind those who approached that access to the marked space required

79. On vases depicting the preliminary washing of the ritual slaughterer's hands before a sacrifice, the attendant extends the vessel of pure water *(chernips)* with his right hand; Van Straten (1995) figs. 30–35. Pimpl (1997) emphasizes that a vase depicting Apollo himself at a *perirrhanterion* shows the god extending his right hand toward the basin; Oxford C 27; *LIMC* II (1984) s.v. Apollo, no. 469. On the meaning of the right hand, Hertz (1960, reprint of 1909 edition).

80. Taking the verb in its literal sense, with the prefix as in LSJ, s.v. περί, F.2: "completion of an orbit and return to the same point." For verbs of purification or expiation compounded with *peri-*, see Pfister (1935) *RE* Suppl. 6:149–51; Parker (1983) 226 n. 100, and 225–26 (emphasizing the symbolic nature of gestures implying encirclement). The new *lex sacra* from Selinous describes a purification ritual where, after sacrificing a piglet to Zeus, the performer is instructed to withdraw and turn himself around (περιστραφέσθο); Jameson, Jordan, and Kotansky (1993) 16 B.5, with 43, for discussion of the possible meanings of this term. Those leaving a house where a corpse was laid out for burial used a branch of laurel for sprinkling about themselves with water; schol. Eur. *Alc.* section 98. Trygaios at Ar. *Pax* 957 commands the slave to "go around the altar on the right side." Pliny *NH* 28.25 describes the Roman ritual of turning around in place.

81. Sprinkling "around about" oneself would not have been the same act as washing or bathing, which, when required for ritual, was normally described by the verb *louesthai,* "to wash (oneself); to bathe." The fact that Plato must argue that ritual baths and "ritual sprinkling" (περίρρανσις) have the same effect—to make a person "clean" (καθαρός) in body and soul (Pl. *Cra.* 405b)—indicates that they were in fact separate acts, even if differing only in degree.

82. For the risk of pollution to the entire community because of the taint of a single individual, see Parker (1983) 279,

83. Aeschin. 1.21, 3.176, both with scholia; see also Lucian *Sacr.* 2–3, *Pseudol.* 23 (for a dirty mouth); Poll. 1.8. Cf. Pl. *Leg.* 6.778d. Several fragments have been found near the *tholos* and the *bouleuterion;* Pimpl (1997) 117.

a special gesture and special behavior.[84] The space within the Athenian *perirrhanteria* was a restricted area,[85] a privileged space associated with the responsibilities of citizenship. The gesture of sprinkling a personal boundary could therefore be considered a prerequisite for participation in the public ritual of the *agora* and a basic requirement for collective political life. Murder,[86] accepting payment for sexual favors,[87] or toleration of a wife's adultery[88] could disqualify a citizen from the ritual of the *perirrhanterion*, exclude him from the political area of the *agora*, and thereby cut him off from the activities of citizenship. Diogenes registers scorn for the man who assumes that sprinkling oneself with the water from a *perirrhanterion* will erase the effects of any sort of error or personal failure. In the same way, Theophrastos takes a dig at the overanxious sprinkler who performs the rites at every opportunity. Neither author doubts the propriety of the ritual of the *perirrhanterion* correctly performed, but both have scorn for those who perform the ritual too much and too often.[89]

Contamination of a sacred space, whether deliberate or inadvertent, required ritual repair; consequently the boundaries of a sacred area needed routine maintenance. The most common act of purification required cutting the throat[90] of a newborn piglet[91] and walking around the perimeter of the designated area while letting the blood drip from the carcass. The procedure was described by the Greek phrase *peritemnein choiro*, "to cut a

84. *Horoi* marking a sacred precinct, whether inscribed or not, always implied a warning. Sometimes special instructions were given. The stones say things like "No building allowed in the sanctuary" (*IG* VII 422); "No trash dumping" (*IG* II^2 2631, 2632).

85. Poll. 1.8: ὁ εἴσω περιρραντηρίων τόπος, "the place within the *perirrhanteria*." Cf. Eur. *Ion* 434–35: ἀλλὰ χρυσέαις πρόχοισιν ἐλθὼν εἰς ἀπορραντήρια. Pimpl (1997) 120 summarizes the two major positions on whether this area was the whole *agora* (the scholiast on Aeschin. 3.176, who says there were two *perirrhanteria*, one on each side of the entrance to the *agora*) or a special, bounded space within the *agora* (Aeschin. 1.21: ἐντὸς τῶν τῆς ἀγορᾶς περιρραντηρίων).

86. Lucian, *Sacr.* 13.2: "the public notice says: do not allow within the *perirrhanteria* anyone who is not pure of hand." See also Eur. *Stheneboia* F I. 16–19 Diggle; Dem. 24.60.

87. Aeschin. 1.19 (male prostitution), 21 (inserted law).

88. Aeschin. 1.183; [Dem.] 59.84–87; Harrison (1968) 1: 35–36.

89. Diog. Laert. 6.42; Theophr. *Char.*

90. Apollon. 4.700–709; Circe cuts the throat of a piglet and sprinkles with its warm blood the hands of Jason and Medea as expiation (λυτήριον) for the death of Apsyrtos. The piglet used to purify the assembly at Athens is called ἱερεῖον in schol. Aeschin. 1.23; the rite is described by the verbs θύειν and σφάζειν in schol. Ar. *Ach.* 44.

91. Apollon. 4.708: the piglet is still a suckling pig. Cf. Eur. *Stheneboia* F I.18: ἐπισφάξας νεόν.

circuit with a piglet"—a procedure so mechanically performed that it is rarely even mentioned in the literary sources.[92] After the circuit was completed, the used carcass (κάθαρμα or καθάρσιον), now irredeemably polluted,[93] had to be thrown outside the boundaries of the city into a place where no one would dare to step. Such places included the no-man's land between the outer boundaries of one *polis* and the next, the empty triangular space at a *triodos* where three roads came together,[94] and the sea.[95]

Symbolic marking of a perimeter was done to create, maintain, or restore ritual purity. At Delos, tracing with a bleeding piglet the sacred perimeter of the island or the boundary of the sanctuary was a regular part of the scheduled maintenance supported by public funds. Annual accounts include the prices for the individual piglets for purifying the entire island,[96] for the piglet to purify the sanctuary of Apollo on the first day of each month,[97] and for the individual piglets used once a year to purify the Thesmophorion for the Thesmophoria.[98] Where purification with a piglet was required, it was normally carried out in anticipation of a regularly scheduled ritual. At Athens, circumambulation with a piglet preceded any communal meeting: around the *pnyx* for the assembly (immediately after the prayer delivered by the herald and in full view of those assembled),[99] around the *bouleuterion*, the place where the council met, and around the theater before dramatic performances.[100] Enclosure indicated eligibility for

92. The title of the ritual attendant who performed the rite was *peristiarchos*, the *katharsia* were called *peristia;* Istros *FGrH* 334 F 16.

93. Schol. Aeschin. 1.23.

94. The empty space where three roads met; Johnston (1991).

95. Dem. 54.39, for carcasses of the piglets used for purification mentioned together with the Hekataia normally found at crossroads; a scholion on Aeschin. 1.23 says the dead piglets were thrown into the sea. Of the objects used in healing purifications, whose disposal was derived from that of objects used in traditional purifications, some were hidden in the earth, others thrown into the sea, and others carried away to the mountains, "where no one will touch them or tread on them," *Morb. Sacr.* 1.99–102.

96. Purification of the island is listed frequently in the Delian accounts, for example, *IDelos* 290.71, 246 B.C.E. (χοῖρος τὴν Νῆσον [κ]αθάρασ[θ]αι, "a piglet: for purifying the island").

97. In the accounts, the piglet used to purify the sanctuary is often the first item listed for the month; see *IG* XI.2 203.32, 34, etc., 269 B.C.E.: *Ληναιῶνος· χοῖρος παρὰ Νίκωνος τὸ ἱερὸγ καθάρασθαι* (Lenaion: a piglet from Nikon for purifying the temple).

98. *IG* XI.1 204.68–69, 268 B.C.E.: *χοῖρος τὸ Θεσμοφόριον καθάρασθαι.* For a collection of relevant texts, see Bruneau (1970) 26–75.

99. Aeschin. 2.158.

100. Schol. Ar. *Eccl.* 128 (assembly); schol. Aeschin. 1.23 (assembly and theater; the piglets are called μικρὰ χοιρίδια); Harp. s.v. καθάρσιον (the assembly, the

inclusion,[101] and marking a perimeter created group solidarity and provided a formal mechanism to inspire order and encourage cooperation.

If the purity of a sanctuary was compromised, no one could sacrifice until sacred status was restored through rituals of purification. At Delos, after the entire island had been purified by Nikias in 426, it was polluting to give birth,[102] have a dog, burn or bury a corpse,[103] or even raise pigeons on the island.[104] After 426, a sudden death anywhere on the island or even a corpse washed up on the beach required remedial ritual with a piglet at public expense.[105] Special precincts elsewhere had similar strict requirements. In Attika, when a corpse was found on the Rharian Plain (agricultural land near Eleusis sacred to the Two Goddesses), the expense for the piglet to purify the land appeared in the Athenian accounts.[106]

Tracing a new boundary with the blood of a suckling pig could also create a temporary sacred space for an ephemeral ritual event. At Delos, annual accounts for the procession preliminary to the Dionysia included costs for cleaning and preparing the streets and the price of the piglet to purify the parade route and the *skene* in the theater.[107] A regulation about processions of Dionysos and Zeus Soter in the Peiraieus contains similar requirements.[108] There the *agoranomoi* were in charge of preparing and grading the streets through which these processions passed. The street was considered pure only as long as the ritual required it, and until the cere-

---

theater, and all public meetings of the *demos*). In schol. Ar. *Ach.* 44, the piglet is called *delphax,* and his death explained as retaliation for harming Demeter's crop.

101. This is implied by the quotation at schol. Aeschin. 1.23 of Ar. *Ach.* 44: "Come here, so that you are within the (boundary of the) *katharma*" (πάριθ' ὡς ἂν ἐντὸς ἦτε τοῦ καθάρματος).

102. The purification was carried out because of an oracle. After 426, anyone about to give birth or die was removed to the island of Rheneia; Thuc. 3.104. The Delian requirements after 426 are unusual for the extent of space involved. Ordinarily such regulations were confined to a particular sanctuary or part of a sanctuary. Paus. 2.27.1 describes similar regulations at Epidauros, where *horoi* all around the sacred grove of Asklepios mark the area: "Men do not die there nor do their wives give birth within the *peribolos.*"

103. For dogs and the dead, Str. 10.5.5 (486c).

104. Because they soiled the sanctuary. The guano of doves was such a problem that the priests collected it and sold it; *IG* XI.2 147.18; 144A.21; 161A.43; 162A.39; 287A.20, 23–24, with discussion by Bruneau (1970) 419–20.

105. The epigraphical evidence is collected by Bruneau (1970) 50. The island had to be purified from accidental death, a corpse washed up on the shore, or an unexpected birth or miscarriage.

106. *IG* II^2 1672.119–20.

107. *IG* XI.2 203A.38; 269 B.C.E.

108. *IG* II^2 380; early fourth century B.C.E.; see Owens (1983) 44–50.

mony took place, anyone who defiled the processional route by pouring wash water or human waste into the street had to pay a fine. The flexible system allowed streets and spaces normally not maintained as sacred to qualify as space ready for ritual. The state of purity achieved by this process lasted only as long as the area was not contaminated by a proscribed activity, and the space so marked reverted to normal status as soon as the ritual performance was finished.

The people of Kolophon maintained that the gods themselves had ordained the locations of their sanctuaries, but they also assumed that by legislative procedures they could consult the gods when it became necessary to change the arrangement of the city's space. There was always a certain flexibility in the rules. We have seen that space could be temporarily designated as sacred. A designated space compromised because of neglect or carelessness could be recovered by legislative intervention. Sanctuaries whose boundaries had been eroded by agricultural, domestic, or even cemetery encroachment could be redefined and reconsecrated. The Athenians organized a massive reclamation process in the late first century B.C.E. when they passed legislation to restore fifty-two properties. These parcels were divided by the decree into shrines *(hiera)* and precincts *(temene)* of the gods and heroes on the one hand, and public reservations *(demosia ore)* and public buildings *(demosiai oikiai)* on the other. Dedication (the verb is *kathieroun*) as well as restoration *(apokathistenai)* were necessary because, as the ordinance itself says, "it is a matter of ancestral custom that no one give birth nor die in any of the sacred precincts."[109] The decree of the Athenians ordained that traditional sacrifices and processions be restored and that the old terms for leasing sacred and public land be followed. The need to appeal to ancestral custom is itself an indication of a certain administrative indifference, but someone must have been paying attention, because in at least one project of sanctuary restoration an oracle was consulted to establish the correct procedure.

MAPPING THE URBAN COMMUNITY

Like her "mother" city, Paros, Thasos was a harbor town on an island. Both mother city and daughter city were grape growers and wine producers, both were fortified, and both had sanctuaries inside as well as outside the city wall. Thasos, however, positioned in the northern Aegean with her

109. *IG* II^2 1035; Culley (1975, 1977), for explication.

harbor directly facing the visible Thracian coast, was close enough to the mainland to control her own vineyards there but far enough away to profit from the defense that distance could provide. The original colonists had brought from Paros the sacred fire, the images of their gods, and the special sacred objects necessary to establish traditional rituals from home in their new city. The list of divinities at Thasos included Zeus, Apollo, Artemis, Athena (called Poliouchos, "she who holds the city"), the Charites (the Graces), Peitho (Persuasion), Demeter, Kore, Herakles, Hera, Poseidon, Dionysos, Pan, and the Dioskouroi. Thasos was unusual in that it had a double *akropolis,* with Athena Poliouchos on one peak and Apollo Pythios on the other.

A walled city on a wooded island, Thasos gave the impression of a bastion in a barbarian land, protected by its gods and preserved by its rituals. Sanctuaries, public buildings, residential areas, and open spaces were symmetrically arranged. The *agora* was located on level ground near the harbor. A recently discovered inscription describes a protected space in the town center, bounded by the *prytaneion* (a building where important town officials dined), *symposion, argyramoibeïon* (the coin exchange), and the sanctuary of the Charites. The *agora* itself was surrounded by a ring of important sanctuaries (for Poseidon, Dionysos, Artemis, and Herakles); and two major residential areas, one to the east, the other to the west, reached as far as the wall that encircled the whole town. That wall, interrupted only by a series of tall towers and massive gates, climbed the rugged coastal hillside on the east to the high double *akropolis* above, then proceeded west along the crest of the *akropolis* before swinging back north to the harbor and drawing a line between the living city and its cemetery outside the wall to the west.

The wall divided the ordered political life of the protected space inside from the rugged landscape outside. Sculptural decorations at the gates of the city emphasized the distinction. At each gate a relief represented either a specific local divinity or an important communal ritual. The imagery and its placement sharpened the distinction between inside and outside. Gods and heroes, still in place, recall the festival processions of peacetime. In one relief, Hermes leads the Charites to their sanctuary in the *agora;* in another he conducts Artemis to the city by chariot. A giant Silenos, part horse, part man and companion to Dionysos, still marches towards the theater. Other scenes catch critical moments in important rituals, such as the *anakalupteria* (nuptial unveiling) of Hera before Zeus, model for the city's marriages, or a *theoxenia* (entertainment of a visiting divinity) commemorating the meal that followed a sacrifice. The divinities in procession face inward, moving toward the center of the city. Invited to attend their own festivals, they are presented in the act of responding to the hymns and prayers of their worshippers. Only Herakles turns towards the wilderness outside. He kneels on one knee, facing west, with bow strung and arrow in position, ready to strike any attacker that threatens the city. The companion relief that depicted Dionysos on the same gate has been lost, but the inscription identifies them both. Herakles was a major hero at Thasos, and his fenced precinct inside the town enclosed a row of dining rooms where the men of Thasos banqueted in his honor.

The fortification wall represented the physical integrity of the city. Thasos could be maintained in warfare even when cut off from its famous vineyards on the mainland, as it was when besieged by the Athenians under Kimon in the 460s. The Thasians protected their wall with the deities that protected the city. Near the wall's weakest point, on the huge lintel of one of the gates, a citizen named Parmenon added a symbol to protect the wall itself—an enormous carved image intended to terrorize intruders and freeze invaders in their tracks. Two giant eyes stare straight ahead, creating the dangerous, aggressive, and direct, head-on gaze that Greeks always tried to avoid.[110]

Demeter was located just outside the Thasian wall, a typical position for her in Greek colonial *poleis* both east and west. The women of Thasos gathered in this small sanctuary for the Thesmophoria, celebrated on the island in the late summer to prepare the land for the fall planting. Near the Thesmophorion an open precinct with several modest altars recognized the Thasian *patriai*, traditional groups that protected lineage. Patron divinities include Zeus Patroos (preserver of the patriline), Zeus Ktesios (protector of the storeroom), Zeus Alastoros (avenger), Athena Patroie (preserver of the patriline), Athena Mykesie, Artemis Orthosie (who sets upright), and the nymphs called Kourades. An inscription indicates that at the sacrifice for Athena Patroie, women were allotted sacrificial meat. The altar of Demeter and the altars of the *patriai* belong together, the one concerned with reproduction and nutrition of the family and the other protecting lineage and family identity.

The gods brought order to the landscape and structured the space inside the town. The sanctuaries determined the layout of the city, anchored its residential districts, and oriented the streets that connected one district to

110. The gates are described in detail by Picard (1962). The Thasian examples are a variation on fearsome traditional guardians of the city gates, for which see Faraone (1992) 18–35.

another. The largest building in any city was its largest temple. At Thasos, this was probably the temple of Athena Poliouchos high on the western *akropolis.* Athena was important, but Artemis, here located in the town center, was also powerful. Thasian coins, however, displayed not these gods but Herakles, Demeter, and Dionysos accompanied by his retinue of satyrs and nymphs, projecting an imagery that suggests a *polis* contending with fierce neighbors in a fierce landscape.

The message of the imagery on Thasian coins contradicted the ordered way in which the Thasians organized space within and outside their city wall. Outside the wall, point-to-point distances from the little harbor on the southern side of the island were posted on a late Archaic inscription found at Aliki.[111] Inside the wall, the gods of Thasos were closely involved in the organization and maintenance of space. Supervision of routine street-cleaning (and, by extension, purification of public spaces) was the responsibility of the *polis* in concert with its major sanctuaries. Actual duties, however, were divided between representatives of the corporate body of the *polis* and individual property owners.

A recently discovered inscription collects the rules about protecting public space and, in so doing, describes the major landmarks of the town.[112] The stone preserves two separate legal enactments, each containing several regulations. As a whole, the enactments cover three different but related subjects: routine street-cleaning and street maintenance, precautions to assure the purity of major civic arteries for scheduled events,[113] and protection of a special central area reserved for communal ritual and meetings.[114] Like texts recording other early laws, this one begins abruptly, without preamble:

> From the street of the shore : ------------------------
> ---------------- of the sanctuary of Herakles : from
> the street of the sanctuary of the Charites : in this

111. *LSAG*² 71a.

112. Duchêne (1992). The partially empty line at line 18 divides the text into two separate enactments organized according to the agent to whom the fines were paid (the first to Apollo Pythios and the *polis;* the second to the *polis,* with Artemis Hekate overseeing the collection of fines beginning in line 41). Fines in the first paragraph are a flat fee for a one-time offense; fines in the second paragraph are cumulative, based on either the total number of offenses or the number of days an offense lasted.

113. For a very different interpretation, see Graham (1998).

114. The stone stele was found underwater in the town harbor. Because the surface of the stone has suffered considerably since it was taken from the water, some of the original readings can no longer be verified.

street it is forbidden to construct a threshold : and do not draw water for ---------: and do not build any wells (?): and do not erect --------: and do not make --------: Whoever does any of these things in violation of what has been inscribed : must pay one hundred *staters* to Apollo Pythios : and one hundred to the *polis* : and the magistrates under whom he commits the violation are to exact payment : but if they do not, they themselves owe : the double penalty to the god and to the *polis* : and if in any way the penalty has not been recorded against the one committing the violation, he is not to pay it : who did not commit this (violation?) --------let him receive --------let him be : whenever he does the same (?), at that time he is to use the building. Each inhabitant is to keep the street clean in front of his own house : but if no one lives in (a house), the responsibility belongs to the one to whom the house belongs: and the *epistatai* are to clean (the streets?) : themselves each month : and if anything falls in, they are to perform the --------: and the street from the sanctuary of the Herakleion as far as the sea the *epistatai* are to clean it : and one must remove the stuff from the inhabitants and the things on the street whenever the *archoi* (magistrates) give the order; whoever does not do any of these : according to what has been written : one-sixth *stater* for each day let him owe to the *polis* : the *epistatai* are to exact payment and they themselves are to keep half : no one is allowed to go up on the roof of the public buildings (or shops?) in this street to see a sight : and a woman is not to gaze (like a spectator?) out of the window : with respect to any infraction : the inhabitant owes to the city a *stater* for each one : the *epistatai* are to exact payment and they themselves get to keep half : from the part of the balcony that juts out into this street : do not build a gutter : if anyone does build one he owes one-half of one-sixth *stater* for each day : half to the *polis* and half to the *epistatai* : and the *epistatai* are to exact payment : from the sanctuary of the Charites as far as the buildings where the *argyramoibeïon* is located : and

where the *symposion* is located : and as far as the street
going past the *prytaneion* : in the area bounded by these no one is to
throw in manure nor solicit; whoever commits any of these violations
must pay one-half of one-sixth *stater* to the city for each infraction as many times
as he commits : it; the *epistatai* are to exact payment and
they keep half themselves : but if they do not
they owe double to Artemis Hekate.[115]

The interpretation of this text is not entirely secure, but we can notice some important structural issues. The first law (1: lines 1–18) forbids permanent construction for private use of specific installations that would impede movement on at least one major street. The landmarks defining that street (as far as can be determined from this battered part of the stone) are the street of the embankment, the sanctuary of Herakles, and the street of the sanctuary of the Charites. The fine is extremely high—100 *stater*s—because the issue is permanent structures—specifically, stone thresholds extending out into the street, wells, and water channels.

The second paragraph (2: lines 19–49) contains four separate regulations. This series begins with a regulation for general maintenance of streets throughout the town (2a: lines 19–30): each resident is responsible for the street in front of his own house.[116] In the case of the space in front of an unoccupied house, the owner is responsible, and the *epistatai* are responsible for a regular monthly cleaning. One specific street—the street from the Herakleion to the sea—is singled out for special treatment. Responsibility for this street lies with the *epistatai.* Four injunctions rules regulate behavior along this street. First, when the senior magistrates, the *archoi,* give the order, the *epistatai* must remove whatever the inhabitants put out and whatever is on the street. Fines for violating this injunction are reckoned on a daily basis, payable to the *polis* at the rate of one-sixth of a *stater* for each day. The second regulation forbids men to climb on the roof of any publicly owned building to observe a scene in the street; and the

115. Examples of early laws: *IG* XII suppl. 347 no. 1 (Thasos); *IDelos* 509. Punctuation and spacing of the translation approximate the layout of the Greek text on the stone. Hyphens indicate words and letters no longer visible when found. Double dots reproduce the actual punctuation on the stone.

116. Cf. Eur. *Phaethon* 54–58 Diggle, for daily housekeeping and fumigation at the doorways of the house. Cf. Eur. *Andr.* 163–69, for sprinkling fresh water from a gold vessel as part of the duties of cleaning house.

third prohibits a woman from peering out a window.[117] The head of each household is assessed one *stater* for each violation, payable to the *polis.* The third regulation in this section (2c: lines 36–41) refers to the same street and forbids the construction of a drain pipe from a second floor balcony. Fines are assessed on a daily basis, payable, as in the two preceding regulations, to the *polis.*

The fourth and final section (2d: lines 41–49) differs from the first three provisions of the second law in that it is concerned not with a building or a street but with a defined space in the center of the city whose area is bounded by four visible landmarks: the sanctuary of the Charites, the *argyramoibeïon* (silver coin exchange), the *symposion,* and the road alongside the *prytaneion.* No one is to toss manure *(kopros)* within this area. The second clause in this regulation, contained in a single verb, forbids soliciting in this space.[118] Fines are assessed at a *hemiekton* for each offense, payable to the *polis,* with Artemis Hekate as the ultimate authority.

The injunction against accumulation of *kopros* in this central area refers to an inevitable product of animal sacrifice: the intestinal residues of slaughtered victims.[119] The regulation to keep an important central area of the city free from such matter defines it as an area where animal slaughter was a regular activity; but precisely because it was an area of sacrifice, it had to be kept clean. The provision to keep this sacrificial area free from manure identifies it as a space similar to the top of the Athenian *akropolis,* likewise an important central ritual area and likewise protected in the early fifth century by rules for the disposal of the manure of sacrificial animals.[120]

117. The interpretation here is close to yet differs from that of both Duchêne (who suggests that clearing the streets served ritual as well as hygenic purposes) and Graham (1998) 22–40 (who argues against a ritual background and interprets two of the prohibitions as regulations about prostitution). Graham's argument focuses on individual expressions ("window," *oikema demosia, tegos*), assumes that any disreputable woman was a prostitute, and does not consider the structure of either the text or the fines. The early date, the problems in reading some of the words, and the difficulty in identifying major landmarks suggests that we do not yet have enough external evidence to be confident of any interpretation.

118. For the discussion about the meaning of this verb, see Graham (1998) 38. The present third person singular imperative form προιστάσθω can be taken as either middle or passive.

119. The evidence for disposal of animal dung at the time of sacrifice is explained by Németh (1994) 59–64.

120. *IG* I^3 4 B.11. At Athens, the following were not allowed on the *akropolis:* birth, death, dogs, goats or goat sacrifice, equipment for baking bread, and animal dung *(onthos);* Jordan (1979) 28–30.

Urban space at Thasos was organized around major sanctuaries and religious monuments. Major streets are here described by their relationship to sanctuaries, and it is the sanctuaries that anchor the town.[121] The *polis* of the Thasians is concerned with protecting several categories of public space: streets, publicly owned buildings, and a restricted area for public ritual at the heart of the city. The ordinances, concerned with the uncertain boundaries between public space and private property, emphasize personal responsibility in the context of public services. They also recognize different kinds of offenses: obstructing traffic by building permanent structures that encroach on the public thoroughfare, failing to maintain routine sanitation in public thoroughfares, and compromising the special status of a central area of the town. Penalties are calculated in cash. Payment is owed to the gods and to the *polis* because the gods have a stake in the efficient operation of the city.

HIERARCHIES OF SACRED SPACE

Sacred space was not all the same. Some places required no human agency in order to qualify for protection. In this category were springs,[122] rivers, and natural heights,[123] all of which required respect.[124] Another group comprised those places marked by natural events, like the precincts of Zeus Katabaites, struck by the god's lightning and therefore considered so dangerous that no human could safely enter.[125] Others were shielded from human contact because they were sharply disputed: the Pelargikon at Athens[126] and the ἱερὰ ὀργάς between Attika and Megara, sacred to Demeter.[127] Still other spaces, like the Athenian *agora*, were artificially marked and kept sacred by ritual because important activities and communal institutions needed protection.

121. For roads as boundaries of sacred precincts, see *IG* I^2 887a–b; 892–895; II^2 2630, discussed by Lalonde (1991) 11.

122. *CID* I.10.

123. Aeschin. 2.90, with scholia (for a mountain in Thrace called Sacred Mountain); Callim. *Hymn* 4.70. For the Athenian *akropolis*, see Dem. 19.272.

124. Rudhardt (1958) 224–25.

125. Poll. 9.41; *Etym. Magn.* 341.6.

126. Thuc. 2.17; *IG* I^3 78.54–59.

127. Thuc. 1.139, where a piece of land between Attika and the Megarid, under dispute and therefore undivided for agriculture, is described as *aoriste* (without internal boundaries). Under the protection of Demeter and Kore, it is considered to be *hiera* (sacred).

Some sacred spaces required more protection than others—a fact Thucydides makes clear when he describes the forced migration of Attic farmers and villagers into Athens at the time of the Peloponnesian War:

> When they arrived at the city, a few people had their own houses and others had a place of refuge with friends or relatives, but many took up residence in the deserted areas of the city and in all the sanctuaries and hero shrines except the *akropolis,* the Eleusinion, and any other place firmly closed off.[128]

Thucydides distinguishes between sanctuaries that could be inhabited in times of emergency and those that could not, recognizing those spaces where it was possible to deal with the needs of the body—sleeping, eating, urination and defecation, sexual activity—and the specially marked areas where such activities were impossible, for instance, the top of the *akropolis.* Here, as an inscription of the late Archaic period makes clear, the presence of cooking utensils and the disposal of manure were forbidden.[129]

The top of the Athenian *akropolis,* one of the places Thucydides describes as "firmly closed off," had a special status. Considered naturally sacred, this area differed from places that had been made sacred, such as the Athenian *agora* ringed with internal *perirrhanteria*[130] or the specially designated area in the center of the town of Thasos. Even the little sanctuaries ringing the cliffs of the *akropolis* did not claim the same status as the top. According to Thucydides' distinction between habitable and inhabitable places, the little sanctuaries would probably not have been available for occupation during the annual siege of the Lakedaimonians. Nevertheless, it is clear from a scene in Aristophanes' *Lysistrata* that all sanctuaries did not share the same requirements regarding sexual purity. In that play, the poet assumes a distinction between the cave of Pan on the north slope and the sacred areas on the heights. Pan had been formally installed in the cave after the battle at Marathon,[131] and his altar was nearby.[132] Aristophanes assumes that the cave of Pan tolerated sexual activity because he places the aborted seduction of Kinesias by Myrrhine in this place[133]—perhaps even the same cave where Euripides had located Apollo's rape of Kre-

128. Thuc. 2.17.
129. *IG* I³ 4 B.10–15.
130. For an *agora* described as sacred *(hiera)* cf. *BIGM* IV 50, line 3 (van Effenterre and Ruzé [1994] I 89, no. 19).
131. Lucian *Bis Acc.* 9; *Dial. Deorum* 22.
132. Eur. *Ion* 938.
133. Ar. *Lys.* 889–953, with notes by Henderson (1987a) 67, 164, 179.

ousa.[134] Pan clearly did not forbid casual entry, and apparently even sexual intercourse in his precinct would not have been an insult.[135] The interchange between Myrrhine and Kinesias implies that, although Pan might tolerate (and even encourage) sexual play in his precinct,[136] the protected status of the sanctuaries on top of the heights (where temple personnel could not even cook their own meals)[137] would have made it impossible for Myrrhine to return to her comrades above without washing first.[138]

Like the Archaic *agora* at Athens, with both external and internal boundaries, a single sanctuary could contain more than one kind of space.[139] An Athenian decree setting out the terms for leasing the *temenos* of Neleus and Basile and the adjacent *hieron* of Kodros, Neleus, and Basile makes this clear. The Athenians claimed that Neleus, son of Kodros, was founder of many Ionian cities of the Asian coast. Kodros was an early, legendary Athenian king whose tomb was thought to mark the spot where he had fallen in battle.[140] According to Thucydides' system of classification, his precinct would have been considered a *heroön* (hero-shrine) and therefore available for domestic occupation in the early years of the Peloponnesian War. The date of the decree, 418/7, places it just thirteen years after the forced migration of the Attic population into the city and only three years after the peace of Nikias had allowed Attic farmers to return to their land. By adopting the decree, the *boule* and *ekklesia* were apparently following a policy of tightening the rules for sanctuary occupation.[141] Leasing out sanctuary land for cultivation would discourage squatters from taking up residence in minor sanctuaries and would ease public financial responsibilities because leasing would enable sanctuaries to generate income from

134. Eur. *Ion* 10–13. Euripides, however, describes the cave as *adyta,* "not to be entered" (938).

135. Pan, in fact encouraged behavior very different from that required by other gods. Normally the act of sacrifice called for ritual silence to avoid saying anything of ill omen. Pan, however, required noise. Cf. Men. *Dys.* 433–34: "One should *not* approach this god in silence."

136. Located on the north slope of the *akropolis* but outside the gated precinct on top; Travlos (1971) 471, with photos and plan 418–21, figs. 536–39.

137. *IG* I^3 4 B.5–6.

138. Ar. *Lys.* 912–13, with Henderson's note.

139. Birge, in Birge, Kraynak, and Miller (1992) 96–98 for boundary stones to demarcate a special area within a sanctuary.

140. South of the *akropolis* or just outside the old city wall. Outside the wall: Lycurg. *Leoc.* 86; Bekker, *Anecdota Graeca* 1: 192.32–193.3. Pausanias 1.19.5 points out the spot in the context of the shrines along the Ilissos. *IG* II^2 4258 locates the grave below the *akropolis.*

141. *IG* I^3 84; *LSCG* 14. Wycherley (1960) 60–66 suggests that the *boule* has initiated a leasing policy to clear out the squatters.

their own resources for subvention of public sacrifices. The decree dates from the period just before the Athenians resumed war and coincides with a revival of Athenian interest in displaying traditional ties to Ionian cities. Neleus, though not the object of a cult elsewhere in Attika, became a powerful symbol as founder of Miletos and the Milesian cult of Artemis Kithone. His tomb is at the Milesian festival site of Didyma.[142]

The decree distinguishes the *temenos* of Neleus and Basile (planted with at least two hundred olive trees) from the *hieron* of Kodros, Neleus, and Basile.[143] The steps taken to secure the lease were under the jurisdiction of the *basileus,* the Athenian official traditionally responsible for public cults. Procedures for surveying and laying out the boundaries of the area had to follow "the law of sacred precincts."[144] Special officials in charge of marking boundaries surveyed the site[145] so each area could be fenced off—the *hieron* at the renter's expense,[146] the *temenos* from the funds of the *poletai.* Balancing the need for income with public responsibility for maintaining the special status of a *hieron,*[147] the decree recognizes the distinction between the *hieron,* fenced separately to discourage secular incursions, and another space, here called the *temenos,* under public jurisdiction but designated for private use and fenced to protect the trees planted on the lot. The *temenos* could be rented out and cultivated;[148] the *hieron,* its special status and sacred area indicated by a boundary stone *(horos),*[149] could not.[150]

142. Robertson (1988) 230–39. For a recent discussion of using this tradition to maintain ties to Ephesos and Ionian history, see Herda (1998).

143. The term *temenos,* usually meaning a bounded cultic space, is more restricted in use than *peribolos,* which can refer to the boundary or wall of a city as well as a wall around a sacred area; see Birge, in Birge, Kraynak, and Miller (1992) 236–37. In this text, however, the term *temenos* is used for the space marked out for the orchard.

144. ὁ νόμος τôν τεμενôν, line 25.

145. Οἱ ὁρισταί, enjoined to "mark out these sacred boundaries" (ὁρίσαι τὰ ἱερὰ ταῦτα, line 7), so the project could be carried out as reverently as possible (εὐσεβέστατα, line 8). For ὁρισταί, cf. the decree from the Peiraieus, *IG* II^2 1177.

146. *IG* I^3 84, 30–37.

147. A *temenos,* when rented out, could not be exploited as freely as privately owned allotments. A lease from Herakleia forbids graves on sacred land leased out for cultivation; *IG* XIV 645.137.

148. The renter is to have jurisdiction over the water (called "the water from Zeus," τô ὕδατος τô ἐγ Διός) flowing into the irrigation ditch, but the trees cut to maintain the ditch are sold for wood and the proceeds turned over to Neleus *(IG* I^3 84, 20–22).

149. "*Horos* of the *hieron,*" Travlos (1971) 332–33; mid-fifth century.

150. A similar distinction is made in *IG* XII.1 103 (Buck 103; *LSCG* 136; fourth- or third-century Ialysos, sanctuary of Alektron); Goldstein (1978) 315.

Local regulations for sacred space depended on local tradition. At Olympia, the entire area between the Alpheios and Kladeos rivers was protected,[151] but within this area the administrators of the sanctuary recognized three degrees of sacred status in and around the sanctuary: the stadium, the Altis (the walled space, originally "grove," where most of the sanctuaries were located), and restricted areas within the Altis. The shape and needs of the sanctuary changed as it grew, and development affected rules for use. Originally the stadium had overlapped the area occupied by sanctuaries, but when the Altis was enclosed by a stone wall, the wall separated the stadium from the Altis. The stadium remained connected to the Altis, however, by a passageway that functioned as an entrance. Contestants and their judges (the Hellanodikai), after making an oath sacrifice together, had to pass through the Altis to reach the "hidden" entrance to the stadium.[152]

The Altis itself was not a restricted area, but designated spaces within its boundaries were reserved for rituals not shared by all. Restricted areas included the ash altar of Zeus (its upper level off bounds to females),[153] the throne of Zeus inside his temple (protected by screens from the view of visitors),[154] the fenced precinct of Hippodameia (open once a year and only to females),[155] and the *peribolos* and temple of Hades (open once a year and entered only by the priest).[156] The stadium itself was not fenced but had its own rules. Adult women (but not *parthenoi*) were excluded at the time of the games[157] except for the priestess of Demeter Chamyne. As the only

151. Paus. 5.6.7; Xen. *Hell.* 7.4.29–30, with Goldstein (1978) 297 pointing out the natural boundaries.

152. Paus. 6.20.8; the entrance (εἴσοδος) is called Κρυπτή, "hidden."

153. Paus. 5.13.10.

154. Paus. 5.11.4. The temple of Zeus was off bounds to anyone who ate of the black ram sacrificed to Pelops; 5.13.2–3.

155. The precinct of Hippodameia in the Altis at Olympia, about one *plethron* in area, was enclosed by a fence (θριγκῷ), and only the women delegated to sacrifice to her could enter; Paus. 6.20.7.

156. Paus. 6.25.2–4. According to Pausanias, the Eleans were the only people who had a sanctuary of Hades. It was open only once a year because people go down to the realm of Hades only once.

157. Paus. 6.20.9. Plutarch, *Thes.* 19, finds it remarkable that on Crete, in the days of Minos and Theseus, men and women sat together as spectators at athletic events.

adult woman permitted to view (θεᾶσθαι) the games, she watched from a seat on a white marble altar directly opposite the Hellanodikai.[158]

Similar rules governed the use of special areas within other sanctuaries. Sacred space reserved for intimate personal contact with divinity (mysteries, oracles, or incubation) was accessible only to those qualified by special purification. In such cases, payment of fees and closely monitored participation in rigidly structured preliminary rites defined ritual eligibility.[159] Examples of temples associated with mysteries or initiation include the Telesterion at Eleusis, the Anaktoron and Hieron at Samothrace,[160] and the sanctuary of Despoina at Lykosoura; an example of a temple associated with an oracle would be the chamber of the Pythia at Delphi. For incubation, examples include the sanctuary of Amphiaraios at Oropos, the dormitories *(enkoimeteria)* at Epidauros, and the *abaton* in the sanctuary of Asklepios at Corinth. Some sanctuaries were partitioned, with one area more restricted than others. As in the case of the *hieron* and *temenos* of Kodros, Neleus, and Basile, hierarchies of space could be recognized within a single enclosure. In one example at Chalkis, the wall around the entire sanctuary (called τὸ ἱερόν) was distinguished from the *peribolos* around the *temenos*.[161] Special rules for a defined space within a sanctuary indicated critical or unusual ritual and sacrifices whose procedures recognized special powers of a divinity. When the meat from sacrifice had to be consumed on the spot,[162] dining areas or accommodations for ritual eating could be reserved for delegated specialists or distinguished participants. As a result, dining complexes for sacred meals could be walled off from the rest

158. Paus. 6.20.8–9 on the priestess of Demeter, chosen from among the women of Elis.

159. Requirements varied. Access to the Telesterion at Eleusis would have been limited to those who had participated in preliminaries at Athens; the rear chamber of the Anaktoron and the Hieron at Samothrace were available only to those who achieved *myesis;* see Fraser (1960) 2: 117–20 nos. 62–63, for the inscriptions. The *adyton* at Delphi required preliminary sacrifice; Parke and Wormell (1956). The *abaton* in the Asklepieion at Corinth was separated by a stairway from the rest of the temple; Roebuck (1951). The dormitory at the Amphiareion at Oropos was restricted. Those wishing to undergo healing rites put at least nine obols into the treasury box *(thesauros)*, had their name recorded, and were admitted to the *enkoimeterion;* Petropoulou (1981), text on page 49, lines 20–23 for payment; 39–43 for recording of names. At Pergamon, candidates had to sacrifice a piglet as well as purify themselves before entering the little *enkoimeterion;* see *IPergamon* 8.3 B.161. For throwing 3 obols into the *thesauros* at Pergamon, see B.8.

160. Fraser (1960) nos. 62–63; Cole (1984) 26–27.

161. *IG* XII.9, 906, Chalkis, third century C.E.

162. The parameters of such sacrifices are discussed by Scullion (1994) 103–12.

of the sacred area.[163] Other areas—for instance the sanctuary of Hades at Olympia—were closed off to all but priests and priestesses. Similar restricted areas included the *anaktoron* at Eleusis;[164] the walled grove of Artemis at Pellene;[165] the enclosed chamber or *adyton* behind the cella in certain temples, particularly those of Artemis but also the temple of Athena Poliatis at Tegea;[166] the area sacred to Apollo Karneios in the temple of Asklepios at Sikyon;[167] and the temple of Aphrodite at Sikyon.[168]

The system of ranking areas within a sanctuary assumes that some spaces were more sacred than others, but there is no term in the language that measures the degree of difference.[169] Conflict, violence, and warfare were not supposed to occur in sanctuaries. We can detect different levels of protection, but it is difficult to describe the system. The sacred truce that guaranteed the inviolability of participants at a festival was a temporary procedure for a temporary event. In the Classical period, the ritual of supplication called *hikesia,* earlier connected to the body of the ruler, was now associated with a sacred space or a particular altar. These were places that provided protection for those in fear of abduction or violence. For those at risk if they left the sanctuary, an intermediate secure space, demarcated and considered to be under the god's protection, could provide a temporary living space. Often a grove, referred to as a *bebelon alsos,* "a grove where one could step," such an intermediate area within the boundaries of a sanctuary could offer protection to people in times of stress.[170] By the Hellenistic period, permanent protection was available by means of a formal declara-

163. Goldstein (1978) calls attention to those at Eleusis, Troizen, and Paros.

164. Also called *megaron,* Hsch., s.v. For entry restricted to the Hierophant, see Ael. Fr. 10; Mylonas (1961) 69, 84, 230.

165. Paus. 7.27.3, located on the road to the city (Pellene was on a hill). The priests were from local families and selected according to the reputation of their *genos.* They swore their greatest oath by this Artemis.

166. Only the priest and only once a year; Paus. 8.47.5.

167. Paus. 2.10.2; only the priests could enter the inner room of the temple.

168. Paus. 2.10.4; only the female *neokoros* (for whom it was not right to go to a man) and a virgin *loutrophoros* (bathwater-bringer) could enter. Others had to stand at the entrance to the temple in order to view the statue and pray to it.

169. Rigsby (1996) 6–10.

170. Aesch. *Supp.* 509. Sinn (1993) 98–101, for distinctions between outer and inner precincts in the same sanctuary. Sinn points out, 102, that Polybius, 5.7–8, recognized the advantages of a protected area, preferably on a high ridge if inland (e.g., the Lykaion in Arkadia). An island off shore (sanctuary of Poseidon on Kalaureia) or a rugged promontory on the coast (Athena at Sounion) were also practical for offering asylum. For a detailed analysis of the situation at Perachora, see Sinn (1990) 53–116.

tion of *asylia* that recognized specific sanctuaries as specially protected areas.[171]

The level of sanctity attached to a particular space was a measure of the caution expected of those who would cross its boundaries. Particular areas, like the grove of the Semnai Theai at Kolonos, were considered so charged with divine power that they could not be entered at all.[172] Some accounts seem exaggerated—for instance the description of a sacred cave of the bees on Crete, birthplace of Zeus and so not to be entered by god or human. Here each year, so it was said, the blood from the god's birth welled up, and fire burst forth. Other spaces inspired great fear. Signs from the gods, communicated by events of nature, impressed those who avoided places struck by lightning; for instance, the enclosure of Zeus Kataibates on the Athenian *akropolis*,[173] the enclosure of Zeus Kataibates in the Altis at Olympia,[174] the grove of the Semnai Theai at Kolonos, the *sekos* of Semele at Thebes,[175] and the fenced grove of Demeter and Persephone at Megalopolis[176] were permanently fenced off to remind people of danger. Zeus Lykaios on Mt. Lykaios in Arkadia inspired similar caution. His sacrifice was performed in ritual silence (ἐν ἀπορρήτῳ), and anyone who entered his *temenos* would not only leave no shadow but would die before the year was out.[177] The dread associated with this particular precinct was so strong that it survived even the move to Megalopolis at the time of the fourth-century synoicism of Arkadia, when a new stone *peribolos* was built for Zeus Lykaios in the headquarter city. Replicating the god's mysterious space on the mountain, the new stone wall encircling his space was not to be breached.[178] Too dreadful to approach, some gods were even too dreadful for speech.[179] The grove of the Semnai Theai at Kolonos, like the enclosure of Zeus on Mt. Lykaios, was so sacred that speech was not allowed at

171. The epigraphical evidence is collected and analyzed by Rigsby (1996).
172. Soph. *OC* 37, 39, and 126.
173. *IG* II^2 4965: Διὸς Κα[τ]αιβάτο[υ] ἄβατον.
174. Paus. 5.14.10.
175. Eur. *Bacch.* 10–11.
176. Paus. 8.31.5.
177. Paus. 8.38.6; Polyb. 16.12.7; cf. Plut. *Quaest. Graec.* 300a–b (who says the Arkadians distinguished between those who entered deliberately and those who did so inadvertently); Hyg. *Poet. Astr.* 2.4; Eratosth. [*Cat.*] 1. For Pausanias's claim that someone was turned into a wolf at this sacrifice (8.2.6), see Buxton (1987) 69–74.
178. Paus. 8.30.2. A cave of Apollo, Herakles, and Hermes, who had the title Spelaites, allowed entrance; Paus. 10.32.5.
179. Van der Horst (1994) 1–25; Pulleyn (1997) 184–87.

all.[180] A prayer that cannot be spoken, like a precinct without entry or a man without a shadow, is a sign of an anomalous divinity or a "twilight zone where the dark world of the dead encroaches upon the social order of the living."[181]

180. Silence for the Semnai Theai: Soph. *OC* 130–33, with Henrichs (1994) 43 n. 78, and Pulleyn (1997) 162.
181. Henrichs (1994) 46.

3 Inventing the Center

REGIONAL SANCTUARIES

Any attempt to describe the religious practice of the ancient Greek *polis* must take into account the contradictions between the tradition of political autonomy for the individual city and the broader context of a shared culture and shared traditions. It is difficult to understand how a landscape so fractured by geology, and a political system so resistant to political centralization, could produce a common culture of religious practice or a shared ideology of divinity. For consistency in religious practice we must look to traditions and institutions that transcended the *polis*. From the archaeological evidence of ritual activity and of gifts to the gods it now seems clear that in the early centuries of the Iron Age, institutions were already being nurtured at sites that would later become the great regional sanctuaries. In the tenth and ninth centuries, concentrations of surplus wealth collected not in settlements but in regional centers beyond the borders of local communities.[1] Such places came to be protected by hallowed protocols that encouraged peaceful interaction between competing communities. The context of neutrality, protected by appeals to the divine, provided security for arbitration and negotiation.[2] Sanctuaries profited from the role they played and derived prestige from procedures that claimed divine support for human decisions.[3] Those sanctuaries whose divinities transcended local borders and whose rituals mediated competition and neutralized aggression

1. A coherent account of the archaeological evidence is found in the work of Morgan (1990, 1993, 1996, 1997).
2. Sinn (1993).
3. Parker (1985).

influenced the processes of exchange, interaction, and negotiation that helped to shape the common institutions of the *polis*.[4]

The great innovation of the early Iron Age was the creation of isolated sacred space, defined by deposits of valuable gifts for the gods and the dedications of sacred equipment used for animal sacrifice and communal banquets.[5] Terracotta dedications, followed soon by gifts of bronze, begin to appear at Olympia in the tenth century and at Delphi and Delos in the ninth. Dedications preceded buildings by about two hundred years, and the three emerging ritual centers at Delphi, Delos, and Olympia were already attracting visitors and participants from afar. By the eighth century, other important sanctuaries were also active on a regional level: at Thermon in Aitolia; at Aigira in Achaia; and the Heraia in the Argolid, at Perachora, and on Samos.[6] In this early period, the contests of Poseidon at Isthmia, of Zeus at Nemea, and of Argive Hera at Prosymna[7] served only local clienteles, but festivals at these sites were already creating nodes of cooperative activity and models of ritual authority. The permanent structures that were built by 700 only confirm the strong incentives for collective action already in place.[8]

Some sanctuaries had a longer reach than others. Migration of Greek communities across the Aegean, to Sicily and Italy in the west and to the Black Sea in the north, encouraged long-distance ties that strengthened the authority of the most important sanctuaries and helped to shape a common culture of ritual practice. The new cities in the west and the trading cities around the isthmus maintained strong relationships with the sanctuaries at Delphi and Olympia in the Archaic period, and they commemorated these ties with generous donations.[9] Several levels of interaction fueled rapid change, and sanctuaries at both local and regional levels followed similar patterns. Early development reflected one of two general models. Territories with a single major population center—the feature that typically de-

4. Sourvinou-Inwood (1988a, 1990).
5. Rolley (1983).
6. Morgan (1991) 141–44.
7. Billot (1997).
8. Coldstream (1977) 317 counted a dozen sanctuaries with votives by the ninth century and seventy sanctuaries (thirty of them with buildings) by 700 B.C.E.
9. Morgan (1990) 16. The influence of the wealth of the Western Greeks was visible at Olympia in Pausanias's day because of the treasuries dedicated by cities such as Selinous, Sybaris, Gela, Metapontum, and Epidamnos; Paus. 6.19.8–15. The connections between Olympia and the west are described by Philipp (1992) 91–122. The epigraphical evidence at Delphi reveals strong interest from Magna Graecia and Sicily; Rougement (1995) 157–92.

fined a *polis*—tended to focus on a regional sanctuary near a territorial border.[10] Areas without a concentrated population center, whose populations were united by claims of ethnic or tribal identity and resided in scattered settlements, required a regional sanctuary more centrally located in the territory.[11] In the eighth and seventh centuries, such sanctuaries were more important than towns in defining community.[12] In Phokis and Thessaly, where populations tended to be dispersed without a dominant central settlement, political organization took the form of a loosely organized league or amphictyony. At first, this northern group was centered on the sanctuary of Demeter at Anthela, but after the First Sacred War, the amphictyony extended its influence to include the sanctuary of Apollo at Delphi.[13] In the territory of Corinth on the isthmus, high concentrations of valuable offerings at Isthmia and Perachora[14] indicate that the energy expended on these sanctuaries was a better indicator of community strength than the level of development at the town site of Corinth itself.[15] At other sites, moreover, even rather ordinary ceramic remains could be a sign of influential ritual. On Samos, votive deposits at the Heraion—cups, bowls, and other dining equipment—target the area around the central spring as a focus of complex and regular ritual dining. Groups met here for feasts before permanent buildings were constructed,[16] and the Heraion grew wealthy with the gifts of travelers, visitors, and the local elite long before the *polis* of Samos put down long roots.[17]

As the young communities grew, the assertion of political identity and claims to territory inevitably produced conflict. Local disagreements could

10. For example, Argos; see de Polignac (1995a).

11. Morgan (1994) and (1997), stressing, however, that all large regions were not alike.

12. The institutions of early cooperation on the regional level are sketched by Forrest (2000), who describes the cooperative efforts of Thessalians around Anthedon, of Peloponnesians around Kalaureia, of eastern Dorians around Triopian Apollo on Knidos, of Ionians at Mycale, the Boiotians at the Ptoion, and the Aitolians at Thermon. He speculates that Lefkandi may have hosted such an organization on Euboia but it did not last.

13. The date of the first Pythia, perhaps as early as the seventh century, has been discussed most recently by Fowler (1998) 15.

14. Morgan (1994) points out that Perachora received far richer votives than Delphi in the last quarter of the eighth century.

15. Morgan (1994).

16. Kron (1988). See Davies (1997) 32 for the suggestion that *eranos*-sponsored dining (meals supported by donations; potluck) was as important as sanctuary-focused dining ritual.

17. Morgan (1994).

be handled by local leaders, but conflicts between larger groups required more widely recognized mechanisms for adjudication of disputes. Collective ritual practice at the major sanctuaries provided an apparatus for mediation. Ritual traditions provided procedures to regulate aggression and competition,[18] to ratify agreements, and to moderate warfare. Temple precincts created a space protected by a god, where laws and treaties of alliance could be displayed and decisions publicized. When diplomatic procedures failed, the results of war could be confirmed by display of the arms and armor taken in battle.

Major sanctuaries encouraged standardization of legal procedures and provided mechanisms for sanctioning policy and condoning political innovation. Zeus and Apollo, both concerned with individual and collective behaviors, actively promoted recognition of "divine ordinances" *(themistes)*.[19] Communities recognized such ordinances as issuing from a divine source and therefore consulted oracles of Zeus at Dodona[20] and oracles of Apollo at Delphi, at Didyma in Ionia, and at the Ptoion in Boiotia to elicit divine approval for legislative decisions and divine support for judicial procedures. An example of this process can be observed in a formal legal pronouncement *(rhetra)* of the Eleans deposited at Olympia.[21] This pronouncement represents the community speaking in one voice to itemize and define the procedures for the prosecution of serious crimes. Until the synoecism, union, of Elis in 471, the people who called themselves Eleans[22] recognized no single town center but looked to the sanctuary of Zeus at Olympia as central authority for the region[23] and used the *bouleuterion* and *prytaneion* in the center of that sanctuary as their own.[24]

18. Morgan (1990) 39–49, for the early festival circuit.

19. "Decrees of the gods," or even "laws"; for *themis* as an abstract concept in Homer and personified Themis associated with "social order" in early poetry, see Stafford (1997) 158–60; for the earliest depiction of Themis, on the great *dinos* of Sophilos, sixth century, see Shapiro (1993) 218, where he also mentions the earliest testimony for Themis at Delphi, identified by inscription as the charioteer of Dionysos on the Siphnian frieze, also sixth century.

20. Parker (1985); Morgan (1989).

21. *IOlympia* 2 (Buck 61; *SEG* 41.391; before 580).

22. *SEG* 46.463, for the collective ethnic title used in a new law on wrestling, 525–500 B.C.E.

23. Walter (1993) 119. Elean decrees set up in Olympia include *IOlympia* 1–5, 7, 9, 12, 16; see Hansen and Fischer-Hansen (1994) 87 n. 241, for further discussion.

24. In Pausanias's day the hymns sung in the *prytaneion* at Olympia were in the Doric dialect and the Eleans still had their own *hestiatorion* (dining room) in the *prytaneion;* Paus. 5.15.12.

Olympia is the only Greek site where both buildings commonly associated with a *polis*—a *prytaneion* and a *bouleuterion*—have actually been found,[25] but Olympia was never itself a *polis*. Zeus at Olympia was closely connected with early Elean law, and the technical vocabulary of the first recorded laws of this area shows that political and judicial procedures were constructed with expectation of his support. In the *rhetra* of the Eleans, bringing a charge is described in terms of a curse,[26] because curses publicly sworn guaranteed that the gods were involved in punishing a crime. A curse publicized the consequences of divine disapproval and emphasized the burden of heavy pollution *(agos)* attached to one who violated a standard considered endorsed by the gods.[27] The *pinax* (plaque) that records the text of the *rhetra* of the Eleans was dedicated (declared sacred) at Olympia, and the fines were paid to Zeus, arbiter for all Eleans. As a direct participant in the judicial process, the god protected the words of the text as well as the judicial procedures. Zeus at Olympia thus ratified the judicial apparatus by which the Eleans operated. His reputation traveled far beyond the range of Elis. Because the sanctuary was convenient to the sailing route to the west, Olympia attracted participants from the wealthy colonies of Italy and Sicily as well as from its own Peloponnesian neighbors.[28] Procedures performed and recorded at Olympia were therefore widely disseminated.

The special status of Olympia was protected by a sacred truce, the result of a deliberate decision confirmed by oath.[29] Several accounts, all fictitious, share the same three claims: 1) that the territory of the Eleans was sacred and inviolable; 2) that the Eleans did not take sides in war; and 3) that the truce resulted from a Peloponnesian decision.[30] This tradition exaggerates the neutrality of Olympia, known to have entered into alliances with indi-

25. Hansen and Fischer-Hansen (1994) 86.

26. *IOlympia* 2 (Buck 61; *SEG* 41.391). The verb "to bring a charge" (later *κατηγορεῖν*) is here *κατιαραίειν* (to put under a curse")—Elean dialect for *καθιερεύειν*, "to render sacred," in the original meaning of "render someone sacred, in terms of what is abhorrent to the gods," in other words, "to utter an imprecation against someone." Parker (1983) 191–92 discusses the meaning of *agos* in this context. Osborne (1997) 79 emphasizes "prosecution and the limits of responsibility" as a general judicial concern of early *poleis*.

27. Parker (1983) 191–93.

28. Philipp (1992) 29–51. A new *lex sacra* found at Olympia mentions Lybians, Cretans, and people from Epidamnos; *SEG* 47.448.

29. Ephoros *FGrH* 70 F 115, as quoted in Str. 8.3.33; discussed by Rigsby (1996) 41–42. Ephoros says that all Eleia was declared sacred and that no one could bring in weapons.

30. Diod. Sic. 8.1; Polyb. 4.73.9–10; Phlegon *FGrH* 257 F 1.

vidual cities;[31] but the claim of neutrality confirms that the sanctuary aspired to a special status invoked every four years with the proclamation of the sacred truce for the Olympic games. Monuments in the sanctuary reflected the significance of that truce and promoted the authority of the agreements that marked the close of important wars. Pausanias describes a *diskos* dedicated by Iphitos on which he could read the truce proclaimed by the Eleans at the Olympic games.[32] A statue of Zeus, dedicated by the Greeks who defeated Mardonios at Plataiai in 479, stood in front of the *bouleuterion* at Olympia, facing the rising sun.[33] Nearby, a bronze stele recorded the conditions of the thirty years' truce sworn between the Athenians and the Lakedaimonians in the fifth century.[34] Every truce required an oath, and Zeus as Horkios, the god of oaths, was always the tacit partner to every agreement. His statue in the *bouleuterion* at Olympia inspired an unusual level of respect because it represented the god holding not one thunderbolt but two, one in each hand.[35] Zeus Horkios at Olympia needed two thunderbolts because he presided over the altar in the *bouleuterion* where, in the presence of their fathers, brothers, and the umpires who judged the events, athletes swore a special oath to compete fairly and to avoid cheating.[36]

Apollo was another divinity with important legal functions, and his judicial authority extended beyond regional borders. At Delphi, he was recognized as a major divinity, consulted by cities on questions of pollution, correct performance of ritual, and legal procedure. The *Homeric Hymn to Apollo* presents Themis as the female personification of right, established custom, and social order.[37] As Kourotrophos, nurse of the god, Themis attended the infant Apollo after his birth on Delos. She fed the divine child not on milk, the food of mortal infants, but on nectar and lovely ambrosia, the food of the gods.[38] Apollo responded by declaring, "The lyre and curved

31. Rigsby (1996) 43, on *Staatsverträge* 2:110, for alliance with Heraia in the sixth century B.C.E.

32. Paus. 5.20.1.

33. Paus. 5.23.1–3. Other statues of Zeus dedicated by Greek cities faced the rising sun, but the one dedicated by the Roman general Mummius from the booty of the Achaean War, faced the sunset; Paus. 5.24.8.

34. Paus. 5.23.4.

35. Paus. 5.24.9. Zeus as god of oaths protected the agreements by which cities created their political institutions. For early dependence on oaths, see Gehrke (1993) 49–67.

36. This oath was sworn on the cut pieces *(tomia)* of a boar; Paus. 5.24.9–10.

37. Stafford (1997) 158.

38. *Hymn. Hom. Ap.* 124–25.

bow shall be dear to me and I shall declare for men the unerring will *(boule)* of Zeus."[39] The hymn assigns to Apollo the responsibility of communicating his father's decisions to the human community. Apollo's pronouncements enforced the standards by which human inquirers measured their own behavior and by which new cities determined appropriate procedures and sought approval for collective decisions.[40] His major sanctuaries at Delphi, Delos, Didyma, and the Ptoion in Boiotia—sites well removed from major settlements,[41] like the sanctuary of Zeus at Olympia—provided neutral locations and uncontested spaces that furthered the communication required to standardize procedures of negotiation.[42]

Greek cities consulted Apollo at Delphi because they recognized the god as an authority on legal issues.[43] A hymn of Alkaios claimed that Zeus himself sent Apollo to Delphi and to the Castalian spring in order to "proclaim a *dike* and *themis* for the Hellenes."[44] Apollo at Delphi was consulted by communities in times of local disaster or political strain and in times of political innovation, when new cities were being settled or new cults established.[45] His major tasks included the settlement of disputes about pollution and the affirmation of correct procedures for purification. Local disasters, described as plague *(loimos)* and famine *(limos)*, were explained as punishments for violation of purity requirements. Apollo, as the god who could both send and prevent plague, was the appropriate authority for cities and their representatives trying to create acceptable procedures for resolving crises and restoring and maintaining the health of the community. When they consulted the oracle, cities sought approval for ritual procedures by submitting plans to the god's scrutiny—a process that contributed to the standardization of the rules for purification and conferred authority on local procedures. The tradition is preserved for us in the preamble to a famous law on pollution from Kyrene, claimed to be delivered in Apollo's own voice.[46]

39. *Hymn Hom. Ap.* 131–32; cf. 394–95 for the *themistes* of Apollo at Delphi.
40. Parker (1985); Morgan (1989).
41. Schachter (1992), on sanctuaries of Apollo.
42. Morgan (1989).
43. The Lakedaimonians, with their "Pythioi"—two special advisors to the kings—had an especially close relationship with Delphi; Hdt. 6.57; Xen. *Lac.* 15.5. On the relationship between Sparta and Delphi: Parke and Wormell (1956) I 82–98.
44. Alc. F 307(c) LP; 308(c) Campbell (Himer. *Or.* 48.10–11, Colonna 200–220) for a prose paraphrase of the hymn.
45. Rougement (1995) 157–92.
46. *LSS* Suppl. 115.

On the local level, Apollo supported the process by which cities made decisions and protected citizens from capricious leaders.[47] In the sixth century, the Ozolian Lokrians posted in Apollo's sanctuary a law containing the conditions for establishing a new colony.[48] The first part of the text lists procedures for inheritance and land division in the new territory. Punishment meted out to those who transgressed the law is stated in the form of a curse endorsed by consecrating the text to Apollo himself.[49] Displayed where all could see it, the inscribed text expressed the will of the community and specified the penalties for political leaders *(damiourgoi)* who might exploit the decision for personal gain. The second part of the inscription, listing penalties for any leader who profited from the law, is inscribed upside down to indicate the power of the curse contained in it.[50] A famous seventh-century law from Dreros makes a similar point. This law, inscribed on the wall of the temple of Apollo Delphinios, limited the term of the local executive officer *(kosmos)* and gave the conditions for his oath of office.[51] At Gortyn, sixth-century regulations about the local leading political office *(kosmos)* were also inscribed directly on blocks of the wall of Apollo's local temple.[52] The early laws displayed in sanctuaries or inscribed on temple walls shared common characteristics because they were written to resolve conflicts. The privileged location demonstrated that such laws derived their authority from the god himself.[53]

47. Hölkeskamp (1992) 87–117 discusses the implications of publishing early laws in sanctuaries, without, however, mentioning the ritual mechanisms for protecting the law. Thomas (1995) 72–73 emphasizes the religious sanctions and points out that "sanctions are in the hands of the gods."

48. *IG* IX^2 I (3) 609 *(GHI* I^2 13; 525–500 B.C.E.), possibly from Naupaktos.

49. Ibid., lines 14–17: *ὁ δὲ τετθμὸς ἱαρὸς ἔστο τô Ἀπόλλονος τô Πυθίο*, "This established ordinance is sacred to Apollo Pythios."

50. Wrongdoers had to dedicate any profit to Apollo, and the profit itself, probably reckoned in precious metal, had to be deposited in the sanctuary to be melted down and made into a statue.

51. *GHI* I^2 2, 650–600 B.C.E.

52. *ICrete* 4 14g–p, 2.

53. At Phaistos, a sixth-century inheritance law (to be decided by the *agora,* the assembly) was inscribed on the wall of a monumental building, obviously a temple; *AsAtene* 56 (1978) 429–35; *SEG* 32.908, 550–500 B.C.E., line 1: "The law is proposed for approval by the *agora.*" For thematic coherence and the involvement of the god, see van Effenterre and Ruzé (1994) 94; Hölkeskamp (1994); and Gehrke (1995) 13–35. Thomas (1995) stresses the original oral transmission of legal provisions and argues that public display in a sanctuary attributed to written rules a status they would otherwise not have had.

FINDING THE CENTER

The location of Apollo's most important sanctuary became an expression of his authority. Delphi is positioned on the steep lower slopes of Mt. Parnassos, far from the nearest city. The site is so remote and the slope so steep that the earliest foundation myth describes the god's attendants, conveyed to Delphi from Crete, as unable to imagine that they could sustain themselves in a place with no room to grow food or pasture animals.[54] To convince them to stay, the god assured that they would be handsomely supported from the animals brought to the sanctuary for sacrifice and the gifts given as dedications.[55] Apollo's attendants are presented as farmers who expect to work for their bread. The god's promise that they would live without toil *(ponoi)* sounds like Hesiod's description of a time when gods mingled with humans and people dwelled "apart from hard work and sorrow," living freely on the earth's bounty.[56] The implied analogy between a golden age and the new sanctuary at Delphi was a sign of the special status and the unique reputation of Apollo in his temple high on Mt. Parnassos.

Delphi was remote but also central. For later Greeks, Delphi was the physical center of the earth,[57] the distances measured by Zeus himself.[58] The *omphalos*, or "navel," of the earth was located here in the temple of Apollo.[59] At Delphi, established communities could consult a god whose messages encouraged self-reflection, and here they could find a god whose pronouncements sanctioned the collective authority necessary for stability and continuity. The claim that Delphi was the precise middle point of the universe[60] elevated Apollo without challenging the role of Zeus—the god identified in epic with *dike*, "right decision," and represented as supporting the pronouncements of his son.[61] Apollo's administrators did not create

54. *Hymn. Hom. Ap.* 529–30. Leto promised the Delians that in spite of the island's agricultural poverty, they would be supported from the wealth produced by a ritual center (51–60).

55. *Hymn. Hom. Ap.* 532–37.

56. Hes. *Op.* 112.

57. Eur. *Ion* 5–6: ὀμφαλὸν μέσον; cf. 223.

58. Agathem. 2.2; Plut. *De Def. Or.* 409e (with doubts, calls the story an "ancient myth"); Varro *Ling.* 7.17 (with criticism); Str. 9.3.6 (attributes the story to Pindar); Romm (1992) 63.

59. For the actual location of the *omphalos* at Delphi (in a *naiskos* constructed next to a wall, *CID* II 49 AI, ca. 340 B.C.E.; 62 IIB, ca. 335 B.C.E.), see Amandry (1993) 263–76. The *omphalos* is mentioned five times in the temple accounts.

60. Romm (1992) 64 n. 44.

61. The Pythia was seated next to the gold eagles of Zeus when she delivered her prophecy to Battos; Pind. *Pyth.* 4.4.

policy, but they provided procedures whereby cities could ascertain the possibility of divine approval for policies already decided or already planned.[62] The status of Delphi depended on its appearance of neutrality because Apollo could be trusted only if his sanctuary could appear to be free from the influence of individual communities. After the First Sacred War, Delphi was put under the authority of the regional representatives of the Pylaian Amphictyony at Anthela,[63] thus formalizing the claim that Delphi belonged not to its residents alone but to the whole region and, by extension, to all Greeks. The site's remoteness, isolation, and relative difficulty of access all contributed to the idea that Delphi was not a normal place but a spot close to the gods.

Although described as a *polis,*[64] Delphi was not a typical *polis.* Her residents appeared to work no agricultural territory of their own, and the community had no status independent of the sanctuary. Recognition of Delphi as the center of the earth created the image of central stability and established the kind of authority Greek cities needed. Delphi's central role reflected a symbolic organization of the landscape that reinforced notions of geographic centrality and cultural hierarchy. Mythic narrative, early historiography,[65] and political discourse imagined a world with Hellenes at the center surrounded by different ethnic groups arranged in a series of concentric rings, foreigners *(xenoi)* in the first outer ring, followed by barbarians, then wild men, and finally monsters *(agrioi)* in the outermost ring, dwelling at the very edges *(eschatiai)* of the world. Beyond the farthest boundaries of the inhabited world, the streams of Ocean created a cosmic circle beyond which dwelled the four winds. Every winter Apollo journeyed to the land of the Hyperboreans, a mythical people "beyond the North Wind," believed by some to have assisted in the foundation of his oracle at Delphi.[66] Like the privileged beings of Hesiod's generation of gold, these Hyperboreans were ignorant of sickness, old age, suffering, war,

62. Parker (1985); Malkin (1987) 17–91.

63. Hdt. 7.200. The Amphictyony was in charge of rebuilding the temple after 548; Hdt. 2.180.

64. Arist. F 487 Rose: Aristotle wrote a *Δελφῶν πολιτεία*. Delphi is said to have had both a *bouleuterion* and a *prytaneion;* Hansen and Fischer-Hansen (1994) 86–87. The local institutions of the *polis* had to be accommodated to the institutions of the Amphictyony. For the formulas of political decision, see Rhodes and Lewis (1997) 126–40.

65. Shaw (1983). See now Sassi (2000) 26–33.

66. Paus. 10.5.9; the first temple was made of laurel, the second of beeswax and feathers sent from the Hyperboreans.

death, and retribution[67] and lived forever, without the restrictions of human status. The god's annual journey created a mythic connection between Delphi at the center of the earth and the powerful forces at its outermost limit. This connection sharpened the authority of the sanctuary for Greeks as well as for those from other lands who came to consult the god.

On the Greek mainland, the sacred center of each *polis* was linked by roads to the sacred center of each local, ex-urban sanctuary and ultimately to Delphi itself, the center of all. Myths of Delphic stability reflected confidence in a coherent network connecting all communities to a recognized center, with each *polis* organized around a ritual space that provided the point from which the distance to a central place in the outside world was measured. At Athens, that distance was measured from the altar of the twelve gods in the agora, the place Pindar calls the "navel *(omphalos)* of the city *(asty)*."[68] Major roads were procession routes, physical reminders of the network of regular processions that connected the city center to the territorial sanctuaries of its *chora* and to the superregional sanctuaries. Major routes leading out of Athens were named for the important ceremonial processions that traveled to sanctuaries outside the city. The gate facing Phaleron was called "the gate by which the *mystai* march to the sea,"[69] and the road to Eleusis was called "the Sacred Way" in honor of the procession to that border sanctuary. Boundary markers *(horoi)* and road signs oriented residents to the major sacred authorities. Delphi was recognized by a *horos* in the *agora* that marked the route of the major sacred procession to Delphi, the Pythaïs.[70] The text announced: "*Horos* of the sacred road by which the Pythaïs proceeds to Delphi."[71]

The myth of Delphic centrality conveyed a message of security, in sharp opposition to the challenges faced by cities protecting a local landscape. A city's neighbors could be its fiercest enemies. Representations of the larger world replicated the experience of the individual *polis,* imagined as a secure center surrounded by its agricultural territory (crops planted on the plains and lower hillsides), and the whole bounded by fringe areas, *eschatiai,* or edge zones—the mountains shared with neighbors or the sea that defined the shore. Boundaries between cities were important and were defined in

67. Pind. *Pyth.* 10.34–44. On the Hyperboreans, see Romm (1992) 60–63.
68. Pind. F 75.3.
69. *IG* I³ 84.35–36.
70. Plutarch tells us that the road leading into the sanctuary itself was the one local residents called "sacred"; Plut. *Quaest. Graec.* 296.
71. Lalonde (1991) 29, H34; fourth century B.C.E.

several ways. Inland *eschatiai* were the marginal lands beyond a city's cultivated fields. Such lands when located on mountain slopes were used for pasturage and considered public space (ὄρη δημόσια, "public mountains") in the same way that the public space at the heart of the city—the *akropolis* and the *agora*—belonged to all.[72] Beyond such *eschatai,* a city's lands ended in the transitional space marking the borders between the territory of one *polis* and the next. Inland boundaries between one territory and another were more like a belt than a simple line. Whether high mountains or deserts, borderlands were desolate by nature (χῶραι ἔρημοι, "deserted lands"),[73] left uninhabited because they were contested (χῶραι μεθόριαι, "lands in between")[74] or because they were so sensitive that they had to be maintained as neutral zones (κοιναὶ χῶραι, "lands held in common") protected by the gods.[75]

Delphi was not the only central point on the imagined map. Intermediate-level regional sanctuaries brought local communities together. The temple of Aphaia on Aigina was one such temple. Located outside the *polis,* the sanctuary was a place of worship for men and women alike. Votives dating from the Geometric period through the early Classical period suggest that males and females worshipped the kourotrophic Aphaia separately. The largest group is similar to votives found elsewhere for divinities associated with childbirth or the raising of children: seated females, worshippers, animals with young, jewelry, perfume jars, and most striking, relief plaques depicting a standing woman offering her breasts for nursing. This group, reflecting the interests of women, stands in contrast to the weapons and male figurines clustered at other sites in the sanctuary. The two very different concentrations of votives define the goddess as protector of both family and tribe, representing the collective unity of both men and women in this local island confederacy.[76]

On the island of Lesbos, "the sanctuary at Messon (midpoint)," as it was known,[77] served several cities and synchronized the festival calendars of

72. Robert (1960) 196–97.

73. Daverio Rocchi (1988) 31–47, on these distinctions.

74. Characterized by shared sanctuaries, such as those in the area between Messenia and Lakonia; Paus. 3.2.6.

75. For example, the *hiera orgas* between Megara and Athens, left uncultivated and under the protection of the Eleusinian goddesses (schol. Thuc. 1.139.2).

76. Sinn (1988) 149–53, for the split between offerings from males and offerings from females at the sanctuary of Aphaia on Aigina.

77. τὸ ἰρὸν τὸ ἐμ Μέσ[σῳ], or "in the middle" (τὸ ἐμ μέσσῳ). For a fuller description, see Robert (1969) 300–15. The place has been identified with a site that

all of them.[78] For the competing cities on the island this sanctuary provided a secure place for negotiation. Hellenistic decrees indicate that the cities of Lesbos (Mytilene, Methymna, Antissa, and Eresos) met here to conclude formal agreements. The significance of the site was expressed in the name for one regional festival, "Days for Turning around the Middle" (μεσοστροφώνιαι ἡμέραι). Alkaios calls the sanctuary "a great *temenos* shared in common" (τέμενος μέγα ξῦνον) by all Lesbians and shared as well by three gods: Zeus, god of suppliants; an Aiolic goddess associated with the birth of all (perhaps Hera); and Dionysos Omastes, "eater of raw flesh."[79]

Alkaios, in exile near the site at Messon, described this sanctuary as located among the *eschatiai*, the most remote areas of the island.[80] *Eschatiai* were on the edge, whether in the mountains or on the sea, and even central spaces like Delphi could be described as land "on the edge" *(eschate ge)*.[81] The great sanctuary on Lesbos was geographically central but considered politically remote, beyond the territorial claim of any individual *polis*.[82] The four cities on Lesbos that met here competed for space and authority. Located at the farthest point from all populated areas, this sanctuary was a place for shared festivals in times of peace, for negotiations in times of stress. The sanctuary also served the island's women, and females from all the cities of Lesbos assembled here to be judged for their beauty.[83] When the women celebrated the rites of Hera or Dionysos, the males excluded from these rites could hear from afar the echo of the women's sacred ululation.[84] Regular celebration of joint festivals was a sign that the women

---

preserves the ancient name, "Messa," near Kryoneri. Labarre (1994) 415–46 follows the discussion of Robert. See now Spencer (2000) 72, for the archaic temple at Apothiki, at the edge of the territory of Eresos.

78. For the *poleis* on Lesbos, see now Labarre (1996).

79. Alc. F 129 (LP).

80. Alc. F 130 col. ii (LP).

81. Schol. Aeschin. 1.97: ἐσχατιαί εἰσι τόποι ἔσχατοι τῆς χώρας περατούμενοι ἢ εἰς ὄρη ἢ εἰς θάλασσαν. On the term applied to both mountainous regions and the boundary between shore and sea, compare Harp. s. v. ἐσχαταί.

82. Robert (1969) 303, quotes Koldeway, who visited the island in 1890: "Die wenigen antiken Häuserreste an drei getrennten Stellen in der Nähe des Tempels sind kaum seine Kome zu nennen. So lag der prächtige Bau abgesondert in der Einsamkeit."

83. Scholia in Homerum, *Il.* 9.130, for women competing with regard to their beauty at a sanctuary of Hera.

84. Alc. F 130B LP.

of the entire island could safely congregate and therefore indicated that the four cities were at peace.[85]

CIVIC CENTRALITY

Any Greek *polis* was both a composite of smaller, internal groups and also part of a larger network of local and regional organizations, linked by ties of ritual.[86] The internal population of any *polis* was divided in many ways; group boundaries were not always coterminous but intersected according to gender, age, kinship, social status, profession, citizenship, or residence. Ritual worked in two ways: It molded individuals into groups, and it created opportunities for any one of those individuals to represent that group at a higher level of the ritual process. Just as the male head of the household *(kyrios)* could represent the family in the collective sacrifices or rituals of the *polis,* so, too, could an individual represent an age class or another segmented group at a collective ritual—whether that of the local *polis,* the region, or a pan-Hellenic sanctuary. The ritual structure was dynamic and fluid. The *polis* was only one stage in the process, but it was the level of organization at which most Greek communities chose to represent themselves politically and symbolically to the outside world.

Cities organized local institutions by taking into account the relationship between their own central place and the wider ritual network beyond their own boundaries. Significant rituals were associated with the *prtyaneion,* a physical space in the center of the city enclosing the community's common hearth and its sacred fire.[87] The fire in the *prytaneion* looked both inward and outward. Within the city, the fire represented the skills required for civilized life; keeping the fire tended meant the life of the city would continue.[88] Sharing fire from a common source at a regional sanctuary emphasized traditional ethnic bonds and acknowledged the connection of each *polis* to a larger ritual network. The civic hearth symbolized the integrity of the individual *polis* and, as its symbolic center, connected that *polis* to every other community that partook of the same fire. The process

85. For the delicate balance between peace and local unrest, see Spencer (2000) with reference to earlier studies. Mytilene was subject to internal stasis, but for the other local *poleis,* tension was mediated by shared sanctuaries.

86. Sourvinou-Inwood (1988a, 1990).

87. *IG* II^{2} 1053.10, 1051c.23.

88. Vernant (1983) 141–42.

encouraged the kind of permanent diplomatic and political contact that made Hellenic communal institutions possible.

The *prytaneion* marked a space at the same time both sacred and political—an area marked off by ritual but also a place to exhibit public contracts and important civic regulations,[89] a space where the gods could be shown to acknowledge diplomatic contacts and agreements between cities. The *prytaneion* was also the place for significant public feasts. It was the dining area set aside for the meals awarded to important political officials, generous local benefactors, and successful local athletes, as well as prestigious foreign visitors and designated representatives from cities abroad. The institutions of the *prytaneion* symbolized difference based on privilege and achievement and, paradoxically, conferred equality by recognizing hierarchy. The ceremonies of the *prytaneion* created community by defining differences between those qualified to participate and those not allowed to enter. Normally only privileged male citizens and highly placed public officials were eligible to use the *prytaneion;* foreigners, even those of high status, were received by invitation only. If we were to make an analogy with domestic space, we would have to say that the *prytaneion* was similar not to the whole house[90] but to the dining area. The dining area of a Greek house was the *andron* (men's room), where the adult males of the family could entertain invited male visitors. Like the *andron,* a privileged area inside the house, the *prytaneion* was a privileged space inside the city, reserved for those deserving special honors, whether local citizens or foreigners. The innovation introduced at Athens in the fifth century, when an additional building for dining, the circular *tholos,* was built in the *agora,* was not imitated in other cities. The *tholos* at Athens served as the communal place for feeding public officials. The *prytaneion* continued to be the site for dispensing special honors in the form of banquets—*sitesis* for citizens, *xenia* for foreigners.[91] Only citizens had access to the hearth itself.

The *prytaneion* was like the *andron* of the house in another important respect. Wives and daughters of citizens did not eat in the *andron* with their male relatives when male guests were present. The *prytaneion* was likewise a place reserved for the banquets and feasts of public guests, and

89. Solon's legislation, for instance; Plut. *Sol.* 25.

90. Although Plato calls Kallias's house the *prytaneion* of wisdom for the Greeks; Pl. *Prt.* 337d.

91. For the distinctions between the arrangements for the meals, see Schmitt Pantel (1992) 147–77.

adult, married women were not invited. Exclusion was expressed in terms of protecting the city's sacred fire, whose special sanctity could be preserved only if sexually active, married females were not present. That is, the fire on the city's hearth had to maintain a level of purity impossible to achieve in the presence of the women responsible for reproduction. Females supervised the fire of the city, just as they supervised the fire of the household,[92] but the women associated with the public sacred fire had to be "finished with sexual relations" because the sacred fire was "pure and undefiled."[93] This requirement was expressed at Naukratis by a rule paraphrased in the following way: "It is not possible for a woman to go into the *prytaneion*, except for the flute-girl,[94] and a chamber pot is not to be carried into the *prytaneion*."[95] Wives and chamber pots are listed together because both threatened the purity of the sacred fire. The fire in the *prytaneion*, like the fire in the household, deserved respect. The rules at Naukratis recognized that the gods required separation of female impurity from the city's sacred fire.

The *prytaneion* was a place for creating male community and male solidarity. The hearth in the *prytaneion*, like the hearth in the home, defined a space for rituals of incorporation. In order to protect the honor conferred on visiting dignitaries, rules of access were governed by a hierarchy of privilege, and meals were offered according to a hierarchy of distribution.[96] Privileged foreigners could be invited to eat in the *prytaneion* but they remained outsiders and their participation was only temporary. At Athens, local ephebes also used the *prytaneion*. As adolescents in training for citizenship, they began as outsiders who would eventually become insiders. The ephebe's initial visit was a brief first step in a process that would eventually culminate in full adult membership in the political community. In the Hellenistic period, the process of incorporation was gradual, beginning with collective "sacrifices of entry at the common hearth" (τὰ εἰσιτήρια ἐπὶ τῆς κοινῆς ἑστίας), supervised by the priest of the Demos and the Charites. After the sacrifice, the ephebes moved in procession to the sanc-

92. For the hearth of the city replicating the hearth of the family, see Gernet (1981) 322–39; Schmitt Pantel (1992) 93–94.

93. Plut. *Num.* 9.6: γυναῖκες πεπαυμέναι γάμων . . . φλόγα καθαρὰν καὶ ἀμίαντον, on the sacred fire at Delphi being rekindled from the sun after the Persian desecration.

94. Starr (1978).

95. Herm. in Ath. 150a. *SEG* 24.361, includes a chamber pot in a list of cooking pots for public feasts. See Schmitt Pantel (1992) 306.

96. *IG* I³ 77; *IG* II² 40.

tuary of Artemis Agrotera, just outside the city wall.[97] The *prytaneion* represented the enclosed center of the city; the sanctuary of Artemis Agrotera, near the city but outside, represented the outer boundaries of the rural territory, where the ephebes would later spend a period of military training before achieving recognition as full members of the assembly of male citizens. The sacrifices at the common hearth introduced the ephebes to the city's political core. Later, when they swore their oath to serve the *polis,* they would swear by the gods and borders of Attika, by the crops and the boundary markers *(horoi)* themselves. The oath of the ephebes, sworn at the sanctuary of Aglauros on the east slope of the *akropolis,* tied the ephebe to the city's ritual core and at the same time bound him to her territory and external borders.[98]

The traditional sacrifices and festivals of the *polis* recognized the gods on whose sufferance the *polis* continued to exist, but the system of public administration was always flexible, allowing changes in ritual and welcoming new divinities when the need arose. The *prytaneion* was the place for announcing new public rituals and for introducing new gods to the local pantheon. Procedures varied from city to city. Some cities recognized new gods by the same rituals they used to recognize new citizens. In other words, they could naturalize a god just as they naturalized foreigners. The people of Thurii, for instance, in gratitude for help from Boreas (the North Wind) in defeating the navy of Dionysios of Syracuse, welcomed the god to Thurii by giving him a house, a plot of land *(kleros),* and a grant of citizenship.[99] At Athens, new gods were granted public sacrifice[100] and treated not as naturalized citizens but as privileged metics, foreigners allowed to reside indefinitely in Attika and granted the privilege of owning property, *enktesis.* A third-century decree of the Athenian assembly granted *enktesis* to the Thracian goddess Bendis.[101] Her worshippers, the *orgeones* of Bendis, thereupon built her a temple in the Peiraieus. She was recognized later with a procession from the *prytaneion,*[102] connecting her sanctuary to the ritual center of the city and recalling with every annual performance that original introduction.

97. *IG* II^2 1006, 1008, 1011, 1028; *SEG* 15.104; 21.476; 24.189; *Hesperia* 16 (1974) 170; Miller (1978) appendix A 195–202. See also Parker (1996) 187.
98. Siewert (1977); Ober (1995).
99. Ael. *VH* 12.61.
100. *IG* I^3 136.
101. *IG* II^2 337.
102. *IG* II^2 1283, third century B.C.E.

Prytaneia were found in regional sanctuaries as well as in the local *poleis.* At Olympia, the *prytaneion* was a meeting place for the people of Elis.[103] At Delphi, the same institution provided a communal space for representatives of all Hellenic cities.[104] The *prytaneion* in the regional sanctuary was the source of the sacred fire that nourished and sustained the whole ritual system. When a local ritual fire was extinguished, or was compromised by pollution, it had to be renewed with sacred fire from a central sanctuary. After the Persian invasion and the battle at Plataiai, the entire territory of Plataiai was considered defiled. To mark renewal, the Greek generals appealed to Apollo Pythios to confirm and support the procedures for reinitiating civic ritual. Delphi granted an altar for Zeus Eleutherios, "Zeus, Sponsor of Freedom," but commanded that it not be used until all fires throughout the land were extinguished and new fires lit with pure fire from the common hearth at Delphi.[105] The Pythaïs—the Delphic festival of Apollo to which many cities sent a publicly sponsored pilgrimage to observe the rites *(theoria)*—seems to have been the occasion for bringing new fire to home cities. At Athens, at least, the new fire seems to have been brought annually during the month of Thargelion, a month of purification and new beginnings. Herodotus mentions a *theoria* from Chios to Delphi, and later epigraphical evidence confirms regular Athenian participation in these rites.[106] For cities in and around the Aegean, new fire was brought from the Aegean center of Apollo on Delos.

The network of civic institutions represented by the *prytaneion* was widespread. Solid epigraphical evidence indicates *prytaneia* in upwards of ninety *poleis,*[107] and there is good archaeological evidence for several more.[108] Most epigraphical evidence is Hellenistic, but the possibility of

103. Xen. *Hell.* 7.4.31 (the population is called Elean, not Olympic); Paus. 5.15.8 (Hansen and Fischer-Hansen [1994] 87–89).

104. See Miller (1978) 187–89 for the relevant sources. In the *prytaneion* at Delos there was a statue of Apollo standing on an *omphalos; ID* 1417B I.89–102.

105. Plut. *Arist.* 20.4. The runner who brought fire to Plataea collapsed and died after running the 125 miles; he was buried in the sanctuary of Artemis Eukleia.

106. Hdt. 6.27; Parker (1983) 23, 25. The sarcastic remarks of Plato and Theopompos about a Delphic pronouncement proclaiming Athens the "hearth of Hellas" belong to a later time. See Pl. *Prt.* 337d; Theopomp. in Ath. 5.187d; and Miller (1978) 157, for comment.

107. There are ninety-five sites on the list assembled by Hansen and Fischer-Hansen (1994) 31–34.

108. Miller (1978) 67–91; one of Miller's original requirements for the identification of architectural remains as a *prytaneion* was the presence of a fixed hearth;

flexible architectural arrangements in earlier periods makes it likely that the scanty evidence going back to the sixth century does not tell the whole story. Reciprocal relationships between cities were already well established by that time, and Herodotus's evidence for early *prytaneia* at Sikyon[109] and Siphnos[110] supports an earlier date. *Prytaneia* are also identifiable at Halos,[111] Tenedos,[112] and Athens[113] by the fifth century.

The early epigraphical and literary evidence for *prytaneia* suggests a strong association with the eastern Aegean; etymology indicates an Ionic source.[114] The earliest epigraphical reference is from Sigeion, an important Aeolic site located directly on the Hellespont. Phanodikos, an emissary from Ionic Prokonnesos, was remembered here by the record of his gift. More or less the same text is inscribed twice, in two different dialects, on the same stele:

> I am of Phanodikos, the son of Hermokrates, from Prokonnesos. He gave a *krater*, a *krater*-stand, and a strainer to the people of Sigeion for the *prytaneion*.
>
> I am of Phanodikos, the son of Hermokrates, from Prokonnesos, and I gave a *krater*, a stand, and a strainer to the people of Sigeion for the *prytaneion*. But if I suffer anything, may the people of Sigeion, take care of me; Haisopos and his brothers made me.

The upper transcription is in the east Ionic dialect of Prokonnesos, a colony of Miletos and Phanodikos's home city. The lower is in the official Attic dialect used by Athens at Sigeion, an Aeolic community at that time under

---

see page 11. Local variation, however, may have allowed a more flexible arrangement, perhaps even duplicating the portable hearths known from domestic contexts, on which see Jameson (1990) 192–95. Miller now concurs; Hansen and Fischer-Hansen (1994) 34 n. 48. There is new evidence from Kassope; Hoepfner and Schwandner (1994^2) 98–101.

109. Hdt. 5.67 (seems to refer to a precinct rather than a building because it had a *temenos* inside).

110. Hdt. 3.57, indicating a building in Herodotus's day, described as decorated with Parian marble.

111. Hdt. 7.197.

112. Pind. *Nem.* 11.1–9.

113. Plut. *Sol.* 19.3.

114. *Prytaneion*, "place of the *prytanis*," is formed from the title of an administrative official, often eponymous in Ionian and Aiolic cities; Geschnitzer (1973) 730–815. Like *tyrannis*, another well-used Greek political term of debated origin, *prytanis* seems to be an eastern word. A Greek suffix signifying place *(-eion)* has been added to a stem that is obviously not Greek. Chantraine (1974) 3: 944, connects it with political titles in Etruscan and early languages in Asia Minor. The proper name "Prytanis" occurs in *Il.* 5.678 (for a Lycian companion of Sarpedon in a list of others with "redende Namen").

Athenian control.[115] This inscription, implying a bouquet of dialects, represents a variety of Greek speakers from a variety of homelands. The two versions are recorded together not because east Ionian readers could not read Attic or because Attic speakers could not interpret Ionic spellings but to represent to the Athenians in control of Sigeion the distinct identity of Phanodikos himself. The monument, taken as a whole, is unusual in that it seeks to represent identity by making linguistic distinctions. It seems a good bet that by the sixth century, Athenians, Aeolians, and Ionians were all familiar with the rituals of the *prytaneion,* and that its institutions were recognized on all sides of the Aegean.

RITUAL NARRATIVES OF CENTRALITY AND JUDICIAL SUCCESS

The exact location of the *prytaneion* in Athens is a matter of dispute,[116] but recent discoveries suggest that this structure was part of an early *agora* located to the east of the *akropolis,*[117] not far from the cave of Aglauros on the steep east slope. Location is of some consequence because the Athenian *prytaneion* anchored two important and closely related rituals: the Dipolieia, the sacred plowing of a special field below the *akropolis,* and the Bouphonia, "rites associated with ox-murder." Timed to coincide with the last full moon of the Athenian year, the Dipolieia on 14 Skirophorion, just before the summer solstice, concluded the year's administrative and ritual cycles and prepared the way for the transfer of some of the city's highest political offices to a new slate of magistrates on the first day of Hekatombaion.[118]

Skirophorion, the turning point of the agricultural year, was an appropriate month to mark the end of one year and the beginning of the next. It fell after the early summer harvest, when the grain stalks left behind in the

115. Jeffery in *LSAG*² 72, 366, 371 no. 5 43–44, 416 and pl. 71, nos. 43–44, 575–550 B.C.E. Jeffery suggests that the stone was cut and the Ionic lines carved in the quarry at Prokonnesos, and that it was then brought to Sigeion, where the Attic version was added in a different hand. This process seems unnecessarily complicated. The *krater, krater*-stand, and wine strainer were equipment for the symposium that would have followed a public banquet in the *prytaneion.*

116. Robertson (1986) 147–76; Miller (1978) 225.

117. Dontas (1983) 57–60, and 62: "It is to the east of the Akropolis, in the heart of the modern Plaka, that the political center of Athens in aristocratic times is to be found." Miller (1995) 211–12 (with notes 83–92), 236–7.

118. Burkert (1983). For variability in the calendar of offices, see Rhodes (1981) 406–7, 517.

dry fields were plowed under in preparation for the next season's plowing and sowing.[119] The festivals that gave the month its name were the Skira, in honor of Athena and Demeter. The Skira included, among other events, a nocturnal celebration for women celebrated locally, and a procession by religious officials to the village of Skiron, located on the Sacred Way *(hiera hodos)* connecting Athens and Eleusis. According to an inscription seen by Pausanias at Skiron, this was the place where the hero Phytalos received Demeter when she authorized the first harvest. In exchange for his hospitality, Demeter gave him the first fig tree.[120]

Plutarch informs us that there were three sacred plowings in Attika. He names them in this order: one at Skiron, a second on the Rharian plain at Eleusis, and a third "under the *polis* at a place called Bouzygion."[121] Plutarch's use of *polis* to mean *akropolis* suggests that he is using an early source. Any connection between these plowing ceremonies and the deme sacrifices called Proerosia (the local preplowing ceremonies of late summer) is not indicated, but the three plowings described by Plutarch clearly had a distinctive status. Each marked a significant location in Attika: first, the *akropolis* at the center; second, the Rharian plain at Eleusis near the external border with Megara; and third, Skiron, midway between Athens and Eleusis.[122] The series as a whole celebrates the introduction of agriculture and Athena's reception of Demeter. The three locations are the important elements. The Rharian field, traditionally Demeter's first stop in Attika, was the field that supplied the grain for the bread used in Eleusinian ritual.[123] The purity of this field was therefore carefully maintained. Skiron had a sanctuary of Athena and represented the midpoint of the ties between the major divinity of the central settlement and the major divinity of the Attic periphery. The priestess of Athena and the priests of Poseidon and Helios left Athens and processed to Skiron.[124] The procession likely had two parts, one beginning from the political center at Athens, the other from the ritual center at Eleusis. Moving in opposite directions, they met

119. Foxhall (1995b) 98–99.

120. Quoted by Pausanias at 1.37.2, where he says it decorated the grave of Phytalos.

121. Plut. *Conj. Praec.* 144b.

122. Near a river named for Skiros, a seer from Dodona buried at the site; Paus. 1.36.4; Burkert (1983) 136, 140. *FGrH* 328 F 14 (IIIB supplement 286–89) collects the sources for the Skira.

123. Paus. 1.38.6; Brumfield (1981) 172.

124. *FGrH* 328 F 14 Philochoros.

at Skiron, a midpoint, where the third sacred plowing underscored the ritual unity between Athens and Eleusis.[125]

We cannot reconstruct the sacred plowing at Skiron or the one on the Rharian plain, but it is possible to sketch out the implications of the ritual at Athens. Plutarch's term "Bouzygion" identifies a field "below the *akropolis*" with Bouzyges, the Attic hero said to have been the first man to yoke an ox to the plow and the first to plow the soil.[126] The Bouzygion, where this event took place,[127] must have been associated with another field, the one Hesychios calls the "field of hunger," located by Zenobius "behind the *prytaneion*," a field the Athenians left untilled.[128]

The ceremony of the first plowing belonged to a cycle of myth about the introduction of agriculture, reenacted annually to renew protection of the community from the curse of collective famine, *limos*. The ritual plowing made an explicit connection between successful agriculture, the physical health of the population, and the political and judicial health of the city. The plowed field reminded the people of the rewards of cooperation with the gods; the untilled field reminded them of the punishments of failure. They could make this connection because as he plowed the field of hunger, the official who played the role of Bouzyges offered public curses on behalf of the *polis*, curses directed against three kinds of people: those who failed to share water, those who failed to share fire, and those who failed to give accurate directions to the lost.[129] These curses emphasized the social sig-

125. As a bidirectional process it both unifies and recognizes the distinction between the territory's various geographic zones. Graf's dichotomy between centrifugal and centripetal processions, (1996) 54–65, is too schematic and does not take into account the possibilities of a single ceremony that includes both.

126. Hsch. s.v. *Βουζύγης*. Jameson (1951) 54 locates the field below the *akropolis*, near the sanctuary of Demeter Chloe. See *IG* II^2 5006.

127. Vernant (1983) 157 understands two separate fields.

128. Hsch. s. v. *λιμοῦ πεδίον*; Zen. 4.93: *λιμοῦ πεδίον . . . τόπος γάρ ἐστιν οὕτω καλοῦμενος. καὶ λέγουσιν ὅτι λιμοῦ ποτε κατασχόντος, ἔχρησεν ὁ θεὸς ἱκέτειαν θεῶν, καὶ τὸν λιμὸν ἐξιλειόσασθαι. οἱ δὲ Ἀθηναῖοι ἀνῆκαν αὐτῷ τὸ ὄπισθεν τοῦ πρυτανείου πεδίον* (Field of hunger . . . for there is a place so called. And they say that when once a famine held them in its grip, the god responded to a supplication of the gods with an oracle, and they put an end to the famine with expiation. And the Athenians left untilled for it the field behind the *prytaneion.)* Robertson (1998) locates the "field of hunger" and the *prytaneion* below the eastern heights of the *akropolis.*

129. Leutsch and Schneidewin (1958) I, app. I 388, s.v. *Βουζύγης*, parodied by Diphilos in Ath. 6.238f–239a. The Spartan refusal of fire to Aristodemos, the only Spartiate to return from Thermopylai alive, was equivalent to a curse; Hdt. 7.231. On the conjunction of planting and cursing, see Pulleyn (1997) 80–81. See

nificance of fire and water and implied that if the *polis* tolerated anyone who did not meet the minimal social obligations of communal life, its own population deserved starvation. Public recitation of the curses at the time of the plowing ceremony demonstrated that successful agriculture depended on fulfilling the obligations of communal responsibility.[130]

Each year the ox that drew the plow met his own death in the Bouphonia, the "ox-murder rituals" for Zeus Polieus that followed. An ox, so necessary to the agricultural way of life, would have been an unusual and expensive sacrificial victim. The exceptionality of the victim highlights the anomaly of the ritual and suggests that it marked an important transition. Originally, in Attika, a god of mountaintops,[131] Zeus protected the heights of the city.[132] Associated with Athena Polias, he was worshipped at the highest point on the *akropolis* within a walled precinct under the open sky.[133] His epithet "Polieus" referred originally not to his political functions but to the location of his altar.[134] The Dipolieia incorporated two events: murder on the *akropolis* and a ritual trial in the *prytaneion*.[135] The dispute turned on the definition of murder and the nature of responsibility.[136] The trial took place at the *prytaneion* because in the sixth century this was where texts of important laws and legislative pronouncements were exhibited. The ritual narrative of murder on the *akropolis* and trial in the *prytaneion* connected the ritual center of the city

---

schol. Soph. *Ant.* 255, for a fourth curse, directed at those who allowed a corpse to remain unburied.

130. For another sacrifice where a bull associated with the sowing is consecrated, the impact of the ritual is made clear by the prayers for peace, wealth, and successful harvest that accompany it. See *SIG*^{3} 589.7, 26–31.

131. Schachter (1992) 42–43; Langdon (1976). Parker (1996) 29–32 takes a slightly different position.

132. Cornutus, *Epidrom.* 20, describing Athena.

133. Brackertz (1976) 202–3; Schwabl (1972) 354. "Polieus," as used of Zeus at Athens, referred first to the location of his open-air altar on the *akropolis* and only later to his political functions in the context of the developing city.

134. The title "Polieus" is used in the early *lex sacra* listing the regulations for the Dipolieia at Athens; *IG* I^3 232.26–27, between 510 and 480 B.C.E. It does not appear again at Athens until 429/8: *IG* II^2 383.139–40. The title does however appear on archaic votives on the *akropolis* at Thera; *IG* XII (3) 363.

135. Paus. 1.24.4, 28.10. Pausanias explains the trials of inanimate objects in the *prytaneion* by the trial of the axe at the Bouphonia. The original meaning of the festival must have been "*akropolis* rites for Zeus." Zeus is associated with the *akropolis* in *Il.* 6.257.

136. The main sources are Theophr. in Porph. *Abst.* 2.28–30 and Paus. 1.24.4, 28.10.

to its political center[137] and brought Zeus into the judicial processes of the *polis.*[138]

The ox chosen for the ritual was slain in an unusual sacrifice where the animal was held responsible for its own death.[139] Enticed to eat grain placed on the altar as a preliminary offering,[140] the animal was slain by human hands wielding both axe and knife. Intended as an act of execution, the act of killing was treated like a murder. The resulting argument transferred responsibility from the human slayer and the ox to the murder weapon, but because two weapons had been used, it was not clear whether criminal liability belonged to the ax that stunned the animal or the knife that slit its throat. The trial concluded with a decision: Although the axe was responsible for the death, the knife was the instrument polluted by the crime. Therefore this weapon had to be thrown into the sea.[141]

The unusual rituals of the Bouphonia have misled interpreters to exaggerate the age of the ceremony. Associated in myth with one of the earliest Athenian kings, either Kekrops or Erechtheus,[142] the Bouphonia were described by fashionable trendsetters in the late fifth century as bizarre and archaic.[143] Accepting this assessment, modern interpreters have explained the rituals either as an expression of distress over the violence of killing or as a narrative about the introduction of agriculture. Such interpretations emphasize the abnormal killing of an abnormal victim[144] but minimize the

137. Connor (1987) 173–74, on ritual as the connection between sacred and political space.

138. Where his epithets Agoraios (god of the *agora*), Boulaios (god of the civic council), Bouleus (god of decision-making), Horkios (protector of oaths), Hikesios (protector of suppliants), and Xenios (protector of foreigners), indicated the characteristics that made political life possible; Schwabl (1972).

139. Burkert (1983) 138 n. 12 points out that it was a crime to kill such an animal.

140. Cooked into a *popanon,* a sacrificial cake, according to a scholion on Ar. *Nub.* 585, or *pelanos,* according to Porph. *Abst.* 2.30.19

141. The dispute provides a ritual precedent for the legal requirement explained at Aeschin. 3.244: "Wood and stones and iron, though without voice or reason, if they fall on a person and kill, are banished beyond the frontiers" (trans. Parke [1977] 163).

142. Kekrops: Euseb. *Chron.* 472; Hsch. s.v. "Dios thakoi," (does not name a king); Erechtheus: Paus. 1.28.10.

143. Ar. *Nub.* 984.

144. Burkert (1983) 136–43 explains the rite in terms of anxiety in a period of transition mixed with guilt for killing the ox, the working partner of the agriculturalist; Durand (1986) explains the ritual in terms of the primordial introduction of agriculture.

significance of an unusual ritual, namely, the resolution of a dispute by means of a judicial procedure in the *prytaneion*.[145]

The change in venue for the decision sharpens the emphasis on the trial. The movement from *akropolis* to *prytaneion* connects the procedures of the *prytaneion* with the most hallowed ritual site in the city and suggests that the segment at the *prytaneion* was the original reason for the entire sequence. The trial scene at the *prytaneion,* like the trial scene in Aischylos's *Oresteia,* represents judicial process as the solution to the problem of assessing responsibility for violence.[146] The ritual that celebrated the first plowing of Attic soil, a first occasion, becomes the template for the ritual trial, also a first occasion. The celebration of a "first occasion" is not a primitive event but a self-conscious commemoration of an institution already in process. The trial of the weapons therefore could not be early, even though Aristophanes implies that some of his contemporaries thought it was.[147] For one thing, the trial could be no older than the introduction of the Athenian judicial procedure it celebrates. The trial solves the dilemma of deciding between competing appeals for justice, and by distinguishing between pollution and legal responsibility, it concludes with a mature debate about violence and public validation for the community's procedures for dealing with crime. The plow-ox was a trusted animal on whose contribution the entire community relied.[148] By assigning to this important agent the role of victim, the Bouphonia posed the problem of coming to a decision and connected the contributions of agriculture to the city's judicial process.[149] The solution to the murder, elevating legal procedure over revenge, established justice for the plow-ox and asserted that successful agricultural production was contingent on judicial solutions for violence—a theme already

145. Two problems require solution: the status of a murder provoked by the victim's assent and the problem of assigning responsibility to an inanimate object. An example of the second predicament occurred at Olympia (Paus. 5.27.9–10) when a little boy died from jumping up suddenly and hitting his head on a bronze dedication. The Eleans had to consult Delphi because they could not remove a dedication, even one believed responsible for a death. The oracle advised purifying the statue by the means of the *katharsis* customarily used for purification of *akousios phonos* (unintentional murder).

146. As Katz has clearly demonstrated (1992a) 177–78.

147. Notably, the Aristophanic character who claims the Bouphonia is old-fashioned is the up-to-the-minute pseudo-intellectual named "Worse Argument" (also known as "Unjust Discourse").

148. Isager and Skydsgaard (1992) 18, with n. 36.

149. Pulleyn (1997) 80, for connection of plowing and the administration of justice in the figure of the Eleusinian Triptolemos, who established laws (Xenocrates F 98 Heinze) and, in the afterlife, served as judge (Plat. *Apol.* 41a).

articulated by Hesiod. Finally, the link between *akropolis* and *prytaneion*, expressed in ritual and emphasized every time the murder and trial were reenacted in sequence, connected two important central places[150] and demonstrated that the judicial procedures of the *polis* required the same divine protection as its physical spaces.

150. For the shrine of Erechtheus on the *akropolis* described as ἐν μέσῃ πόλει, see Eur. *Erechtheus* IV. 90 Diggle.

4 The Ritual Body

HEBE'S HENS AND HERAKLES' ROOSTERS

The *Homeric Hymn to Apollo* celebrates Delos as a major meeting place for Ionians, who traveled to the island "together with their children and modest wives" to take part in Apollo's major festival.[1] There the visitors heard local maidens sing hymns to Artemis, Apollo, and Leto—hymns understood by all because the girls could imitate the sounds of "all the tribes of men."[2] From the hymn we can infer that the festival had a tradition of open admission and that the audience could be male or female, old or young, local or foreign. Thucydides quotes the hymn and adds that Ionians and their neighbors came to observe[3] as well as to participate. Choruses performed at Delos until after the Persian Wars, when Aegean politics brought the festival into decline.[4]

It is rare to find a description of a festival so explicit about the festival's constituency. We do know that the Eleusinian mysteries were famous for including all who spoke Greek and for being open to male and female, slave and free—as long as they could pay.[5] Festivals like the Panathenaia were undoubtedly for everyone,[6] and at Magnesia in the Hellenistic period the

1. *Hymn. Hom. Ap.* 147–48.
2. Probably not the same as the chorus of women mentioned in the Delian accounts of the fourth through second centuries; see Bruneau (1970) 270–75 for a catalogue of the relevant inscriptions.
3. Thuc. 3.104.3: *ἐθεώρουν*.
4. Thuc. 3.104. In Thucydides' day the Ionians went to the Ephesia instead.
5. For the fees, *IG* II^2 1672.207: 30 drachmas for two people.
6. The speaker of [Dem.] 59.24 assumes that even a foreign woman of ambiguous social status, reputed to have been born a slave, could accompany the Thessalian Simos to the Panathenaia at Athens.

entire city came together for the installation of a new cult statue for Artemis Leukophryene. On this occasion men, adult women, and choruses of unmarried girls *(parthenoi)* all performed important roles. Those who observed the procession included young boys released from their lessons and slaves excused from their work.[7] Moreover, Xenophon made it very clear when he founded a new sanctuary for Artemis at Skillous that gender did not have to be a bar to participation.[8] Apart from such rare descriptions, however, we can seldom be confident about the composition of a festival's clientele. There is usually no evidence about distinctions between active participants and observers; and in those cases where inscriptions or an ancient author does give information about particular requirements, it is more likely to concern private organizations than the big public festivals. At Aigale, for example, a private association invited to a sacrifice and banquet "all the citizens present in Aigale and all the local residents and foreigners and any Romans present, including the women."[9] The specificity of the invitation suggests that a certain exclusivity was the norm. In the case of major public festivals, there are examples where free and even slave women shared in the meat of a public sacrifice,[10] but we should not assume that women were always included in every big city festival.[11]

7. *LSAM* 33 A.26–31, second century. For another all-inclusive clientele—this one for Artemis of Ephesos—see Xen. Eph. *Ephesiaka* 1.2. Van Bremen (1996) 146–54, on the issue of female representation at public banquets, emphasizes segregation by gender; see *IG* XII.5 668. Schmitt Pantel (1992) 134–45 stresses a difference between women's feasting at the Thesmophoria (mediated by the financial support of males) and the banquets of males (defined by the blood of sacrifice); but see now Osborne (1993).

8. Xen. *An.* 5.3.7–13. All the men and women in the area were invited to participate in festivals at the new sanctuary.

9. *LSS* 61.55–57, second century C.E. A whole *choinix* of grain was allotted to each man, one-half to each boy (lines 72–74). Ephebes and other young men took part in the procession of the sacrificial victim (lines 46–49).

10. Osborne (1993) demonstrates that the argument for a strict contrast between male and female roles, as represented by Detienne in Detienne and Vernant (1989), does not take into account the variety of information in the sources, in particular the detail of the epigraphical evidence.

11. At the Athenian Hephaistia even metics were included, but women are not mentioned; *IG* I^3 82; Osborne (1993) 404, comparing *IG* I^3 244. For the absence of women among those invited to public banquets, see Schmitt Pantel (1992) 380–408, esp. 397–99. Women were more likely to be invited to a public feast when the divinity was especially associated with women's life and experience, for instance, the invitation extended by the female priest of Artemis at Kyrene; *IGRR* I 1037. For the Panathenaia—a festival, one assumes, for all Athenians—the fact that particular women had specific ritual responsibilities should not be taken as evidence that Attic wives were routinely part of the audience.

Several issues determined constituency, and there was no single pattern. Eligibility could be based on a stable characteristic or defined in terms of purity from a temporary condition.[12] Stable characteristics were gender,[13] ethnicity,[14] age,[15] residence,[16] kinship,[17] citizenship,[18] and even language. Temporary conditions that interfered with definitions of purity were of two kinds: physical states and flexible attributes. The same physical conditions that divided humans from gods determined categories of pollution. Most important were bodily processes: sexual activity, childbirth, and death. Flexible attributes would have included wearing certain clothing, eating certain foods, and bringing iron weapons into the sanctuary. Such specific requirements were rarely topics for literature and therefore are not usually recoverable without the testimony of an ancient witness or detailed information from an inscription once posted at the entrance to a sacred space.[19] Whether recorded in writing or not, local rules must have been well known and well understood even if not always well observed. Ritual error constituted impiety *(asebeia)*, and failure to observe the rules put everyone at risk. Compliance was therefore a concern of the entire community. It was necessary to obey the rules and important for each individual to see that everybody else did, too.

Plato makes a distinction between women's celebrations *(heortai)* where men were permitted and those rituals where women were to worship alone. Plato is not confined by the messy boundaries of real life because he is designing his own system. In the delegation of real ritual responsibilities gender was often a consideration; but gender is never a simple category, and

12. *IG* II^2 1035.10–11.

13. Cole (1992).

14. Hdt. 5.72: Spartan Kleomenes was stopped by the priestess of Athena on the Athenian *akropolis* because he was Dorian. Distinctions based on ethnicity were operative in the fifth century; Hdt. 1.144, 171; 6.81. On the relation of ξένοι (foreigners) to local civic cults, see Gauthier (1972) 45–47. The epigraphical evidence for exclusion of ξένοι is collected by Butz (1996) 75–95, who relates the requirement to the "rise of the polis."

15. For οἱ παῖδες and οἱ νυμφίοι participating in sacrifices, consult *SIG*^{3} 1024.33–34, Mykonos.

16. *GHI* 20.1–4, for the distinction between ἄποικος and ἔποικος; Butz (1996) 95 n. 89.

17. *GHI* I^2 20. 4.

18. *IG* XII.5 225.

19. Nilsson (1967^3) I 783 argues that "eine tiefe Kluft zwischen der Religionsübung der Frauen und der Männer bestand," but such a division, although sometimes discernable, is not easy to define.

the relationship between gender and ritual is not always transparent. Greeks worshipped in groups,[20] and various factors could influence both a group's composition and the assignment of roles and duties within a group. Divisions could be related to function. Life-cycle ceremonies, because they prepared an age cohort for gender-specific social roles, were segregated by sex,[21] as were certain public rituals targeted at a sensitive goal. In general, public rituals of war, athletics, and political life were restricted to adult males, and rituals of reproduction were limited to females. Worship of male divinities, however, was not the exclusive province of men; the worship of female divinities was not limited to women; and even in cases where gender lines were clearly drawn, distinctions of gender did not apply to all situations.

Certain female divinities, like Eileithyia,[22] Kourotrophos,[23] the Genetyllides,[24] and Aphrodite Kolias,[25] had ceremonies for women alone, but it is also obvious that at least Eileithyia and Aphrodite could and did receive offerings from males. Some rituals—in particular, certain rites of Demeter and Dionysos—had an exclusively female clientele,[26] but except for the Thesmophoria (which apparently everywhere excluded males), local rules show considerable variation.[27] Some festivals required women to sacrifice

20. Arist. *Pol.* 1280b33–35. See also Mikalson (1983) 83–90.

21. Brelich (1969).

22. Hesch. s.v. Eileithyia: "a woman's goddess." For the ritual responsibility of the wife and mother, see Eur. *Phaethon* 245–50 Diggle. The leading female of the household had special authority to lead the household ritual and to organize the dancing at wedding ceremonies.

23. The evidence is collected by Price (1978).

24. Divinities invoked by women in childbirth; Ar. *Lys.* 2, *Nub.* 52, with scholia; *Thesm.* 130.

25. Worshipped in conjunction with the Genetyllides in the Attic deme of Kolieis. See Ar. *Nub.* 52; Stra. 9.1.21; Paus. 1.1.5; *Suda* s.v. *Γενετυλλίς*; Raubitschek (1974).

26. The evidence is extensive. The following represents only a selection. Dionysos: at Erchia (*SEG* 21.541 Δ .33–40), Thebes (Eur. *Phoen.* 1751 with scholia; Paus. 9.12.3; the *thalamos* of Semele: *τοῦτον δὲ καὶ ἐς ἡμᾶς ἔτι ἄβατον φυλάσσουσιν ἀνθρώποις*); Demeter: Paros (Hdt. 6.134), Attika (Ar. *Thesm.* 1150), Megalopolis (Paus. 8.31.8: sanctuary of Kore at Megalopolis; women could enter at any time, men only once a year). Zeitlin (1982) 129–57 emphasizes the issue of gender.

27. The little cave sanctuary outside Pharsalos, a local shrine, was for families. The inscription invites husbands and wives, boys and girls. Some of the divinities listed are associated with health and with raising children, for instance, nymphs, Pan, Hermes, Apollo, Herakles, Cheiron, Asklepios, and Hygieia; *IThessaly* 90–94, nos. 72–73; with English translation and comments, Larson (2001) 16–18.

without males present. As a result, we know from inscriptions that women banqueted alone on sacrificial meat[28] for Athena at Thasos,[29] for Semele and Dionysos at Erchia in Attika,[30] and for Demeter and Kore in Messenia.[31] Dionysiac ritual is equally confusing to the outsider. At Methymna, a supervisor of women *(gynaikonomos)* stood at the door to see that no male tried to enter the women's ceremonies,[32] but at Miletos, men and women participated together in a sacrifice to Dionysos "for the sake of the city," even as women worshipped without men at both a Dionysiac ceremony in town and at the special rites *(teletai)* of Dionysos in adjacent rural communities.[33] To complicate the picture, segregation by gender could be limited to a particular event in the course of a festival, as at the Attic Haloa, which called for a women-only banquet in honor of Demeter concurrent with an exclusively male banquet in honor of Poseidon.[34] A similar pattern must have been the norm at Mykonos, where there was a sacrifice to Demeter Chloe on the same day as a sacrifice to Poseidon that allowed no women at all.[35] A recently discovered decree from Teos, however, requires that a proclamation be made at the Dionysia and the Thesmophoria—a strategy that seems designed to ensure that both males and females heard it, therefore implying that the audience for the Dionysia was entirely male just as that of the Thesmophoria was entirely female.[36] The pattern was slightly different at a seven-day festival to Mysian Demeter near Pellene in Arkadia, where men and women worshipped together for several days except for one ceremony that required the women to worship by themselves for one night.[37] At Gambreion, a small *polis* near Pergamon, when the voters decided to post a new regulation on public mourning, they had it set up in two places where the women of the community would surely see it.

28. Osborne (1993).
29. Rolley (1965) 447 no. 6; *LSCG* 113 (fifth century).
30. Erchia, calendar of sacrifices, *LSCG* 18*A*.44–51 and Δ.33–40, where in sacrifices to Dionysos and Semele the meat is handed over to the women.
31. *IG* V.1 364, lines 8–10.
32. *LSCG* 127.
33. *LSAM* 48. Burkert (1985) 245 points out that the Thesmophorion at Delos received dedications appropriate to males; see Bruneau (1970) 28.
34. Deubner (1932) 60–69.
35. *SIG*[3] 1024; Robertson (1984) 1–16. The women fed on pork from a pregnant sow; the men ate meat from a lamb "with testicles." At Kos in a private sanctuary of Herakles, dining was segregated by gender in separate buildings—an *andreia* for the men and a *gynaikeia* for the women; *LSCG* 177; Herzog (1928) no. 10; *SIG*[3] 1106.
36. Şahin (1994) 1–40; *SEG* 44.949.
37. Paus. 7.27.9–10; Olender (1985) 36 n. 156.

They chose not a public site in the *agora* but the Thesmophorion and the temple of Artemis Lochia, apparently assuming that these two sanctuaries were the only public places in town that all citizens' wives would be certain to visit.[38]

Where there were sharp divisions, the formulas of exclusion are quite explicit. Restrictions posted in sanctuaries use expressions that mean "no female allowed" (*ou themis gynaiki,* "it is not right for a woman"; *ouch hosion gynaiki,* "it is not in accord with sacred rules for a woman"). Public rules deploying explicit technical language were posted to protect male sanctuaries and male rituals.[39] Similar technical language excluding males was used in female speech on the stage but apparently not on stone when the issue was gender alone. The examples from drama include the chorus of Aristophanes' *Thesmophoriazusai,* who describe their grove as a place "where it is not right *(ou themis)* for men to see the rites of the goddess." Euripides' Melanippe, when listing the ritual contributions of women, includes service to the Moirai and the Eumenides and defines such service as "not holy *(ouch hosia)* for men" to perform.[40] Men had more opportunities to make public pronouncements and publish ritual requirements, so they were more likely than women to post signs. Women knew the rules but rarely had access to the process of creating formal documents. Melanippe, who claims that women made a more important ritual contribution than men, tries to argue that women have a more direct access to the divine. She attributes a high value to the women who transmit the intent of Apollo and to the priestesses at Dodona who reveal the thoughts of Zeus, as well as those to who tend the Moirai and the Eumenides. The three priestesses of Zeus at Dodona were interviewed by Herodotus when he visited the site, and they were well informed about the historical tradition of the cult; nevertheless, he felt he had to check their story against that of the other local inhabitants.[41] Melanippe has a stake in glorifying the female contribution to the ritual life of the *polis,* but few female characters in tragedy would share her opinion. Others, excluded from religious ceremonies, complain of feeling deprived.[42]

38. *LSAM* 16.

39. *LSCG* 82; *LSS* 63; *LSS* 88–89; *LSCG* 96; *LSCG* 124; *LSS* 56.

40. She says: *ταῦτ᾽ ἐν ἀνδράσιν μὲν οὐχ ὅσια καθέστηκ᾽*; Eur. *Melanippe Desmotis* a.15–16, from a papyrus fragment published in 1907; see D. L. Page (1962) 112; see Ar. *Thesm.* 1150–51.

41. Hdt. 2.155.

42. Soph. *Oed.* 1490–91 (Antigone); Eur. *El.* 310 (Electra); Eur. *Tro.* 452 (Kassandra); see Mikalson (1982) 217.

The Moirai and the Eumenides were divinities concerned with the vitality of children, with lifeblood, and with the future of the family. Women's ritual activities and dedications were always related to the family. They worshipped in the context of the family, for the sake of the family, or with the goal of reproducing the family. The asymmetrical relationships of family life were therefore replicated in ritual situations, where even when females worshipped alongside their male relatives or husbands, they did not always share the same privileges or responsibilities. Although votive reliefs of the fourth century often depict male and female family members joining together in private sacrifices,[43] males and females are represented as maintaining different roles and exhibiting different functions. Representations of families in ritual recognize a male adult as head of any group. Even in situations where a dedication is made in the name of a female, reliefs depicting the family procession to the sacrifice put the male head of the family in the lead. It is also important to notice how often women are depicted with children. In scenes on fourth-century reliefs depicting a banquet after a sacrifice, 75 percent show husband and wife eating together, and of these about 70 percent include children.[44]

Asymmetrical responsibility in sacrificial duties is also evident in the distribution of sacrificial meat. An Athenian association stipulated equal shares to male members *(orgeones)* and free women (their wives), with half shares for sons, daughters, and a single female attendant per family, but it was the men who received the meat and distributed the shares.[45] In a family cult at Halikarnassos, the women shared in the feast and received a portion equal to that of their husbands,[46] but on Tenos a new wife introduced to her husband's phratry with the sacrifice of a billy goat was not invited to the dinner that followed.[47] In a sacrifice to Artemis Pergaia at

43. Several examples in van Straten (1987); Golden (1990) 30–32 discusses the inclusion of children in family rites. The presence of women in these depictions is assumed to indicate their prominence by Vikela (1994) 171; Foxhall (1995b) 97–98; and Sourvinou-Inwood (1995) 118.

44. Van Straten (1992) 281–82.

45. *LSS* 20.17–23; for male as mediator, see Detienne in Detienne and Vernant (1989) 112.

46. *LSAM* 72; Halikarnassos, third century, a cult for the founder, his descendants—both male and female—and their spouses. In *LSAM* 73 the wives of the *prytaneis* play a special role in the preparation of a sacrifice (Halikarnassos, third century). In *LSAM* 79.20, first century, both men and women participate.

47. *LSS* 48, fourth century; see Osborne (1993). As van Bremen (1996) 32 n. 82 points out, the *stephanephoros* Archippe may have subsidized a banquet for male magistrates, but nothing in the text (*SEG* 33.1036) implies that she herself at-

Halikarnassos, the priestess had to make sure that the wives of the *prytaneis* received equal portions of the meat.[48] At Delos, the Posideia for Poseidon and the Eileithyiaia for the goddess of childbirth were celebrated in the same month, possibly at the same time (the annual accounts are listed together). Poseidon's meat (beef, pork, boar, sheep, goat, and sausage) probably fed the entire body of male citizens (numbering more than one thousand), who also had a budget for wine, fruit, nuts, barley, chick peas, and seasonings (total number of items, 26; total budget, 600 dr.). Eileithyia's menu would have fed no more than about seventy women. They ate a very frugal meal: one sheep, some wheat, a little cheese, some vegetables and dried fish, and a small amount of nuts (total number of items, 14; total budget 40 dr.).[49] When women worshipped alone, their fare could be modest. Women took a leading role only when there were no men present. To be sure, a women could issue a prayer on her own[50] or, on occasion, even curse in her own name,[51] but if a male were present, he was in charge.[52]

Women subscribed to public campaigns for temple construction and restoration, as well as to other important civic projects, but they almost always appear in the documents as financial appendages to husbands or guardians and are only rarely mentioned without a guardian at all.[53] Women appear here, as elsewhere, almost always in the context of the family. When subordinate family members are listed with the male head of family, it is much more common to find a son than a wife, and more common to find a wife than a daughter. Except for a very few cases where women made significant contributions in their own right, the donations for which women are listed without a head of family are for token amounts and/or for women's cults (a temple of Demeter at Messene, restoration of textiles and decorations for

---

tended. Schmitt Pantel (1992) 88 points out that there is no evidence that the bride attended the *gamelia.*

48. *SIG*^{3} 1015 (*LSAM* 73); Osborne (1993) 399; compare *SIG*^{3} 1044, where meat for sacrifice is divided equally between men and women.

49. The accounts for these meals are analyzed by Linders (1994), with a translation of the menu for 173 B.C.E. on page 73.

50. Men. *Dys.* 660–61 (but a male is shouting advice); Pulleyn (1997) 169.

51. *IG* II^2 4348; Pulleyn (1997) 169. Voutiras (1998), for a new curse tablet, issued by a woman.

52. Aubriot (1992) 85, for Penelope's prayer and the compensation due to her from Odysseus's accumulation of *charis* (*Od.* 4.762–66, 767: ὀλόλυξε). The *ololyge,* in some circumstances invoked like a prayer to summon a god, was an opportunity for female invocations, especially in a crisis or special situation; Pulleyn (1997) 179–80.

53. The epigraphical evidence has been collected by Migeotte (1992).

Athena at Lindos, a symbolic donation of five drachmas each for moving the temple of Demeter at Tanagra). Recent analysis of the evidence for private subscriptions at Delos confirms the broader picture. There, in a series of group donations for the Sarapeion in the second century B.C.E., women are named only with their husbands and constitute a small fraction of the whole.[54] When women subscribed alone, individual donations were very modest. The same difference operated in making dedications at Delos. Collective familial dedications could be quite impressive, but when women made dedications on their own, or even if a small group of women made a dedication together, such gifts were always small, whether it was a matter of gifts to Isis and Sarapis or to more traditional divinities like Artemis, Aphrodite, and Kore.

In the Greek ritual system males and females could not always share the same ritual space. Distinctions were expressed in a number of ways. For a rite of incubation in the dormitory of the Amphiareion at Oropos, women and men slept apart, the men in the space to the east of the altar, the women in the space to the west.[55] The contrast between east and west is the contrast between dawn and evening, light and darkness, and life and death, and the sleeping arrangements assume that women naturally belong to the less propitious place. In some rituals, women had no place at all.

At Thasos in the mid-fifth century a rule displayed at the entrance to the sanctuary of Herakles announced:

> For Herakles of Thasos it is not right to offer a goat or a piglet; and it is not right for a woman to take part.[56]

At Messene a similar sign posted at a sanctuary of Demeter, Despoina, Kore, and Plouton, regulated the local Eleusinia. It says:

> [The ritual specialist] will sacrifice to Demeter two little fat male piglets and a loaf of bread with sesame seeds, which the (female) child will [consume?], and no male will be present.[57]

Comparison of these two texts suggests a ritual antithesis between Herakles and Demeter. Demeter's space and Demeter's ritual contain what Herakles' space and ritual exclude.

54. Le Dinahet-Couilloud (1996) 391–92.
55. *IG* VII 235; *LSCG* 69. 43–47.
56. *IG* XII suppl. 414; *LSCG* suppl. 63, lines 1–4.
57. *IG* V.1 364, lines 8–10; published originally as *CIG* 1464, from a copy by Fourmont; *LSCG* 63.

Thasos is not the only place where Herakles was so particular. His antipathy to females was so strong that in Phokis he was called "Woman-Hater" (Misogynes),[58] and a well-known proverb stated: "A woman does not go to a shrine of Herakles."[59] Aelian tells an anecdote that clarifies the implications of that proverb. He describes two adjacent sanctuaries, one of Herakles and the other of Hebe. The hens of Hebe never visited the roosters in Herakles' sanctuary, but Herakles' roosters had to visit Hebe's hens.[60] The roosters had no reservations about consorting with the hens, however, so long as the interchange was limited to Hebe's sanctuary, but they bathed in the pure water of a perennial stream flowing between the two sanctuaries before returning home to Herakles. The issue for the roosters was clearly pollution from sexual intercourse, a temporary problem easily solved by a bath.

The roosters' behavior can be explained by well-known traditional pollution requirements. Categories of ritual purity and pollution reflect issues of cultural concern and social anxiety. The roosters washed before returning to their own sacred yard because they were considered polluted by sexual contact, usually described in terms of pollution from a female source. Greek women, identified with their bodies and subject to physical conditions beyond their control, were as a consequence completely excluded from some male rituals.[61] Certain rituals of Herakles belonged to this group.

58. Plut. *De Pyth. Or.* 403 f, where the priest was normally an old man because the post required that the holder not associate with a woman during the year of service.

59. Leutsch and Schneidewin (1958) 1:392 no. 88. At Erythrai, only Thracian women could enter a sanctuary of Herakles; Paus. 7.5.8.

60. Ael. *NA* 17.46. Not all cults of Herakles excluded women entirely. In real life, ceremonies of Herakles and Hebe celebrated union in the form of marriage. A sanctuary of Herakles, Hebe, and Hera on Kos had separate dining chambers for the men *(andreia oikia)* and for the women *(gynaikeia oikia)*. In a *xenismos* of Herakles himself, bastards *(nothoi)* could share in the sacrifice but not in the priesthood (*LSCG* 177.101–11). Sokolowski (1956) 157 explains exclusion of women in terms of dining restrictions, arguing that women were excluded from banquets where men reclined on couches. In *LSAM* 72.41–42 (a private cult at Halikarnassos, third century) women are mentioned separately from male banqueters.

61. Women were excluded from the worship of Ares at Geronthrai in Lakonia (Paus. 3.22.7), from the *adyton* of the temple (and therefore consultation of the oracle) at Delphi (Plut. *De E* 385c–d; cf. Eur. *Ion* 219–22), the temple of Aphrodite Akraia on Cyprus (Strab. 14.682), the Herakleion at Erythrai (except for Thracian women; Paus. 7.5.8), and from several sacred areas associated with heroes: the *hieron* of Herotimos at Klazomenai (Apollon. *Hist. Mir.* 3.4 Giannini 122); the grove of Eunostos at Tanagra (Plut. *Quaest. Graec.* 300f–301a); the grove of Orpheus in

Women played no part in rituals of preparation for or resolution of armed conflict and were systematically excluded from the contexts of politics, war, and athletics.[62] Restrictions were especially strong in sacred spaces associated with recognition of male authority and the validation of male prestige. The most important of such spaces—the hearth in the *prytaneion,* the stadium at Olympia, and the *adyton* where Apollo delivered his oracles at Delphi—were centrally located focal points of male competition, negotiation, and decision. Female ritual presence in support of significant male ceremonies in any of these places had to be diluted by standards of purity so demanding that the woman had to be completely separated from her reproductive function.

The relative significance of different kinds of sacred space was very evident at Olympia. Particular areas were reserved for female rituals, but the most prestigious spaces were, to some extent, male preserves. Male exclusivity was most noticeable during the quadrennial games. At this time the only females allowed inside the stadium were young unmarried girls *(parthenoi)* and the priestess of Demeter Chamyne.[63] Pausanias reports, without comment, that any mature woman who appeared on the sanctuary side of the river during the prohibited days had to be thrown off a cliff on nearby Mt. Typaion.[64] Aelian would even have us believe that it was easier to keep flies off the raw meat of animals slaughtered for sacrifice than to keep women out of the stadium.[65] The women, he says, needed external control, represented by a law that kept athletes from sexual encounters while training.[66] The rule about athletes and sex, as well as Pausanias's information about the cliff on Mt. Typaion, suggest a concern that females

---

Thrace (Conon *FGrHist* 26 F 1 (XLV.6); the sacrifice for the Agamemnonidai at Tarentum ([Arist.] *Mir.* 840a3).

62. Graf (1984); Schaps (1982).

63. Paus. 6.20.9. Cf. the custom at the Olympic festival at Ephesos in the Imperial period, where wives of men who paid for the festival had the privilege of observing the games and were called by the official term *θεωροί*; Robert (1974) 176–81. For the epithet "Chamyne," see Sansalvador (1992) 166–80, who compares it to "Chamynaia" (*IG* V.1 1390) and translates it as "sleeping on the ground."

64. Paus. 5.6.7, the law of the Eleans.

65. Ael. *NA* 5.17. Aelian tells this story twice, once at the expense of the Elean women and a second time, 11.8, at the expense of the flies on Leukas.

66. Aelian claims that the flies surpassed the women in self-control because they stayed away by an act of will. Aelian likes the story about the self-control of flies so much that he omits a significant anecdote that demonstrates their reputation as a nuisance. The Elean flies were actually known as prototypical party-crashers, the sort of uninvited guests the Greeks called "parasites" (Antiphanes in Athen. 4f). They presented such a challenge to the sacrifices that the sanctuary had to pro-

could compromise the athletes' strength and competitive edge.[67] The rule that excluded women from the games, however, like the rules excluding women from the heroic cult of Herakles, has a deeper meaning. The pollution code reflected distinctions of gender basic to the society and differences crucial to the whole system of honor and prestige. The complete absence of sexually active, fertile women at the time of the games sends a clear message that the athletes and their audience needed the attention of the gods to maintain the institutions the games required.[68] Flies and women were a concern because the consequence of their presence was estrangement from divine support. When Plutarch tells us that at Tanagra a drought sent everyone scurrying to find out whether a woman had polluted the *temenos* of Herakles the Woman-Hater, we know that pollution from female contact was a real issue.[69] Exclusion of fertile women from the stadium at Olympia only confirms the special status that victory at the games conferred.

At Olympia, the women of Elis celebrated rites for Hera in a sanctuary reserved for them in the Altis. Rituals were managed by a special board, the Sixteen Women of Elis. This group represented prominent local families and supervised the females who participated in festivals for Hera and Dionysos. Young women and girls had their own footraces in the stadium at Olympia, but these contests were not scheduled during the Olympic games and never achieved the significance of the male competitions.[70] Male contestants, who came to Olympia from the whole Greek world, were identified with their home cities. The Elean girls who competed in footraces for Hera represented local families, and their contests could never confer the reputation male athletes garnered for competing in the great games for Zeus.

---

vide them with an ox of their own, which was sacrificed first as a decoy to distract them from the meat at the sacrifice and banquet.

67. Pl. *Leg.* 8.840a: an athlete touched neither woman nor boy during an entire year of training for the Olympic games; Flav. Philostr. *Gym.* 1.48, for the negative effects of sexual activity on the athlete's ability to compete. Aelian's description of the sexual abstinence of bulls in competition is based on the same assumption; *NA* 6.1 (where he includes an athlete, a musician, an actor, and a pancreatist). Sansone (1988) 70, heavily influenced by Burkert (1983), derives this sensitivity from early hunting ritual, with no real evidence.

68. According to Hippocratic theory, the excess moisture of females was a problem for athletes and a threat to their strength because they had to convert moisture to sweat; Hanson (1992a).

69. Plut. *Quaest. Graec.* 40.300f; Parker (1983) 279 makes the same point.

70. Perlman (1983); Scanlon (1984).

Within the area of the Altis, sites associated with powerful male rituals were off-limits to females. One such place was the ash altar of Zeus, the surface of which was considered so charged with divine presence that ashes from the daily sacrifice were never hauled away. These ashes remained piled up on the altar like a miniature mountain rising up to the sky. Mature women and *parthenoi* could ascend by stone steps as far as the base *(prothysis),* but only males could climb the steps cut in the accumulated ash to sacrifice at the top.[71] As a metaphor for the hierarchy of sacred spaces, the ash altar provided a daily reminder that Olympia created and preserved a protected space that all Greeks recognized as safe for competition. The stadium was like the *prytaneion* at the center of the individual *polis* or the *adyton* in the temple at Delphi—places that had to be secure for exchange of sensitive information. The sacred truce, reenacted every time the festival came around, kept the sanctuary safe for athletic competition, even at times of war. Ritual exclusion of women and the harshness of the threats directed against them protected the sanctuary, mitigated tensions of competition and recognized the special demands of Zeus, the divinity who guaranteed the oaths that bound all cities to the truce and all athletes to fair play.

"WOMEN, DOGS, AND FLIES"

Flies polluted sacrifices because they eat offal and feed off corpses.[72] Aelian was not alone in comparing the habits of flies with the habits of women. The Athenian historian Phylarchos once mentioned a sanctuary of Kronos that had a sign that must have said, "No women, dogs, or flies."[73] Women were classified with polluting animals because they could not control the natural processes of their bodies. A sanctuary at Lindos posted a sign prohibiting from a sacred area a man in recent contact with the miscarriage of a woman, dog, or donkey,[74] and another cautioned about recent contact with a corpse, a woman in childbed, or a parturient dog.[75] Contact with a

71. Paus. 5.13.8–11.

72. Ginouvés (1962) 239–42, on rites of purification at the time of a death; Parker (1983) 32–48, on death and pollution.

73. *FGrH* 81 F 33. For the Roman context and a different interpretation of dogs and flies, see McDonough (1999), esp. 475, on dog-flies and pollution—a suggestion, however, not supported by the Greek evidence.

74. *LSS* 91, third century C.E.

75. *LSAM* 51.

woman in childbirth and contact with a corpse appear together because birth and death were human conditions that compromised relations with the divine. The Athenian law that prohibited birth and death in a sanctuary measured the same concern.[76] When Peisistratos purified Delos, he purified only as much area as could be seen from the temple. When Nikias purified the island in 426, he extended the circumference of the protected area and applied the same rule to the entire island.[77] As a result, birth and death were no longer permitted anywhere on Delos. By applying to the entire island requirements normally used only for sanctuaries, Nikias called attention to the revival of the Ionian Delia, now converted by the Athenians to a penteteric festival under their own control.[78]

Birth and death were treated together in pollution regulations because both are transitional states, both involve risk, and the outcome of both is not easy to predict. In birth and death boundaries of the body are breached, identity is ambiguous, and the individual can be imagined to inhabit two realms. Birth is a visible physical transition, but the transition associated with death is not so obvious. In the Homeric tradition, death is described with images of the soul passing out of the body or the breath crossing the barrier of the teeth,[79]—experiences portending the final journey from the world of the living to the home of the dead.[80] Women, whose bodies were considered more permeable than those of males, were assumed to be less compromised by contact with situations where boundaries are crossed. Because female physical processes obscure body boundaries,[81] women were assigned responsibilities for presiding over transitions for others, whether at the beginning or end of life.[82] The ritual for a corpse and the funeral ceremony, like a family's obligations at the time of birth, sharpened the dis-

76. *IG* II^{2} 1035.10–11; on this text see Culley (1975) 207–23; (1977) 282–98; *SEG* 36.121.

77. Thuc. 3.104.

78. The Delia became an Attic liturgy in 426/5 B.C.E.; Schmitt Pantel (1992) 189. For Nikias's leadership in reorganizing the ceremonies, see Plut. *Nic.* 3. Plutarch describes an inscribed column set up by Nikias at Delos to preserve traditions for the ceremony. Plutarch emphasizes that he took care to consult decrees and dedications in order to corroborate the traditional accounts; Plut. *Nic.* 1.1.

79. The images are discussed by Garland (1981) 47–48. For the "barrier of the teeth," see Hom. *Il.* 9.408–9.

80. On death as a journey, see Garland (1981) 45, 54, table 3.

81. Carson (1990, 2000).

82. [Dem.] 43.62, for legislation limiting the responsibility of preparing the body for burial to female family members over the age of sixty; Kurtz and Boardman (1971) 144; Garland (1985) 24, with 138.

tinction between life and death, thereby creating the illusion of control. Females, being intimately involved with both birth and death, were also associated with the hazardous and polluting aspects of both.[83] Birth and death were in fact so powerful that the mother in childbed and the corpse before burial were classified along with murderers as not only polluted in themselves but able to pollute others. A *lex sacra* from Cyrene states:

> The woman in childbed shall pollute the roof . . . she shall not pollute (anyone) outside the roof unless he comes in. The man who is inside, he himself shall be polluted for three days, but he shall not pollute anyone else, not wherever this man goes.[84]

The woman who had just given birth *(lecho)* polluted the house and anyone who entered it. Families who had a new child therefore marked their doors to announce a birth. In Attika, they hung at the door a wreath of olive for a boy and a piece of woolen fleece for a girl.[85] With respect to the gods, anyone who entered the house during the period immediately after a birth was considered temporarily polluted and therefore subject to whatever sanctuary restrictions might apply. Although it is the process of birth that offended the gods, the language of the regulations focuses on the mother and identifies her as the source of pollution.[86]

This ability of females to pollute others involuntarily measures the risks associated with birth.[87] Consequently, periods of exclusion were longer for the woman in childbed than for others in the same house. At Eresos, with respect to entering a sanctuary of a goddess, a *lecho* was considered pol-

83. In Is. 6.41, the women of the family prepare a corpse for burial, "as is fitting."

84. *LSS* 115A.16–20, translated by Parker (1983) 336. For the contagion, Eur. *IT* 381–84; Porph. *Abst.* 4.16 (classifying recently parturient women and corpses together).

85. Hsch. s.v. *stephanon ekpherein.* Cf. schol. Theoc. 2.11; Ephipp. in Ath. 9.370c; and Phot. s.v. *rhamnos.* Theophrastos's superstitious man "was not willing to visit a woman in childbed": *οὐκ ἐπὶ λεχὼ ἐλθεῖν ἐθελῆσαι,* 16.9; Wächter (1910) 27–28.

86. The Greek expressions can all be translated as "from the female giving (or having given) birth": *apo lechous,* Fraser (1953) 45 (Sokolowski's text, *LSS* 91.15, is wrong); *apo tekouses, LSAM* 12.7; *apo tetokeias, LSS* 54.5.

87. Wright (1987) 227, for special restrictions on those able to pollute others. Douglas (1975) 54–55, following Durkheim, argues that "dangerous powers imputed to the gods are in actual fact powers rested in the social structure for defending itself, as a structure, against the deviant behavior of its members." For a concise summary of traditional modern views, see Ortner (1984) 298–304. Greek attitudes, as they pertain to gender, are explored by Carson (1990) 135–69.

luted for ten days, but those in contact with her for only three.[88] At Lindos, a new mother had to wait twenty-one days after childbirth to enter a sanctuary of Athena, but those in contact with her for only three.[89] Miscarriage and abortion, compounding birth and death, also compromised ritual.[90] At Kyrene, a visible embryo polluted like a death and an invisible embryo polluted like a birth.[91] The longest waiting period on record, which was for miscarriage, was forty-four days, compared with nine days for a live birth in the same regulation (for Isis and Sarapis).[92] Elsewhere, pollution from miscarriage was treated like pollution from birth.[93] The mother is often confused with the process. The blurring of the distinction between the two is nicely illustrated in a text from Lindos. The woman who has just given birth is polluted for twenty-one days (but those who visit her for only three), but in the same regulation it is contact with miscarriage, whether that of "woman, dog, or donkey," that results in a forty-day defilement.[94]

Ritual restrictions for females were based on situations associated with

88. *LSCG* 124.6–7, second century. It is important to note that the period of confinement after childbirth does not correspond to the normal period of lochial bleeding. For women making sacrifices to Asklepios while "girded up and walking out the lochia," see *LSAM* 52B.10–11, Miletos, first century C.E.; cf. *LSCG* 77D.13, sacrifice for a *lecho* at the time of birth, on which see Parker (1983) 52 n. 74.

89. *LSS* 91.16; Lindos, cult of Athena, third century C.E. In *LSCG* 171, private cult of Artemis, Zeus Hikesios, and Theoi Patrooi, second century, the waiting periods for contact with a woman who has given birth or one who has had a miscarriage are the same—ten days.

90. The terms used are *ektrosis, ektrosmos,* and *diaphthora;* Ilberg (1910) 3. *Diaphthora,* because it can be used of a dog or donkey, *LSCG* 91.11, does not imply induced abortion. See Parker (1983) 355.

91. *LSS* 115B.24–27; Artemis, fourth century.

92. Te Riele (1978) 326, Megalopolis, cult of Isis and Sarapis, second century. This high figure of forty-four days is consistent with other texts from the second century and later, where the number of days was usually forty. The exposure of a live infant may be an issue in another proscription; *LSS* 119.7, 12, Ptolemaïs, first century. See Bingen (1993), however, for suggestions about improving the text. For forty days (miscarriage and exposure) at Smyrna, see *LSAM* 84.3–5 (Bromios, second century C.E.).

93. *LSCG* 154A.23–24, Kos. Another Koan text may equate the time period for miscarriage with that for death; the stone is broken away at the crucial spot. Herzog (1928) 15, followed by Sokolowski, reads *pente* (five), equating miscarriage with death. Parker (1983) 50, suggests *tria* (three), equating miscarriage with birth.

94. *LSS* 91; third century C.E. Forty days has a biblical ring, but in Greek gynecological folklore approximately forty days frequently defined stages of prenatal and postnatal development. See Roscher (1909) 82–105; Jones (1987) 229; on forty days in the gynecology of other cultures, see Parker (1983) 48 n. 59. Forty days is a normal outer limit for the period of postnatal lochial bleeding and therefore a perceptible marker of ritual ambiguity.

reproduction, but evidence is not consistent for all stages. The evidence for restrictions concerning birth—a process in which female moisture is spilled and boundaries of the body are crossed—is the most explicit. The evidence for restrictions with regard to pregnancy (which, in Hippocratic terms, consumes excess moisture) and lactation (which puts moisture to work) is scant; these situations are mentioned only once or twice.[95] Menstruation, in which female moisture is lost, is better represented (in at least six regulations),[96] but in contexts considered problematical: four of the six menstrual prohibitions are from immigrant cults (Isis and Sarapis, the Syrian gods, a Hellenistic cult in Egypt, and Men Tyrannos),[97] and the other two are from late texts.[98] Most commentators therefore assume that these texts express concerns not typically Greek.[99] Menstruation is almost never mentioned in Greek texts outside the scientific and philosophical literature. Nevertheless, there are some indications that menstruation could be of concern in a ritual context.

The most striking description of the effects of menstruation is found in a disputed passage in Aristotle's essay on dreams, where the dreamer's imperfect vision is compared to a woman's gaze corrupted by menstruation.[100] Relying on a conventional theory of projectile vision, the author explains that menstruation causes a disturbance of the blood that can be detected when a menstruating woman looks into a bronze mirror. The disturbance, carried to her eyes and projected through the air, strikes the surface of the mirror and stains it with a bloody cloud.

This description of the menstruant's gaze assumes a direct pathway between the eye and the womb. Hippocratics described the eye as an en-

95. With reference to a cult of Despoina in Lykosoura. The generic participle is in the masculine; *LSCG* 68.12–13, third century.

96. The involuntary pollution at *LSS* 115 B.7–8 could be menstruation, but see Parker (1983) 37, 346.

97. Te Riele (1978) 362; *LSS* 54.7–8, 119; *LSCG* 55.5–6.

98. *LSS* 91, third century C.E. (a woman can enter the sanctuary after menstruation if she has wiped herself off, *sesamene*, line 16); Immerwahr (1971) 237, second or third century C.E.

99. Farnell (1904); Parker (1983) 100–103 contributes a very sober and detailed discussion, but his negative conclusion is perhaps too strong.

100. Arist. *De Somn.* 459b–460a. Many commentators regard this passage as an interpolation; for the most recent summary, see Gallop (1996) 145. Frontisi (1997) 150–51 accepts Aristotle as author, argues that mirrors were especially associated with women, and argues that the belief in menstrual pollution suggested by this passage must have been widespread.

trance to the body's interior, opening into a channel extending as far as the uterus.[101] The eye was a window for diagnosing reproductive dysfunction because it gave access to the condition of the blood.[102] Tests to determine a woman's readiness for conception assumed the existence of such an interior pathway. When midwives and medical practitioners wanted to test a woman's reproductive organs, they rubbed a red stone on her eyelid. The appearance of a red stain confirmed that her "channels" were "open" and that she was ready for intercourse.[103] Doctors even claimed to be able to predict a heavy menstrual flow by detecting a mist hovering in front of a woman's eyes.

The negative effects of menstrual blood are expressed by the image of its power to deform vision. This idea was implicit in descriptions of agricultural ritual, where menstrual blood, precisely because it was "disturbed," was considered a powerful antidote for crop failure. Agriculturalists said that a menstruating woman walking among cucumbers would make them bitter,[104] but they also claimed that a menstruant could rid a garden of caterpillars.[105]Plutarch reports that farmers used both menstrual rags and the blood of moles to avert hail.[106] The connection between menstrual blood and the blood of moles is no coincidence; both were considered able to corrupt vision. The blindness of moles was related to the quality of their blood.[107] Fluctuations in moisture due to the menstrual cycle represented fluctuations in the quality of women's blood. The cyclical accumulation of menstrual blood created excessive wetness that could deform vision. When a woman achieved a drier condition, her moisture was more concentrated; and when she fasted, she was driest of all. The saliva of a fasting

101. On the Hippocratic notion of a *hodos* (path, road) within the female body, connecting all orifices to the uterus, see King (1998) 28, 68.

102. For the whites of a woman's eyes turning red after abortion, see *Epid.* 5.53 (V.238.8); Dean-Jones (1994) 201–2, on the connection between the eyes and the reproductive system.

103. *Nat. Mul.* 99 (122 Trapp); translation from Hanson (1995b) 291. The same test was used for infertility; Arist. *GA* 747a10–18.

104. *Geopon.* 12.20.5. See 12.25.1 for a menstruant's negative effect on rue.

105. *Geopon.* 12.8.5–7: A farmer who had a menstruating woman—barefoot, with hair let loose, clothed in a single garment, and wearing no belt—walk three times around garden and then up the middle would find that the caterpillars disappeared.

106. Plut. *Quaes. Conv.* 700e.

107. The eyes of moles are covered by a thick layer of skin because the eyes' development is "stunted"; Arist. *HA* 491b; 533a.

woman was therefore beneficial for bloodshot eyes because fasting eliminated moisture and made a woman drier.[108] Menstrual blood, as Pliny reports, could rust iron,[109] drive away hail and storms,[110] and undo spells;[111] and a woman's menstrual blood could be removed from her clothing only by her own urine.

The power of menstruation to deform vision is consistent with Aristotle's argument that menstrual blood is a kind of inferior sperm, insufficiently concocted and therefore not as pure as the male product. According to this model, because menstruation rids the female body of impure matter, the process eventually culminates in a cleansing *(katharsis)*.[112] Aristotle's description of menstruation as expulsion of excess blood identifies the process as a transitional state and assumes that the female becomes as pure as she can be only after the process is complete. Hippocratics, more concerned with the process of menstruation as a means of achieving balance between wet and dry, nevertheless also identified blood flows of women as cleansing or purification.[113] For this reason they defined the period immediately after menstruation as the best time for conception.[114]

The description of the menstruant's gaze in Aristotle's essay on dreams assumes a popular superstition warning a menstruating woman not to look in a mirror lest she not see her reflection there. Failure to see a reflection in a mirror, like the failure to cast a shadow in sunlight,[115] is a symptom of abnormality. Menstruating, like stepping into a precinct with no entrance or traveling so far that the sun casts no shadow,[116] created a situation of rit-

108. Plin. *NH* 28.76.

109. Plin. *NH* 7.64. For the power of menstrual blood, Weinrich (1928)—more an indication of early-twentieth-century irrationality than ancient ideology—and Parker (1983) 103 n. 116.

110. Plin. *HN* 28.76.

111. Plin. *HN* 28.70.

112. Arist. *Gen. An.* 728a; 777a. Aristotle's description of menstruation as *katharsis* is consistent with the remark attributed to another fourth-century writer, the orator Demades, who is said to have called a woman whose menstrual period was late *akathartos*, "uncleansed"; Ath. 99d–e.

113. Menstruation: *Superf.* 33; afterbirth: *Mul.* 1.78. For other examples, see von Staden (1991) 51 n. 30.

114. *Mul.* 1.24 (Littré 8.62.20–21); Dean-Jones (1994) 153.

115. According to Pausanias, 8.38.6, any human or animal entering the forbidden zone—the sanctuary of Zeus Lykaios in Arkadia—did not cast a shadow and died within the year.

116. Pausanias adds that in a place called Syene, so far away that it lay on the borders of Ethiopia, at a certain time of year even in sunlight it was impossible to cast a shadow; 8.38.6.

ual ambiguity.[117] Hesiod's warning about the temporary danger of a woman's bathwater belongs to the same category as the caution about the mirror and suggests a similar wary respect for menstruation.[118] The lack of evidence for ritual prohibitions for the menstruant before the Hellenistic period is no guarantee that such restrictions did not exist then. Restricted access to sacred space and communal sacrifice would not have been out of place. Mirrors were used in ritual, and the connection of the stained mirror with vision is consistent with rituals where clear vision was required. For instance, when Pausanias visited the temple of the goddesses at Lykosoura, located directly below the sanctuary of Zeus on Mt. Lykaios, he noticed a mirror in the sanctuary:

> As you go out of the temple there is a mirror fitted into the wall. If anyone looks into this mirror, he will see himself very dimly indeed or not at all, but the actual images of the gods and the throne can be seen quite clearly.[119]

If gods could have a bright reflection and ordinary humans a dim one, it is possible that the menstruant had no reflection at all.

Up to this point, in discussing the impact of gender on ritual restrictions, we have considered those physical processes exclusive to females. Ritual restrictions also recognized activities that involved male and female equally. The most obvious activity was the sexual act, which was generally prohibited in sanctuaries. Heterosexual activity within the boundaries of a sacred place was punished severely. At Olympia in the Archaic period, a breach of a god's *temenos* required an expensive sacrifice to satisfy the offended divinity:

> If anyone fornicates in the sacred precinct, (the authorities) shall make him expiate it by the sacrifice of an ox and by complete purification.[120]

Heterosexual sexual activity outside a sanctuary was of concern only if recent. Compared with pollution from childbirth, contact with a corpse, or participation in a funeral, the pollution from sexual intercourse was almost inconsequential. Accepted as a regular and necessary part of adult life, intercourse normally required only minor ritual attention. Sexual activity at

117. Implied in Ach. Tat. 4.7.7, where it is said that it is not right *(ou themis)* for a man to have intercourse with a menstruating woman, although he is permitted to fondle and kiss her.

118. On the challenge of menstrual blood to males, see Shanzer (1985).

119. Paus. 8.37.7, trans. Jones.

120. Ziehen no. 61; Buck 261–62 no. 64.

night in fact might require no special delay[121] and that in daytime only a bath.[122] For males, as far as ritual was concerned, regular heterosexual intercourse, or "to go to women," was an indication of physical maturity.[123] Once a male had made the initial transition to sexual maturity, the act itself was of little ritual concern so long as it did not disturb a sacred space. The language of sanctuary regulations reflects common usage. A man who has just "come from a woman" is a man who has just had sex. Inscriptions use the abbreviated expression "from a woman" *(apo gynaikos).* The first epigraphical example dates from the fourth century,[124] but the idiom is used by Herodotus and probably represents colloquial speech. Herodotus employs the expression to make the point that the Greeks, like the Egyptians (who did not engage in intercourse with women in sanctuaries or enter a sanctuary coming "from women" without washing), had stringent regulations about mixing sexual activity and sacred space.[125] It is important to notice that Herodotus sees the issue entirely from the male point of view. Other euphemisms also assume that males associated the pollution of sexual activity with female contact, as in this inscription from a precinct at Tegea:

> "Nor can a male [enter, if he] goes to a female."[126]

The tendency to express concerns about sexual purity from a male point of view indicates that the audience for most of these texts was male.[127] Although sperm could pollute,[128] and although sexual intercourse polluted the female as well as the male,[129] the colloquial language for sexual contact

121. Plutarch suggests putting at least a night's sleep between the sexual act and a visit to a sanctuary; *Quaest. Conv.* 655d. Night was thought more appropriate for sex than day; Dikaiopolis at Ar. *Ach.* 1221, with a new coinage: σκοτοβινιῶ.
122. *LSS* 115 A.11–13, fourth century.
123. Describing this age as "the time when they go to women;" *LSCG* 51.41, 161–178 C.E. The corresponding idiom for females assumes a single sexual partner; see Paus. 2.10.4.
124. *LSAM* 29.4–5, Metropolis, cult of Mater Gallesia.
125. Hdt. 2.64; his observation is generally ignored in modern scholarship.
126. *LSS* 31.6, Tegea, fourth century, probably a sanctuary of Apollo.
127. We can usually, but not always, assume that a text using the expression *apo gynaikos* was intended for a male clientele. For an exception at Maionia, 147/6 B.C.E.; *LSAM* 18.
128. Hes. *Op.* 733–34; Cf. *ekmiainomai,* "ejaculate," Ar. *Ran.* 753 with scholia; Parker (1983) 76 n. 9. For the possibility of wet dreams as a source of pollution for young men, see Parker (1983) 342 on *LSS* 115 A.40–42.
129. Ar. *Lys.* 911–12.

implies that when a male was concerned about sexual pollution, he identified his female partner as the source.[130]

Maintaining boundaries between humans and gods[131] required separating those activities that defined the human condition—birth, sexual intercourse,[132] and death—from sacred spaces. Because males and females were assumed to differ in their ability to control body boundaries, and because some involuntary female physical processes were treated as sources of contagious pollution, females were subject to more restrictions. A female in childbed, at the moment of her greatest contribution to family and community, was defined in ritual terms as farthest from the divine. There are several reasons. Childbirth was a time of transition for both mother and infant. The level of anxiety about the ritual status of the parturient reflects both the risk and the significance of the process. Ritual danger is a marker of anxiety; it also a marker of great social value. The experience of childbirth therefore had important ritual consequences.

BODY LANGUAGE AND RITUAL GESTURE

Although both mothers and fathers prayed to have children,[133] and although entire families worshipped together,[134] women were the most likely to be responsible for ritual activity centered on reproduction, children, and family maintenance. In those cases where the female ritual role differed from that of the male, concern for children and anxiety about the family were decisive elements. When Plato claims that women were more likely

130. Vaginal secretions were considered unclean; Ar. *Eq.* 1284–87; Parker (1983) 99 n. 101. Heterosexual intercourse is twice described from both the male and the female point of view; both examples are later than the second century. See *LSAM* 12, Pergamon, Athena Nikephoros, after 133; *LSS* 119, Ptolemaïs, first century. Gender neutral terms like *apo synousias* (*LSCG* 139.14) or *apo aphrodision* (*LSS* 108; Habicht [1969] 168 no. 161.12) are less common.

131. Pind. *Nem.* 6.1–6.

132. Mythical accounts of sexual intercourse in a sanctuary have a special meaning; see Burkert (1983) 60 and n. 11.

133. Ar. *Pax* 1325; *Thesm.* 286–91 is a parody of such a prayer; cf. *IG* II^2 4588: [Φ]ίλη ταῖν θεαῖν [ε]ὐξαμένη τοῦ παιδίου, "Phile, having prayed to the two goddesses for a child." More examples for the sake of children: *IG* II^2 4403 (to Asklepios), 4593 (for the sake of a daughter), 4613 (to Herakles); van Straten (1974) 177 n. 142.

134. Theophrastos's *deisidaimon* takes his wife and children with him to religious celebrations: Theophr. *Char.* 16.11.

than men to make dedications,[135] it is important to remember that a large proportion of the dedications women made were not for themselves but on behalf of children or members of their family.[136] Even so, Plato exaggerates. One survey shows that where it is possible to distinguish female dedicants from male, men outnumber women by more than ten to one.[137] Another survey, this one limited to the epigraphical evidence on Delos, finds frequent offerings to Artemis, Eileithyia, and Demeter by women, but in the case of Artemis, more offerings by males than by females.[138] Males give more expensive gifts (women rarely dedicate statues, for instance) and are more able to make donations on behalf of wife and children. The difference is perhaps best summed up by noticing that women operate in a narrow range of ritual situations, bound by the interests of the family, but males move easily between public and private contexts.

The tension surrounding distribution of ritual responsibility was a theme for tragedy, where distinctions between male and female obligations are often presented not only as problems but also as opportunities to display differences in male and female language and gesture. The *parodos,* entry of the chorus, in Aischylos's *Seven against Thebes,* is a formal entreaty for deliverance of a city from impending attack. The text represents a debate about the meaning and efficacy of female rituals of crisis. When the women of Thebes enter the orchestra, they notice the distant cloud of dust that signals the approach of an enemy. As the noise grows, they struggle in desperation to find a ritual remedy. They begin by using conventional epithets to invoke specific divinities and then accelerate to formal requests ornamented by the rhetorical language of traditional Greek prayer.[139] Their goal is to avert destruction for themselves and avoid slavery for their daughters. Aischylos exploits the formal language of prayer to convey dependence on the gods, but the terror of the women converts an ordered plea for help into a desperate display of supplication. Instead of addressing the gods in the normal stance for prayer—that is, standing with hands raised

135. Pl. *Leg.* 909e–910a.

136. Most of the statues of priestesses honored for service to a divinity are found in sanctuaries of kourotrophic goddesses; see Kron (1996).

137. See Kron (1996) 160–61. Kron uses figures based on Raubitschek's collection of inscribed dedications from the Athenian *akropolis* (250 by males; 18 by females) and Lazzarini's collection (804 by males; 80 by females), though warning about the difficulties of interpretation of fragmentary texts.

138. Le Dinahet-Couilloud (1996) 388–89.

139. Alliteration, asyndeton, and repetition of key formulas; described in detail in the commentary of Hutchinson (1985) 55–75, on lines 78–180.

in formal greeting, palms facing out[140]—the women fall down on their knees to embrace the gods and beseech them with tears and groans. They grasp statues of the gods placed in the orchestra and imagine themselves as making offerings of wreaths, robes, and sacrifices.[141]

Their leader, Eteokles, is horrified. The enemy has not yet arrived at the gates of the city, but the women have already resorted to gestures and words appropriate only after a wall is breached or a city has fallen. Eteokles' rage at the women's erratic behavior turns into contempt for the whole female sex. He blames the women for any future erosion of courage and cites their fear as responsible for the ruin of family and city. In place of the gods addressed by the women, Eteokles prefers his own: Zeus, Earth, and the Erinyes of his father's curse (69–77); yet he is unaware that such a prayer would destroy himself as well as his sibling rival at the gates. For Eteokles, the women have erred thrice. They have performed their ritual in the wrong way (183–86), they have left the inner world of the home to influence public strategy outside (200–201), and they have usurped the formal prebattle rituals reserved for the men who must fight (*sphagia* and *chresteria,* 230–32). Eteokles would allow them to pray, but only under his direction, their only permitted gesture a wordless, ecstatic ululation—the female equivalent of the ordered military paean of soldiers preparing for battle (268).[142]

Eteokles' reaction is more complicated than it seems at first glance. His vicious attack on the whole female sex (187–95), although a generic catalogue of female faults,[143] is not a simple misogynistic outburst but emphasizes significant differences between male and female reactions to crisis. For Eteokles, the dangerous issue is timing. The women of Thebes have performed a ritual act normally reserved for the last resort. Only in desperate situations were threatened victims expected to fall down on their knees and grasp the statue of a divinity.[144] Evidence from vase paintings—Kassandra seeking protection from Athena while pursued by Ajax, Helen grasping

140. Plut. *Phil. et Tit.* 2.3: *χεῖρες ὕπτιαι* ("hands palm up"). Cf. [Arist.] *De Mundo* 400a17: *πάντες οἱ ἄνθρωποι ἀνατείνομεν τὰς χεῖρας εἰς τὸν οὐρανὸν εὐχὰς ποιούμενοι,* "We all stretch our hands to the sky when we make our prayers." For the material evidence, see Neumann (1965) 78–80.

141. Hutchinson (1985) 55.

142. Zeitlin (1990) 109–10, on Eteokles and male attempts to regulate female expression.

143. Hutchinson (1985) 75. See Foley (2001) 47–53 for a response.

144. Alroth (1992) 12–21; van Straten (1974) 183, several nonmythological examples.

Apollo's knees, or Orestes seeking protection from Athena as he escapes from the Erinyes—makes this clear. Beseeching a statue was like beseeching a god, but kneeling converted a prayer to supplication, inappropriate before battle and, if performed too soon, a sign of ill omen, portending failure. Kneeling was a sign of submission, and Eteokles knows that any sign of weakness is a sign of defeat.

Eteokles' reaction is consistent with conventional concerns. The vocabulary of ritual language and ritual gesture compelled worshippers to correctly match specific requests to specific divinities, to call the divinity by the right name, and to choose the ritual appropriate to the situation.[145] Eteokles may be convinced that the women have chosen the wrong time for a gesture inspired by panic, but he does not suggest that such behavior is always inappropriate. Aischylos builds the entire play on the meaning of visual symbols[146] and lays out two ritual programs and two modes of interpretation, one male, one female. In the end it is Eteokles, not the chorus, who misinterprets the signs. As the enemy approaches the women of Thebes, long accustomed to observation instead of direct participation, have a keener eye than he for the meaning of the "silent cloud of dust."

The Theban women call their prayers *litai,* a term more common in poetry than prose and used to express urgency. The women of Thebes also imply urgency by their need to kneel. Relatively rare, kneeling was reserved for narrowly defined situations. In Greek tragedy it is only women who kneel, in comedy only slaves, and neither kneels except in situations of grave distress.[147] Although Xenophon does say that the sound of a sneeze made his whole army fall down in fright to supplicate Zeus Soter,[148] the only other male known to kneel in worship is Theophrastus's *deisidaimon* (the superstitious man)[149] who, in his excessive anxiety about ritual observance, acts more like a woman than a man.[150] The literary evidence is consistent with the evidence on Attic dedicatory reliefs. In this corpus little

145. Bremer (1981) 194–95. Determining the proper procedure could even involve consulting an oracle; *IG* I^3 7.1–12. See Parker (1985) 304; Versnel (1981) 5–11.

146. Zeitlin (1990).

147. Women: in addition to Aesch. *Sept.,* only Eur. *Alc.* 162–64, on behalf of her soon-to-be-motherless children; slaves: Ar. *Eq.* 30–31.

148. Xen. *An.* 3.2.9.

149. Theophr. *Char.* 16.5.

150. Polybios describes a kneeling male (γονυπετῶν) as "acting like a woman" (γυναικιζόμενος, 32.15.7–8).

girls can imitate their mother's gesture of kneeling,[151] but none of these examples shows a male kneeling before a god.[152] The gods to whom females appeal are all "helping" divinities:[153] Zeus Meilichios or Zeus Philios, Artemis, the Eleusinian deities, Herakles, Asklepios, heroes and heroines (e.g., Leukothea and Palaimon), and nymphs.[154] Women kneel to strengthen requests for themselves, but more often they take to their knees on behalf of another—a sick person or their own child.[155] When the women of Thebes pray for protection to the gods of the city, they are clearly frightened for themselves, but their plea is on behalf of the city, its residents, and, especially, their own children. Their most anxious prayers are for their daughters, the cohort of young unmarried girls *(parthenoi)*, who in defeat would be the war's most vulnerable victims. Their mothers describe them as already in supplication, their minds on inevitable enslavement.[156]

"I WRITE THE OATHS OF A WOMAN IN WATER"[157]

Reproductive concerns and family responsibilities shaped female access to the language of public ritual. The social roles and biological functions

151. An inventory from the Erechtheion describes a piece of sculpture depicting "a woman with whom a little girl has fallen forward" (*προσ[πέπ]τοκε*, *IG* I² 374.180–82); van Straten (1974) 161–62.

152. Van Straten (1974) 159–89, with references to earlier studies. Of van Straten's twenty-six examples, only one kneeling person can be definitely identified as male, and even he goes down on only one knee. Van Straten is reluctant to include this late example, but the divinity addressed is Asklepios, and as van Straten points out, Aelius Aristides describes himself singing a hymn to Dionysos Lysios in the same pose: *καὶ ἔδει τὸ γόνυ τὸ δεξιὸν κλίναντα ἱκετεύειν τε καὶ καλεῖν Λύσιον τὸν θεόν* (2.435, 38 Keil). Pulleyn (1997) 190 stresses the rarity of this gesture for males, isolating a vase painting that shows Ajax kneeling just before his suicide.

153. Van Straten (1974) 177: "those whom a Greek might think of as *σωτῆρες* or *ἐπήκοοι*." The deities where children are present include Zeus Meilichios or Zeus Philios (combinations include kneeling woman, adult male, younger boys, younger girls, older boy with ram, and older girl with basket); Artemis (kneeling woman, deer, fragment of plaque); Demeter, Kore, and Iakchos Ploutodotes holding the infant Ploutos (kneeling woman); Plaimon, Pankrates, and Leukothea (kneeling woman, male, and two children).

154. Described in detail by van Straten (1974) 162–74.

155. Van Straten (1974) 177 n. 142, on prayers for children.

156. Aesch. *Sept.* 111.

157. *Ὅρκους ἐγὼ γυναικὸς εἰς ὕδωρ γράφω*; Soph. *TrGF* F 811 Radt, with parodies.

that separated male and female were also reflected in ritual language. Ritual cries are a case in point. The female cry, represented by the verb ὀλολυγεῖν, could accompany sacrifice; but its direct corollary, the ritual cry of males, ἀλαλάζειν, was sounded only on the battlefield.[158] Homer assumes that females, although in epic never represented as wielding the ax or knife in sacrifice, were normally present at the precise moment of the kill to shriek in ululation, no matter which deity was being honored. Women were not always present at a sacrifice, however, so the ululation could not have been a universal requirement for sacrifice. In the context of the family, moreover, the same ritual cry marked moments of great anxiety, whether of jubilation or horror.[159] The female cry that in sacrificial contexts signaled the moment of death could announce, in the life of the family, the moment of birth.[160] The ululation required to summon Athena at a time of critical danger was a service to the community that only its women could provide.[161]

Sound was important. Women's voices, higher and shriller than men's, varied with age. Changes in the female voice were associated with biological development, and ritual assignments recognized a correlation between genre and sexual status. The notion that sexual intercourse deepened the female voice[162] marked the public choral performances of unwed maidens as especially sweet. The actual sound of the female voice must have carried important associations and implications.[163] The authority of the virgin's voice in tragedy, the association of older women with lamentation, and the requirement that Apollo's attendant be unwed concentrated attention on the sound of the female voice.

158. Aesch. *Ag.* 594: ὀλολυγεῖν is a γυναικεῖος νόμος (spoken by Clytemnestra); Pulleyn (1997) 178–81. Xen. *An.* 4.3.19 makes a clear gender distinction. See McClure (1999) 52–53 (for distinction between *ololyge,* the female cry of jubilation, and *alalage,* the male war cry); 110–111. The *ololyge* is associated with mature women (Sappho F 44 L-P), but free status is not necessarily a qualification (Xen. *An.* 4.3.19). Ritual cries were divided by gender because male and female had different ritual roles. When Medea uses a ritual cry normally used by men, Sophokles is making a point about Medea's attempt to usurp a position normally held by males; Soph. F 534 Radt: ἀλαλαζομένη.

159. Horror or exultation: Aesch. *Ag.* 28 (ironic to the hearer), 587, 595, 1118, 1236; *Cho.* 386, 942. See Haldane (1965) 37–38.

160. Theoc. 17.64.

161. Eur. *Erechtheus* F 351 Nauck^2.

162. Armstrong and Hanson (1986) 97–100.

163. Iphigeneia's voice, when she sang for her father, is described as pure: ἁγνᾷ . . . αὐδᾷ (Aesch. *Ag.* 245). Sapph. 153: παρθένον ἀδύφωνον.

Some assignments were unique to females, for instance, the formal lament over the dead. In epic poetry and Attic tragedy lamentation is a female responsibility. Although legislation to curb public lament targeted and limited females,[164] the same legislation recognized the obligations of close female kin at the time of a death. In the world of the classical city-state, lamentation was no longer a public event but belonged to the intimate cycle of family ritual. The females who sang laments at the time of a death performed a service. They bridged the worlds of the living and the dead,[165] but because the lament itself also divided the dead from the living, female performance also buffered male family members from the taint of death. Finally, because females controlled the content of laments, they had a role in shaping family tradition and collective memory.[166]

Other differences in ritual language are not so obvious, but it is clear that social restrictions and relative isolation for women shaped female discourse. Ancient commentators recognized a certain conservatism in ordinary female speech patterns,[167] a fact that suggests conservatism in female ritual speech.[168] Traditional ritual language and traditional ritual songs had long roots in the past. Genres associated with the female life cycle, women's work, and the ritual of family life are mentioned by commentators, and there seems to have been little distinction between genres of ritual and genres of women's everyday life.[169] The weak boundaries between women's

164. Garland (1989); Holst-Warhaft (1992).

165. McClure (1999). For a summary, see Johnston (1999) 101–2; more details, especially with reference to tragedy, in Foley (2001) 19–55, 144–77.

166. Seremetakis (1991).

167. For women as a "separate speech community," see McClure (1999) 27–27, 123–25, 260–61, etc.

168. Ancient commentators noticed that female speech preserved archaic pronunciation (Pl. *Cra.* 418c) and old-fashioned forms of address. Archaic forms of address, *ὦ μέλε, ὦ τάν, ὦ οὗτος, ὦ τάλαν,* once in general use, were by the classical period apparently used only by women; schol. Pl. *Tht.* 178e; schol. *Ap.* 25c; *Suda, ὦ μέλε, ὦ τάν;* Gilleland (1980). But see Sommerstein (1995). Other characteristics include a predilection for particles (to indicate emotional speech) and high-pitched voices; McClure (1999) 38–39.

169. Genres include, for tasks: the *ioulos* (spinning song), *ailinos* (the song of those who weave), the *himaios* (the song for grinding grain; see *PMG* 869); for ritual: the *oulos* (or *ioulos), Demetroulos,* and *Kallioulos* (hymns in honor of Demeter), the *ioupingos* (for Artemis), the Linus song, and the song women sang at the swing festival for Erigone. Songs for the life cycle of the family: *humenaios* (wedding song); *katabaukalesis* (lullaby); and the *olophurmos, goos, threnos,* and *ialemos* (songs of lamentation); Ath. 14.618d–619c, discussed briefly by McClure (1999) 39–40.

social roles and their ritual functions influenced speech practice. Comic parodies of female language in Aristophanes' plays show that some exclamations are gender specific. The male Strepsiades can swear by Demeter,[170] and female characters can swear by Zeus, but an oath by Apollo is considered a man's expression.[171] Women most often swore by female divinities—Aphrodite, Hekate, Aglauros, or Artemis[172]—and the oath "by the Two Goddesses!" (τὼ θεώ, Demeter and Kore) was so closely identified with females that it was considered inappropriate for a female in male disguise.[173]

The exclamatory oaths used by women in casual conversation[174] differed markedly from the promissory oaths of Athenian males in public life or the reciprocal oaths sworn by males in arbitration and litigation. Exclamatory oaths such as "by Artemis!", "by the Two Goddesses!", or "by Aglauros!" had no legal status and served only to provide emphasis or punctuate normal conversation. Limited access to the complete ritual language of oath and oath sacrifice was in fact a measure of female political and economic disability. At Athens, a woman had access to the judicial system only through a guardian *(kyrios)* and did not participate directly in a public trial. A woman could provide sworn testimony in pretrial arbitration,[175] but like children, women appeared at jury trials as mute characters, exhibited only to inspire pity for male relatives.

In Attic tragedy, women could swear two-party oaths[176] and even re-

170. Ar. *Nub.* 121.

171. Ar. *Ecc.* 160.

172. Aphrodite (*Lys.* 556); Hekate (*Thesm.* 858; *Lys.* 443, 738); Aglauros (*Thesm.* 533); Artemis (*Thesm.* 517, 569); Nilsson (1967[3]) I 783.

173. Ar. *Ecc.* 155–58, with McClure (1999) 242, for the parody here. The same expression occurs elsewhere in Aristophanes' plays: *Thesm.* 383, 566, 718, 897; *Lys.* 51, *Vesp.* 1396. For other remarks on female speech in Aristophanes, see Taaffe (1993).

174. Gender bias in exclamatory oaths was noticed originally by Ziebarth (1892) 10–14.

175. Mirhady (1991) 79–80, 82–83. When a woman was required as a witness, there were special arrangements for securing her testimony. A woman (who could not speak in court, directly initiate a suit herself, or offer an oath challenge) could still be the object of a curse designed to make her mute when testifying. The procedure is not understood by Gager (1992) 119–20. For judicial curses directed at women, see Gager, 126–27, nos. 39–40. In both examples, females are neither the principal litigants nor the primary targets.

176. Creon asks Ismene to take an oath (Soph. *Ant.* 535); Deianeira mentions an oath (Soph. *Trach.* 378) that Lichas did not swear (314–19); Klytemnestra's references to oaths occur in a context where she has assumed a male role (Eur. *IA* 831–32, offer of *engyesis* to Achilles; 866, offer to disregard the need for an oath).

quest an oath,[177] but women's oaths were limited to situations of private life. A woman swore in litigation only when she had a direct connection to a male relative involved in dispute, or possibly when a case concerned her directly.[178] A woman could be charged with murder[179] or impiety,[180] but her own name did not have to be used in court. A woman's testimony was sought only when no one else could have known what she knew. Because female experience was confined to the life of the family, women were consulted only in cases and procedures concerned with family affairs. Disputes requiring a woman's oath concerned kin, property, or inheritance.[181] At Athens, the issue most likely to require a woman's testimony was paternity, the sort of thing only a mother could know for sure.[182] When Plangon swore an oath about the paternity of her children, she swore at the Delphinion, where she must have sworn by Apollo, but women otherwise swore by female divinities.[183] At Gortyn, if an oath of denial was required of a woman in a divorce proceeding, she swore that oath by Artemis in the sanctuary called the Amykleion.[184] Artemis protected mothers and children, but as the divinity women called upon in childbirth,[185] she was also the one whose wrath women had most cause to fear. In spite of this check on fidelity, women had a reputation for not keeping their oaths. In a lost play by Sophokles, a character complains that a woman's oath to forswear

177. Iphigeneia asks Pylades to exchange oaths; he swears by Zeus, she swears by Artemis; Eur. *IT* 735–65.

178. Lys. 32.13; Diogeiton's daughter offers to swear on her children that her husband had deposited money with Diogeiton. In [Dem.] 47.50 a women whose husband is party to a dispute is said to have sworn at the Palladion about the mistreatment of a freedwoman by the prosecutor. For a woman's sworn testimony at the Delphinion, see Is. 12.9. Evidence for women's oaths in legal actions is discussed by Leisi (1908) 13–15 and Lacey (1968) 160, 174.

179. Antiphon 1.

180. Is. 57.8; Hyperides F 30.

181. Humphreys (1986). Cf. Kydippe, who swore an oath about whom she would marry; Parke and Wormell (1956) 2.383.

182. Is. 12.9: "Who was more likely to know this than she?" Arist. *Rh.* 1398b, for the belief that women can be counted on to identify the fathers of their children. Men. *Karchedonios* F 2: "For no one knows who his own father is—we all assume it, or take it on trust" (trans. Arnott).

183. As they also usually prayed to female rather than to male divinities; Aubriot (1992) 80–81.

184. *ICrete* IV 72 III.6–9; Buck 316 no. 117, and 325. Female divinities also offered protection to women, as in the case of the mother who sought protection in a sanctuary of Eileithyia when mistreated by her son; Is. 5.39.

185. Men. *Georg.* 112 Sandbach, daughter of Myrrhine, in labor offstage, cries out to Artemis when she is about to give birth.

sex, even if taken in the midst of the pains of childbirth, could be easily forgotten later in a moment of sexual passion.[186]

The only arena where the oaths of a female had teeth was that of public ritual service. Major priesthoods were government offices, and priests and priestesses, like magistrates taking office, were often required to swear an oath to perform their duties in accordance with the community's laws.[187] A woman had to swear a promissory oath when accepting ritual responsibility to serve as a priestess in the city's public cults[188] because in this position she could act on behalf of the *polis*. In fact, ritual service was the only type of service where a female could represent the city. In recognition of this responsibility, priestesses could sign documents, issue public curses,[189] appoint their own assistants,[190] testify in court, and even initiate lawsuits.[191] Service as public priestess converted a female to a male, but only in her capacity to carry out the duties of the office.

SERVING THE GODS

Regulations for service to the gods were normally the same for priests, priestesses, and general worshippers. Few priesthoods required professional commitment, lifelong service to a divinity was not common, and priests and priestesses could serve more than one divinity at a time. Every city organized a complex calendar of festivals, and complicated rituals were performed regularly for generations. Each sanctuary had its own schedule, and sacrifices might be performed annually, monthly, or, in some cases, daily; buildings needed regular maintenance; and gifts dedicated by worshippers required care and preservation. The administration of sanctuaries and performance of rituals were the responsibility of sanctuary staff working together with officially appointed priests and priestesses.[192] In order to

186. Soph. F 932 Radt.

187. *IG* II^2 1175.21–24; Garland (1984) 84, for speculation about oaths of ritual specialists.

188. Oath of the *gerarai*, administered by the wife of the *basileus;* [Dem.] 59.78, Athens. Elsewhere: *LSCG* 65, Andania; *LSCG* 175, Antimacheia; *LSS* 127, Athens, Imperial period (priestess swears oath on taking office that she will protect the temple furnishings). On the oath at Antimacheia, Krob (1997) 448–50.

189. Plut. *Alc.* 22.

190. Kron (1996) 141.

191. [Dem.] 59.115–17; Ath. 13.594b; Kron (1996) 141 n. 13.

192. Cleomenes, attempting to seize the Athenian *akropolis*, was stopped by the priestess when he tried to breach the *adyton* of Athena. She was seated on a chair in front of the door, as guardian of the temple's inner chamber. We have here

function, the ritual system relied on a well-informed general public, cooperative officials, engaged legislatures, and generous benefactors. Management of festivals fell under the control of elected magistrates,[193] and legislative assemblies were responsible for regulating and funding public ritual and supervising public sanctuaries.[194] Except for hereditary priesthoods, most offices were technically open to the general public, and although some priesthoods could be purchased for life, terms of office were usually limited to one year. As a result, there would normally have been a steady turnover of ritual personnel. Specialized knowledge and experience were therefore rarely required, and men and women alike had to be well acquainted with the traditions and rituals of local cults, the schedules of local festivals, and the responsibilities of ritual attendants.

In the assignment of priestly offices, although asymmetries are obvious, issues of gender are not always easy to analyze. Priesthoods were assigned to individuals by inheritance, selection, or election by lot, as well as by purchase.[195] Procedures, however, were not everywhere the same. Inheritance was common in the earlier periods,[196] selection by lot was an innovation of democratic Athens in the Classical period, and appointment by purchase was the typical procedure in Hellenistic Asia Minor, the Black Sea coast, and some new foundations. Females of designated families could inherit gentile priesthoods, but, with rare exceptions, descent was reckoned in the male line.[197] At Epidauros, the female priesthood of Mnia and Ayosia seems

---

a rare example of directly quoted female speech. She says to the Spartan king: "O Lakedaimonian stranger, go back and do not come into the sanctuary; for it is not right for Dorians come in here"; Hdt. 5.72.

193. *Ath. Pol.* 54.6–7, individual festivals; 56.3–5, *archon;* 57.1, *basileus;* 58.1, polemarch. For a list of religious officials, see Arist. *Pol.* 6.1322b18–30.

194. Garland (1984) on the limitations on the responsibility of priests, esp. 78–80, on the authority of the Athenian assembly and its jurisdiction over civic cults.

195. Hereditary priesthoods must have relied on selection by lot when there was more than one eligible candidate, but the reverse situation—a lack of candidates—was the more likely problem. See Clinton (1974) 52–53 for the list of Dadouchoi at Eleusis indicating a succession of at least eighteen generations, with the office passed back and forth between two families. The Athenian procedures are discussed by Aleshire (1994) 325–37, who argues that for inherited priesthoods, sortition from a list of eligible candidates was a common practice. Appointment by election (a show of hands) was rare; see Turner (1983) 120–28. The Athenian procedure is discussed by Aleshire (1994) 325–37, where she indicates that sortition from a list was a feature of political developments in the early fifth century B.C.E.

196. Turner (1983) 35–58, for a partial list.

197. For control by important and influential families, see Turner (1983) 15–20; Garland (1984) 84. Lewis (1955) 5 suggests that succession could occasionally be transferred in the maternal line; Kron (1996) 140 n. 7 describes the case of the

to have been transmitted from mother to daughter,[198] and in the Attic deme Semachidai, the priestess of Dionysos claimed descent from the daughters of Semachos, the male founder of the deme and its cult.[199] The maternal line was normally recognized only in cases where the paternal line failed to produce a candidate or where citizenship as a qualification for priestly service was defined by both affinal and collateral lines.[200] In general, the status of her father's family determined a female's eligibility.[201] For the purposes of ritual a woman remained her father's daughter, even after marriage.

Hereditary offices for females were most common in cults of Demeter or Athena.[202] The most famous priesthood of Athena was that of Athena Polias at Athens—a lifelong obligation controlled by an elite kin group, the Eteoboutadai.[203] When selection by lot was introduced at Athens for the city's highest political offices, it also began to be used for filling new priesthoods, male and female alike. The first known priesthood to employ this procedure was that of Athena Nike, introduced after the mid-fifth century, when Perikles built a little temple for the goddess on the *akropolis* and the

---

Eteoboutadai, where succession passed from father's daughter to eldest son's daughter—but to father's daughter's daughter in cases where there was no son.

198. Broadbent (1968) 18–23.

199. Steph. Byz. s.v. Σημαχίδαι; Turner (1983) 31. The priestess of Aphrodite Kolias came from another Attic priestly family, the Kolieis; Turner (1983) 38; Parker (1996) 304–5.

200. A female candidate for the priesthood of Artemis Pergaia at Halikarnassos had to demonstrate that her family on both sides had been citizens *(astoi)* for three generations; *LSAM* 73 (third century).

201. For this reason Attic women, even when married, were given patronymics on all public documents; for the epigraphical evidence, see Hansen et al. (1987); Scafuro (1994) emphasizes the connection between status of father and status of daughter. Cf. King (1998) 60, noticing that women described in the Hippocratic corpus are referred to not by their given names but by either patronymic or their husband's name. A woman's first name was normally not used in public unless she was dead.

202. Turner (1983) 39.

203. The same family also controlled the priesthood of Poseidon Erechtheus. A member of this family, Lysimache, who served for fifty-three years, held the office for a good part of the late fifth century. The names of at least twenty-five of the women who held the office between the fifth and second centuries are known; Lewis (1955). Mantes (1990) 43 gives a summary; *IG* II^2 1456 is a list of dedications by women, probably priestesses of Athena. The support of the priestess's husband contributed to the success of her office; see *IG* II^2 776.240 (praise for the priestess of Athena Polias's husband for his piety and generosity); see van Bremen (1996) 272–73.

assembly created a new priesthood for her.[204] All Attic women whose parents were citizens *(astoi)* were technically eligible to apply.[205]

Where priesthoods were awarded by purchase, male offices commanded far higher prices than female. The average price for a male priesthood was 1700 drachmas, but the average for a female office was only 350. Dionysos had the most expensive priesthood on record, at Priene, where the fee could go as high as 12,002 drachmas—a far cry from the lowest recorded price, only 10 drachmas, for Ge (Earth) at Erythrai.[206] Disparities in costs resulted from unequal status.[207] Purchasing a priesthood was equivalent to accepting a liturgy, the subsidizing of a public rite or benefit. The most prestigious offices were reserved for the wealthiest men, who were under obligation to accept. Wealthy males who subsidized public ritual were compensated by remission of taxes and by the special honors and privileges extended by the office itself.[208] A female, on the other hand, appears to have been under liturgical obligation only in cases where responsibility fell to her family, and then only in the absence of father or brothers.[209]

Women rarely acted with complete financial independence, even when they held public office. Husbands or sons regularly mediated between administrators and a priestess, and they stood in for wives or mothers in situations where women could not be present.[210] The son of the priestess of Aglauros at Athens, for instance, formally accepted the honors the assembly granted to his mother for her service.[211] The *kyrios*, guardian, of the

204. *GHI* I^2 44; the inscription establishing the priesthood may be earlier than the temple.

205. Lewis (1955) 1–12; *GHI* I^2 44 and 71; Turner (1983) 54. Parker (1996) 126 points out that we may not have the earliest example of sortition.

206. Turner (1983) 168–73.

207. A woman did not necessarily purchase the office herself; the husband of the priestess of Artemis Pergaia at Halikarnassos acted on her behalf; *LSAM* 73.

208. The priest of Dionysos at Priene could choose from two levels of payment, both of which excused him from other public liturgies. The discount price exempted him from subsidizing public torch races, athletic contests, horses, official embassies to sanctuaries, and the gymnasium. The higher price relieved him of funding ships, public finances, temple construction, and loans to the state; *LSAM* 37.24–32. Perquisites of priestesses could be considerable. The priestess of Demeter at Athens took in upwards of five hundred drachmas, that is, one obol per initiate every year; Kron (1996) 141.

209. Discussed in detail by van Bremen (1996) 1–26, 30–31, 50–59, 62. When a female held the title of *prytanis* or *stephanephoros*, she was fulfilling a family obligation, and the title, which was simply ceremonial, carried no political responsibility. Some civic titles held by women were even bestowed posthumously.

210. Dontas (1983).

211. Dontas (1983).

priestess of Artemis at Miletos reported her bills to the authorities by submitting a list of those who failed to give her the perquisites from the sacrifices she monitored.[212] In Attika, wealthy husbands subsidized deme banquets at the Thesmophoria for their wives.[213]

Holding a priesthood could be a means for financial gain. Both priests and priestesses received a share of the meat of animals sacrificed, were sometimes paid for their public service, were eligible for honors accorded by a group or city for services rendered, and could even qualify for burial with public honors at public expense.[214] Priestesses of Demeter were especially well rewarded. At Eleusis, the priestess was not only supplied with a house; she also received part of each initiate's fee and enjoyed legal privileges equivalent to those of male citizens.

Managing a priesthood could also require financial responsibilities. In the Hellenistic period, the purchase price for a priesthood amounted to a liturgy, a responsibility borne by the family in the name of the current member. The occasional appearance of women's names in texts concerned with such obligations is due to the inherited status and wealth of the family, not to the energy, resources, or achievement of the individual female office holder.[215] Such liturgies mandated subsidies for buildings, sacrifices, ceremonies, and festivals, and the offices associated with them consumed but did not create wealth.

Distribution of priesthoods tended to follow the social distinctions of gender, with male divinities ordinarily served by priests and female divinities by priestesses.[216] At Athens, this was true for the major city priesthoods, except in the civic administration of the Eleusinian mysteries. Elsewhere there were exceptions—and the sex of attendants did not always match the sex of the divinity. Patterns of appointment suggest that it was far more common for a female divinity to be served by a male than for a male to be served by a female, but all female divinities were not the same. Some, most prominently Athena[217] and Aphrodite, were more likely to be

212. *LSAM* 45, 380/79 B.C.E.
213. Is. 3.20, 8.18.
214. Kron (1996) 140–42.
215. Well documented by van Bremen (1996).
216. Kron (1996) 140 n. 6, for a bibliography of earlier discussions. At Ephesos and Metropolis, Ares had a female priest; *IEphesos* 3416, *SEG* 43.844. However, Ares at Metropolis was worshipped with the female Areia. See note 221.
217. Athena Lindia had a priest. After 40 B.C.E., his wife was included in references to his euergetism; van Bremen (1996) 134–45.

served by males;[218] and others, namely Artemis, Demeter, and Hera, were more likely to be served by females.[219] When a male and a female divinity were worshipped together, a single ritual specialist was almost always male.[220] Male gods, on the other hand, rarely had a priestess or female attendant,[221] and when they did—especially in the case of Apollo or Dionysos[222]—the situation was exceptional. Women who served Apollo were bound by special demands of purity because they attended the god in his prophetic role. Such a female had to be either too young to marry (a *parthenos)* or too old to bear children. Above all, she had to stay away "from the gifts of garland-loving Aphrodite."[223]

For Dionysos the nature of the ritual and the sex of his worshippers seem to have determined the sex of his attendants. Where he was worshipped by male and female together, Dionysos needed both a priest and a priestess.[224] Where he was associated with the theater and a male clientele,[225] his major ritual specialist was always a priest. As god of the theater, his only female attendant was the *kanephoros* who marched in his procession. She was a *parthenos* because she had to be sexually neutral. Where his clientele was strictly female, Dionysos's ritual specialist was also fe-

218. *IG* II^2 5067: the Muses have a priest.

219. Demeter at Eleusis had both priestess and priest, but the position of priestess seems to have been the older office; Clinton (1974) 76; Garland (1984) 96–104. Generalizations are not possible; Artemis Epipurgidia had a priest (*IG* II^2 5050).

220. The material is collected by Holderman (1913) (selections translated into Italian in Arrigoni and Gentili [1985] 299–330). Holderman's lists, 32–50, are generous for the literary sources, are out of date for the epigraphical sources, and do not include male divinities served only by a priest (by far the largest category). The Greek mainland has a higher proportion of female attendants for female divinities than Asia Minor; see also McClees (1920); Jordan (1979) 28–36; Turner (1983); Burkert (1985) 98.

221. Holderman (1913) 52–53, for priestesses for Zeus, but all refer to late or indigenous cults of Asia Minor. Others include Asklepios at Pergamon, *IGR* 4.508; Ares at Selge in Pisidia, *ISelge* 20 (wife of an official); Pan at Lykosoura, Paus. 8.37.11; Pluto at Eleusis, *SIG*^{3} 1039.28; Poseidon at Kalaureia, Paus. 2.33.2. See also Turner (1983) 186. Epie of Thasos, in service to Zeus Eubouleus, served voluntarily in what seems to have been a female office; van Bremen (1996) 26 n. 52.

222. Priestess of Dionysos: *LSCG* 18 (Erchia, Attika), 28 (Athens), 166 (Kos); Dionysos Anthios, *IG* II^2 1356; *LSAM* 48 (Miletos).

223. *Hymn. Hom. Dem.* 101–2.

224. Miletos, *LSAM* 48.

225. Some examples include: Athens, *IG* II^2 5022 (Dionysos Eleuthereus), 5060 (Dionysos Melpomenos); Priene, *IPriene* 174 (Dionysos Phleus); Aristophanes' Dikaiopolis claims that the priest of Dionysos invited him to a feast; Ar. *Ach.* 1087.

male.[226] At Miletos in the Hellenistic period, Dionysos had a major public priest and a major public priestess, but he also had both priests and priestesses who officiated at bacchic ceremonies in the city's outlying territory. At the Dionysiac Katagogia, the public priest and priestesses led the priests and priestesses of Dionysos Bakchios in a public ritual that lasted from dawn to dusk. The priestess, in addition to presiding at sacrifices, also represented the city by supervising the Dionysiac initiations in the countryside. She performed a special sacrifice "for the sake of the *polis*," distributed sacred equipment, and received perquisites when any woman offered a sacrifice to Dionysos. She also collected biannual payments from other women who performed initiations in the countryside or throughout the island territories of the *polis*.[227]

The prominent role of female ritual specialists in both public and private cults of Dionysos at Miletos was a consequence of the many Dionysian rituals restricted to female participants. In many cases, therefore, it is the gender of the clientele that makes the difference. Dionysos's ritual ambidexterity can be detected in other manifestations of his multiple identities. He was unusual in that he could be invoked by the same title as his worshippers[228] and, being capable of many visual surprises, could be depicted as human or divine, young or middle-aged, in masculine form or feminized.[229] Having androgynous features, he could even appear costumed as one of his own female worshippers.[230]

Herakles, who rarely deviated from the heroic model, was especially vulnerable to the ritual challenge of females. He had a female attendant only at Thespiai, where the priestess had to remain a *parthenos* and serve him until death.[231] These exceptional requirements minimized her ritual threat and solved the problem of the hero's vulnerability to the presence of a sexually active adult woman, but this is not the whole story. Local myth explained the unusual requirement of permanent virginity as a punishment for the first priestess, Thespius's fiftieth daughter. Perpetual virginity

226. For a priestess of Dionysos at a sacrifice restricted to women, see *LSCG* 18 A.50, Δ.39, Attic deme of Erchia. Priestesses of Dionysos were not, however, restricted to all-female groups; Holderman (1913) 51.
227. *LSAM* 48.
228. Cole (1980).
229. In Dionysos's earliest known appearance on stage, he wears a *krokotos* (Greek equivalent of a party dress) and is taunted by the Thracian king Lykourgos as a "womanish man"; Aesch. *Edonoi, TrGF* F 61 Radt. For the feminized Dionysos, cf. Eur. *Bacch.* 150, 233–36, 353, 453–59, 464; Loraux (1990) 38; Turcan (1958).
230. Bremmer (1999).
231. Paus. 9.27.6.

was imposed because she had refused Herakles when, as guest of her father, he had slept with each of her forty-nine sisters in a single night. The story pattern of a young girl's refusal of a god's advances is similar to that of Apollo's failed seductions and seems designed to account for the ritual anomaly of a female who subverts her social role of wife and mother for a ritual end. The risks of female sexuality were handled differently in Phokis, where Herakles, called "Woman-Hater," was served by a celibate male.[232] At Antimacheia on Kos, the risk of a real female attendant was minimized by dressing the hero's priest in women's clothing and having him wear a *mitra*, a special headgear otherwise worn only by women.[233]

The unusual precautions taken at Thespiai, Antimachia, and the unnamed sanctuary somewhere in Phokis indicate special concerns. Although Herakles was a model of male strength and virility, he was nevertheless considered vulnerable to female influence. His mythical servitude to Omphale,[234] although a source of shame, and his lifelong experience of Hera's antagonism do not completely explain the exclusion of women from his ritual. The answer is in the ritual itself. Herakles, like Dionysos and Achilles, could wear women's clothing.[235] A change of clothing is a feature of life-cycle festivals, and these festivals were marked by requirements of gender. In the case of Herakles, the feminized hero provided a model for ritual cross-dressing—an experience males had to successfully negotiate in order to cross over to adult status.[236] Normally a source of ridicule,[237] feminine attire was not a problem for males if ritual required it. Successfully performed and successfully completed, temporary cross-dressing signaled achievement of maturity and demonstrated to the rest of the male community a candidate's eligibility for adult life.[238] The ambivalence and anxi-

232. Plut. *De Pyth. Or.* 403f–404a, explaining the substitution of an older man (for whom a year of sexual abstinence would be no hardship) for a younger one.

233. Plut. *Quaest. Graec.* 304c explains the *mitra* by claiming that Herakles, defeated in a wrestling match, had to escape dressed as a Thracian woman. He uses the same episode to explain a Koan custom in which bridegrooms wore women's clothing on the first night of marriage. Nilsson (1906) 453 argues that Herakles ἐς *Κονίσαλον*, worshipped at Kos, was a phallic god of marriage (*SIG*[3] 1027; Ar. *Lys.* 982, with scholia; Hsch. s.v. *Κονίσαλος*).

234. Soph. *Trach.* 248–57; Loraux (1990) 26.

235. Loraux (1990).

236. On ritual transvestism, see Leitao (1995) and Bremmer (1999).

237. Aristophanes' jokes at Agathon's expense (Ar. *Thesm.* 88–208, passim) or the female clothing worn by Euripides' *kedestes* when invading the women's rites at the Thesmophoria (Ar. *Thesm.* 249–65) are good examples.

238. Artem. 2.3, for a married man to dream of cross-dressing portends disease or even loss of his wife; but for unmarried men to dream of wearing women's cloth-

ety associated with such rituals, however, is indicated by Herakles' subordination to Hera at Didyma, where the language of ritual, insulting to Herakles, calls him a "womanish man" (θηλυπρεπὴς φώς).[239]

Heroes rarely had female attendants, but Sosipolis, a local hero of Elis, was an exception. Paired with Eileithyia, he "preserved the city" by enacting a ritual that imitated the first night of the newlyweds. Sosipolis was worshipped with Eileithyia in a divided temple—the outer chamber for the goddess of childbirth and the protected inner chamber for the hero alone. Married women and *parthenoi* worshipped the goddess of childbirth in the outer chamber, but only the priestess, with a white veil drawn over her head and face, could approach Sosipolis himself.[240] Limitation of access to the god's statue affirmed the powerful nature of a ritual on which the city depended. Like a bride on the first night of marriage, veiled for *anakalupteria,* the ritual where she would reveal herself to her husband for the first time, the priestess entered the hero's chamber alone. Her sexual status protected her because, although dressed as a bride, she was not really a *parthenos* but an old woman, protected by age from the real dangers of sexuality and sexual experience. Nevertheless, her ritual enactment isolated the event the city needed. Celibacy was not the only possibility. Other rituals emphasized reproductive aptitude. Designed to promote fertility and successful childbirth, some even required sexually active married women of childbearing age.[241] When sexual maturity was symbolically significant, unmarried and postmenopausal women could even be excluded.[242]

Requirements of purity for ritual specialists and temple personnel did not normally differ from those for ordinary worshippers. Sexual abstinence was rarely required for more than a few days,[243] and standards for male and female attendants were, on the whole, similar. Where long-term

---

ing is not ominous because it represents a necessary stage on the journey to adulthood. The story of Alcibiades' dreaming about wearing his mistress's clothing was obviously thought to portend his death; Plut. *Alc.* 39.1–2.

239. *IDidyma* 501.9; Loraux (1990) 21.

240. Paus. 6.20.2–3. There was a similar division between old and young women in the ritual of Aphrodite at Sikyon; Paus. 2.10.4. The *neokoros,* an adult female for whom it was οὐ θέμις (not in accordance with laws fixed by custom) to go to a man, was assisted by a *loutrophoros,* a virgin who served for a year.

241. Delaney (1987; 1991) 35–48, for the same distinctions in modern Turkish agricultural society; for a fuller account, see Delaney (1991).

242. A sanctuary of Demeter at Sparta required that all participating women be married and explicitly prohibited both *parthenoi* and widows from serving as priestess; Beattie (1951) 46–58.

243. *LSCG* 151A.42: *anti nyktos.*

requirements did occur, they marked a divinity's ritual in a special way. Pausanias never systematically discusses the issue of sexual purity, but his descriptions do distinguish between virginity, marital chastity, and sexual abstinence—conditions that singled out females and governed female service more often than male. Temporary abstinence was a condition of service for both males and females, but marital chastity, permanent or long-term sexual abstinence, and permanent virginity were normally required only of females.[244]

At Andania, both males and females took an oath to perform ritual duties, but only the females had to swear to marital fidelity. Priestesses concluded their oath:

> "and I have also lived my life together with my husband, in accordance with divine and human law."[245]

In Achaia, the priestess of Ge Eurysternos at Aigai not only had to abstain from sexual intercourse during her term but, before assuming office, she had to swear that she had not had intercourse with more than one man. As part of the ritual to test her oath she was required to drink bull's blood, a substance considered poisonous.[246] At Athens, an ancient inscription preserved a sacred law that set standards for the wife of the *basileus.* One of the three leading magistrates in the city, the *basileus* administered most of the major city festivals and sacrifices. The wife of any man aspiring to the office of *basileus* had to be daughter of a citizen and at the time of her marriage a *parthenos,* without experience of sexual contact "with any other man."[247]

244. Except for the priesthood of Artemis at Orchomenos, where both priest and priestess served for life in permanent purity, sexual and otherwise; Paus. 8.13.1 (the text is corrupt). The evidence for sexual abstinence for priests and priestesses has been collected by Fehrle (1910) 75–111 and summarized by Turner (1983) 174–231.

245. *LSCG* 65.2–6.

246. Any priestess dishonest about her marital history was punished immediately; Paus. 7.25.13. Oath by bull's blood is problematic; see Hirzel (1902) 183–84 and Turner (1983) 209. For test of an oath by water, see Phil. *VA.* 1.6; cf. the fictitious test for virginity (with sound of the syrinx of Pan) at a cave behind the temple of Artemis at Ephesos, Ach. Tat. 8.6. Versnel (1994) 151 discusses the evidence for ordeal by fire as a test of virginity for the priestess of Artemis Perasia in Cilicia.

247. [Dem.] 59.75–76. Achilles Tatius 8.12 describes a procedure where the water of a spring of Artemis could rise up to cover (and invalidate) an oath of virginity written on a card and tied around the neck. Cf. Eust. *Phil.* 8.72 for a test of virginity by water from a fountain of Artemis in Artykomis.

Although Apollo, Herakles, and even Poseidon[248] had priestesses who had to remain *parthenoi,* unmarried priestesses were more frequent in cults of female divinities, especially Artemis[249] but also Athena,[250] the Leukippides,[251] Aphrodite,[252] and Demeter.[253] Unmarried attendants of a virgin goddess imitated the sexual status of the divinity whose ritual, associated with stages of the female life cycle, demanded virginity until marriage.[254] Unlike attendants of Apollo, who had to be professional virgins, young women who served a goddess were expected to marry when they reached maturity. Consequently, they served for limited terms. The evidence for *parthenoi* who served sexually mature divinities like Aphrodite and Demeter is more difficult to analyze, but such service also seems to have been considered appropriate preparation for marriage.[255]

Frequent formal recognition of the service of young, unwed priestesses, especially in the cult of Artemis, indicates the high value placed on control of female sexuality. Proclamation of a daughter's service, publicized by dedicating a statue with an inscribed base, testified to the depth of parental investment in the sexual status of daughters. Virgin daughters on the point of marriage reflected a family's success, because a child was an "ornament *(agalma)* of the home."[256] A count of all commemorative statues at Delos reveals that the only stage of life where statues of females were displayed

248. On Kalaureia, a *parthenos* served Poseidon until she reached marriageable age; Paus. 2.33.2. For a priestess of Poseidon at Thebes, see *IG* VII 2465.

249. Especially in myth. Greek mainland (all from Peloponnese): Artemis Knagia near Sparta, Paus. 3.18.4; Artemis Hekate in Aigeira (Achaia), Paus. 7.26.4–5; Artemis Laphria at Patrai, Paus. 7.18.12; Artemis Triklaria in Patrai, Paus. 7.19.1. Asia Minor: Ephesos, Paus. 8.13.1, Strab. 14.641; Plut. *An Seni* 795d-e (three stages are equivalent to three age grades); Sidyma (Lykia), Benndorf, *Reisen* I 75–77.

250. Athena Triteia (Achaia), Paus. 7.22.8–9 (female); at Pellene, Polyaen. 8.59.

251. Near Amyklai two young girls, called "fillies," *poloi,* served Hilaeira and Phoebe, daughters of Apollo; Paus. 3.16.1, Hsch. s.v. πωλιά.

252. Aphrodite in Sikyon, Paus. 2.10.4. The priestess was a *parthenos* who served one year; the *neokoros* was a woman for whom it was "no longer right to have intercourse with a man."

253. Kleioboia, priestess of Demeter at Thasos, is described by Pausanias as "still a *parthenos*"; Paus. 10.28.3.

254. In a lost play of Sophokles, the king of Tegea tries to avoid the predicted death of a son at the hands of a grandson by keeping his daughter, Auge, in service as priestess to Athena; Soph. *Aleadai,* argument, in Radt, *TrGF,* p. 140.

255. The priestess of Artemis Triklaria at Patrai was a *parthenos* who served until marriage; Paus. 7.19.1. The *kanephoros* of Hera at Argos (as well as the one at Phalerion in Italy) is described as a child "pure of marriage," ἁγνὴ γάμων παῖς; Dion. Hal. 1.21.

256. Aesch. *Ag.* 208, of Iphigeneia.

in numbers equal to those of males is adolescence.[257] Daughters were commemorated as often as sons because adolescent ritual roles for girls were as important as the adolescent ritual roles of boys.

The requirement of permanent virginity was confined for the most part to prophetic cults of Apollo. Held to the same standard as that of the Delphic Pythia, a Sibyl at Kyme was still called *parthenos* when she died at the age of ninety because she could claim that she had never submitted herself to a man.[258] Herophile, another Sibyl, who was *neokoros,* temple warden, of Apollo Smintheus at Alexandria Troas and a professional prophet, poet, and writer of hymns, claimed to have remained a *parthenos* during her long life of giving oracles.[259]

Where standards for purity required permanent abstinence, a woman beyond menopause was considered a reliable appointment.[260] Like Demeter in search of her daughter, disguised as an old woman uninterested in sexual activity, a postmenopausal woman was done with Aphrodite.[261] Free from sexual pollution, she presented no risk to men, nor was she sexually at risk herself.[262] The priestess of Artemis Hymnia at Orchomenos was a woman who had had "enough sexual intercourse with men."[263] She was similar to the sixty-year-old priestess of Artemis Lochia at Stobi, whose purity could be affirmed by an oracle from Apollo at Klaros.[264] Older women were safe for assignment to special ritual duties[265] and filled the critical posts of tending the fire in cults of Hestia or the sacred flames at

257. Le Dinahet-Couilloud (1996) 395–97.

258. *MDAI(A)* 17 (1892) 16–18.

259. Paus. 10.12.1–6. For "Herophile" as a generic name for Sibyls, see Parke (1988) 24, 65–66, 69 n. 30.

260. Men were rarely required to meet such standards; Plut. *De Pyth. Or.* 403f–404a.

261. *Hymn Hom. Dem.* 101–2.

262. Bremmer (1987) 192. Drew-Bear and Lebek (1973) 63.10, translate the description of an applicant for a priesthood of Athena Polias at Miletos as eligible because "she had previously obtained her share of Aphrodite." The text is reprinted with commentary by Fontenrose, (1988) 199–25 no. 25, who explains that the Milesians are asking for dispensation to appoint a married woman as priestess of Athena Polias, though the position normally required virginity. Because the woman had already "had a share of Aphrogeneia's (Aphrodite's) gifts," the oracle agreed that she remained first in line for the hereditary appointment.

263. Paus. 8.5.11–12.

264. Wiseman (1973) 153–55 errs in assuming that the priestess *served* for sixty years.

265. Plato makes sixty the minimum age for ritual attendants; *Leg.* 6.759d. Henderson (1987b) 110–17 emphasizes the honor granted to older women.

Athens and Delphi.[266] Older women, like the *gerarai* of Dionysos at Athens,[267] the *geraraides* who served Athena at Argos,[268] or the four aged priestesses of Demeter at Hermione, served in groups.[269] At Athens, the Dionysiac *gerarai* whose sexual abstinence was a function of age, qualified for service by swearing the following oath:

> I live a holy life, and I am clean and pure from all that is not pure and from intercourse with a man, and I will celebrate the Theoinia and the Iobakcheia for Dionysos according to custom and at the established times.[270]

Violation of the rules for sexual purity was a serious failure and deserved punishment by the gods. A priestess of Artemis at Patrai was sacrificed along with her lover to stop a plague sent as punishment for sexual violation of the goddess's sanctuary.[271] Virgin priestesses residing in a sanctuary were an attractive temptation,[272] but females were more likely than males to be punished for the violation of a sacred space, even when the cause was rape. Although adult males were expected to be able to control their sexual urges,[273] permanent masculine virginity was unknown and long-term male abstinence extremely rare.[274] For a male, even a short-term requirement could be considered a burden. A young priest of Herakles Misogynes who could not abstain from sex for the year of his term was ab-

266. Plut. *Num.* 9.5: εἴτε ὡς καθαρὰν καὶ ἄφθαρτον τὴν τοῦ πυρὸς οὐσίαν . . . εἴτε τὸ ἄκαρπον καὶ ἄγονον.

267. [Dem.] 59.73; *Etym. Magn.* 277.35, s.v. γεραραί; Hsch. s.v. Γεραραί.

268. Hsch. s.v. γεραράδες· αἱ τῶν ἀρίστων ἀνδρῶν γυναῖκες (*gerarades:* the wives of the best men). See Turner (1983) 213.

269. Paus. 2.35.6–9; they transgressed sacrificial convention by killing the victim themselves. Subversion of normal procedure was emphasized by locating the slaughter not at the altar outside the building but within the temple. The same story is told by Aelian, *NA* 11.4, with, however, only one priestess and a bull as victim.

270. Quoted at [Dem.] 59.78. Such oaths are parodied by Aristophanes, *Lys.* 187–237; see Henderson (1987a) 91–96.

271. Paus. 7.19.2–4. In myth such punishments were severe. Atalanta and Melanaion were changed into animals for breaking the prohibition against sexual intercourse in a sanctuary; Apollod. 3.9.2; Hyg. 185.

272. More than one sanctuary is supposed to have replaced a young priestess with an older woman in order to minimize risk. According to tradition, a *parthenos* at Delphi was raped by a Thessalian; Diod. Sic. 16.26. After a virgin priestess was raped in the sanctuary near the cult statue, the administrators of the cult of Artemis Hymnia at Orchomenos changed the requirements and accepted an older woman as priestess of Artemis; Paus. 8.5.11–12.

273. Dem. 54.14; Xen. *Mem.* 2.1.4–5; Cole (1984) 97 n. 4. Sexual acts with a female dependent of another citizen or sexual acts in submission to another male were discouraged; on male *sophrosyne* and *enkrateia,* Just (1985) 177–84.

274. The priest of Artemis at Orchomenos in Arkadia is unusual; Paus. 8.13.1.

solved from any responsibility by an oracle that said: "The god allows all that is necessary."[275] Plato recognized the same problem and therefore fixed the minimum age for priests in his imaginary Magnesia at sixty.[276]

Regulations for males were more likely to require youth than age. Prepubescent boys served Zeus,[277] a prophetic cult of Apollo,[278] and Athena at Tegea[279] and Elateia.[280] The interesting transition for males was the one between childhood and adolescence, and ritual requirements for boys and young men were less concerned with issues of sexual experience than with the physical evidence of maturity. Boys were carefully scrutinized as they approached puberty, and any sign of a beard terminated childhood and eligibility for childhood service. For the young girls described as *parthenoi* (unmarried), social status—more visible than technical virginity—was the important factor.[281]

Stricter purity requirements for women than for men underscore the association of women with procreation. The Andanian inscription, stressing loyalty of wives to husbands, was consistent with Greek social values. The social system distributed prestigious administrative responsibilities to men but not to women, required sexual loyalty of wives but not of husbands, and punished females but not males for sexual infractions. Formulas of praise for wives stress the importance of the marriage bond. The marriage of Epigone and Euphrosynos at Mantineia is a model:

> She was united with him in a happy marriage; their two lives were yoked together and they were linked in body and mind.[282]

275. Plut. *De Pyth. Or.* 404a; Fontenrose (1978) 263 classifies this response as historical; compare Artem. 1.79; Brown (1988) 84.

276. Pl. *Leg.* 759d; cf. Arist. *Pol.* 1329a27–34. Parker (1983) 87, on Plato's acknowledgment of difficulties in meeting purity requirements. At Ephesos a temple builder *(neopoios)* gave a ceremonial dinner for sanctuary personnel to celebrate his achievement in maintaining ritual purity; *IEphesos* VII.1 195–96 no. 3263.21–22; *BE* 1982.308; *SEG* 31.957.

277. At Aigion (Achaia), Paus. 7.24.4. Pausanias says that at one time the priest was a boy chosen for his beauty who served until his beard grew. In his day the priest was a man who served an annual term.

278. The priest of Apollo Ismenios at Thebes was a boy from a respectable family who wore laurel leaves, was called *daphnephoros,* and served for one year; Paus. 9.10.4.

279. Paus. 8.47.2–3.

280. Athena Kranaia, Paus. 10.34.8. The boy, chosen young enough to ensure that his term ran out before his beard grew, served for five years.

281. Sissa (1990a) insists on physical status.

282. *IG* V.2 278 (trans. van Bremen [1996] 138).

Although philosophers and orators encouraged sexual fidelity in husbands,[283] epigraphical evidence reflects the social reality. Regulations assume that sexual experience for married women should be linked with reproduction for the sake of the family, but for married men sexual experience, not necessarily connected with marriage,[284] was its own reward.[285]

THE DELPHIC BEE

Differences in ritual standards for males and females reflect social divides. Expressed in terms of maintaining sanctity of special areas of sacred space, these requirements convert the female body to a marker of sacred status. Sacred areas considered more important than others were distinguished by special standards of purity. Attendants, who represented with their own bodies the purity of the sanctuary,[286] had to be careful. The most important ritual offices required sanctuary personnel to undergo purification procedures normally used only for the sanctuary itself.

Pausanias describes such procedures when he introduces the Sixteen Women of Elis, who administrated female rituals at Olympia. They wove the robe for Hera, presided at a festival for Dionysos, supervised the footraces of young women, and managed the choral dances of the local heroines, Physkoa and Hippodameia. They had to be mature, married women (γυναῖκες) belonging to the privileged class, and first in "age, status, and reputation."[287] Their clientele was female; their rites, except for those of Dionysos, honored female divinities; and at least one of their sanctuaries, the *hieron* of Hippodameia, was reserved for women alone. Their rituals of purification were considered so important that even Pausanias viewed them as unusual. The Hellanodikai—the judges who presided at the quadrennial games—and the Sixteen Women of Elis had a special status. Pausanias says that they had to leave the sanctuary to purify themselves (middle voice)

283. Foucault (1986) 166–67.

284. Sex with a prostitute required a longer waiting period than intercourse with a wife (Lindos in the third century C.E.); *LSS* 91.17–18.

285. A private cult at Philadelpheia in Lydia required that sexual relations be limited to spouses; Barton and Horsley (1981), for *LSAM* 20. The penalties for women who failed to comply are expressed in far stronger language than the penalties for men. An adulterous woman is "full of endemic pollution" (38) and able to contaminate others.

286. Parker (1983) 175–76 describes ritual attendants as "walking temples."

287. Paus. 5.16.5–6.

> with a piglet suitable for purification, and with water. They have the purifications at a spring called Piera. If you cross the plain from Olympia to Elis, you come to the Pieran spring.[288]

Pausanias does not say that the Sixteen were required to refrain from sexual activity for the term of their service, but the emphasis on their advanced age implies that he did not consider this an issue.

Special standards of purity called attention to central-place sanctuaries. Ritual specialists had to meet high levels of purity at places like Delphi, sacred seat of an important amphictyony; Olympia, site of the most important pan-Hellenic competitions; and Kalaureia, island sanctuary of Poseidon and headquarters for an important early Peloponnesian amphictyony. The Pythia, originally a *parthenos,* had to be purified with a singular rite before every consultation; the priestess of Poseidon on Kalaureia had to be a *parthenos;* and the Sixteen Women of Elis were subject to the same ritual purifications as the Hellanodikai.

Females who served Demeter were set apart by high standards of purity. The best evidence comes from Kos, where a synoecism in 366 necessitated consolidation of local *leges sacrae* under a single authority. Earlier regulations preserved on whitened boards were collected and transferred to stone. Local community festivals of Demeter were subordinated to a central authority, and procedures for priestesses of Demeter were standardized. Impurity from sexual contact was only one among several concerns. Regulations for the priest of Zeus Polieus and the priestesses of Demeter distinguish keeping oneself pure (ἁγνεύεσθαι) from making oneself pure (καθαράσθαι) from filth (μυσαρός). Polluting conditions were divided into two categories: those that involved contact only by propinquity or touch, and those that involved intimate contact, for instance, eating. Like the procedures for the Hellanodikai and the Sixteen at Olympia, the procedure had three parts: cathartic purification with blood, ritual sprinkling with water from a golden vessel, and propitiatory sprinkling of grain.[289] Casual contact with impurity could be rectified by merely a circuit of sprinkled water and a circuit of sprinkled grain, but intimate contact, especially contact with certain foods, required purification with blood. The priestess of Demeter had to keep herself pure (ἁγνεύεσθαι) in the following way:[290]

288. Paus. 5.16.8.

289. The word *prospermeia,* known only from this text, refers to the sprinkling of grain from a vessel.

290. In this and the following quotation, square brackets enclose material restored by Herzog in the original edition. His restorations are based on parallel pas-

> She is not to associate in any way with anything] foul or filthy, nor is she to eat at a hero's feast nor set foot in a *heroon* [nor go into a house] in which a woman gave birth or aborted a child during three days from the [day the woman gave birth or miscarried nor] is she to go into wherever a person [died during three days from the day on which] the corpse was carried out, nor is she [to touch any] carcasses, nor eat of any animal [that has been strangled (?)].[291]

The priestess of Demeter and the priest of Zeus Polieus had to avoid anything polluted, whether a feast of a hero, a place of recent childbirth or miscarriage, the house of a dead person, or an animal carcass, and probably also meat from any animal that had not bled in sacrifice.[292] Before undertaking any ritual responsibility on behalf of the deme or the *polis,* a Koan priestess of Demeter had to demonstrate her separation from polluting contact and show that her body no longer carried even the symbolic residue of any of the other forbidden pollutions on the list:

> If it happens to the priestess to do any of these foul or filthy things, so as to err because she ate any [of these foul or filthy things, let her cut a boundary around herself with a female piglet][293] and let her [purify (or cleanse) herself and sprinkle around herself] (with water) from a golden vessel and from a *prospermeia,* [but if any] of these other things happens, let her sprinkle around herself from a golden vessel and from a *prospermeia* [and let her be pure].[294]

The Koan ritual mandated a level of concern not recorded for priesthoods of other divinities. If the priestess ate of an animal whose meat had been sacrificed to a hero, her body was polluted by ritual intimacy with the dead.

---

sages in other parts of this text and other Koan texts of the same series. Parentheses in the translated text enclose alternate translations of my own.

291. Herzog (1928) no. 5; *LSCG* 154 IIa.22–27. I have punctuated the text to indicate its fragmentary state. Key terms having to do with purification procedures, however, although sometimes bracketed here, are restored according to formulas for the priestess of Demeter at Isthmos (*LSCG* 154 IIb) and the procedures for the priest of Zeus Polieus (*LSCG* 151).

292. There are textual problems at this point.

293. Text is reconstructed by Herzog (1928) no. 15, 5A.14, comparing the same procedure for the priest of Zeus Polieus, where a male piglet is used: *περιταμέσθω χοίρωι ἔρσενι.*

294. Herzog (1928) no. 5, lines 28–30. Herzog's text makes the piglet female, in opposition to the male piglet specified in the purification rites for the priest of Zeus Polieus. Piglets are often required to be male (especially those sacrificed to male divinities: *IRhPeraia* 1.2 11.2, *LSCG* 63, 64). A female piglet is listed at Tralles (*ITralles* 248.7), and the pig for sacrifice by a woman in Alexandria at Her. 4.15 is female.

For the stain of eating forbidden meat, she had to "cut" circuit boundaries with the blood of a piglet. Other impurities were corrected by sprinkling around herself a circuit of pure water and a circuit of seeds from a *prospermeia.* No other ritual specialists are mentioned. This fact, together with the use of the middle voice for the verb of purification,[295] implies that the priestess performed the series of rituals on herself.

The three substances, blood, water, and grain, belong to two different categories—one polluted, the other pure. Spring water and blood were opposites, with different ritual characteristics and different ritual functions.[296] When Heraklitos criticizes ritual practice, he draws attention to this opposition :

> Those that purify themselves (from blood) with blood are raving mad, in the same way as a person who steps in mud and tries to clean himself with mud would appear to be raving mad if anyone ever noticed him doing this.[297]

Parker deals with the problem of these apparently self-contradictory procedures by emphasizing similarities. He assumes that the mechanics of purification depended on the absorptive character of the material used for the procedure, whether that material was considered pure itself (e.g., spring water or Apollo's branch of laurel) or polluted (e.g., blood, mud, sulfur, or pitch).[298] Such substances, he points out, whether "clean" or "dirty" in themselves, had to be discarded after use because both the pure and the impure worked by absorption.

The procedure is actually more complicated. Different kinds of substances were required because two different processes were involved. Agents of purification, like pharmacological substances, could be homeopathic or allopathic. Homeopathic substances are believed to effect a change by replicating the situation they aim to correct. Allopathic substances, believed to work in the opposite way, correct the balance by introducing a substance that acts in direct opposition to the offending condition. The difference between the two processes is made clear by a discussion in the *Sophist* where Plato compares a method of argumentation to the processes of purification. The purifications of medical practice as well as the *katharmoi* of ritual are analogues to a method of logical discrimination he calls "diacritics," a

295. Cf. Theophr. *Char.* 16.12.
296. Cf. Eur. *HF* 1324.
297. Heraclit. F 5.
298. Parker (1983) 226–32, on substances used for purification.

method of argumentation that divides the better from the worse.[299] According to Plato, agents of purification that divide the pure from the polluted work in two different ways: either like a sponge or like a cathartic drug.[300] The one absorbs, the other expels. He says that "diacritics," like purification rituals, "cut" a line (227c–d) separating the better from the worse (226d), keeping the worse outside and the better in (227d). For the act of separation Plato uses the technical terminology for "cutting" a ritual boundary and inscribing the boundary of a sacred space (*τέμνειν, συντέμνειν* 227c–d). According to his metaphor, the priestess's circuit with the blood of a dead piglet created a boundary that separated her body from the taint of eating forbidden food. She accomplished this division by cutting a line with a substance that separated any possible taint or impurity on the outside from what was inscribed within. The blood of the dead piglet, impure like the impurity it was designed to attract, was a homeopathic substance. Like a sponge, the blood of the slain piglet absorbed the impurity so it could be removed.[301] Because the circuit drawn with the blood of the piglet transferred pollution to its carcass, the carcass itself had to be discarded.[302] Drawing a circuit with pure water, on the other hand, like using an allopathic substance, reinforced the boundary by keeping impurity out. By circumscribing her body with pure water from a pure vessel, the priestess demonstrated herself as untouched by the polluting object, which was now outside.[303]

Heraklitos, who would have been familiar with procedures like those at Kos, calls attention to the paradox of purification ritual. If we look beyond his scorn, we can see the logic of the practice he despises. Smearing mud on the surface of the body, being a homeopathic process, would not pollute the skin. Like a second skin, the mud could absorb any "muddy" or polluting substance previously contracted, and, when removed, could testify to the purity of the skin and therefore of the body beneath.

The terminology of purification stresses the process of creating active

299. Pl. *Soph.* 226c–d.

300. Pl. *Soph.* 227a.

301. Pliny, who identifies this process as Greek, calls it sympathy; *NH* 28.84.

302. Like the Hekataia, "the meal left for Hekate," the remnants of the carcass of the piglets used for purification were left at a *triodos;* Dem. 54.39.

303. [Plut.] *Aet. Rom. et Graec.* 263e: *τὸ πῦρ καθαίρει καὶ τὸ ὕδωρ ἁγνίζει,* "Fire takes away impurity, water restores the original state of purity." Rudhardt (1958) 163–64 distinguishes between *καθαίρειν,* the elimination of impurities (such as those associated with murder), and *ἁγνίζειν,* restoration of purity after contact with the impurities associated with the life cycle (childbirth, sex, and funerals).

boundaries. Inscribing a boundary with a homeopathic substance like the blood of a piglet removed the taint of blood by drawing it out. The idea of "cutting" a boundary is essential. Plato makes this very clear when he uses the language of maintaining and disputing political boundaries as a second analogy for his philosophical method (231a–b). The image of political boundaries assumes complete encirclement, an idea emphasized in the many Greek terms for purification compounded with *peri-*, "around."[304] Creating a new boundary was part of recovery.

Purification with pure water was ubiquitous and took many forms. Purification with the blood of a piglet, however, was reserved for very special or very dangerous situations. Special situations included, in addition to purification of murderers, the rites at Olympia for the Hellanodikai and the Sixteen Women, rituals of Demeter everywhere, and the purification of encirclement that defined the space for the male community in public places, such as the assembly or the theater. At Kos, the triple procedure of blood, grain, and water emphasized the special level of purity necessary for one who moved across the specially challenging boundary dividing the gods from human experience. A priestess of Demeter could not import any trace of impurity from her domestic life or personal experience to the place where she fulfilled her ritual responsibility to the community. The special form of purification for the priestess of Demeter at Kos puts her personal ritual on the same level as the procedures for the officials of a central-place sanctuary, such as the Hellanodikai and the Sixteen Women of Elis. Attendants of Demeter were held to a high standard because the goddess's ritual was fundamental to the *polis* and to the success of both *polis* and family.

The special procedures for the priestess of Demeter at Kos explain why the priestess of Demeter Chamyne at Olympia was permitted to observe male athletic events. She was the only adult female at Olympia whose purity made comparison to a fly out of the question. Priestesses of Demeter were so highly respected that the only insect to which they could be compared was the bee. Demeter's priestesses were called Melissai, "bees," because honey bees had a reputation of sexual purity.[305] These dutiful atten-

304. For example, "purify around," "purification around," "sprinkle around," "wipe all around," "cut all around," "pour all around," etc. Examples are collected by Pfister (1935) 149–52.

305. Schol. Pind. *Pyth.* 4.106c; Eur. *Hipp.* 73–77 and scholia; Parker (1983) 83 n. 37; Borthwick (1991) 560–63. On Paros, "Melissai" was the title for the women who abstained from intercourse for the Thesmophoria; Apollod. *FGrH* 244 F 89. Melissos, king at Paros, had sixty daughters whom Demeter instructed about the sufferings of Persephone when she gave the Parians her mysteries. The priestess

dants had to maintain such high levels of ritual purity because they were in charge of the special ritual objects that legitimated the community.[306] These objects had to be transported whenever a population moved—a fact illustrated by Polygnotos of Thasos in his famous painting at Delphi, in which he showed the priestess Kleiobeia carrying the sacred objects of Demeter to Thasos during the original migration *(apoikia)* from Paros.[307] Kleiobeia deserved a place among the famous heroes in the underworld because of her important role in the foundation of Thasos and because she met the standards her office required.

Kleiobeia was both priestess of Demeter and a *parthenos*. Normally, however, adult women who served the goddess were expected to marry and to have children. At Athens, the priestess of Demeter Thesmophoros had a reputation for maintaining strict purity, but when she was not required to perform duties on behalf of the goddess, she led a normal life. Both Demeter's worshippers and her ritual attendants rarely had to maintain long-term abstinence.[308] At Athens, the priestess of the Thesmophoroi had a husband,[309] and at Eleusis, the priestess of Demeter and Kore, named by patronymic (as was the custom),[310] had children.[311] These women could mix ritual responsibility with family life because the purification rites required for meeting Demeter's demands were so strenuous and therefore all the more powerful. At Delos, inscribed accounts list the piglet for mandatory purification of the Thesmophorion. At Eleusis, even the priestess's sacred residence had to be purified. The fees paid to purify the "sacred house where the priestess dwells" are listed in the Athenian accounts along with

---

Timo, who showed Miltiades how to cut through the sanctuary of Demeter when he was besieging Paros, was not reliable. The Pythia, however, did not blame her for allowing Miltiades to intrude on "sacred places not to be talked about with a man" but was satisfied with his punishment; Hdt. 6.134.

306. The priestess of Demeter Thesmophoros was an example of strict purity; Lucian *Tim.* 17, with Parker (1983) 90 n. 65.

307. Paus. 10.28.3.

308. Fehrle (1910) 104.

309. Broneer (1942) 265 no. 51, line 2, early second century, Athenian *agora.* Clinton (1974) 71 identifies her as priestess of Demeter and Kore at Eleusis. He does not explain, however, why the title is not in the more common Attic dual (e.g., Arist. *Thesm.* 83, 282. 297; *Ecc.* 443; *IG* II^2 1363, Eleusis).

310. Vestergaard et al. (1985).

311. Clinton (1974) 68–76; for priestesses of Demeter and Kore who had children, nos. 6, 10, 16. For the priestess's special house in the sanctuary, *IG* II^2 1672.127, 329/8 B.C.E.

the sum for the two piglets purchased to purify the sanctuary.[312] The priestess received the same treatment as the sanctuary.

Purity requirements for priestesses of Demeter, for Apollo's Pythia, the Women of Elis, and the Hellanodikai were so strict because the stakes were so high. Purity regulations are not just window dressing; they have social content. Purity codes not only reflect social divisions; they also indicate what a group really cares about. Any space whose activity depended on mutual recognition by potentially competitive political bodies needed divine protection. The *megaron* of the Thesmophoria, the *adyton* at Delphi, and the stadium at Olympia were such spaces. Rituals at Olympia were enacted in support of contests that represented the skills associated with waging war. Successful performance of such rituals was impossible without protection of a sacred truce announced months in advance of the beginning of the events. The games therefore represented the kind of peaceful interaction impossible to achieve in the competitive environment of ordinary political life. Regional oracles, especially the one at Delphi, operated the same way. City administrators submitted decisions to the Pythia to garner the support and approval their own procedures could neither achieve nor guarantee.

According to Pausanias, the gods paid the most attention to the Delphic oracle, the Olympic games, and the Eleusinian mysteries. He rates these celebrations on the basis of their public reputation and the impact of their sanctuaries.[313] Eleusis, however, was not the only place where the significance of Demeter was recognized and commemorated. Her most important festival, celebrated wherever Greeks settled, was the Thesmophoria, a public celebration managed by local administrations. At Athens, the Thesmophoria was administered in the deme. Demeter's Thesmophoria did not even always require a building. In Phokia, Demeter's little sanctuary at Anthela near Thermopylai was modest in the extreme and very different in scale from the public, ornamented sanctuary at Delphi. Nevertheless, Demeter was a regional divinity on a par with Apollo, and her sanctuary, a meeting place for the representatives of the participating states, was administered by the Pylaian (or Delphic) Amphictyony. Demeter, except for the anomaly of Eleusis, was rarely associated with a central-place sanctuary. Rather, she was recognized everywhere because her rituals were local, decentralized, and performed at the level of the smallest component of the *polis*.

312. *IG* II^2 1672.126–27.
313. Paus. 5.10.1.

The sexual status of Demeter's priestesses is an indicator of the status of her local rituals. Her priestesses were called Melissai because of temporary requirements to imitate sexless but active insects. At Delphi, Apollo's priestess had to imitate the bee on a permanent basis. Pindar's nickname for the Pythia was "Delphic Bee,"[314] a metaphor that also called attention to the harsh sound of her voice, reputedly projected through her body by will of the god and through no act of her own.[315] Other characteristics of the insect are even more relevant, especially the close connection between conscientious labor[316] and physical purity. If the tradition is reliable, the sexual status of the Delphic Pythia was guaranteed in earlier periods by youth[317] and in the Hellenistic period by age. In Diodorus's day the Pythia had to be a woman[318] past menopause[319] dressed in the clothing of a *parthenos,* a costume that marked her as equivalent to a female totally unacquainted with sex and childbirth.[320] Although an old woman, she stood in for a child.[321]

In order to emphasize the Pythia's close relationship to the god, access to the oracle was tightly guarded, and the priestess herself performed complicated preliminary purifications that separated her from the human community. The responses of the god were delivered in the *adyton,* a restricted

314. Pind. *Pyth.* 4.60–61: the oracle spoke "with the spontaneous sound of the Delphic bee," μελίσσας Δελφίδος αὐτομάτῳ κελάδῳ.

315. Cf. *Hymn. Hom. Merc.* 552–63 for the three sisters *(parthenoi)* who dwelled under a cleft of Parnassos as prophets. If fed on honey, they were willing to speak the truth. Herodotus mentions a Thracian oracle of Dionysos, where the one who gave the oracle was female. He compares her procedures to those at Delphi; Hdt. 7.111. For the mechanics of possession by a god in divination, see Maurizio (1995), with perhaps too much emphasis on the agency of the Pythia. Dewald (1981) 111–12 stresses the passivity of the Delphic priestess.

316. Eur. *Erechtheus* F 370K.85–86 (IV.85–86 Diggle): "of the much-laboring bee," πολυπόνου μελίσσης.

317. Aischylos, however, implies an aged priestess in the Classical period; Aesch. *Eum.* 38.

318. Actually, two women in rotation, with a third held in reserve; Plut. 414b.

319. Pythia in Delphi, Diod. Sic. 16.26.6 (for the age requirement); prophetess of Apollo at Argos, Paus. 2.24.1; priestess of Apollo in Epirus, Ael. *NA* 11.2; Sibyl at Kyme, Lyk. *Alex.* 1278–79. See also Parke and Wormell (1956) 1:35–41; Parker (1983) 93. On privileges associated with older women, see Henderson (1987b), esp. 115.

320. Blok and Mason (1987).

321. Aesch. *Eum.* 38; cf. the ambiguous γυνὴ παρθένος of schol. Eur. *Or.* 165. This ambiguity is misunderstood by Sissa (1990a), whose description of the oracular process requires that the Pythia be a real virgin. For the possibility that the Peleiades, "Doves"—priestesses of Zeus at Dodona—were old women, see Strab. 7.7.10–12; Parke (1967) 62; Bodson (1978) 101–2; Parker (1983) 93.

area of the temple. Other women did not enter this space, and they did not normally submit requests directly to the Pythia herself.[322] Her immediate audience was therefore exclusively male. Her sexual purity, replacing ties to husband and family, made her available for receiving and transmitting the voice of the god.[323] The rules that governed the Pythia's body earned special ties to Apollo and secured her location in a very sacred place at the center of the earth, but only if she met a standard of purity so strenuous that it completely removed her from the human cycle of sexual experience and genetic reproduction. In order to be considered an extension of the god, she had to achieve the status of a permanent "non-person"[324]—a status to which, it seems, only a sexless female could aspire.

322. Plut. *De E* 385c–d, where a Delphic riddle *(ainigma)* needing explanation is quoted: "It is possible for no woman to approach the place where the oracle is given (*χρηστήριον*)." Euripides' Ion tells the female chorus that they cannot step over the threshold (reading Hermann's *βαλόν* in 221) of the *adyton* (figuratively called "hollows"): *οὐ θέμις, ὦ ξέναι* (Eur. *Ion* 220–22). Although Fontenrose (1978) 217 n. 26 assumes from Ion's remarks (226–28) that women could have approached the oracle, he does not distinguish preliminary rites from the consultation itself. Ion indicates that females approached the altars (*ἐς θύμελας*) and even entered the inner temple (*ἐς μυχόν*), but it is clear that they did not have access to the restricted area where the Pythia actually spoke. Opportunistic mythical accounts credit responses to Telesilla of Argos (in response to her inquiry about her own health; Plut. *Mul. Virt.* 245c) and to Teiresias's daughter Manto, "founder" of Klaros (Paus. 7.3.1–2; 9.33.2); Parke and Wormell (1956) 2:38 no. 85 (Telesilla); 9 no. 20, 210 no. 523 (Manto). In the Hellenistic period, on very rare occasions, Delphi honored female performers with *promanteia; SIG*³ 689, 711; Pleket (1969) 16–18 no. 6. They even invited one of them to the *prytaneion.* These three awards to women from other cities are exceptional cases (among the hundreds of examples of *promanteia* being awarded to males); the honoring of a female, highly unusual itself, seems to have neutralized gender.

323. Fehrle (1910) argues that purity was a requirement because the priestess was considered married to the god; Sissa (1990a; 1990b), basing her description on Hippocratic notions of an interior tube connecting the vagina with the mouth, argues that virginity implied a body open to receive the power, and therefore the voice, of the god himself. For corrections to Sissa's description of Hippocratic female anatomy, see Hanson (1992a) 61–62 n. 58.

324. The expression is from Schachter (1992) 10.

5 The Plague of Infertility

MALE REPRODUCTIVE ANXIETY

The women at Aristophanes' Thesmophoria suggest that those who produced sons for the city should receive public honors at the Stenia.[1] Their audience knew, however, that honors for women were not publicly proclaimed at festivals and that the Stenia, a festival that excluded males, would not provide the platform for celebrity that public proclamation at the Dionysia gave to men.

Women did not deserve public honors for raising children because the maternal impulse was considered a fact of nature. Xenophon's Sokrates makes that clear when he distinguishes the "desire for creating children," *eros teknopoiias*,[2] from sexual passion, *aphrodisia*, and recognizes it as innate in both male and female. The impulse to nourish children, however, he attributes to mothers alone.[3] He argues that men choose their wives on the basis of their ability to bear healthy children,[4] and that although fathers contribute material support, it is mothers who share their own sustenance in pregnancy and risk their lives in childbirth without knowing how their

1. Ar. *Thes.* 830–45.

2. Cf. Eur. *Ion* 67: ἔρωτι παίδων. See also Arist. *EN* 1155a: the affection of parent for child is natural; 1158: but it is not the same as the affection of child for parent.

3. Xen. *Mem.* 1.4.7. Xenophon ranks the love of parents for children above the love of children for parents, brothers for brothers, wives for husbands, and comrades for comrades; *Hier.* 3.7. He says nothing about the love of husbands for wives. Cf. Lycurg. *Leoc.* 100: it is a natural characteristic for all women to love their children.

4. Xen. *Mem.* 2.2.4.

pains will be rewarded.[5] Mothers make sacrifices because they have a natural affection for their infants.[6]

Fatherhood was nevertheless considered a blessing. The Greek attitude is abundantly clear in Herodotus's tale about Solon's visit to Kroisos, ruler of the Lydians and one of the richest men of his day. When Kroisos asked Solon to name the most blessed *(olbiotatos)* person he knew,[7] he was surprised to hear Solon's answer: "Tellos the Athenian." Solon explained that Tellos had lived to see his son's sons and had died fighting on behalf of his city. Kroisos did not understand that Solon rated successful family life and service to the community higher than personal fortune, military success, or political power and so did not grasp the explanation. When told that second place went to Kleobis and Biton, two young men from Argos who died young, without wealth, he was dumbfounded. The reason, however, is simple. When the oxen did not come home from the fields in time to draw their mother's cart to a scheduled festival, they dragged the cart with their mother in it to Hera's sanctuary themselves. Impressed by their achievement, the Argive men blessed them for their strength, and the Argive women blessed their mother for her children. When the mother then asked Hera to grant her sons a gift, the goddess bestowed the greatest gift she could: to live not one day longer but in her temple to fall asleep forever with the praise of their countrymen still ringing in their ears. Herodotus calls this the best fulfillment a life could have. He agrees with Solon, who measured Tellos's prosperity by the health and number of his children,[8] and for Kleobis and Biton deemed exemplary service for their mother their highest achievement and an early, painless death their greatest reward.

Kleobis and Biton are called *olbiotatoi,* "most blessed," because the goddess fulfilled the Argives' benediction. Herodotus's verb for the Argive people's act of blessing (μακαρίζειν) refers to a ritual speech act called *makarismos,* a public, ritual pronouncement of happiness, prosperity, and blessing from the gods. Like a curse, a *makarismos* was directed at another person and required the participation of the gods, but its purpose was to

5. Xen. *Mem.* 2.2.5. On the risk to mothers, see Demand (1994). The only women honored for childbirth were those who died in the act: Vedder (1988) 161–91.

6. Xen. *Mem.* 7.21–22, 24–35; Lycurg. *Leoc.* 100. See also Arist. *EN* 1155a, where the *philia* of parents for children and children for parents is natural, but, in 1158b, not the same because "father" and "son" are not equals.

7. This story is told in Hdt. 1.30–31.

8. Foxhall (1995a) 133–34, for a slightly different interpretation of this fable.

wish good fortune instead of bad.[9] The blessing most people aspired to was reproductive success.[10] Solon's reply to Kroisos suggests that reproductive success was a sign of prosperity, and Kroisos's failure to understand portends the loss of his kingdom and death of his only viable son—deprivations equivalent to the heaviest curse a man could bear.[11]

Solon's Greek contemporaries would have understood the difference between a Lydian potentate who evaluated wealth in terms of gold and their own poets, who measured a man's happiness by his progeny[12] and a city's prosperity by the fecundity of its women and the health of its children.[13] Reproductive anxiety is a common theme in Greek literature and when described from the male point of view, is influenced by concerns about female fertility and wives' sexual loyalty.[14] Responsibility for sterility and for failure in childbirth was usually attributed to the female. Families desperate for children resorted to drugs, incantations, and amulets, and even traveled to visit healing sanctuaries and oracles. In Attic tragedy Andromache dispenses drugs *(pharmaka)* to Hermione to deprive Neoptolemos of a child,[15] and Medea offers drugs to Aegeus to help him "sow" one.[16] Midwives were often consulted. Plato's Sokrates describes his own mother as a professional midwife—a woman who knew incantations and remedies for reproductive problems.[17] Few early incantations survive, but the later tradition is rich

9. The gift of the goddess is not bestowed without irony. *Makarizein* elsewhere in the narrative is a symptom of presumption; see Hdt. 7.18.3, 7.45–46.1, 9.93.4. Arist. *Rh.* 1367b33–34, makes a distinction between *makarismos* and *eudaimonismos* on the one hand, and praise and encomium on the other. The early literary evidence for *makarismos* is collected by Dirichlet (1914).

10. *Hymn Hom. Ap.* 14, for the terminology (if not the form) of a *makarismos* for a mother. For the *makarismos* of parents on account of their children, see Dirichlet (1914) 28–32; Ar. *Thes.* 845 may be a parody of such formulas.

11. Hdt. 1.44–45. Herodotus's praise of Tellos is a *makarismos* for a father, the opposite of the traditional curse. Herodotus recognizes the depth of a father's emotional investment in a son when he describes the Persian custom of keeping young sons with the women until five years old to protect fathers from the distress of the death of a son in infancy; Hdt.1.136.

12. Ar. *Ach.* 254–56, with schol. on 255; Aristophanes uses the term *makarios.*

13. *Od.* 19.108–14; Ar. *Pax* 1325; Eur. *Andr.* 418; *Ion* 472–80; Raepsaet (1971) on the reasons for having children.

14. For the theme elsewhere in Herodotus, see Dewald (1981) 122, I.A.2.

15. Eur. *Andr.* 32–33, 157–58, 355–56.

16. Eur. *Med.* 717–8.

17. Pl. *Tht.* 149b–e. Plato's analogy makes it clear that midwives used both drugs and incantations; *Men.* 80a; *Char.* 156d; *Tht.* 149d. Cf. Xen. *Mem.* 2.6.10 and Ar. *Nub.* 135–39; Tomin (1987) 99–102.

with a variety of spells and charms. One class of spells was designed to control the uterus.[18] Another series of specialized incantations was intended for a husband who wanted to subdue a wife's womb,[19] and substances were used to test a woman's ability to receive her husband's seed.[20] Amulets were worn, attached to the body or clothing,[21] to remedy reproductive problems[22] and to aid delivery.[23] The evidence of the surviving examples indicates a belief system consistent with the descriptions of female physical nature in Greek scientific literature.[24]

Reproductive anxiety is also a frequent theme in the questions men put to oracles. Fifth- and fourth-century examples from the oracle of Zeus at Dodona show that the inquiries of ordinary people were concerned above all with crops, professions, and the ability to have children. Requests to oracles in Classical literature repeat the same themes. Euripides' Ion, at Delphi, assumes Kreousa and her husband are visiting Apollo's sanctuary for

18. Plin. *HN* 28.81 associates a collection of gynecological remedies he calls *monstrifica* with the name of Lais, attached to a variety of texts on gynecological matters; Aubert (1989) 429 n. 12. From Pliny's comments it seems that she was connected with abortifacients.

19. *Pharmaka* were used to control the uterus; Eur. *Andr.* 32–33, 157–58; *Med.* 717–18; Hyp. F 67 (Jensen). For other references see Aubert (1989) n. 47, with a recipe for a mixture applied to a male to secure exclusive entitlement to his partner's womb: "Take an egg of a crow and the juice of the plant crow's foot and gall of a river electric eel, and grind them with honey and say the spell whenever you grind and whenever you smear it on your genitals. This is the spell that is to be spoken: 'I say to you, womb of NN, open and receive the seed of NN and the uncontrollable seed of the IARPHE ARPHE (write it). Let her, NN, love me for all her time as Isis loved Osiris and let her remain chaste for me as Penelope did of Odysseus. And do you, womb, remember me for all the time of my life, because I am AKARNACHTHAS.' Say this while grinding and whenever you rub your genitals, and in this way have intercourse with the woman you wish, and she will love you alone and by no one else will she ever be laid, just by you alone" (translated by E. N. O'Neil in *PGM* XXXVI.283–94). For similar commands to the womb, cf. Kotanksky (1994) 360–68 no. 61, a Greek charm found in a grave in Nubia, third or fourth century C.E. Hanson (1995b) 283 discusses the general appeal of amulets in the eastern Mediterranean.

20. Hanson (1995b) 291.

21. Pl. *Resp.* 726a-b. See Faraone (1990) and Hanson (1995b) on amulets. The amulet worn by Perikles, as reported by Theophr. *Ethics* (F 463 Fortenbaugh; Plut. *Per.* 38.1–2), had no reproductive value.

22. Examples in Bonner (1950) 88–89.

23. *Mul.* 1.77 (8:172 Littré), quoted by Hanson (1995b) 288: "Smear the fruit of a wild cucumber already white on wax, wind up on crimson fleece, and affix around her loins."

24. Hanson (1995b) 284.

one of only two reasons when he asks, "Have you come for the sake of fruit of the earth or for the sake of children?"[25]

At Dodona, visitors wrote their questions for the oracle on small lead tablets and submitted them to Zeus. Men's queries are concerned family and fatherhood, anxiety about the fertility of their wives, and the possibility of reproductive failure.[26] The inquirer wrote on a little strip of lead in his own dialect and his own handwriting, then rolled or folded it and labeled the outside with a letter. The variety of scripts and alphabets and the idiosyncratic grammar make individual examples very difficult to date, but the corpus as a whole extends from the late sixth century to the middle of the third century. Visitors expected the god to take an interest in very personal matters.

These men asked the oracle not only about their fields and property, but whether they should marry, how they might have children (especially male children), and whether their wives' offspring were truly their own. A Greek husband was anxious to produce male children[27] and needed confirmation that any child born to his wife was really his.[28]

1. Gods. Good fortune. Euandros and his wife consult Zeus Naios and Dione: to which of the gods or heroes or *daimones* should they pray and sacrifice in order to fare better and more well, both themselves and their household, both now and for all time?[29]

2. About his belongings, offspring, and wife: by praying to which of the gods may I fare well?[30]

25. Eur. *Ion* 303; cf. 423–24. See Dougherty (1993) 257–58 for the issue linked to colonial discourse.

26. A large proportion of the published tablets from Dodona record private inquiries, all but one from males. The single identifiably female writer is concerned about her health; Parke (1967) no. 15.

27. [Dem.] 43.12; Xen. *Oec.* 7.12; Aeschin. 3.111; Ar. *Pax* 1325; Mikalson (1983) 25.

28. Lys. 1.33; discussed by Gardner (1989) 52 in connection with adultery. As Gardner shows, if a child who is not the father's is introduced into a family, it is the *oikos*, not the father, that suffers the taint. A similar view is argued by Konstan (1994) 224 in a slightly different context. In the case of the hereditary kingship at Sparta, doubts about paternity were taken seriously, as the case of Demaratos indicates; see Hdt. 6.61–69.

29. Parke (1967) 263 no. 1. Translations follow but do not exactly reproduce those of Parke. Publication of these tablets has been slow. Parke's collection in appendix 1 can be supplemented by *SEG* 15.385–409; 19.426–32; 23.473; 24.454; J. Robert and L. Robert, *BE* 1939.153; 1957.584; 1959.231; 1961.171. See now Christidis, Dakaris, and Votokopoulou (1997) 55 no.1 (*περὶ γενεᾶς*).

30. Fifth century, unfolded; Parke (1967) 264 no. 3.

3. Hermon: by attaching (himself) to which of the gods may there be offspring from Keretaia, beneficial sometime for his livelihood(?).[31]
4. God: Gerioton asks Zeus about a wife, if it is better for him to take one.[32]
5. Herakleidas asks Zeus and Dione for good fortune and asks the god about having children: if there will be any from his wife, Aigle, the one he now has.[33]
6. Kallikrates asks the god if there will be offspring for me from Nike, the wife whom he has, by remaining with her and praying to which of the gods.[34]
7. God. Good Fortune. Anaxippos asks Zeus Naios and Dione about male offspring from Pilistoa, his wife: by praying to which of the gods may I fare best and most well?[35]
8. . . . or should I take another one (female)?[36]
9. . . . whether she might have children if she is intimate with me.[37]
10. . . . (if it is) better for Onasimos to get a wife for himself.[38]
11. . . . for Kleanor about paternal offspring from Gontha, his present wife.[39]
12. Lysanias asks Zeus Naios and Deona if the infant is not from him with which Annyla is pregnant.[40]
13. . . . asks if it is better and more profitable for him to take a wife and will there be children to take care of Isodemos in his old age and is it better for him to go to move to Athens and become a citizen there.[41]

Families had good cause to be concerned. Birth rates were low, and infant and child mortality high. Early cemetery population counts do not al-

31. Parke (1967) 264 no. 5.
32. *BE* 1939.153 no. 37; Parke (1967) 265 no. 6.
33. Parke (1967) 265 no. 7.
34. Parke (1967) 265 no. 8.
35. *BE* 1959.231; Parke (1967) 266 no. 9.
36. *BE* (1939) 153 no. 39.
37. *BE* (1939) 153 no. 27, in Corinthian alphabet.
38. *BE* (1939) 153 no. 14, in Corinthian alphabet.
39. *BE* (1939) 153 no. 15, in Corinthian alphabet.
40. Parke (1967) 266 no. 11.
41. Guarducci, *Epigrafia* 4 84.

ways include young children, but where they do, they confirm high rates of very early death. Among eighth-century burials at Pithekoussai, 27 percent were infants or stillborn infants and 39 percent of the others were children.[42] At the Pantanello cemetery at Metapontum in the fifth century, 40 percent of the cemetery population was children in spite of the area's good agricultural resources.[43] The grief of parents is not easy to measure,[44] but a high proportion of the inscribed tomb monuments at Athens in the sixth century were for adolescents, and in the North Cemetery at Corinth, where 536 graves were excavated, child burials have 60 percent more vases than adult burials.[45] Lineages were fragile, and many landholders must have died without an heir. At early Iron Age Knossos, where women and children were buried with men in what appear to be family tombs, 44 percent of the tombs served only two generations.[46] Public sentiment emphasized ancestors and ancestral tradition, but in actuality family cycles were of short duration. Family memory at Athens rarely claims to extend beyond grandfathers,[47] even for elite families. Among group burials at Metapontum, family lines do not persist through more than three generations. Classical tomb reliefs at Athens emphasize family groups, but it is the nuclear family that is stressed, not the extended lineage.[48] The material evidence is all the more striking when considered in the context of the rates of reproduction for agricultural societies. At Metapontum, where 50 percent of the infants born did not reach sexual maturity and the life expectancy of females was only thirty-eight years, even if every marriage produced progeny, each adult woman would have had to complete at least six successful pregnancies to simply maintain the population.[49] The odds of success could not have been good. In agricultural societies in general, about one in three families fails to produce a son and one in six fails to produce

42. Ridgway (1992) 51–53.
43. Carter (1998) 144.
44. As Golden (1988) 152–63 recognizes.
45. Blegen (1964) 78–79.
46. Cavanagh (1991) 99.
47. Thomas (1989) 124–26.
48. Death is a disruption of the lineage; Osborne (1996) explains the prominence of women on Attic funerary monuments after 500 B.C.E. in terms of the drive to perpetuate the *oikos* and validate the status of parents. Humphreys (1983) 108–19, however, reports that of the six hundred fourth-century Athenian epitaphs with deme affiliation, most are for single individuals. The most frequent combination (88 examples) is that of husband and wife; with husband, wife, and child second (50 examples).
49. Carter (1998) 512.

any children at all.[50] The high rate of maternal mortality is another factor in slowing rates of reproduction.[51]

The language of formal Greek betrothal makes it clear that production of children was the purpose of marriage.[52] The *engyesis,* the pledge exchanged between the bride's father and the groom, exploits an agricultural metaphor to define the relationship between husband and wife.[53] Menander preserves the formula:

> Well, then, I pledge (ἐγγύω) my daughter to you, young man, for the plowing of legitimate children, and I am giving, in addition to her, a dowry worth three talents.[54]

The agreement was made before witnesses because the ritual of *engyesis,* "betrothal," was one of the events that identified children from the union as *gnesioi* (belonging to the family) and therefore legal heirs to family property.[55] The formula identified the male as the active partner in sexual intercourse and the woman as the passive field waiting to receive his seed—ideas natural in a language where verbs of sexual connection were used in the active voice only of the male.[56] The agricultural metaphor reflects the

50. Morris (1986) 107. Reproductive rates can be estimated, but real data is rare. On female infertility, Sallares (1991) 104, with reference to the reputation of Troizen. Even in the families of Roman emperors, where the desire for successors was pressing, few emperors had more than one son, and even those who did often survived their own children. Neonatal and childhood mortality was the great risk, and fathers were often disappointed. For the emotional impact on a father who lost five only children, each dying before the next was born, see Fronto, *De Nepote Amisso,* 2 and 4, quoted by Scheidel (1999) 267.

51. Demand (1994); see *SEG* 44.1729 on epitaphs for those who have just given birth.

52. Cf. Xen. *Mem.* 2.2.4.

53. Greek metaphors expressing homology between human and agricultural reproduction have been widely noted, in detail by Edmunds (1981) 221–38. For the imagery of agriculture in the wedding ceremony itself, see Redfield (1982).

54. Men. *Dys.* 842–46 Sandbach; the same formula is repeated by Menander in *Mis.* 444–46 Sandbach; *Pk.* 1012–15 Sandbach; *Sam.* 726–28 Sandbach; and in several fragments. Cf. Clem. Al. *Strom.* 2.23 for the symbolism of sowing; Carson (1990) 146.

55. The agreement was marked by an exchange of pledges *(pisteis)* between the two men. See Men. *Dys.* 308, where Sostratos indicates that he loves Myrrhine so much that he is ready to pledge (πίστιν ἐπιθεὶς διατελεῖν στέργων) to take her even without a dowry. For the distinction between *pistis* and *horkos,* see Arist. *Rh.* 1375a10: ὅρκους δεξιὰς πίστεις ἐπιγαμίας. The father offers a pledge of daughter and dowry (δίδωμι), and the young man accepts (ἔχω, λαμβάνω, στέργω, Men. *Sam.* 729).

56. Bain (1991) 51–77. Cf. Aesch. *TrGF* F 13 Radt: σοὶ μὲν γαμεῖσθαι μόρσιμον, γαμεῖν δ' ἐμοί, "It is your lot to get yourself married, but it is mine to

asymmetrical relationship between husband and wife and makes it clear that a wife produced children for her husband's family. It was natural to describe the male progenitor as sower in a language where *sperma* could refer to the seed of both plants and animals, and *gone*, "offspring," was used for children as well as for the fruit of the earth.[57]

Reproductive success was evidence of a city's judicial maturity, an idea illustrated by Hesiod with his comparison of the city of "straight judgments" (*dikai itheiai*, 225–26) with the city of "crooked judgments" (*skoliai dikai*, 250). His descriptions assume a close connection between reproduction and judicial process. The city of crooked judgments is marked by a sterile landscape and reproductive failure. Visited by hunger (λιμός) and pestilence (λοιμός), its people waste away, the women no longer bear children, and households decline.[58] The signs of a successful city are the opposite: successful agriculture, successful animal husbandry, and successful childbirth.[59] The city that gives straight judgments is a city that blooms, where peace nourishes the young, the earth gives forth its bounty, and

> the oak in the mountains bears acorns at the tips of its branches and honey in its midst, the woolly sheep are heavy with fleeces, the women bear children resembling their fathers,[60] and these people flourish forever with good things.[61]

---

marry." For γαμεῖν as the act of sexual intercourse itself, Robert (1967) 77–81; cf. Eur. *Ion* 72.

57. Aischylos describes Oidipous as one who "by sowing the chaste furrow of his mother where he was nourished, brought forth a bloody root" (*Sept.* 753–56). When Sophokles' Kreon tells his son Haimon to give up Antigone, he says, "arable fields of other woman are (always available)"; Soph. *Ant.* 569.

58. Hes. *Op.* 243, following West (against Solmsen) in accepting lines 244–45 as part of at least one of the principal versions of the poem.

59. Hes. *Op.* 225–36.

60. Technically, γονεύς means the one who engenders seed—in the singular, "father," but in the plural, usually "parents." There are two possible distinctions to draw here: one contrasts children who resemble their parents with children who look like monsters, and the other compares children who look like their father to children who do not. For the city, the first was important; for the individual father, the second. The sign of a successful father was sons who resembled him; Quint. Smyrn. 5.527: υἱὸν ἐοικότα πάντα τοκῆι. In the keen competition for reputation, women scrutinized other peoples' children to identify any who did not resemble their fathers; Ath. 190e: πάνυ γὰρ αἱ γυναῖκες διὰ τὸ παρατηρεῖσθαι τὴν ἀλλήλων σωφροσύνην δειναὶ τὰς ὁμοιότητας τῶν παίδων πρὸς τοὺς γονέας ἐλέγξαι. To know one's father was a sign of civilization and indicated the success of the institution of marriage, at Athens attributed to Kekrops; Ath. 555d. Helen is the first to recognize whose son Telemachos is; *Od.* 4.138–46, and from Ar. *Thesm.* 514–16, it is clear that babies, especially male babies, were supposed to resemble

Judicial responsibility is delegated to males who exploit the earth, and reproductive responsibility is allotted to females, equated with the soil. Objectified and classified with other means of production, women take their place among the possessions of men: tilled fields, woodlands, and flocks. Agricultural and reproductive success is evidence of judicial propriety. Hunger (λιμός, 230) and doom (ἄτη, 231)—punishments from the gods—do not visit those who make straight judgments (230).

Hesiod's catalogue of the signs of judicial success imitates a *makarismos;* his catalogue of the signs of judicial failure echoes the opposite. The city of crooked judgments suffers the traditional punishments of the formulaic curse incorporated in every formal oath, which threatens failure in the primary areas of male productivity. The oath of the Athenians at Plateia in 479 illustrates a version of the formula used by Hesiod:

> And if I abide by the conditions inscribed in the oath, may my city be without disease, but if (I do) not, may it be sick. And may my city be unravaged, but if (I do) not, may it be destroyed. And may the earth bring forth fruits, but if (I do) not, may it be barren. And may the women bear children resembling their fathers, but if (I do) not, monsters. And may the cattle bring forth (offspring that look) like cattle, but if (I do) not, monsters.[62]

Sterile earth and barren wives were signs of broken oaths and promises not kept—a theme that recurs in one of the most elaborate Greek curses on record, the curse paired with the oath of the Pylaian Amphictyony:

> If anyone violates these conditions, whether as representative of the *polis,* private person, or member of an ethnic community, let them be

---

their fathers. For Aristotle, the best result of the successful concoction of semen at conception results in a male child who looks like his father; the second best, a male who looks like his paternal grandfather; and the third, a male who looks like his mother. Female children are lumped together in fourth place, and last of all come monsters—divided between children who resemble no member of the family and the real monsters, children born with too many hands or feet; *Gen. An.* 767a36–b5. For more examples, see West (1978) on *Op.* 235. For a discussion of monsters in this sense, see Lenfant (1999). This is a good place to recall the curse of Demaratos's mother on those who would doubt her oath to secure her son's paternity: "Do not lend a word of belief to any other tales of your birth. I have given you the whole and absolute truth. For Leotychides and all who tell stories like his: may their wives all bear them sons by their muleteers" (Hdt. 6.69, trans. Grene).

61. Translation follows West. Compare *Od.* 19.108–14; the list of items reflects an ancient Mediterranean tradition; see Levit. 26 and Deut. 28.

62. *GHI* II no. 204. Because the text was not inscribed until the fourth century, many believe the oath is not genuine.

> under a curse (*enages*) of Apollo, Artemis, Leto, and Athena Pronoia . . . may their land not bear fruit; their women not bear children resembling their fathers, but monsters; nor their flocks bear young according to nature; and may they have defeat in war, law court, and *agora* and complete destruction for themselves, their family, and their lineage.[63]

Curses like this were a regular part of the formulas by which citizens were bound to political obligation and collective responsibility, and they were required components in the formal agreements between cities. They are included in the texts of the treaties and public documents by which cities established and maintained diplomatic relations with their peers.[64] The rhetoric of oaths and curses recognized that bonds to family were stronger than ties to peers or ties to the city and that ritual expressions of unity were therefore needed to create the artificial bonds that maintained the male community. Like fields and animals, wives were rated as valuable productive property that was at risk. Healthy children represented the community's success, and failed birth and diseased or deformed children marked a city's collective failure.[65] The consequences of breaking an oath were said to be dire. The child of Oath pursued and punished those who swore falsely or who broke an oath:

> The child of Oath has no name, no hands, no feet, but he is swift in pursuit, until, grasping a man's whole house and lineage, he destroys it utterly.[66]

Political responsibility was premised on an alliance of eligible males, each representing his own family. Every oath defined the family as security for the citizen's loyalty to the community. Treason was punished by a kind of death that wiped out the family and its future; punishment included appropriation of property, destruction of the family home, and denial of hereditary privilege to the condemned man's children.

63. As preserved in the manuscript of Aeschin. 3.110–11. Curses like these, originating in the Mesopotamian cultures of the Sumerians and Akkadians, were widespread in the eastern Mediterranean. Similar patterns occur in the oaths of other Greek cities; Strubbe (1991) 49 n. 35, for the Near Eastern material, and n. 34, for the Greek material.

64. For a similar catalogue, cf. Eur. *Hel.* 1327–37, where the mother of the gods, in sorrow for her daughter, wastes the crops in the fields, the offspring of the people, the flourishing herds, the sacrifices to the gods, and the sweet spring water.

65. For the prayer for blessings, cf. Aesch. *Suppl.* 630–710, esp. 674–79, for successful harvests and successful childbirth. The same prayer appears on Athena's lips at the close of Aesch. *Eum.* 1025 ff., until the text fails.

66. Hdt. 6.86.

Deformity and stillbirth were symptoms of pollution, which, whether individual or collective, could defile the entire community. Sophokles emphasizes this repeatedly when he describes the curse on Oidipous as a curse on his people and his land as well as a curse on himself. When the priest describes the city struck by plague (28: λοιμός), the land is as sick as its people, "wasting together with the budding fruit of the earth, wasting in the pastures of the herds, wasting in the barren childbirth of the women" (25–27).[67] Sophokles reverses Hesiod's images of the city in success to describe the city in distress:

> Neither will the offspring (ἔκγονα) of the famous earth show increase nor do the women recover from their labor of cries with [the birth of live] children.[68]

The perverted marriage of Oidipous and Jocasta, direct cause of the city's misfortune, is described in agricultural metaphors that closely link sterility of the soil, *limos,* and sterility of the population, *loimos.* Oidipous describes Jocasta as "same sown" (by himself and Laios)[69] and himself as "sower of the same wife" as his father.[70] The chorus calls Jocasta Oidipous's "paternal furrows," plowed by his own father,[71] and the messenger reverts to the same metaphor when he describes Oidipous as reaching "twice his mother's furrow (ἄρουραν), furrow of his own and furrow of his children."[72] His children are growing plants,[73] and the distress of the city is reflected in the sterility of his daughters, who were ineligible for marriage, their infertility described in terms of barren land.[74]

Human infertility was a plague sent by the gods, a pestilence, a communicable disease. It was not a problem for individuals but a problem for the entire population. As Hesiod puts it, the whole city suffers for the misdeeds of one man:

> Often even the whole *polis* suffers on account of one evil man, who does wrong and contrives outrageous deeds, and on these people the

67. For agricultural imagery in this play, see DuBois (1988).
68. Soph. *OT* 171–73.
69. Soph. *OT* 260: ὁμόσπορον, passive verbal adjective: literally, "same-sown."
70. Soph. *OT* 460: ὁμόσπορος, active verbal adjective; see Jebb's note *ad loc.*
71. Soph. *OT* 1211. Cf. Eur. *Ph.* 18: μὴ σπεῖρε τέκνων ἄλοκα, "do not sow the furrow (wife) with children."
72. Soph. *OT* 1257–58. He plowed the place where he was sown (1485) and plowed the one who bore him (1497).
73. Soph. *OT* 1376: βλαστοῦσ' ὅπως ἔβλαστε.
74. Soph. *OT* 1502: χέρσους φθαρῆναι.

> son of Kronos sends from the heavens above great disasters, hunger,
> and plague together, and the people keep dying.[75]

When Aischines quotes the same lines in his speech against Kteisiphon, he is reminded of the language of oracles.[76] Thucydides, who is himself contemptuous of such oracles, nevertheless reports that during the plague at Athens, many people believed their suffering had been predicted by oracles threatening plague *(loimos)*, misunderstood as oracles threatening dearth *(limos)*.[77] The words *limos* and *loimos* chime together in many literary versions of the traditional oracles identified with Delphi.[78] Most appear in mythical narratives emphasizing the pervasive anxieties of a people concerned about the vitality of the land and the health of their children.[79]

BODIES OF WATER AND MINIATURE LANDSCAPES

Similar anxieties about illness and sterility pervade the corpus of the early medical writers, whose works reflect the concerns of contemporary medical practitioners and the people they treated. Reproductive failure was a primary target for practitioners, and the earliest Hippocratic writings were gynecological catalogues—remedies and procedures collected for practical use.[80] These collections preserved traditional therapies used by midwives and "wise women," recording them for the new, literate practitioners of the late fifth and early fourth centuries: male physicians who claimed to treat disorders of the female reproductive system.[81] Practical rather than theoretical, these new texts put the female body at the center of discussions about diagnosis and treatment of reproductive failure.[82]

75. Hes. *Op.* 240–43. Hesiod's description of the disasters suffered by the cursed in the last line, rich in assonance and alliteration, is especially ominous.

76. Aeschin. 3.136.

77. Thuc. 2.54.

78. Parke and Wormell (1956) 2:10–11, 13, 72, 83, 108, 125, 158, 169, 179, 200, 221, 237, 210, 388, 390–91, 398, 487, 493, 572.

79. However, in the late fourth century B.C.E. a real father, attributing his daughter's successful and easy birth to a Delphic response, named her "Delphis" in recognition; *FdDelph* 3.1 560 (*SEG* 3.400).

80. The Hippocratic gynecological catalogues are among the earliest extant examples of Greek prose; Dean-Jones (1994) 10.

81. Demand (1994) 94.

82. Hanson (1992a 33–35 and (1992b) 36–37 for the distinction between the gynecological catalogues and the theoretical works of the Hippocratic corpus; and Hanson (1989) 40–41 for the influence of the female tradition. On methodology in

Theory followed fast on the heels of practice,[83] and concerns about reproduction were a major incentive to those developing systematic theories about conception and embryology. Explanations of reproductive processes, like the earlier catalogues of practical remedies, focused on the female body as a problem to be solved. Descriptions of the mechanics of reproduction assumed a sympathy between the human body and the natural world, and theorists argued that the health of a population was influenced by the local landscape. Female fecundity was now a function of the environment and local weather patterns. This idea is most systematically developed in the Hippocratic *Airs, Waters, Places,* where the author attempts to demonstrate the influence on health of location and orientation of a city and the nature and availability of its water. Here, local environment is a key to diagnosis, and regulation of moisture a sound therapeutic strategy. Exposure to the four winds and the sun is considered vital because wind and sun are regulators of heat and cold, dry and wet, and so determine the composition of the soil, the characteristics of the local water supply, and therefore, the disposition of the bodies of local residents. Health is achieved by maintaining a balance between the opposites: heat and cold, dry and wet. Disease is the result of excess, which can be tempered by diet and lifestyle—the only conditions the physician could modify.[84]

The first half of *Airs, Waters, Places* presents a typology of city environments. In each environment the reproductive capacity of the city's women is the best indication of the community's health. The best location for a *polis* is facing the east wind; the best water comes from high ground. In a town facing east the women are prolific, childbirth easy, and the population healthy. Towns facing south might be well endowed with water, but exposure to excessive moisture makes their women suffer from vaginal discharge, sterility, and miscarriage; too much moisture inflicts children with convulsions and asthma; and for males, it leads to diarrhea, dysentery, fevers, skin eruptions, and hemorrhoids.[85] Towns facing north have hard, brackish water, which makes the men sinewy and causes them to suffer constipation, pleurisy, oozing from the eyes, and even epilepsy; it makes the women sterile, causes them to suffer from painful menstruation

the *Epidemics,* Demand (1994) 45–46 makes a distinction between case history and close observation of the individual case. For self-conscious literacy in the *Epidemics,* cf. King (1998) 57.

83. Hanson (1991).

84. King (1998) 169 for disease as an indication of loss of self-control, reversible only if the physician can assert control over the patient.

85. *Aër.* 3.

and childbirth, and contributes to poor milk, infections, convulsions, and anorexia.[86]

The effect of the water supply on a population's health is determined by its source: stagnant water comes from marshes or lakes, hard water from rock springs, sweet water from high ground, and brackish water from rain or melted snow. For men, lake or marsh water contributes to dysentery, diarrhea, enlarged spleen, and fevers; but for women, it causes excessive uterine moisture, which is in turn responsible for tumor, discharge, painful childbirth, and false pregnancy.[87] Seasonal changes and extremes of climate are dangerous, with special problems occurring at the transitional periods marking the chronological turning points of the year: winter and summer solstices and autumnal and vernal equinoxes.[88]

The second half of *Airs, Waters, and Places* distinguishes the great regional environments of the world, with Europe at the center as the standard by which all other regions are measured. Each area has its own climate and ecology, local populations are identified with the landscape they inhabit, and the reproductive capacity of females is the index of local health. The Scythians, farthest to the north and dwelling on barren soil in a cold and harsh climate, are small but "fleshy," with "watery" joints because the water they drink comes from melted snow.[89] As a consequence, they are physically flabby, mentally sluggish, and unprolific. The men are weak and the women fat. Habit and local custom exaggerate their weaknesses. Riding horseback reduces male sexual appetite; and in females, excessive weight weakens sexual desire and clogs the cervix with soft fat. Menstruation is scant, conception difficult, and the Scythian birth rate low.[90]

Transitional areas dividing the three major geographical areas of Europe, Asia, and Africa have a more variegated terrain and produce a more diverse population. Some people are like "wooded and well-watered moun-

86. *Aër.* 4.

87. *Aër.* 7. Environmental factors may have contributed to population decline at Troizen in the fourth century B.C.E. Theophrastos attributed a local problem of sterility to the wine (*HP* 9.8.11 Wimmer); Aristotle explained it by the custom of marrying too early (*Pol.* 1335a). Sallares (1991) 104 and n. 480 gives the background.

88. *Aër.* 11. For water as a primary theme in the discovery, see Jouanna (1994) 28–29; on water and the city, Ath. 2.42–43; 2.46b–c.

89. *Aër.* 19.

90. *Aër.* 21. Deviation from this standard is explained, paradoxically by social status. Female domestic servants, presumably non-Scythians, active and slender, conceive as soon as they "go to a man."

tains," others like "thin and arid soil," some like "meadowy and marshy places," and others like "a flat plain or dry, parched earth."[91] Excess moisture is identified with female characteristics, and places with too much moisture are described as producing feminized plants and crops.[92]

Hippocratic therapies emphasize a close relationship between body and landscape, and water is an important element of irrigation in both realms. The landscape becomes a metaphor for the body, and images of the landscape can be analyzed to design cures for afflicted parts. Dreams have therapeutic content, and dreams of an ordered landscape promise health when the dreamer is able

> to see clearly and hear distinctly things on the earth; to walk safely and run safely and swiftly without fear; to see the earth smooth and well-tilled and trees flourishing, laden with fruit and well-kept; to see the rivers flowing normally with water clear and neither in flood nor with their flow lessened, and for springs and wells the same. All these things indicate the subject's health, and that the body, its flows, the food ingested and the excreta, are normal.[93]

In dreams, rivers represent circulation of the blood; foul streams indicate problems with the bowels; floods signify disease, storms at sea, and stomach disorders; and bare earth means terminal illness.[94]

Health is most easily achieved in cities that, like the typical Greek temple, face east and the rising sun.[95] Populations are grouped by gender, and children are classified with men. Health is possible when both male and female live in harmony with the landscape, but because female hydrology is more complex than that of the male, the female has a more complex relationship with the land. Sterility is the primary concern. Hippocratic therapy divided female from male because Hippocratic theory recognized the

91. *Aër.* 13.

92. Hanson (1992b) 250.

93. *Vict.* 4.90 (about dreams, fourth century B.C.E.), trans. J. Chadwick and W. N. Mann. On the theoretical basis for medical analysis of dreams, see Oberhelman (1993) 127–33. The author of this book distinguishes two kinds of dreams—those sent by the gods and therapeutic dreams resulting from the soul's ability to understand conditions of the body. Natural phenomena (both celestial and terrestrial) exist in symbiosis with the body; the medical practitioner must therefore consider the symbolism of dreams in devising successful therapies for a patient.

94. For cases that illustrate the correspondence between a dream and an illness, see Ruph. Eph. *Quaest. Med.* 5 (Gärtner 34–36), translated by Oberhelman (1993) 142. Dreams are signs of the future; King (1998) 102.

95. *Aër.* 5.

female body as a body at risk, tested by the physical demands of reproduction. The female differs from the male in both substance and operation.[96] Female flesh is described as more moist than male flesh, as porous and spongy, soaking up liquid as a fleece soaks up water.[97] Fluctuations in female moisture are described in terms of the landscape, and the same tests used by farmers to measure moisture of the soil were used to test female moisture.[98] Circulation of underground water provided a model for circulation of moisture within the female body.[99] Blood moves like water rising from or flowing through the earth, and menstrual blood is described as welling up like water rising from springs. The female circulatory system is a riverine system with all blood vessels leading to the uterus.[100]

For the Hippocratic theorist, the reproductive female is a miniature agricultural landscape,[101] one that must be managed, tended, and stimulated in order to reproduce the family.[102] Female health depends on regulation of internal moisture, and the quality and quantity of menstrual blood are diagnostic clues to health and illness. Difficulties in menstruation are correctable by pregnancy, when the uterus regulates the distribution of moisture by absorbing the blood otherwise expelled in menstruation.[103] Hippocratic theorists assumed that because menstruation ceases in pregnancy, menstrual blood remains in the uterus to become the primary matter from which the embryo is constituted.[104] Regular menstruation is a sign

96. Laqueur (1990) argues for a single model of the body for both male and female, but by reducing his subject to the representation of genitalia, he minimizes Greek distinctions in the substance of male and female bodies.

97. Process described at *Mul.* 1.1 (8:12.6–14.7 Littré); Hanson (1992a) 51–52, on "feminization" of wetness. The female is identified with water in *Reg.* 1.27.1–2; Hanson (1995a) 295.

98. Hanson (1992a) 37, for the use of fleece for hydroscopy.

99. At the sanctuary of Hera at Koroneia, Hera's springs were shaped like breasts and water was likened to flowing milk; Paus. 9.34.3–4.

100. *Nat. Puer.* 2.10.1, for an analogy between the porosity of the soil and the porosity of female flesh; Hanson (1992a) 37, 40, etc.

101. She was made from earth (and water), cf. Hom. *Il.* 7.99; Hes. *Theog.* 571; Loraux (1993) 78 n. 36. West's note on 571 gives many examples, going back to Homer. To insult his allies, Menelaos makes them females made of female stuff by using the feminine form of the ethnic and calling them "water and earth": "Achaiides, no longer Achaioi . . . but you all be water and earth (ἀλλ' ὑμεῖς μὲν πάντες ὕδωρ καὶ γαῖα).

102. Eur. *Erechtheus* F I.22–23 Diggle, for a "crop" of children. See also Hanson (1992a) 40–41.

103. Dean-Jones (1994) 126–27.

104. Dean-Jones (1994) 152–54.

of health, and female wetness must be carefully monitored, especially at critical times of female bleeding and fluctuation in female body liquids. The most critical moments are the initial onset of menstruation, pregnancy, lochial bleeding, and lactation. These are the periods when the female body is most productive—but also when it is in transition and therefore least stable.

Most theorists acknowledged a female role in gestation,[105] but the nature of conception continued to be a subject of vigorous philosophical and scientific debate.[106] Ignorance of female physiology encouraged speculation, since claims could not be tested by direct observation.[107] Assumptions were rarely challenged, and serious contradictions between theory and reality were never resolved. At Athens, where restrictions on eligibility for citizenship in the mid-fifth century eventually resulted in a new definition of maternity, some of that debate took place on stage. Aischylos, who presents the discussion about responsibility for conception as a contest between paternity and maternity, seems to have been the first to problematize these issues in the theater. The outcome of *Eumenides,* the final play in the *Oresteia* trilogy, hangs on establishing a definition of parenthood and an explanation for the process of conception. The solution is successfully argued by Apollo, who represents a radical view:

> A mother cannot be called the parent of a child;
> she is but the nurse of the newly sown embryo.
> The one who leaps begets, but she, a stranger,
> for a stranger, preserves the sprout, unless a god harms it.[108]

This view did not prevail. In fact, it was even challenged in the second play of the trilogy, where Orestes' instinct for murder is traced to his own mother.[109] Hippocratic theorists argued for an active female role in concep-

105. Dean-Jones (1994) 151: the male could not supply catamenial fluid. Zeus could not produce Athena without swallowing the pregnant Metis, but Hera could engender Hephaistos and Typhon without male intervention; Hes. *Theog.* 927–29.

106. Philosophers debated the female contribution to seed; recent summaries: Lloyd (1983) 86–87; Dean-Jones (1994) 149.

107. Ovaries are not mentioned by a Greek writer before Herophilus in the Hellenistic period; Lloyd (1983) 108–9. Even when noticed, however, ovaries were misunderstood. Herophilus described ovaries as if they were testicles; Herophilus F 61 (von Staden 184–85). Misconceptions among the Hippocratics abound: air and other things flowed through veins along with blood; there was a connection between the mouth and the vagina; Lloyd (1983) 83–84.

108. Aesch. *Eum.* 657–60.

109. Hanson (1992a) 42.

tion.[110] To account for the fact that sons could resemble their mothers and daughters their fathers, and realizing that a child could derive characteristics from both sides of the family, they argued that both mother and father contribute "seed" (*gone*, "sperm").[111] Some Hippocratics even claimed that parents contribute seed from all parts of their bodies. Nevertheless, the Hippocratics always regarded the male product as superior. One author postulates two kinds of seed, stronger and weaker, each produced by both parents. A balance in favor of strong seed produces a male child, a balance in favor of weak seed results in a female child.[112]

Botanical imagery permeates the Hippocratic arguments about gestation,[113] which was explained in terms of botanical cycles. The growing embryo—a seed encased in a membrane—consumes the mother's blood[114] and takes root like a plant, so that the skeletal frame grows like a tree. Assuming a correlation between the health of the mother and the health of the embryo, the writer says:

> In just the same way, plants growing in the earth receive their nutriment from the earth and the condition of the plant depends on the condition of the earth in which it grows. . . . I maintain, then, that all plants which grow in the ground live off the moisture which comes from the ground, and that the character of the plant depends on the character of this moisture. Now it is just the same way that the child in the womb lives from its mother, and it is on the condition of health of the mother that the condition of health of the child depends. But in fact, if you review what I have said, you will find that from beginning to end the process of growth in plants and in humans is exactly the same.[115]

110. Hanson (1995a) 394–98; Dean-Jones (1992) 72–87, for the function of female sexual desire and the physiological aspects of orgasm, as opposed to the psychological.

111. Censorinus says that Diogenes and Hippon followed this view and claims that Parmenides, Empedocles, Anaxagoras, and Alcmaeon described the mother as contributing seed as well as the father (Censorinus, *De Die Nat.* 5.4). Aristotle contradicts Censorinus by attributing to Anaxagoras the idea that the seed determined the child's sex but originated only in the male. Aetius acknowledges Hippon's belief that the female produced seed but says this seed did not contribute to reproduction; he attributes to Hippon the idea that the father contributes the bones, the mother contributes the flesh; Aetius 5.5.1. See Lesky (1951) 52–54.; Lloyd (1983) 87–88.

112. *Genit.* 6.1–2 (Littré 7:478.5–11).

113. Lonie (1969) and (1981) 211–16.

114. Otherwise lost in menstruation; *Nat. Puer.* 14.1–2. The blood is the agent that makes the fetus grow; *Mul.* 1.25.

115. *Nat. Puer.* 22.1, 27.1 (trans. Lonie; Littré 7:544; 7:528).

The mother is simultaneously earth and vessel filled with blood that flows like a river. The embryo's character is influenced by the character of the local water supply, communicated to the embryo through the mother's uterine moisture. The Hippocratic author describes how the child is therefore directly related to the local land and water system. He has transformed an idea, previously passed down as local myth, about the fertilizing power of the local water supply into a scientific claim.[116]

The child thrives in the womb like the trees in the orchards of Hesiod's just city. The trees grow fruit at the tips of their branches; so also, the child's arms grow fingernails at the tips of their fingers, the legs grow toenails at the ends of their toes. Heat causes the bones to contract, harden, and then "send out branches like a tree."[117]

> Once the embryo's limbs are articulated and shaped, as it grows its bones become both harder and hollow. . . . Once the bones are hollow, they absorb the richest part of the clotted blood from the flesh. In due course the bones at their extremities branch out, just as in a tree it is the tips of the branches which are last to shoot forth twigs. It is the same way that the child's fingers and toes become differentiated. Further, nails grow on these extremities, because all the veins in the human body terminate in the fingers and toes. . . . The embryo starts to move once the extremities of the body have branched and the nails and hair have taken root.[118]

Aristotle, whose description of the *polis* is based on the family, privileges male over female;[119] he rejects Hippocratic explanations of conception and attributes the creative power to the father alone. For Aristotle, the mother contributes only matter. Comparing the action of semen on female blood to the action of rennet on milk in cheese making,[120] he says that when the fetus is "set," it grows like "plants sown in the soil,"[121] receiving nourishment through the umbilical cord, which he compares to a root joined to the earth.[122] The fluid produced from the blood of the male (semen—com-

116. Schol. Pind. *Pyth.* 4.104: no marriage takes place without the nymphs. Artemid. 2.38 (on dreams): rivers, lakes, and springs are good for procreation. Theophrastus, in Ath. 2.15, remarks on the child-engendering water of Thespiai. See Dowden (1989) 123 for sources of water as sources for local identity.

117. *Nat. Puer.* 17.2 (Littré 7:496).

118. *Nat. Puer.* 19.1–2, 21.1 (trans. Lonie; Littré 7:506).

119. Arist. *Pol.* 1254b: "Male is by nature superior, woman inferior; the male is that which rules, the female is that which is ruled."

120. Arist. *Gen. An.* 739b20.

121. Arist. *Gen. An.* 739b35.

122. Arist. *Gen. An.* 740a20–35, 740b10; cf. 745b26.

pletely concocted, thoroughly heated, and therefore pure) is superior to that of the female (menstrual blood, *katamenia*—unconcocted and therefore impure, likened to unfinished semen). For Aristotle, the ability to concoct semen confirms the superiority of the male body. Semen makes the superior contribution because it is the source of both form and movement (τὸ εἶδος, ἡ ἀρχὴ τῆς κινήσεως) and is even able to create soul (ψυχή). Male soul is superior to female soul because it is perceptive and sentient. Male soul can create soul in the child; female soul can only sustain but not create soul in another.[123] The inability to achieve complete concoction confirms the inferiority of the female body. Unable to achieve the heat and dryness associated with the male body, the female contributes only physical matter (τὸ σῶμα, ἡ ὕλη). This physical matter, nevertheless, is not entirely passive. Inherited characteristics transmitted by menstrual fluid can influence the final result of the form imposed by the paternal seed.[124]

Hippocratics recognized that in conception the contributions of mother and father were more or less equal, but they regarded the male body as more efficient with respect to its own gestation and later life cycle. Differences in physical characteristics were explained by differences in levels of moisture. Male superiority begins in the womb, where the sex of the fetus has a direct effect on the condition of the uterus.[125] The male fetus, being less moist, is superior to the female in rate of development, lack of complications during pregnancy, and rate of recovery of the mother after pregnancy.[126] Female seed is more moist and therefore weaker.[127] The female fetus, wetter than the male, develops more slowly, quickens later, gives more trouble at birth, and is responsible for a higher level of maternal mortality and a longer period of lochial bleeding.[128] Differential rates of lochial bleeding were based not on observation but on a theory of fetal develop-

123. Because the mother has only "nutritive soul" (θρεπτικὴ ψυχή, *Gen. An.* 741a), she cannot produce the "perceptive soul" (αἰσθητικὴ ψυχή, 741b5).

124. Freeland (1987); see Cooper (1987), for Aristotle's response to Hippocratic attempts to account for the child's resemblance to the mother and the maternal family.

125. Hanson (1992a) 32.

126. Dean-Jones (1994) 104.

127. Hanson (1992a) 53.

128. Hanson (1989) 48–49, for different rates of negative influence on maternal progress for male and female fetuses, as reported in the *Epidemics*. One-third of the case histories in the *Epidemics* describe females; Lloyd (1983) 67 n. 33. A survey of all cases of maternal death in the Hippocratic *Epidemics* reveals that the death rate is eleven times more frequent with a female fetus than with a male; Hanson (1992a) 54.

ment that assumed different rates of liquid consumption for male and female fetuses. Being inherently wetter than the male, the female fetus does not need as much blood during gestation. Consequently the maternal body has more moisture to express after birth. The male fetus, needing more moisture for gestation, is not a liability but rather promotes maternal health as it consumes excess moisture, since maternal health is viewed as depending on disposal of excess blood. Paradoxically, slow development, considered a liability for females in gestation, is an advantage for males in later life. The male ages more slowly because he produces "seed" well into old age.[129] Females, although slow in fetal development, nevertheless age more quickly because they stop producing "seed" at menopause.

For the Hippocratics, female reproductive processes put the whole body at risk. Health problems in females are attributed to uterine malfunction. For males, on the other hand, pathology is the consequence of behavior and activity.[130] In *Epidemics* (where case histories of men far outnumber case histories of women)[131] fever in males is attributed to drinking too much, indulging too frequently in sexual intercourse, or exercising too strenuously, but fever in females is attributed to complications from childbirth, miscarriage, first menstruation, or grief.

Hippocratic protocols were based on several assumptions: Sexual intercourse promotes female health and corrects menstrual problems. Early marriage alleviates menstrual problems in young women. Adult women require regular intercourse to maintain femininity and health. Women deprived of the sexual attention of husbands run the risk of masculinization, a condition that can even be fatal.[132] Childbirth is dangerous, but because pregnancy consumes excess moisture, it has beneficial effects on female health. Pregnancy with a daughter is more hazardous than pregnancy with a son but is nevertheless preferable to the hazards of a barren life.

129. Hanson (1992a) 65 n. 131.

130. Dean-Jones (1994) 119. Even when the disease and symptoms were recognized as the same for women and men, the female experience of the disease is discussed separately from the male experience; see *Epid.* 4.57 (Littré 7: 612, lines 19–21).

131. Dean-Jones (1994) 136 explains the disparity by assuming that women were visiting traditional healers. The fact that women's diseases were explained in terms of reproductive disorders would also reduce the number of conditions discussed.

132. Masculinization of females was an ominous sign among the Pedasians (in Caria), whose priestess of Athena grew a beard if something bad was about to happen. Herodotus reports that this had happened three times; Hdt. 1.175.

In the Classical period, practical therapies as well as the culture at large usually assigned responsibility for reproductive failure to the female.[133] Even Hippocratics, who recognized a female contribution to conception, could describe the pregnant female as a passive, fertile field, attributing any ultimate deformity in her infant to deficiencies in her womb. The author of *On the Seed* illustrates this last idea with a telling example:

> A similar thing happens to trees which have insufficient space in the earth, being obstructed by a stone or the like. They grow up twisted, or thick in some places and slender in others, and this is what happens to the child as well, if one part of the womb constricts some part of its body more than another.[134]

The same point is made by comparing a deformed fetus to a stunted cucumber, misshapen because it was confined to a small pot.[135]

Some Hippocratics compared the period of gestation to the agricultural cycle, which depended on seasonal changes in the underground waterways, fluctuating with changes in porosity of the soil.[136] Others compared the changes in the female body during pregnancy with the yearly weather cycle. Both explanations of variations in female moisture assume that the sympathy between natural cycles and bodily changes was more pronounced for females than for males. The character of the local water supply was important because it not only determined the state of the mother's health but also had an influence on her progeny.[137] When Plato's Aspasia praises the land of Attika, source of nourishment for the Athenian people, she develops the metaphor of the earth as mother; she stresses, however,

133. Males can be described as sterile (Hdt. 6.68, Ariston did not have σπέρμα παιδοποιόν; *Aër.* 21; Arist. *Gen. An.* 746b–747a, etc., on which see Hanson [1991] 265), but except for the water test for semen described by Aristotle, tests for sterility and ability to conceive were designed for the female; *Steril.* 219. As for Roman writers, Pliny blames a plant associated with funerals for male infertility (*HN* 20.114, 26.70) and an adaptor of Soranus, Caelius Aurelian, *Gyn.* 64 (Drabkin and Drabkin 92–93) attributes male sterility to weak sperm. The author of Arist. *HA* 10 concedes the possibility of male deficiency (636b) but describes in detail only female problems. See now van der Eijk (1999) 490–502, esp. 490. Aristotle, *Pol.* 1335a, interpreting an oracle to the people of Troizen, explains that age at marriage is a factor for both males and females.

134. *Genit.* 10.2, trans. Lonie. Deformed infants are the result of accidents in the womb (a blow to the mother) or a deformed or inadequate uterus.

135. *Genit.* 9.2; Hanson (1992a) 38–39.

136. *Nat. Puer.* 24–26; summarized by Hanson (1992a) 55.

137. Arist. *Hist. An.* 519a.

that in conception and gestation the earth does not imitate woman; rather, woman imitates the earth.[138] The same idea is reflected in metaphors of an Athenian brotherhood of citizens, virtual siblings because of their common birth from the soil of Attika.[139]

The identification of the productive female body with the earth was not an idle metaphor but a working concept whose power was recognized by Hippocratic therapies. Doctors prescribed a variety of substances to deal with female conditions. One of the most striking types of recommendations advised both oral and internal application of animal excrement and/or urine.[140] In the Classical period, Hippocratics limited treatment with animal excrement to women's conditions, and only for serious problems of the uterus. Excrement therapies dealt with abnormal excess of fluid, associated with conditions such as sterility, expulsion of a dead fetus, and delayed menstruation. Remedies included the dung of cows and mules and the excrement of mice and birds.[141] Such treatments, prevalent in other ancient Mediterranean cultures, were part of traditional medical practice, but only the Hippocratics restricted such therapies to females.[142] It has been argued that excrement therapy shares certain characteristics with ritual *katharsis,* a process of purification where pollution is removed or cleansed by application of a related polluted substance to soak it up and withdraw it.[143] This description, however, is inconsistent with both Hippocratics and Aristotle, who describe menstruation itself as a form of *katharsis.* In the context of Hippocratic therapy, where health was achieved by balancing diet, moisture, environment, and activity, animal excrement was used in extreme situations because it supplied a defined need. The conditions treated with excrement may have been considered undesirable, even pathological. Nevertheless, they were not in themselves ritually polluting. Physicians believed that levels of female moisture could be so dire as to require exceptional strategies. Pathological levels of female moisture required treatment with extremely dry substances. In Hippocratic terms, excrement was extremely dry, to be used only in situations of extreme and dangerous accu-

138. Pl. *Menex.* 238a.

139. Isoc. 6.124; Lycurg. *Leoc.* 100; Dougherty (1996) 256; Rosivach (1987) 301.

140. Von Staden (1992) 9.

141. Examples listed by von Staden (1992) 9–10.

142. Von Staden (1992) 13–15. Hanson (1998) 87–91 points out that both Dioscourides and Galen later extended excrement therapy to males.

143. Von Staden (1992) 16–20, comparing excrement to the substances used in ritual and influenced by the idea of the power of dirt to purify, as demonstrated by Douglas (1966).

mulation of moisture.[144] Treatment of the uterus with animal excrement therefore corrected what the Hippocratic doctor defined as a threatening imbalance in the fluid content of the uterus. Excrement therapy did not correct a polluting condition; it only corrected a potentially dangerous level of moisture.

Regulation of the moisture of the uterus with a pharmacology of excrement is consistent with the Hippocratic notion of the uterus as a miniature landscape.[145] In agricultural contexts animal excrement was the major material for fertilization; treatment of the uterus with selective types therefore imitated fertilization of a field with manure.[146] Treatment of pathological levels of female moisture assumed an analogy between the female body and the productive landscape of the community. The similarities between excrement therapy and ritual practice have more to do with this analogy than with any similarity between the material means of purification and excrement. The fundamental division acknowledged by ritual was not between pure and polluted materials, nor even between pure and polluted individuals, but rather between sacred and productive spaces. Rites of purification addressed conditions that would transgress this boundary. Excrement therapy targeted pathological moisture, not the natural female processes addressed by sanctuary regulations. Physicians—and midwives—devised extreme procedures to deal with problems inside the female body not because females were trapped in a cycle of polluting conditions but because each woman contained an appropriated space in need of supervision.

Hippocratic theory conceptualized the interior of the female body as a miniature landscape whose moisture levels had to be managed by the sexual intervention of husbands and the therapeutic intervention of physicians. The goal of therapy was health—a condition that, for women, automatically included successful childbirth. The goal of ritual was the right relationship with the gods. Worshippers did indeed pray for children, but they realized that the gods demanded particular behaviors and a certain care to recognize the great divide between human and divine. The arena where that recognition was demonstrated was not the home but the sanc-

144. Recipes advise pounding it into a dry powder; see von Staden (1992) 9–11.

145. As described by Hanson (1992a) 36–41. Hanson (1998) 87–94 deepens the evidence for excrement therapy and broadens its discussion by arguing that it operated according to the principles of Hippocratic humoral theory specifically and the mechanical principles of Hippocratic therapy in general. Cf. Diog. Laert. 9.1.

146. For the evidence of manuring in agricultural contexts, see Alcock, Cherry, and Davis (1994).

tuary. We saw in chapter 4 that the female in childbirth, at the moment of her greatest contribution to the community, was defined in ritual terms as farthest from the divine. She was farthest from the divine precisely because at that moment she was the most like the earth.

BODY PARTS

The Hippocratic emphasis on therapy had an effect on sanctuary development. By the end of the fifth century, the medical community had created a culture of healing practice based on diagnosis and treatment of disease. The new medicine competed with the prevailing religious ideology. In the view of the medical community reproductive failure was due not to *loimos,* affliction sent by the gods, but to *nosos,* illness that could be treated.[147] Sanctuaries of Asklepios responded to the therapeutic model by incorporating procedures that paid close attention to symptoms, diagnosis, and therapy. Services were expanded,[148] filial sanctuaries were established where Asklepios had not been worshipped before, and sanctuary personnel added medical procedures to traditional ritual practices. Managers of such sanctuaries were successful because they offered specific treatments tailored to the individual. Temple personnel practiced a combination of dream interpretation, ritual remedy, and medical therapy.

People dedicated models of body parts to represent specific illnesses or disabilities, either in hopes that a god would cure the affected part[149] or in gratitude for a cure already given. Satisfied customers testified to the positive results of their treatments with sculptured reliefs or representations of afflicted body parts in ceramic, stone, silver, and gold.[150] Such dedications are found in the sanctuaries of a number of divinities, but the greatest variety seems to have been concentrated in sanctuaries of Asklepios. At the Asklepieion in Corinth deposits included ceramic heads, ears, eyes, tongue,

147. Kosak (2000) emphasizes a difference between the Hippocratic notion of disease and an earlier notion of disease as a result of religious pollution. Parker (1983) 235–36 summarizes the evidence for the persistence of belief in divine intervention. Inscriptional evidence suggests that that theory did not percolate very far. For a recently discovered text on the great plague of 165 C.E. (considered a visitation from the gods) and the oracles advising rituals to deal with it, see Graf (1992) 167–79 (*SEG* 41.981).

148. Burford (1969), for the building program at Epidauros, beginning in mid-fourth century B.C.E.

149. Ael. Arist. 52.7 Keil.

150. Van Straten (1981) 105–51, for an extensive catalogue of body parts.

chests, male genitalia, arms, hands, fingers, legs, feet, hair, and a thigh.[151] Inventories inscribed at the Athenian Asklepieion list heads, ears, faces, eyes, jaws, mouths, body trunks (usually female), hearts, breasts, arms, hands, fingers, genitalia (both male and female), and legs.[152] Dedications having to do with care of the body were not necessarily confined to sanctuaries of healing gods. Tiny body parts of gold, electrum, and ivory, representing arms, feet, eyes, ears and a vulva, have been found in deposits at the Ephesian Artemision, dated as early as the late eighth to the middle of the seventh century. Such dedications become common by the fourth century, appearing eventually throughout mainland Greece (including Thrace) and the Aegean islands, as well as at Pergamon, Ephesos, and elsewhere.

To some extent, types of offerings cluster in specific sanctuaries. Eyes were often offered to Demeter, and breasts and vulvae to Artemis and Aphrodite. Occasionally the offerings in a specific sanctuary seem limited to a female clientele, but the more typical deposits, especially those associated with Asklepios, reflect a diverse clientele—male and female, young and old—with concerns for a variety of diseases and disabilities. Body parts carved in stone were offered for the most part to divinities associated with childbirth and women's health.[153] The inventories from the Asklepieion on the south slope of the Athenian *akropolis* record items of gold and silver to be melted down by the sanctuary and list as well not only anatomical dedications but also stone reliefs, crowns, ritual equipment, coins, jewelry, medical equipment, and personal items (including drinking vessels, cooking utensils, and little boxes for cosmetics). On the whole, a higher proportion of the inventoried dedications come from women than from men. Moreover, women had a predilection for certain types of offerings, dedicating most of the jewelry and a greater proportion of the ceramic models of body parts.[154] Men, who were more likely to make dedications as the consequence of hieratic service than as a consequence of illness, dedicated most of the expensive items—the ritual vessels, crowns, and medical equipment. Men and women alike, however, made dedications in hopes of recovery from diseases associated with a variety of limbs and organs, most of the time for themselves, sometimes for other members of their families. Men made dedications on behalf of their wives; fathers and mothers made dedications on behalf of their children; and once, a mother and grand-

151. Roebuck (1951).
152. Aleshire (1989).
153. Forsén (1996), for 171 examples of body parts in relief on stone.
154. Aleshire (1989) 46.

mother joined in a dedication for a young boy. The highest concentrations of body parts are full bodies or body trunks (65 individuals), eyes (154 individuals), legs (41), and arms (23 individuals), but a concern for reproductive problems is also evident, represented by the frequent dedication of breasts (13) and genital organs both male (usually called *aidoion,* but *hebe* once)[155] and female (*hebe,* twice).[156] Among the dedications of ceramic body parts models of male genitalia cluster at the Asklepieion at Corinth, but elsewhere models of female reproductive organs predominate. On the whole, Athenian inventories for the Asklepieion list more dedications from women than from men,[157] giving some support to Plato's claim that women and sick people were the most likely to make dedications,[158] but it is difficult to reconstruct a particular illness from the lists. Breasts and vulvae are also found in sanctuaries of Aphrodite, Kalliste and Ariste, Artemis Kolainis, Artemis at Ephesos, Zeus Hypsistos (second century C.E.), Eileithyia, and Amphiareus dispersed geographically from Greece to Asia Minor and extending chronologically from the sixth century B.C.E. to the second century C.E. A Delian inventory lists two silver wombs.[159]

At Epidauros, inscribed testimonials publicized successful cures. The narratives are formulaic, all in the Doric dialect, apparently composed at the request of sanctuary administrators and recorded by professional scribes.[160] Females are underrepresented in the inscriptions recording extraordinary cures at Epidauros—only seventeen out of the seventy narratives.[161] Male and female ailments belong to different categories. Men suffered from conditions ranging from blindness, paralysis, lameness, lice,

155. As Aleshire (1989) 41 points out, however, the male genitalia dedicated by a mother on behalf of her son (V.161, page 264) need not have been associated with a reproductive disorder.

156. Van Straten (1981) 109.

157. Female dedicants: 51.39%; male dedicants: 45.82%; male and female dedicants together: 2.79%. See Aleshire (1989) 45. Women dedicate models of reproductive organs, lower bodies, and whole bodies on their own behalf; husbands dedicate the same items for their wives (V.133, see 45); and mothers can dedicate such items on behalf of themselves and their children (IV.100). Some women dedicate several reliefs (Sibilla, 15: IV.108; Komike, 2: IV.66 Aphrodisia, 3: IV.75; Philiste, 3: V.100; Archippe, 5: V.100).

158. Pl. *Leg.* 909e.

159. *IDélos* 1442 A.55, 145/4 B.C.E.

160. LiDonnici (1995) 52–69 stresses the possible influence of an oral tradition. Her strongest evidence is the group of inscribed testimonials from Lebena on Crete (discussed 46–47), which exhibit similarities with the dossier from Epidauros (although they employ herbal therapies, not mentioned at Epidauros).

161. Lloyd (1983) 69 n. 40.

tuberculosis, and hepatitis to headache, dyspepsia, and gout. The narratives about women, however, tend to concentrate on reproductive problems, and most female complaints are attributed to either prolonged pregnancy or sterility. The males in myth who visit oracles to find out how to sow a child—figures such as Aegeus and Xouthos[162]—are not represented in the testimonials at Epidauros. Apparently, under the impression that for males sexual performance was equivalent to fertility, husbands anxious to produce progeny sent their wives instead.

STERILITY AND THE CRISIS OF PATERNITY

The philosophical debate about the definition of physical parenthood had practical consequences in fifth-century Athens, particularly during the Peloponnesian War. Tension between competing interpretations of local history was sharpened by the larger political pressures of empire in a period when Athens tried to balance claims for their own unique local origin with a competing claim to be leader of all Ionians. In fifth-century Athens, where metaphor and myth played a more powerful explanatory role than abstraction, citizenship was described in metaphors of kinship. The myth of Athenian autochthony, by which Athenians claimed descent from a king born from the soil, defined Athenians as members of a single family.[163] Perikles' citizenship law of 451, passed less than a decade after Aischylos's *Oresteia* of 458, based citizenship on kinship. By defining membership in the political community in terms of family relationships, and by requiring that both father and mother belong to the hereditary group of Attic families, this law emphasized ties of both collateral and affinal kinship and sharpened the distinction between insiders (men with Attic mothers and fathers) and outsiders (men with a foreign parent).[164] According to this law, only those whose parents on both sides were *astoi* (belonging to the city of Athens) could participate in the *politeia* (the political community). Whoever was "not pure in family" (τῷ γένει μὴ καθαροί) could not participate.[165] The new law required close attention to the status of a citizen's maternal grandfather and therefore to the status of his mother.[166]

162. To which can be added Lyrkos, who asked the oracle of Apollo at Didyma "about engendering children" (περὶ γονῆς τέκνων); Parth. 1.2 (Fontenrose [1988] 228 no. 57, a "legendary" response).
163. Loraux (1993) 37–71.
164. Patterson (1990) 57.
165. *Ath. Pol.* 13.5, 26.4.
166. Scafuro (1994).

The political community at Athens was a community of qualified families, each represented in the external world of the *polis* by its male head.[167] Natural ties to family—stronger than ties to peers, *polis,* or citizens of allied cities—were a model for ritual expressions of unity at the level of deme and *polis.* Myths of local origin, though subject to revision, represented the city as a family. One place where this definition is developed is the contest about Attic identity presented in Euripides' *Ion,* a play that examined competing traditions of ethnic origin at a time when claims for Ionian ethnicity had to be reconciled with the Attic myth of authochthony. The central problem of the play is a crisis of fertility, presented by Euripides as three separate issues: the problem of a family without a child,[168] the problem of a child without parents,[169] and the problem of a people without a father.[170] Kreousa, as the sole surviving child of Erechtheus, is technically an Athenian *epikleros,* the daughter of a father without sons. In order to secure the tradition of Athenian autochthony, she requires a husband to produce an heir for her father.[171] At the time of the action of the play, Kreousa's marriage to Xouthos, a foreigner from Euboia,[172] is a marriage in crisis because it is a marriage without a child.

A debate about the definition of maternity is crucial to the drama's resolution. Hermes' introductory speech sets out the terms of that debate and gives the audience the information they will need to assess the arguments. The audience knows from the very beginning that Kreousa, now visiting Delphi to learn how her marriage might be fruitful, had actually borne a child to Apollo in her youth. That child is Ion, who, unknown to Kreousa, now serves Apollo himself at Delphi. The issue of Ion's paternity is a crisis of identity for the whole Athenian people because their claim to the land of Attika rests on an unbroken line back to their earliest kings, who were born from the soil.[173] Euripides' solution to the play's crisis of family continuity reunites mother and son and confirms Ion, son of Apollo and Kreousa, as heir to the family of the Athenian king Erechtheus. As progenitor of the Athenians, Ion can be an eponymous ancestor for the whole Ionian

167. Recognized by Aristotle, *Pol.* 1259a37–1260b20.

168. Eur. *Ion* 304.

169. Eur. *Ion* 49–50, 109.

170. Loraux (1993) 65, for Athens as a metaphorical family.

171. Kreousa, whose husband is not a relative of her father (she says he is not *astos,* 290), is not actually married as an *epikleros;* Loraux (1993) 203. Saxenhouse (1986) sees the play as a rejection of autochthony and argues for the significance of the female in the revision of the city's foundation myth.

172. Separated from Athens by "watery boundaries"; Eur. *Ion* 295.

173. Eur. *Ion* 20–21, 29–30.

people.[174] The play's resolution also creates a place for the future sons of Xouthos and Kreousa, who will be first in the Dorian and Achaian lines. Most important, Euripides' conclusion rationalizes Athenian claims to autochthony by preserving through Kreousa alone the family line of the Erechtheids.

Euripides emphasizes the crisis of sterility as a crisis of paternity by repeating traditional agricultural metaphors. The image of the father as sower of his child, implying that the mother is only the soil, is introduced first by Hermes, who says that Ion knows neither the father "who sowed him" (τὸν σπείραντα, 49) nor the mother from whom "he grew" (ἔφυ, 50). Hermes uses the image again in the same speech when he describes how Xouthos "remains childless although he has already sown his marriage bed" (χρόνια δὲ σπείρας λέχη ἄτεκνός ἐστι, 64–65). Ion uses the verb when he hears Xouthos's claim to be his father (τοῦτ' ἐκεῖν' ἵν' ἐσπάρημεν, 554), and it is picked up later, in bitterness, by the Presbeutes announcing to Kreousa that her husband has reaped the crop of another woman by sowing a child outside marriage,[175] and finally, in describing the youthful sexual escapade of Xouthos on Parnassos as an "illegal sowing."[176] The sowing of seed, always associated with Xouthos, prioritizes paternity over maternity and privileges the male role in conception, assuming that a "bed" (64–65) once sown should necessarily produce a crop.[177]

Kreousa's discussion of conception within marriage employs a very different language of reproduction and represents a radically different theory of parenthood. For Kreousa, sexual intercourse is not the sowing of seeds into a passive earth but a mixing of substances from two parents (μιγῆναι, 338).[178] Like a Hippocratic theorist, Kreousa describes conception in terms of "seed for children from both (parents)" and assumes that seed from father and seed from mother must be mixed together to create a child.[179] Kreousa, taking sides in the debate about the nature and mechanics of parenthood, redefines maternity for the audience. Euripides converts a theoretical debate about biological conception and parenthood into a political issue whose resolution requires a scientific argument. Kreousa's narrative, for

174. Eur. *Ion* 74.

175. Eur. *Ion* 815: ἄλλης γυναικὸς παῖδας ἐκκαρπούμενος.

176. Eur. *Ion* 1095: ἄδικον ἄροτον; Zeitlin (1989) 163.

177. Hanson (1992a).

178. Hanson (1989) 45, for μειγνύναι and Hippocratic theories of conception; (1995a) 292, for mixing seed from both parents.

179. Eur. *Ion* 406, reading, with Wilamowitz and Diggle, Wakefield's συγκραθήσεται for the ms. συγκαθήσεται.

which Hermes' prologue has already evoked the audience's sympathy, takes center stage and transforms the discussion about parenthood into one about identity by recognizing Kreousa herself as the creative connection to the kings of Attika.

Kreousa's commentary on Ion's origins connects two important myths about Athenian identity. When Athena addresses Ion and Kreousa at the close of the play, the goddess makes a distinction between Ion as son of Apollo and Ion as son of Kreousa. When speaking directly to Ion (1555–70), she emphasizes his relationship to Apollo.[180] When speaking to Kreousa, however, (1571–78), she emphasizes Ion's heritage from the family of Erechtheus, a heritage he can now confer on the people whom Athena calls by her own name, Athenians. By recognizing this heritage, Athena praises the family line preserved and carried through Kreousa.[181] Ion's sons are born from a single root not because Ion is born from Apollo (who, as a god, has no roots) but because Athena recognizes Ion as born from Kreousa.[182] As a miniature landscape, Kreousa replicates the land of Attika; as contributor of maternal seed equal to the paternal seed of Apollo, she guarantees that the child she once nourished with her own blood is a true son of the land.

180. A relationship exploited by the Athenians when on Samos they confiscated estates under the jurisdiction of Athenian gods, at least once that of Ion himself; Parker (1996) 144–46. For the boundary stones of a *temenos* of Ion on Samos, see *IG* I^{3} 1496.

181. And Euripides challenges the Athenian appropriation of Ionian history; see Herda (1998) 1–48, esp. 1–19.

182. Eur. *Ion* 1571–78. Dougherty (1996) 261 emphasizes the role of Apollo, but Athena does not mention Apollo when addressing Kreousa directly.

6 Landscapes of Artemis

BORDERLANDS

In the southeastern quadrant of the Peloponnese, high on Mt. Parnon, there is a place where the ancient borders of Lakonia, Arkadia, and the Argolid came together.[1] The proximity of the fertile Thyreatic plain made this borderland much contested. As Pausanias climbed the narrow, steep path approaching the heights of the mountain, he passed the site where in 548 B.C.E. three hundred Argives were said to have fought with three hundred Lakedaimonians for control of that plain.[2] The site was still marked in his day by the graves of the 597 hoplites who had fallen in that battle.[3]

When Pausanias eventually reached the heights of Parnon, well above the inhabited villages, he came to the actual spot where the border markers (ὅροι) of the Lakedaimonians faced the border markers of the Argives and the Tegeans.[4] Standing at this point, he had reached one of the principal Peloponnesian watersheds, the point from which the river Tanaos flowed down toward Argos. Pausanias tells us that the place where he crossed the borderland between Argos, Arkadia, and Lakonia was named Hermai, for the herms that marked the sensitive triple boundary.[5] These herms, probably one for each *polis,* were the boundary markers that guarded the lim-

1. Paus. 2.38.7.
2. For the battle, see Hdt. 1.82; Thuc. 2.27.
3. There is little agreement on Pausanias's actual itinerary; see Winter and Winter (1990) 221–39, esp. 231.
4. For reports of three piles of stones as boundary markers on a ridge of Parnon, see Pritchett (1979) 3:127–42.
5. Paus. 2.38.7; Pausanias also mentions *horoi* at 8.25.1 and 8.34.6; in 10.4.1 he considers *horoi* essential to the definition of a *polis.*

its of each city's political reach. The area between them was a type of space that belonged to no one.[6] The Greeks recognized the unusual nature of this kind of landscape by calling it *chora methoria,* "borderland" or "space-in-between," acknowledging the strip of liminal land lying between or beyond political boundaries.[7] Like the solid color running between the spots on a panther's skin,[8] such spaces could be broad or narrow, the width dependent on the shape of the local landscape and the turn of local military contest. Strips of borderland divided the territory of one *polis* from another, and like the triangular space at a triple crossroads *(triodos),*[9] a *chora methoria* was a no-man's-land, a place suitable only for disposal of objects so polluted that no one could touch them.[10]

After crossing the isolated space guarded by the herms, Pausanias passed through a forest of oak trees sacred to Zeus "of the Darkness" (Skotias)[11] before taking a right turn to reach the sanctuary of Artemis Karyatis, a sacred precinct surrounded by a grove of nut trees. He describes no building but says that the cult statue *(agalma)* of Artemis Karyatis stood in the open air at a place where the young daughters *(parthenoi)* of the Lakedaimonians danced every year in choral celebrations.[12] Artemis at Karyai was not situated in the borderland between Argos, Arkadia, and Lakonia but nearby, on land claimed by the Lakedaimonians, located within their traditional boundaries and marked as their possession by their festival to the goddess. As Pausanias's narrative shows, however, borders were never secure.[13] His own work describes how once, long before his own day, during

6. For the distinction between *ἔρημος χώρα* and *κοινὴ χώρα,* see Chaniotis (1988a) 31. For mountains as public space (*ὄρη δημόσια*), see Robert (1960) 196–97.

7. The usual terms are: *γῆ μεθορία, χώρα μεθορία,* or simply the neuter plural, *τὰ μεθόρια;* Thuc. 2.18, 27; Xen. *Cy.* 1.4.16; Plut. *Crass.* 22. For especially contested boundary land recognized as neutral territory, see Thuc. 5.41; Sartre (1979) 213–24. For a sanctuary of Hermes Kornisaios in a *chora methoria* between Lato and Hierapytna, see Chaniotis (1988a) 25–30. Daverio Rocchi, (1988) distinguishes border territory deserted because of natural inaccessibility *(chorai eremoi)* from contested border territory *(ge methoria).*

8. Herrmann (1985) 337, on such boundaries in early medieval central Europe.

9. Johnston (1991) 217–24.

10. MacDowell (1963) 85–86, 120–25. In Dem. 23.46: *πέρα ὅρου* means "beyond the boundaries."

11. The grove of oaks still grows on the slopes of Parnon; Rackham (1996) 97.

12. Paus. 3.10.7.

13. Thucydides locates Karyai on the border of Lakonia (5.55.3). Control of this area changed hands often; Cartledge (1979) 152, 297, 300, 319, 322.

a festival for Artemis, Messenians returning from Boiotia had kidnapped Lakonian girls *(parthenoi)* from this very sanctuary.[14]

Hermai was located on Lakonia's eastern border. On Lakonia's western border stood another sanctuary of Artemis, this one of Artemis Limnatis. Located on Mt. Taygetos "in the borderland"[15] between Lakonia and Messenia, the site figured in accounts of the early Messenian wars.[16] Lakedaimonian legend claims that Lakonian *parthenoi* celebrating a festival of Artemis here were attacked and raped by Messenians and had to kill themselves for shame.[17] The incident as recounted by Pausanias provided one of the traditional justifications for the Messenian Wars, remembered and used later as a pretext for Spartan military action in the fourth century.

TYPOLOGIES OF SACRED SPACE

Legends about Artemis reflect the realities of space and place because she was a goddess often located in or near easily disputable areas. Pausanias mentions or describes eighty-six of her sanctuaries, forty-nine of which were in the Peloponnese. Four-fifths of the total eighty-six were located far from settled areas, and of the forty-nine Peloponnesian sites, at least twenty-nine lay outside a city, with eighteen situated on a road between two cities or at a boundary between territories. Pausanias's description of Artemis's Peloponnesian sites indicates that she was expected to be available in border areas, close to the mountain passes that divided one inland territory from another. His examples, however, represent only a fraction of the original total. Brulotte has recorded 175 sanctuaries of Artemis in

14. Paus. 4.16.9–10; the Messenian king Aristomenes even had to kill some of his own men because they had not only captured girls (from the "best families") but also attempted rape. Leitao (1999) considers this incident in the context of initiatory ritual for young men sent to border areas.

15. Paus. 3.2.6: ἐν μεθορίῳ. Two possible candidates for the site of this sanctuary have been located; Brulotte (1994) 236–38.

16. The Spartan king Telechos is believed to have been killed by Messenians at this sanctuary, perhaps about 740 B.C. Late Geometric Lakonian pottery was found at the sanctuary of Artemis Limnatis at Volimnos and also across the border in Messenia, confirming contact between these two areas by 750 B.C.E.; see Cartledge (1979) 99, 112–13. For boundary markers in the area see Giannakoupoulos (1953) 147–58.

17. The Messenian version claimed that among their victims were Lakedaimonian boys disguised as girls (Paus. 4.4.3; Str. 6.3.3). This was actually a sanctuary where the Messenians and Lakedaimonians once celebrated a *panegyris* and *thysia* in common; Str. 8.4.9. Leitao (1999) explains the incident as an element of cross-dressing associated with initiatory rituals overseen by Artemis.

the Peloponnese alone.[18] A significant proportion of these were on mountainsides, in wooded areas, at springs, on rivers or lakes, near harbors, or in a borderland shared by two *poleis.* The epithets of the goddess describe the environment of her sanctuary: Agrotera, Limnatis, Heleia (of the marsh), Koryphaia (of the peak), Kedreatis (of the cedar trees), Karyatis (of the walnut trees), and Kyparissia (of the cypress trees).[19] These descriptions are all the more striking when we notice that Artemis's earliest attested sanctuaries are in the most remote places.

There are several possible ways to explain this pattern. Jost connects the placement of Artemis's sanctuaries with function, distinguishing Artemis at the margins, associated with hunting, from an Artemis in low, marshy areas, associated with fertility.[20] Frontisi, however, emphasizes the rural aspects of the goddess and associates Artemis with transitions between the world of nature and the civilized territory of the organized *polis.*[21] De Polignac translates this contrast into a dynamic relationship between center and periphery and associates Artemis with the early border sanctuaries that defined the limits of a city's agricultural territory and political sovereignty and created a symbolic boundary of both civic and spatial order.[22] He finds a special significance in sanctuaries of Artemis that test the limits of a city's reach, and Artemis has a key place in his argument about the relation between the placement of sanctuaries and the development of the *polis.* Ellinger, who focuses on the sanctuary of Artemis at Kalapodi, also finds significance in boundaries, but he places more emphasis on the dangers of frontier territory and connects sanctuaries of Artemis with military crisis and genocidal contest.[23] Schachter, who stresses that Artemis was to be found at coastal as well as inland sites, develops a more comprehensive interpretation. He finds structural similarities between contested border areas, transitional territories dividing city and countryside, and boundaries between the land and sea. He therefore suggests a more general typology, arguing that these locations reflected the character of Artemis as a goddess who presided over transitions—from wild to civilized, from childhood to adulthood, and, in his words, "from unreadiness to readiness."[24] The Greek language recognized the symmetry between shoreline and mountain fron-

18. Brulotte (1994).
19. For Artemis and trees, Chirassi (1964) 5–6.
20. Jost (1994) 219–20.
21. Frontisi-Ducroux (1981) 25–56; Vernant (1991) 195–206, esp. 197–98.
22. De Polignac (1994) 55–60.
23. Ellinger (1993).
24. Schachter (1992) 39–40.

tier by calling both types of space *eschatia*, "edge" or "furthest limit."[25] Schachter's interpretation recognizes the thematic unity of these spaces but does not fully account for the emotional tension associated with them. Because political boundaries did not always coincide with the boundaries created by the landscape's natural features, there was always a possibility of conflict. It is this dissonance that required the attention of the goddess. Expressed in historicizing myths as the danger associated with her rites, it required attention not only in the period of the developing *polis* but throughout the long life of intercity rivalry for control of the local landscape.

To understand the dangers of protecting border territory, it is necessary to take a look at Artemis in other environments. She could be found on the frontier or at the water's edge, but she was also located at or near the entrance to a harbor[26] or even in the heart of the city, as at Orchomenos, where she was called "Mesopolitis."[27] Of Pausanias's eight-six locations for the goddess, fifteen were in an *agora* or elsewhere within the settled or walled area of the town. In their hymns, poets summoned Artemis from mountains, cities, and waterways.[28] Kallimachos recognizes this variation when he describes how Zeus assigned to Artemis her domain. In Kallimachos's hymn to the goddess, she demands of her father, "Give to me all mountains, and assign whatever city you wish, for Artemis rarely goes down to the city." Zeus grants her wish by proclaiming Artemis "guardian of highways and harbors," but he also gives her cities up to "three times ten, both island and inland."[29]

The inventory of locations for Artemis as given by Kallimachos does not contradict the information we can cull from scrutinizing Pausanias's itinerary. Artemis may have preferred the country, but she was also found in towns. Her sanctuaries were not evenly distributed throughout the Peloponnese, however. In the Argolid, for instance, she was more prominent in the hills of the eastern sector than in the central plain, where Hera was the female divinity of choice and Artemis was only a "visitor" in Hera's sanc-

25. Schol. Aeschin. 1.97; Harpocration, s.v. ἐσχατιά, with comments by Robert (1969) 821.

26. A space called ἐπ' ἐσχατιῇ λιμένος in *Od.* 2.391. In coastal towns she guarded travel by protecting harbors; Brulé (1988) 186–90.

27. "Midtowner"; for two inscriptions of the third century B.C.E., see Brulotte (1994).

28. Menander Rhetor 9.135 Walz; 3.334 Spengel.

29. Callim. *Dian.* 3.17–18, 38–39; for the variety of sites within a specific area, see Lafond (1991) 413, for Achaia.

tuary.[30] Sanctuaries of Artemis clustered in the territories of the cities in the southeastern sector of the region or along the roads passing through the mountains to the northwest on the way to Arkadia.[31] If we examine more closely the nature of the sites she occupied, it becomes clear that a significant defining feature was not so much location, but the character of the space they occupied.

Even in towns, Artemis is distinctive. Rarely found on an *akropolis,* she was more likely to be in the *agora* or at some meeting place.[32] When she was located on an *akropolis,* as at Athens or Aigeira, she was generally not the most prominent divinity, and her sanctuary was not the most striking construction. Artemis did not dislodge Athena. Moreover, even on an *akropolis,* her sanctuary was recognized as a place associated with the natural landscape. That is, when she came to town, Artemis brought the wilderness with her. At Pellene, where she was important to the civic community, citizens swore their oaths in her walled grove, located above the temple of Athena, on the peak that divided the two areas of the city.[33] At Aigeira, she was located on a rocky plateau, with a cistern as water source nearby.[34] At Patrai, as the major goddess on the *akropolis,* she was actually an import, Artemis Laphria. Here her festival was marked by an unusual holocaust of birds and wild animals—wolves, bears, wild boars, deer, and even gazelle.[35] Outside the city, as Pausanias and Kallimachos knew, Artemis was the goddess of thoroughfares. In coastal areas she often overlooked the harbor. In inland areas her sanctuaries were elevated on hills, mountainsides, or even the tops of mountains, but always in direct relation to the roads she protected. Even in towns Artemis could be associated with streets and located at intersections; at Thasos, for instance, her sanctuary

30. *IG* IV.513, a dedication to Artemis at the Argive Heraion. For one god "visiting" in the sanctuary of another, see Alroth (1987) 9–19. The distribution of divinities in the Argolid reflects differences in local identities; Hall (1997).

31. As Fossey (1987) makes clear (see his map, page 81), arguing for Sparta's influence in spreading the cult of Artemis Orthia.

32. At Sparta, Artemis was worshipped at a place called Guardposts on a road leading out of the *agora* (Paus. 3.12.8); with Apollo and Leto at a place called the Dancing Place (*choros;* Paus. 3.11.9); at a place associated with goats at Theomelida (3.14.2); near a racetrack (*dromos:* Paus. 3.14.6–7); and in a well-fortified place on the Issorion (Plut. *Ages.* 32.3). Brulotte (1994) 188 points out that as Pausanias leaves Sparta on the road to Amyklai, he mentions Artemis Knagia, whose priestess was a *parthenos* (3.18.4–5).

33. Paus. 7.27.3; cf. Plut. *Arat.* 32.1–3.

34. The sanctuary is described by Lafond (1991) 415–17.

35. Paus. 7.18.12; he witnessed the sacrifice.

was placed near the *agora* where three roads came together.[36] She was often on a line of communication, where a major road met the major gate or entrance to the town, as, for example, at Sikyon and Thebes.[37]

The theme that unites the most distinctive sites of Artemis is the idea of dangerous or threatened passage. She was particularly associated with places of narrow access, both straits of water and mountain passes—the sensitive places necessary for a city's defense but also the places most vulnerable to enemy penetration. Her inland sites tended to be located, as Pausanias indicates, along main roads, especially where these passed between high mountains. Artemis was imagined to dwell in the mountains,[38] but her sanctuaries were not peak sanctuaries. It is not the mountains themselves that were sacred to her but the narrow passes in between. Mountains associated with Artemis were the mountains located at borders.[39] Artemis as protector was the scout who watched for danger; hence she could be called Proskopa, "Lookout."[40]

The choice of elevated sites and border locations for sanctuaries of Artemis was not accidental but governed by conscious strategic decisions in the context of the developing *polis*. Strategic concerns influenced her coastal locations, because by sea the navigation of bounded or treacherous space required her protection. Coastal sanctuaries of Artemis were therefore located at straits or narrows (northern Euboia, Aulis, Amarynthos, Halai, Salamis, Patrai, Naupaktos), where a river flows into the sea (Amarynthos, Aulis, and Brauron), or on a headland protecting a city's harbor

36. Grandjean (1988) 312–16; 483–84; Schachter (1992) 24.
37. Sikyon: Paus. 2.11.1; Thebes: 9.17.1.
38. Cf. *Od.* 6.102; Eur. *Tro.* 551.
39. Paus. 2.24.5 (Artemis Orthia on Mt. Lykone on the Argive side, with a second temple of Artemis on the far side of Mt. Lykone, on the way down toward Tegea); 2.28.2 (on Mt. Koryphon, at the boundary between Epidauros and Asine, Artemis as Koryphos, goddess at the peak); 3.20.7 (Dereion on Mt. Taygetos); 3.22.6 (in the borderland of Lakonia and Messenia); 4.4.2 (in the borders of Messenia, shared by Lakonians and Messenians); 6.22.1 (at the borders between Arkadia and Elis); 8.5.11 (at the borders of Orchomenos and Mantineia); 8.6.6 and 2.25.3 (on Mt. Artemision, near the source of the Inachos, between Mantineia and the Argolid); 8.13.1 (on a level place on the mountain between Orchomenos and Anchisiai); 8.13.2 (Artemis Kedreatis on a flat peak of the mountain at Old Orchomenos); 8.15.8 (on Mt. Krathis on the borders between Pheneos in Arkadia, and Achaia); 8.23.4 (Mt. Knakalos at Kaphyai); 9.24.4 (on Mt. Kyrtone in Boeotia, Artemis with Apollo and the nymphs, near a tended grove); 10.37.1 (on a high ledge on the mountain between Antikyra and Bulis).
40. At Apollonia, *SEG* 36.559.

(Mounychia,[41] Aigina, Delion on Paros,[42] Kalydon[43]). Her sanctuaries monitored entrances and exits, passage through narrow channels, or movement in and out of protected harbors. Boundary space on the sea was equated with boundary space at a mountain pass. An oracle of Dodona to the Athenians during the period of Macedonian aggression warned, "Guard the heights *(akroteria)* of Artemis." The oracle was interpreted to refer not to the *akropolis* but to Artemis's coastal sanctuary at Mounychia.[44]

In cities where she was not in the *agora* (as at Thasos, Sikyon, Troizen, Aigion), Artemis could be near a gymnasium (Elis, Sikyon), a military camp and race track (as at Sparta), or located at a gate of the fortification wall (Phlius, Thebes). Even when worshipped with another divinity—for instance, Demeter or Asklepios—she was often found at the gate of the more important partner's sanctuary (Epidauros, Eleusis, and Lykosoura).

TURNING POINTS

The placement of temples of Artemis on major ancient highways at regional boundary points reflected the shape of the land and emphasized the relation of political territory to natural landscapes. When located along major land or sea routes, sanctuaries of Artemis did not mark a single point in isolation from the surrounding land but were deliberately placed to mark important divisions within the larger landscape. The boundaries[45] Pausanias so often notices when approaching her sanctuaries defined a critical space associated with the motion of people or armies traveling through a mountain pass, of water flowing through a river[46] or channel,[47] or of ships passing through a strait.

In the mountainous terrain of inland areas, territorial boundaries of a political community were officially recognized by the direction of flowing

41. Palaiokrassa (1991).
42. Schuller (1991) 2–3, especially fig. 1.
43. Dyggve (1948).
44. Plut. *Phoc.* 28.2.
45. In addition to the border sanctuaries listed in n. 39, this chapter, Pausanias locates sanctuaries of Artemis in or near borderlands at Karyai (3.10.7) and between Sparta and Arkadia (3.20.9).
46. Paus. 3.24.9, for Artemis Diktynna on a headland overlooking the sea where a freshwater river flows past.
47. As at Aulis, near the Euripos, marking the boundary between Euboia and Boiotia; Paus. 9.19.6.

water.[48] Pausanias noticed the watershed of the Tanaos river before he crossed the borderland at Hermai on his way to the sanctuary of Artemis at Karyai. Such obvious and natural boundaries were often marked in the landscape by *horoi,* the markers used as reference points in official documents, treaties, and leases. Treaties between states recognized local waterways and watersheds, especially the watershed at the top of a mountain pass, as limits of territorial authority.[49] Sanctuaries of Artemis were located in conjunction with water in records of boundary settlements near Megalopolis,[50] between Messene and Megalopolis,[51] along the Choireos river on Mt. Taygetos,[52] and, outside the Peloponnese, on Crete between Knossos and Tylissos.[53] At this last location political borders were defined with reference to a temple of Artemis, a river, and the direction of the watershed. Again in the Peloponnese, border locations were chosen for Artemis at Pheneos,[54] on the ridge of Mt. Anchisia marking the borders between Mantineia and Orchomenos,[55] and at the peak of Mt. Artemision above Oinoe, near the borders of Argos and Mantineia, at the source of the Inachos.[56] Artemis also guarded a waterway between two heights on the road between Tegea and Argos, where a herm dedicated to the goddess marked an enclosure in a gorge at the foot of Mt. Ktenias.[57] Four of these examples are preserved in treaties that defined boundaries and settled border disputes. Watersheds were used to mark the limits of territorial claims because they could be determined by observation and because sovereignty over sources of water was as important to the life of the city as sovereignty over the land. Artemis is mentioned so often in treaties resolving border disputes because she was identified with those sensitive places where the flow of the water itself divided and changed direction.

48. Daverio Rocchi (1988) 51 n. 4.

49. Jameson (1989) 7–16.

50. *SEG* 17.195.

51. *IOlympia* V.46; *SEG* 11.1189. For description, see Brulotte (1994) 233–34. For border markers in the Peloponnese and elsewhere, see Alcock (1993) 118–20, observing the persistence of local borders even after Hellenistic leagues and treaties should have made them obsolete.

52. *IG* V. 1431. The site is disputed; see Brulotte (1994) 165–66, 235–36.

53. *Staatsverträge* II no. 148b.6–9, treaty between Knossos and Tylissos, about 450 B.C.E.

54. Paus. 8.15.8.

55. Paus. 8.5.11. Tausend (1998) 109 has traced the path.

56. Paus. 2.25.3; 8.6.6; *SEG* 38.314, sixth century B.C.E. See also Brulotte (1994) 126–27.

57. Jost (1985) 163; Brulotte (1994) 78–79.

In coastal and island regions, political territory was demarcated by the water's edge. In such landscapes sanctuaries of Artemis could be located where shorelines faced each other. Like mountain passes, narrow straits were marked by danger,[58] and in times of war such places required special protection. There are many examples. Artemis at Mounychia overlooked the approach to the harbors of Athens. The Artemision on Euboia overlooked the straits guarding the main channel from the north, which Themistocles' strategy identified as the first line of defense against the Persian advance into Greece.[59] A series of Artemis's sanctuaries dotted the shorelines of the narrow strait between Euboia and the mainland at Aulis, Amarynthos, Halai, and Brauron. The Artemision at Aulis just south of Chalkis was very near the Euripos,[60] a point between Euboia and the mainland where the strait narrows and deepens so fast that the water actually reverses its flow many times a day. This waterway was the principal transportation route between Attika and the Hellespont—southward, the route taken by the invading Persian fleet, and northward, the route of Agamemnon's armada on its way to Troy. Safe passage, as the poets knew well, required the good will of the goddess.

In legend and in fact, Artemis was associated with turning back an enemy's attack. At her sanctuary in the Lakonian hinterland near Pyrrhichos she was known as Astrateia (she who disperses invasion) because this was the place where she was said to have turned back the legendary invasion of the Amazons.[61] Artemis was a god of turning points.[62] Her temples were strategically placed and marked critical points of defense in real battles. The Artemision across from northern Euboia overlooked the strait where Themistocles had to turn back after his first naval engagement with the Persians in 480. Artemis's sanctuary on Salamis had a clear view of the strait where Xerxes would in turn yield to him later that year.[63] Artemis also stood guard at critical points of incursion by land. Her temple at Hyampolis

58. At Apollonia in Illyria, Artemis was therefore called *Προσκοπά*, "Lookout" (*SEG* 36.559).

59. Plut. *Them.* 7.2.

60. The harbors of the Euripos (*λιμένες Εὐρίποιο*) are listed by Kallimachos, *Hymn. Dian.* 184, as among Artemis's favorite sites.

61. Paus. 3.25.3; the epithet is puzzling; see Brulotte (1994) 181, 184–85.

62. Hippias of Erythrai in Ath. 6.259b, reading Spanheim's *Στροφαίᾳ* for the ms. *στοφέα*. Cf. the reaction to an imagined epiphany of Artemis during an attack on the territory of Pellene; Plut. *Arat.* 32.

63. Cf. Hdt. 4.87 for the columns used by Darius to mark the Bosphoros, put to use later use by the people of Byzantion to build an altar for Artemis Orthosia.

in the borderland between Phokis and Lokris overlooked the pass that provided entry to the whole Greek mainland for forces from the north. It was here that first the Thessalians, then the Persian land troops, and finally the Romans moved down into Phokis and Boiotia.[64]

BOUNDARIES AND COMBAT

At Athens, Artemis Agrotera—Artemis of the Wilds—was recognized as necessary to the ritual process that formed the male community. Athenian ephebes began their military service with a sacrifice at her little temple just outside the wall at Agrai on the bank of the Ilissos.[65] This experience was recalled with every military campaign. When Athenian hoplites mobilized for battle, they assembled at the sanctuary of Apollo Lykeios. Here, the temple of Artemis at Agrai was directly in their line of vision as they prepared to meet the enemy. In some sense, the male community had to be recreated as a combat force for each engagement.[66] As Agrotera, Artemis inspired the intense emotion male citizens needed to transform themselves into the soldiers war compelled them to become.[67]

Sanctuaries of Artemis marked the spaces where this emotional transformation took place. The actual stages of that transformation were accomplished by ritual,[68] and Artemis's support was necessary at critical moments. Crossing boundaries in times of war, whether by sea or land, was accompanied by specific forms of sacrifice. Artemis's sanctuaries, whether on land at border crossings or on sea at places of embarkation, recognized the sites of emotional challenge, to which, once passed, there was no turning back.[69] As guardian of harbor, strait, or mountain pass, the goddess represented for the men of a marching army or an embarking force the moments of extreme tension experienced when leaving behind the borders of home or the security of the shore.

Marching armies traveled with flocks of animals and carried sacred fire

64. Ellinger (1987) 93.

65. Burkert (1983) 65 and n. 31. The Athenian festival of Artemis Agrotera was associated in the Hellenistic period with the ephebes; for the epigraphical evidence, see Pritchett (1979) 3:174–75.

66. Jameson (1991) 210–11, for the relation between the two sanctuaries; (1980) 224–25, for a description of the sanctuary of Apollo Lykeios.

67. Vernant (1991) 44–57, for the process.

68. For sacrifices before battle, see Lonis (1979) 95–110; Jameson (1991) 197–227.

69. Lonis (1979) 95–104, for a summary of these sacrifices.

for the sacrifices the crises of war required. Spartan kings traveled with flocks of sheep led by she-goats[70] because the Spartans could not engage in battle without the ritual slaughter of a young she-goat[71] for Artemis Agrotera.[72] By cutting the goat's throat, the *mantis,* ritual advisor to the king, determined whether signs were favorable for battle.[73] Goats grazed in the mountains and therefore represented marginal space. Identified with the spatial fringe of the community, they were considered marginal as sacrificial animals. At Athens, they were even banned from the *akropolis.*[74] Sacrifice of a goat, when prescribed by the ritual calendar or a specific ritual, like acknowledgment of Artemis Agrotera, signified an anomalous or dangerous situation.

EPIPHANY AND CRISIS

During battle, Artemis Agrotera inspired soldiers at critical moments—moments sometimes distinguished by the appearance of the goddess herself.[75] A dramatic epiphany of the goddess, accompanied by a flash of light, revealed the moment of crisis or turning point of battle. The Athenians at Marathon, fighting in the light of the almost-full moon,[76] recognized such a moment and associated it with Artemis Agrotera.[77] Later, the Athenians established for her an annual sacrifice of goats, originally one for each of the Persian casualties, but for economy the number was eventually rounded

70. Paus. 9.13.4.

71. Plut. *Lyc.* 22.2; the Greek word is *χίμαιρα,* described by Pritchett (1979) 3:84, as a goat that "has seen one winter."

72. Xen. *Lac.* 13.8; *Hell.* 4.2.20; Plut. *Lyc.* 22; cf. Arist. *Equit.* 660–62; Ael. *NH* 2.25.

73. Jameson (1991) 208.

74. Ath. 13.587a; Varro, *Rust.* 1.2.19–20; von Schwenn (1922) 64.

75. Artemis had a reputation for epiphany in wartime. Plutarch, *Arat.* 32.1–3 describes a priestess of Artemis who turned away an enemy attack with the help of an epiphany of the goddess herself; the goddess's presence in her statue was so powerful that no could look directly at it. A lost work by Syriskos of Chersonesos was devoted to the epiphanies of the Tauric Artemis; *IOSPE* I^2 344. For an inscription at Ephesos referring to a tradition of Greek and non-Greek dedications to Artemis for wartime epiphanies, see *SIG*^{3} 867. Artemis Kindyas was credited with saving Bargylia; Robert (1937) 459–65. For epiphanies of Artemis at Pellene and Knidos, see Pritchett (1979) 3:36–37.

76. Hdt. 6.120.

77. With reservations, Pritchett (1979) 3:172–75. The festival, however, took place on the birthday of the goddess, not the anniversary of the battle; see Rhodes (1981) 650, on 58.1.

down to five hundred.[78] This sacrifice was performed by the polemarch, the official traditionally identified as the military leader.[79]

Some believed that Artemis sent a full moon to the Athenian force at Salamis in 480.[80] On the island, a sanctuary of the goddess[81] overlooked the narrows where the final engagement was fought.[82] In recognition for her inspiration in planning his battle strategy, Themistokles dedicated a little temple to the goddess in the city and called her Artemis Aristoboule, "Artemis Who Gives the Best Advice."[83] Later, during the Athenian festival to Artemis on 16 Mounichion, the ephebes commemorated Artemis's connection with the battle by sailing from her sanctuary at Mounichia to Salamis and back, creating a connection between the sanctuary on the mainland and the sanctuary on the island.[84]

In the last stage of the campaign against the Thirty in 404 the supporters of Thrasyboulos attributed to Artemis the decisive encouragement they needed for their final confrontation with Critias's force. They claimed that the goddess appeared to them on a moonless night as a flash of fire from

78. Xen. *An.* 3.2.12. The original sacrifice (at the Herakleion at Marathon) is the earliest known publicly subsidized sacrifice; Parker (1996) 153. Herodotus gives the number of Persian casualties as sixty-four hundred (6.117). Xenophon explains the eventual reduction to five hundred in terms of the shortage of animals.

79. *Ath. Pol.* 58.

80. Plut. *De Glor. Ath.* 349f–350a, where it is implied that she appeared at full moon. Pritchett (1979) 3:173–76 questions the schedule of events and denies that the battle took place at night. He assumes, perhaps too rigidly, that accounts of divine epiphany must have a rational base.

81. Pausanias (1.36.1) mentions the sanctuary of Artemis and a *tropaion* from the famous battle in the same sentence.

82. Parker (1996) 155 n. 10, following the oracle in Hdt. 8.77, argues for sanctuaries of Artemis on both sides of the strait. Local topography in relation to the battle has been much discussed; references in Roux (1974) 53 n. 1, with discussion of the whereabouts of the local Artemision, 68–69. A decree of the *thiasotai* of Artemis has been found on the acropolis of the town of Salamis. The sanctuary may have stood on the northern shore or at the tip of Cape Kamatero (Kynosoura), named in antiquity for the *tropaion* that stood there; see Hammond (1956) 54. For the *tropaia* erected to celebrate Persian defeat, see Wallace (1969) 293–303.

83. Threpsiades and Vanderpool (1964) 26–36; although the site was in use in the Geometric period, the earliest known votives *(krateriskoi)* seem to date from the period after the Persian Wars. The site was probably a local sanctuary of Artemis well before Themistokles' dedication. The few remains of the original building are dated only roughly to the fifth century. Plutarch associates the epithet of Artemis with the plan of Themistokles (*Them.* 22; *De Herodoti Malignitate* 869d), where it is connected explicitly with the Salamis strategy. For further discussion, see Parker (1996) 155 n. 8 and 216.

84. Plut. *De Glor. Ath.* 349f; *IG* II^2 1011.16, with discussion by Pritchett (1979) 3:176.

her sanctuary on Mounychia. In tribute, when democracy was restored, they dedicated an altar to the goddess at Mounychia and gave her the title Phosphoros, "Torchbearer."[85] The epiphany of Artemis at Mounychia was considered essential to the restoration of democracy and was later recognized when Artemis Phosphoros was included among the divinities named in official prayers of the governing bodies of the *polis*.[86]

THE LAY OF THE LAND

Jost has noted that a high proportion of the epithets for Artemis in Arkadia were formed from toponyms,[87] an indication that she was more tightly bound to particular places than other gods. Many of her temples were placed in direct relation to a natural spring, and others were associated with specific topographical features, whether a flat outcrop on a mountainside, a hollow just below a peak, or a low, marshy area.[88]

Artemis's epithets, which often describe a feature of the site, also indicate strong attachment to place. They often emphasized proximity to flowing water or springs. "Agrotera" ("wild," at Agrai and Megalopolis), "Limnatis" ("marshy," at Tegea, Epidauros Limera, the Messenian frontier, Kalamai, and Patrai), "Limnaia" ("of the marsh," at Sparta and Patrai), and "Heleia" (also "of the marsh")[89] were formed from the names of the natural features that anchored her sanctuaries. Epithets of Artemis connect her to lakes, rivers, springs, and the seashore; they also connect her to woodlands, mountains, and the countryside.[90] The distribution of such epithets indicates a conscious recognition of the local environment. Epithets like "Limnatis" and "Limnaia" were more common in the countryside and were rarely used of Artemis when she was recognized inside the *asty*, where she was more likely to be called Soteira, Eukleia, or Philomeirax,

85. Clem. Alex. *Strom.* 1.24 (163.1); Borgeaud (1988) 157.
86. For example, *IG* II^2 902.8; Meritt and Traill (1974) 183.8, 184.8, 197.7, 240.8, 261.12.
87. Jost (1985) 396.
88. For exceptions at Kombothekra; see Sinn (1981) 29–30 and fig. 1a (early fifth century). Here her temple was actually located on top of a mountain, but an inscribed mirror is dedicated to Artemis Limnatis, "Artemis of the Marsh," suggesting a low-lying place, and creating a juxtaposition between epithet and location. For Artemis and her association with marshes and ponds, compare her epithet "Blaganitis" and her description as "goddess of frogs" in *SEG* 37.539–40.
89. Strab. 8.3.25.
90. Brulé (1998) for comprehensive classification of the epithets of Artemis.

names associated with her role as protector of the city or protector of children and adolescents.

Water was often a focal point in sanctuaries of Artemis, whether she was located on a mountain,[91] in a marshy area, or by the side of a river. One of her earliest temples, the sanctuary of Orthia at Sparta, was located outside the town in a low, marshy area near the Eurotas River.[92] Pausanias also notices water at her sites at Megara, Mt. Artemision in Argos, Teuthrone, Korone, Skillous, Muthone, Phrixa, Lousoi, and Stympalos, and near Trikolonoi, Aulis, and Lilia. Excavation and exploration has established that her temples were oriented around springs at Brauron, Aulis,[93] Amarynthos,[94] Lousoi,[95] Stymphalos,[96] and outside Greece at Kyrene.[97] The groves of trees frequently mentioned in connection with her sanctuaries imply the presence of a good water supply.[98]

Water could both frame and focus the space within a sanctuary of Artemis. At Brauron in Attika, Artemis's sanctuary was designed to emphasize the natural features of the site. Here the goddess presided over an especially lush spring, and her sanctuary overlooked a small harbor where a river joins the sea.[99] Similarity between the natural features of this site and those of other coastal sites of Artemis suggest that such sites were deliberately chosen. The site at Brauron replicated the site of Artemis across the straits at Amarynthos, which was also located where a river flowed into the sea. At Brauron, the precinct, built into the side of a hill, was framed by the sea and harbor directly to the east and the river to the west, such that whether worshippers approached the sanctuary by land or sea, they

91. Pausanias mentions springs in connection with the sanctuary of Artemis on Mt. Artemision (2.25.3) and describes cold water gushing out of the rocks on Mt. Kyrtone in Boeotia, where Artemis was worshipped in a grove dedicated to Apollo (9.24.4).

92. In an area subject to flooding; Dawkins (1929) 15–16.

93. Muthmann (1975) 235–36.

94. Sapouna-Sakellaraki (1992) 240, for a subterranean chamber at Sarantapotamos that might be the location of a sacred spring. This is near the site of Aghia Kyriaki, where extensive votives have been found. For a critical discussion, see Brulé (1993).

95. Reichel and Wilhelm (1901) 15–18.

96. Seiler (1986) 120–29; for doubts about identification this as a sanctuary to Artemis, see Morizot (1994) 204 n. 8.

97. Pernier (1931) 173–228; Chamoux (1953); Wright (1957) 307–10.

98. For a list (at least 22 sites), see Birge (1982) 245 n. 62.

99. Brauron was not an Attic border town but the site of a harbor convenient to the Cyclades, perhaps exploited by Peisistratos for his campaign to establish stronger links with Delos. See Peppas-Delmousou (1986) 255–57.

had to cross a boundary between water and land. Those approaching from the interior crossed a bridge over the river immediately before entering the precinct itself. Architectural structures designed for social ritual emphasized other natural features, including the spring and a shallow rock crevice that provided focal points for ritual. A large *pi*-shaped stoa, built during the last quarter of the fifth century[100] and designed to control entry to the interior of the sanctuary, dominated the area. It contained a series of dining rooms backed on the northern end by an unusual long, narrow gallery, where textiles dedicated by the women of Attika were apparently displayed. Although its east wing was never entirely completed, the stoa was designed to frame an important ritual space, demarcated on the south by the temple of Artemis.[101] The foundation of the temple, cut from the natural rock, almost filled the space between two other natural features—the spring adjacent to the west side,[102] and the rock crevice, a small ravine, to the east.[103]

Water was highlighted at Brauron because water was essential to the ritual of the goddess. Installations for water in her sanctuaries were directly related to her roles as goddess of childbirth and *kourotrophos*, protector of children. *Hydriai*, vessels for carrying water, are prominent among items dedicated in her sanctuaries, and terracotta images of female *hydrophoroi* (water-carriers) are widespread.[104] The young girls who served as ritual water-carriers for Artemis at Didyma in Ionia protected the sacred springs of the goddess and performed ritual *hydrophoria* for sacrifices, libations, and the *mysteria* (rites that could not be divulged) celebrated by the women and *parthenoi* of the city.[105] Water was central to the rituals for women associated with Artemis. It was used for rituals of transition, for purification before marriage and after childbirth, and for rituals associated with raising children. The water surging up from the earth in the sacred enclosures of Artemis was identified with her gifts of both physical and mental health.[106]

100. Bouras (1967).

101. Kondis (1967) 156–206, for a description of the site. The fifth-century temple replaced an earlier building of the seventh or sixth century.

102. Travlos (1988) 63 pl. 62.

103. Travlos (1988) 70 pl. 74.

104. *Hydriae* at Brauron, Ephesos, Sparta, and *hydrophoroi* at Didyma, Patmos, Samos, Lousoi; Diehl (1964) 199–201.

105. *IDidyma* 326, 327, 353.

106. Morizot (1994) 201–16. It was believed that the water of the Stymphalian lake depended on the festival of Artemis; Paus. 8.22.9.

Greek poets assume the unity of all surface water, connected by underground rivers to Okeanos, the generative water of the primordial sea flowing around the earth.[107] The spaces occupied by Artemis, whether in the mountains, on a promontory along a shore, or at an inland spring or marsh, marked significant boundaries between land and water. Major watersheds marked the boundaries that enclosed the territory of the individual *polis*, and they also rimmed the territorial ground water, which, as we have seen, was as important as the native soil in conferring local identity.[108] Within the territory of the *polis*, the local springs and the watery places associated with Artemis and local nymphs were recognized as sources of human fruition, growth, and health. The rituals performed in such places by women of the community marked important stages in the life of the individual, and they also affirmed community integrity. A small, unadorned spring sanctuary dedicated to Artemis on Mt. Megalovouni, at the border between Argos and Nemea, is a good example of the connection between fertility, territorial boundaries, and community identity. A site of worship for women with concerns about reproduction, the place was reached by a steep stairway cut into the stone. The stairway is still in use because this is the only spring in the area.[109] At this remote spot, inscriptions were carved in the living rock for Artemis Oraia, "she who ripens," because she was the goddess who protected infants in the womb and women in childbirth.[110]

UNIFYING CENTER AND BORDERLAND

Artemis never completely lost the characteristics that placed her in or near the kind of borderlands over which the Argives and Spartans had fought in the sixth century. Her earliest sanctuaries, where votives date from the Geometric period, were in mountainous border areas—in Arkadia at places like the western ridge of Mt. Chelos, between Kleitor and Lousoi;[111] on the

107. Hes. *Theog.* 346–47; Rudhardt (1971) 31.

108. *Od.* 13.353–60, where Odysseus greets first the earth and then the nymphs of Ithaka's water sources when he returns to his native land; cf. Soph. *TrGF* F 911 Radt.

109. Mitsos (1949) 75.

110. Hdt. 1.202, 196, 107; Xen. *Cyr.* 4.6.9, on the vocabulary "ripe for marriage."

111. With some of the earliest votives in Arkadia; Jost (1985) 48–51 and Brulotte (1994) 43–57. For a similar sanctuary that may have been dedicated to Artemis about the same time on the saddle between Lousoi and Pheneos, see Tausend (1995), with comments on the sanctuary of Artemis Hemera at the town sanctuary in Lousoi.

frontier between Achaia and Elis;[112] in Boiotia at Mavrovouni;[113] or in Phokis at Kalapodi.[114] As city-states matured and established consolidated centers, they brought Artemis to town. At Kaphyai, a rite *(telete)* for Artemis Knakalesia celebrated in her sanctuary on Mt. Knakalos was balanced by rites at her sanctuary in the city on the plain.[115] The same is true at Aigeira in Achaia, where Artemis, as Agrotera, had a sanctuary in the borderland facing Sikyon and was recognized in town as associated with Iphigenia.[116] The location of the borderland sanctuary had been chosen, so the story goes, because at this spot an invading force from Sikyon had been fooled by the lights of torches tied to the horns of a herd of goats. The temple had been built at the site where the lead female, the most beautiful of all the goats, had chosen to lie down.

Cults on the fringes could be replicated in major settlements, but secondary foundations in town centers did not replace the distinctive rural sanctuaries of Artemis. In Arkadia, new cult sites established in towns to mirror traditional rural sanctuaries were the result of political synoecism.[117] Each region had its own reasons for connecting peripheries to the center. In Attika, Artemis was clearly established at Brauron by the seventh century.[118] Possibly in the sixth century but definitely by the fifth, the Brauronia, celebrated in her honor, had become one of the major quadrennial festivals of Athens.[119] The procession of females to Brauron was a major social event, but it also had political meaning. By connecting an important outlying sanctuary to the political center, it emphasized the unity of Attika.

The Athenians formally recognized the importance of this strategic connection sometime in the middle of the fifth century with the dedication of

112. At the "wall of the Dymaioi," Polyb. 4.59, 4.83; for an inscription, see Lafond (1991) 414.

113. Tomlinson and Fossey (1970) 245–52.

114. Felsch et al. (1987) 1–99.

115. Paus. 8.23.3–4; Kaphyai was the site of a dike that kept the runoff from Orchomenos from flooding the plain. Compare Artemis at Arkadian Orchomenos: as Mesopolitis inside the city wall, as Kedreatis outside the city, and as Hymnia on the frontier with Mantineia; Paus. 8.13.2, with Jost (1985) 115 and Brulotte (1994) 79–85.

116. Paus. 7.26.1–5, 11. See Ellinger (1993) 222–23 for the high concentration of sanctuaries of Artemis in this border area.

117. Jost (1992) 205–38.

118. Rhodes and Dobbins (1979) 325–41.

119. Part of the great Athenian penteteric cycle, administered by the ten *hieropoioi; Ath. Pol.* 54.7.

a *pi*-shaped stoa for Artemis Brauronia on the *akropolis*. This structure, directly facing the Propylaia, gateway to the *akropolis*, was the first building a visitor encountered after passing through that entrance.[120] The new stoa was not a temple, but it shared at least one function with the *pi*-shaped stoa at Brauron. At Brauron, the gallery of the *pi*-shaped stoa displayed the textiles made by the wives of the men of Attika. In Athens, the stoa provided a prominent space to display the stones inscribed with inventories of the dedications made at Brauron.[121] Exhibited at the heart of the city, the inscriptions displayed Attic unity and made visible the political identification of the city with its outer territory. Like the sanctuary of the Eleusinian goddesses nearby on the slope descending toward the *agora*, which represented at Athens Demeter's important sanctuary at Eleusis, the Brauronion on the *akropolis* brought into the city a specific divinity whose reputation, reflected in her epithet, was identified with a specific location on the external borders of the *chora*.

When recognized at or near the nucleated center, Artemis often had the generic epithet Soteira, "preserver,"[122] but she never lost the powerful characteristics so appropriate to her earliest border spaces. Sanctuaries of Artemis, replicating in town the kind of space associated with the goddess at her rural sites, protected the city by creating a unity between the center and its borderlands. This process is illustrated by a pair of monuments set up by Megara to commemorate Artemis's aid in driving out the Persians. After 479, the Megarians erected two identical statues of Artemis Soteira, one in the city of Megara and the other in Pagai, a Megarean village on the border facing Boiotia.[123] This pair of statues recognized the two locations as spatially separate but symbolically interdependent, and both of them as essential to the preservation of the city.

Greek cities created themselves by claiming a coherent landscape. De Polignac explains this phenomenon in terms of the early history of the *polis*, arguing that early communities demonstrated original claims to local territory by controlling major rural sanctuaries.[124] He describes the developing *polis* as a unified spatial construct and argues that a major sanctuary

120. Rhodes and Dobbins (1979) 325–41.

121. Linders (1972).

122. Megalopolis, Paus. 8.30.10; Troizen, Paus. 2.30.7; Phigaleia, Paus. 8.39.5; Boiai, Paus. 3.22.12 (exact location not given); Pellene, Paus. 7.27.3, on the *akropolis* above the temple of Athena. Artemis Soteira at Tegea was apparently located just north of the town; Brulotte (1994) 99–101.

123. Paus. 1.40.3; in 1.44.4, Pausanias calls Pagai a *polis* of Megara.

124. De Polignac (1995a).

in the countryside at or near sensitive borders was a structural and formative element. As we have seen, however, the basic notion of a ritual unity between center and periphery was fundamental to the Greek *polis* throughout the Classical period and marked its continued survival thereafter. As long as they lasted, Greek cities maintained stability by protecting both a nucleated center and external borders.[125] Each independent *polis* depended on a whole community of divinities, each with its own kind of space. Artemis protected boundary lands, tied boundary lands to the center, and prepared communities for meeting military crises in vulnerable places. As Pausanias approached the borderland on his way to Artemis's sanctuary at Karyai, he noticed the tomb of those who had fallen in battle there—the memory still fresh because the borderland was a place where anything might happen.

125. On Crete, this concern for borders was a characteristic of the Hellenistic period, when the population filled up the landscape. See Chaniotis (1998) for treaties.

7 Domesticating Artemis

AT THE MARGINS

The action of Euripides' *Iphigeneia among the Taurians* is set far away from the Aegean, on the northern coast of the Black Sea.[1] When Orestes arrives on a mission to fetch from this place a portable image of Artemis, a crisis is generated by the local Taurian custom requiring any stranger arriving on these shores to be sacrificed to Artemis. Unknown to Orestes, his sister Iphigeneia (whom he believes is dead) is living here in service to Artemis, and she is expected to officiate at her own brother's death. This is avoided when each learns the true identity of the other, but the crisis (how to appease a goddess who demands the death of strangers) cannot be resolved without the intervention of Athena. In a show-stopping epiphany towards the end of the play, Athena announces Athenian ritual as the solution, directing that Orestes install a statue of Artemis at one sanctuary of Attika (Halai) and that Iphigeneia take up service to Artemis at another (Brauron). In imitation of the Taurian rite, the sacrifice at Halai would require not death but merely a show of human blood. Athena announces to Iphigeneia that, as priestess of Artemis at Brauron, she would one day have her tomb in the sanctuary "at the Brauranian steps," where she would receive the garments left behind by women who died in childbirth:

> . . . and they will
> dedicate as ornament for you the fine-webbed woven garments that women

1. Hall (1987) 422–38, for the geography.

breathing out their last breath in childbirth leave behind in their homes.[2]

The Brauronian steps can be seen today, carved into the living rock—a detail Euripides knew his audience would recognize. Other conditions described here, however, are puzzling. For one thing, Iphigeneia's mission to receive gifts made by those who have died has no ritual model. Death in childbirth would constitute ritual failure, an ominous occasion for making a gift in a sanctuary. Granted, Iphigeneia's own death was a prerequisite for her achievement of heroic status, because dying is what heroes and heroines must do, but why here and why now? More precisely, why at this time should Athens be glorifying a Peloponnesian heroine, and why did Athens need a grave and heroine that other cities claimed?[3] Finally, why, in the penultimate decade of the fifth century,[4] did Euripides talk about a *xoanon* (portable image) of Artemis in Attika? We know there were several statues of Artemis at Brauron, at one time even a special *xoanon*,[5] but Pausanias denies that this particular *xoanon* was the one Iphigeneia had brought back from the Taurians.[6] The Persians took this one back to Susa in 480.[7] In fact, several cities claimed to have the "genuine" Taurian statue. Strabo locates one in the temple of Artemis at Halai,[8] another in a temple of Diana at Aricia,[9] still another in a temple of Ma in Cappadocia,[10] and even reports a fourth among the people of Tyndaris in Sicily.[11] For Pausanias, although he mentions a *xoanon* of the goddess at Hermione (where, he says, Artemis was called Iphigeneia), the wooden *xoanon* in the sanctuary of Artemis Orthosia at Sparta was the only genuine article.[12]

2. Eur. *IT* 1462–66:

. . . *καὶ πέπλων*
ἄλγαμά σοι θήσουσιν εὐπήνους ὑφᾶς,
ἃς ἂν γυναῖκες ἐν τόκοις ψυχορραγεῖς
λίπωσ᾽ ἐν οἴκοις.

3. Namely, Megara; Paus. 1.43.1.
4. The date may be about 413 B.C.E., sometime after Sophokles' *Chryses* (dated before 414) and before Euripides' *Helen* (412).
5. Paus. 1.23.7. Euripides calls the statue *bretas, agalma,* and (once) *xoanon.*
6. Paus. 1.33.1.
7. Paus. 3.16.7–8.
8. Strab. 9.1.22.
9. Strab. 5.3.12.
10. Strab. 12.2.3. Pausanias, 3.16.8, is aware of this tradition.
11. Graf (1979) 41 n. 4, and Pritchett (1998) 256–60, collect the evidence.
12. Paus. 2.35.1.

Many sanctuaries of Artemis must have had such a portable image of the goddess.[13] The most powerful were treated with special respect, and some even required a place for safekeeping. For security, many temples of Artemis had an extra interior chamber,[14] usually called the *adyton*, accessible only to the priestess. *Adyta* are found in other sanctuaries, especially those associated with oracles, mysteries, or the incubation connected with healing cults, and in such contexts they were places for special rituals restricted to only a few. Such chambers in temples of Artemis were different, however, in that they were not for ritual but for safe storage of sacred items. Entry was strictly controlled.[15] A restricted-access chamber would have provided a secure place for an image considered dangerous in itself.[16] Threatening images were kept out of sight and were brought out only rarely, under supervision and the protection of ritual.[17] Artemis's temple at Hyampolis was open only twice a year.[18] The image of Artemis Eurynome at Phigalia was so hard to control that it was bound with golden chains, and her temple was opened only once a year.[19] At Pellene, the *xoanon* of Artemis was such an object of dread when taken out on parade that no one would willingly look on it, for it could wither the fruit on a tree or stop an enemy in its tracks.[20]

Respect for the power and danger of an angry god encouraged myths of foreign origin that located violent divinities like Ares, Dionysos, and, in

13. At Messene, the young attendant of Artemis who carried the image *(bretas)* of Artemis Orthia in the ceremony was honored with a statue; *IG* V.1 1032; see Themelis (1994) 114–15 for a summary, and fig. 18 for the statue base. *Hierai parthenoi* performed the *xoanophoria* for the mysteries at Andania; *IG* V.1 1390.29.

14. Travlos (1976), for Brauron, Halai, and Aulis. The *adyton* at Mounichia is essential to the story of the sacrifice there. Hewitt (1909) 89–90 associates Artemis with *adyta* only when her function is exceptional. Hollinshead (1985) is critical of the Attic reconstructions of Travlos, but the pattern is well-established elsewhere. See Felsch et al. (1987) for Hyampolis, Seiler (1986) for Stymphalos, Sinn (1978) and (1981) for Kombothekra, Kuhn (1993) for Thermon, and Pernier (1931) for Kyrene. Recent work at Lousoi indicates that the early temple for Artemis had a separate chamber divided from the cella by a wall. Pottery goes back to the eighth century; Mitsopoulos-Leon (1992).

15. Hollinshead (1999), especially 196–97, emphasizes security for valuable objects but does not even consider the possibility of danger from the objects themselves.

16. Suggested by Graf (1985) 37 for Halai.

17. Hewitt (1909) 89–90.

18. Paus. 10.35.7.

19. Paus. 8.41.5.

20. Plut. *Arat.* 32; Faraone (1992) 138, for the fear aroused by these images. See Graf (1985) 81–98 for the type.

some forms, Artemis far away, at the fringes of the civilized world. Artemis, so often worshipped in border areas, could be explained in her most savage form only as a foreign goddess, imported from a distant and alien realm. Iphigeneia's apprenticeship in the far north, then, is preparation for her service at Brauron. As a victim of violence who is loyal to Artemis, Iphigeneia is qualified to preside over the consequences of violent death in childbirth. Athena's solution satisfies an angry Artemis and a needy Iphigeneia. Both figures were called for at home in Attika, but only if they would protect as well as destroy. Euripides' play was staged during a time of continuing crisis for the Athenians, when Brauron in eastern Attika was under the shadow of a Spartan threat. What better time for claiming the grave of a Peloponnesian heroine and appropriating a talisman of Artemis so strongly identified with Sparta?

THE ANGER OF ARTEMIS

Euripides presents Artemis in her savage form to illustrate that she was a divinity who had to be appeased. Her sanctuaries could be places of refuge in times of stress or conflict,[21] but the protection Artemis offered her female worshippers demanded loyalty in return. When rituals of Artemis excluded males, females had no protection except what the goddess herself could provide. Rural sanctuaries were vulnerable targets, whether they were located in mountain areas, the countryside,[22] or where the land met the sea. Artemis was associated with risk.[23] The attacks on her female worshippers, common in myth and legend, suggest anxiety about the safety of women at her festivals. The plot of Menander's *Epitrepontes*, structured around a rape at the Tauropolia;[24] Euripides' description of Xouthos's recollection of sexual encounter while observing a bacchic rite on Parnassos;[25] and Plutarch's story about the women of Amphissa protecting the Athenian Bakchai while they slept[26] all make the same assumption. Whether alone at a festival or traveling to a celebration, women were an irresistible

21. Sinn (1993).
22. Immediately following his description of the events at Karyai, Pausanias relates the account of an attack on women celebrating the rites of Demeter at Aigila in Lakonia; Paus. 4.17.1.
23. Artemis was found in all three types of places; Schachter (1992) 49–51.
24. Men. *Epitr.* 471–92.
25. Eur. *Ion* 550–54.
26. Plut. *Mul. Virt.* 249e–f.

attraction.[27] In the case of Artemis, early Messenian attacks on Lakonian females emphasized the consequences of interfering with the rites of a neighboring community's women and indicated that drastic punishment could be meted out for cities as well as for individuals.

Successful celebration of female festivals at unprotected border sanctuaries was recognized as pleasing to the gods and was considered a sign of peace, security, and territorial integrity. Lack of respect for the boundaries of another community was expressed in myth by attacks on that community's women. Stories about violation of females were told to demonstrate the gods' involvement in human affairs, to rationalize political alliances, and to justify military aggression. Violation of the safety of females at frontier sites was a sign of ritual failure and indicated that the security of a *polis* was threatened by war with its neighbors. The Spartans long remembered the story of Theseus's abduction of Helen from the sanctuary of Artemis Orthia on the Eurotas when she was still a young girl. The retaliatory invasion of Attika by the Tyndaridai was paradigmatic for a tradition of hostility against Athens.[28]

The Athenians had a story of their own. The sanctuary of Artemis at Brauron—situated as it was on the east coast of Attika, at an important harbor—was a stepping-off place to Delos and Ionia and was open to intrusion from the sea. A Lemnian incursion at Brauron in mythical time became part of the fifth-century rationale for Athenian interference at Lemnos in the early years of the Delian confederacy.[29] According to Herodotus, ancient Pelasgians from Lemnos feuded with the Athenians, kidnapped Attic women from this sacred place, and kept them as concubines *(pallakai)*. The Lemnians attempted to conceal their crime, but they eventually compounded it by killing both the women and their children. Herodotus describes how the Lemnians were later cursed by a three-fold disaster: blight in their crops, disease in their herds, and decline in their birthrate. His narrative incorporates the punishments of the typical curse, a pattern designed to illustrate the consequences of *asebeia* (impiety), where ritual transgression meant that the many could suffer for the mistakes of the few.

The nature of Artemis and the remote location of many of her sanctu-

27. Trygaios and his slave, characters in Aristophanes' *Peace*, recall with pleasure how they took advantage of females in procession to Brauron; Ar. *Pax* 872–75 and passim.

28. Kearns (1989) 158. The consequences of Helen's youth are important for the multiple versions of this story; Lyons (1997) 138–39.

29. Hdt. 6.137–40.

aries define her as a goddess associated with unsettled areas.[30] Paradoxically, the risks of unprotected ritual were a necessary feature of the worship of Artemis. The paradox is usually explained as a consequence of initiation ritual, whereby an individual's transition to a new status is achieved by a temporary reversal of normal communal restraints and a demonstration of successful confrontation with the wilderness,[31] but an explanation that concentrates on individual experience and personal transformation does not take into account the political significance of state sponsorship of female ritual. The ritual system of the *polis* placed more emphasis on creating community than on achieving individual status. Unprotected ritual at a rural site, performed by those who seemed most marginal to the society, was in fact a component of the larger religious system. When the public ritual calendar required women to meet at an unprotected sanctuary at the border of the city's territory, the successful performance of traditional rituals there had a special meaning. The Lakedaimonians who sent their daughters to perform the dances described by Pausanias at Karyai tested Lakedaimonian strength and celebrated Lakonian security by entrusting to Artemis the most vulnerable members of their community.[32] Young girls measured with their bodies the security of the community. So too, in ritual, by dispatching delegations of the community's most eligible daughters for ritual at the farthest reaches of its territory, the city confirmed its own security.

Artemis could protect the borders of the *polis*, but she demanded a steep price. An unreliable female was a threat to the entire community, and stories like the one about the attack on the Lakonian women at Karyai were told to demonstrate that females could expect protection only if they could be trusted. The story about Karyai also shows what could happen if the protection of the goddess was withdrawn. Punishments were particularly severe in cases involving young attendants expected to be *parthenoi* (unmarried) and to remain sexually inexperienced for the term of their service. Mythical narratives associated with particular sanctuaries show how an entire community could suffer for the duplicity of a single female. When he describes how the town of Patrai was punished with plague *(loimos)* and

30. Vernant (1991).

31. Dowden (1989).

32. In myth, the daughter of the king, by volunteering to risk her body, could guarantee the success of her father's military operation. Larson (1995) 101–110 collects the most important Attic examples. For the curious story of Polykrite of Naxos, who saves her city but is destroyed by the *phthonos* of the other women, see Burkert (1979) 73 and Bremmer (1983) 305.

famine *(limos)* because a priestess of Artemis Triklaria entertained her lover in the sanctuary, Pausanias echoes the formulaic curse Herodotus used to describe the punishment of the Lemnians: "The earth no longer bore fruit, and abnormal diseases were responsible for an unusual number of fatalities."[33] Disease and blight could not be stopped until the Delphic oracle instructed the community to sacrifice the girl and her lover and to replicate that rite with an annual double sacrifice. The punishment of Artemis's priestess was so severe because she had violated the standards of purity for the sanctuary and the requirements of sexual purity for service to Artemis. More important, as representative of all the young women in the community, she had also violated the social requirement that young women refrain from sexual experience until marriage.

The story of Kallisto follows a similar pattern. Well known as early as the Archaic period, this popular tale describes how a young *parthenos* was punished by the goddess when she became pregnant.[34] Because sexual experience violated the purity requirements of Artemis, Kallisto was turned into a bear. Vase painters and poets represented the metamorphosis as a personal tragedy, but the message delivered by the goddess addressed more than Kallisto's feelings. Her punishment demonstrated the high value the community placed on control of female sexuality. The fact that the girl was seduced, perhaps even raped (by Zeus, no less), was not relevant. She was punished because her pregnancy revealed sexual experience before marriage.[35]

Myths associated with rites of Artemis at the Attic sites of Brauron, Aulis, and Mounychia also deal with problems of a girl's disobedience. Service to Artemis tested female loyalty and measured the community's success in supervising its women. In the version associated with Brauron,[36] a young girl was scratched by a bear sacred to the goddess because she had teased the animal. When her brothers responded by killing the bear, the whole community began to suffer from an infectious disease *(loimodes*

33. Paus. 7.19.6; compare 6.11.7.

34. Kallisto's tragedy was well known long before the melodramatic scenes of fourth-century Apulian vases. She was included in *The Catalogue of Women* attributed to Hesiod, Fr. 163 Merkelbach and West; she was represented (with a bearskin) on Polygnotus's painting at Delphi, Paus. 10.31.10; and she was the subject of Aischylos's *Kallisto, TrGF* 3:216 Radt. Henrichs (1987) 266 summarizes the evidence.

35. Sissa (1990b) 358, on pregnancy as a visible sign of the loss of virginity.

36. *Suda*, s.v. *ἄρκτος ἢ Βραυρωνίοις*, reading *Φιλαιδῶν* for the ms. *Φλαυιδῶν*. Philaidai is the deme where the sanctuary of Brauron was located; Sale (1975) 268.

nosos) that could be cleared up only if the community established a regularly scheduled ritual, the *arkteia.* Young girls called *arktoi,* "she-bears," therefore, played the part of bears in dances performed for Artemis. In a variant of this story, associated with Artemis at Mounichia, the girl's father had to sacrifice her to the goddess—a deed he avoided by substituting a goat dressed as a girl.

In the Attic stories the entire community suffered for the misbehavior of a single member.[37] The typical penalties—plague or pestilence *(loimos)* and famine *(limos)*—were both associated with Brauron.[38] These were considered serious punishments sent by the gods.[39] Artemis herself was more likely to be associated with plague than famine, and diseases inflicted by Artemis had specific targets and specific consequences. Kallimachos makes this clear in his hymn to the goddess, where, echoing Hesiod, he says that those on whom the goddess smiles have rich fields, healthy herds, and long lives. The unjust, those on whom the goddess frowns, suffer terribly. Plague destroys their cattle, frost destroys their fields, and their women either die in childbirth or, if they survive, give birth to infants who are not able to stand "on upright ankle."[40]

An infant who could stand "on upright ankle," was a healthy child; its stance reflected and confirmed the health of the entire population. Collective reproductive failure was a threat to any community that did not respect the ritual of the goddess. The poet's description draws on a tradition that associated deformed children and stillborn infants with the communal failure resulting from insult to a divinity. The anger of Artemis was especially threatening because it was directed against the next generation. Pausanias reports an example in a story about Kaphyai in Arkadia, where Artemis Kondyleatis was called by the strange epithet Apanchomene, "strangled." According to this story, a group of children once "strangled" her image by tying a noose around its neck.[41] When adults punished the children with death by stoning, the goddess was so angry that she threatened the entire community with extinction by sending a terrible disease that caused all infants to die in the womb. The effects were so severe that the pattern of successful childbirth could not be restored until the commu-

37. The sources are conveniently quoted and analyzed by Sale (1975) 265–84.

38. Schol. Leid. Ar. *Lys.* 645. For the pattern, Bonnechere (1994) 118–20.

39. Delcourt (1938); Brulé (1988) 183–85, 201, 218–22, on plague as a general issue in myths associated with Artemis.

40. Callim. *Dian.* 128. Calame (1997) 167 considers the connection between this idea and the meaning of Artemis's epithet "Orthia" at Sparta.

41. Paus. 8.23.6–7.

nity consulted Delphi, granted normal burial to the dead children, and honored them with the sacrifice normally offered only to heroes. The structure of the tale is familiar: error offends a divinity, who sends punishment in the form of a plague or famine;[42] and ruin is averted only when the community consults an oracle about the appropriate ritual for restoring the normal life cycle.[43]

At Kaphyai it was the statue *(agalma)* of the goddess that was strangled. The goddess herself could not be injured, so she was angry when the children were punished. In fact it was not the goddess but her young female worshippers who were at risk of choking. This is clear from other accounts of the same pattern, such as at Karyai in Lakonia. Here, young girls dancing at a festival of Artemis were threatened with trouble[44] (probably rape) and climbed the nut trees *(karya)* in her sanctuary to escape. Under pressure from attackers, they hung themselves by the neck from the branches and died.[45]

Death by hanging was not an acceptable form of suicide for males, but it was the standard method for females.[46] Mass suicide, however, is a different issue, and this example of failed ritual demands explanation. Female forms suspended from the branches of a tree were apparently not an unusual sight. There is a story that Diogenes of Sinope, known for his caustic witticisms, did not even blink when he caught sight of what appeared to be young girls hanging from a tree. His only reported comment is: "If only all trees bore such fruit!"[47] The variant story about the strangled statue of Artemis suggests that the figures Diogenes saw were not real girls but images or figurines. Pausanias's term for the strangled image is *agalma*, a word that normally refers to a statue of a god, as opposed to a statue of a person *(eikon)*;[48] but *agalma* is also used of apotropaic figures set up to avoid disaster, illness, or doom.[49] In ritual, ceramic figurines could be substituted for real people. At Delphi, the Thyiades carried a doll-like image of

42. Examples collected by Faraone (1992) 57–66, etc.; and Larson (1995) 141–44, etc.

43. Calame (1997) 101, for a similar structure in initiation rituals for Artemis.

44. Lactantius, on Stat. *Theb.* 4.225.

45. Paus. 3.10.7, for the dances; 4.16.9–10, for soldiers' attack on the girls who danced at Karyai. The incident is discussed by Calame (1997) 149–54.

46. Loraux (1987).

47. Reported by Diog. Laert. 6.52.

48. Gernet (1981c) 100–101.

49. Faraone (1992) 54–61, where he discusses the riddle of divinities who also guard against the trouble they cause.

Charilla in the annual celebration of her funeral procession.[50] When the Attic heroine Erigone hanged herself for grief over her father's death, Athenians put an end to the epidemic of copycat hangings she inspired by hanging clay images in the trees.[51] Diogenes' females hanging in trees were therefore probably not real girls but their terracotta images. Publicly displayed as apotropaic dedications to Artemis, such figurines would have been a record of ritual performed and a reminder of the protection earned.[52]

There is archaeological evidence for such figurines. Ceramic figurines associated with promoting female reproductive health are found in two fourth-century Attic contexts: graves (the actual ceramic figurines) and grave reliefs (depicting little girls holding figurines). These figurines are in the form of a headless body without hands or feet. Labeled in inventories from the Athenian Asklepieion as *soma* (body), *somation* (little body), or *soma gynaikos,* (body of a woman),[53] such truncated, nude female torsos represent the reproductive female body. The little girls depicted as holding a fully developed female torso in their arms are obviously too young for the physical changes and rituals that would prepare them for womanhood. Nevertheless, the headless torsos found in graves were put there for a reason: Like the ritual vessels for the prenuptial bath buried with those who died too soon to experience wedding rituals themselves, these torsos were markers of age and social status. A ceramic torso identifies a female who died before she could complete the ritual cycle that would have prepared her for the risks of reproduction. Whether placed in the grave or represented on a grave marker, such a "miniature body" both records a family's loss and confirms the significance of that ritual cycle.

A crucial element in the story of Artemis Apanchomene at Kaphyai is the identification of hanging and choking as female reproductive disorders. The ancient medical profession considered the problem serious. One med-

50. Plut. *Quaest. Graec.* 12.293c–e.

51. For terracotta images, Verg. *Georg.* 2.388–92. For the story, Apollod. 3.14.7; Hyg. 130; Callim. Fr. 178 Pfeiffer; Hsch. s.v. *Αἰώρα, Ἀλῆτις*. See also Jost (1985) 400–401 and Larson (1995) 140 and 204 n. 55. Jost (1985) 401 n. 4 describes a terracotta figurine with a hole in the top for suspension, now in Munich.

52. Cantarella (1985) 65 connects myths of suicide by hanging with swinging rituals. Others, for instance, Nilsson (1967³) I 486–92, exaggerate the significance of the tree.

53. Reilly (1997); for figurines found in a grave, see 155 fig. 32, 156 fig. 33, and 158 fig. 36. For a funereal relief, see 161 fig. 37 (New York: Metropolitan Museum of Art, inv. 20.205). Other examples are mentioned in the partial catalogue, 170 n. 27.

ical writer, attempting to describe the menstrual problems of adolescent girls in terms of Hippocratic theory, explains choking as a symptom of a pathological condition induced by abnormal retention of menstrual blood at menarche.[54] Other symptoms associated with this condition include delirium, fear of the dark, and hallucinations—conditions so dire they could drive a young girl to death. Sufferers tried to drown themselves in wells or even strangle themselves by hanging. The doctor indicates two possible methods of therapy: divination (the more popular) and his own (the more rational):

> And the virgins who are ripe for marriage, if they remain unmarried, suffer this (condition) more at the time of the onset of their menstrual cycle. . . . But relief from this complaint comes when nothing impedes the flow of blood. I order *parthenoi* to marry as quickly as possible if they suffer this. For if they become pregnant, they become healthy. If not, then at puberty or a little later she will be caught by this or some other disease. Among married women *(gynaikes)* it is the ones who are barren who suffer most from these conditions. . . . And when the girl comes to her senses, the women dedicate to Artemis many other things, but especially the most expensive (or carefully finished) of their feminine clothing, because the diviners demand it, but they are deceived.[55]

The doctor prefers a practical solution, but for the women who believed in ritual remedy, successful reproduction depended on the will of a goddess. As the stories show, a girl's belt could become her noose,[56] but Artemis herself was Lysizonos, "she who unties the belt." Just as the goddess could release a woman from the burden of pregnancy, she could also release the blood that caused distress.[57] The girls dancing at Karyai and the girls who hung figurines in trees acted out of fear; but they also acted out of hope, because the female forms hung in trees represented an outcome Artemis's celebrants wished to avoid.[58]

Artemis's epithet "Apanchomene" was appropriate for the effigies of her young female attendants. Artemis could palliate the risks of growing up, but she herself was removed from the reproductive process. Because she

54. I follow here the explanation of King (1983) and (1998) 80–86.

55. *Virg.* 5–6, translation follows that of King.

56. King (1998) 85 points out that Myro made a noose out of her belt; Plut. *Mul. Virt.* 253c.

57. As King (1998) suggests.

58. Jost (1985) 402. For a wooden statue *(xoanon)* of Artemis in a tree, see Paus. 8.13.2.

was immortal, she could not bleed. For young girls who had to pass through menarche and accept bleeding at menstruation and childbirth in order to fulfill biological and social roles, normal periodic bleeding was a positive event. A flow of bright red blood, like the blood flowing from an animal struck in sacrifice, was considered a sign of health both at menarche and after childbirth.[59] The goddess had to remain permanently a *parthenos* and biologically a girl, for she could protect girls, brides, and adult women from the dangers of reproduction only if she herself was immune to its disabilities.[60]

THE CYCLE OF REPRODUCTION

Cities needed the good will of Artemis because the reproductive capacity of its women and the health of its children were measures of success. Service to Artemis required not one but a whole cycle of rituals to mark the stages in the reproductive process:[61] just before puberty; on the eve of marriage; between marriage and first pregnancy; during pregnancy; and at childbirth. Artemis was the gatekeeper at each stage. A mother relived her own experience by participating in her daughter's developmental cycle. No single ceremony was more important than the others; rather, they formed a series of critical transitions that began before the first signs of sexual development, continued through the onset of menstruation and first sexual intercourse, and ended with the birth of a living child.[62] Age divisions were not precise, and the distribution of female rituals according to age cohort was not the same everywhere. At Olympia, *parthenoi* were divided into three groups,[63] and although three groups were typical,[64] there were sometimes four.[65] Precise age limits were not as important as the sequence of experiences. *Partheneia* (though usually translated "virginity") was not necessarily coterminous with sexual inexperience, especially if that experience occurred outside of wedlock. A girl could be called *parthenos* until marriage

59. King (1987).
60. Pl. *Tht.* 149b–c.
61. Sourvinou-Inwood (1988b) 25: these transitions were gradual.
62. King (1983) 122.
63. Paus. 5.16.3.
64. Paus. 3.13.7. Hatzopoulos (1994) 46, reconstructing a three-stage process in Macedonia and Thessaly, notices the frequent appearance of the motif of three daughters in myth as a possible analogy.
65. Theocritus describes as many as four cohorts of sixty girls each; *Id.* 18.24.

even if she had already borne a child,[66] and the status of bride, defined by the Greek word *nymphe*, lasted until the birth of the first child.[67] Physical and social status did not always coincide, but full adult status for a female, described by the word for woman, *gyne*, required childbirth and possibly even a living infant.

Young girls began to prepare for the event of first childbirth at an early age. Even before menarche girls danced for Artemis and, in some places, performed the role of animals, for instance, at Brauron, where they imitated she-bears, *arktoi*.[68] Playing an animal prepared a girl for the experience of pregnancy and childbirth.[69] Acting the she-bear for Artemis was a prerequisite for sexual intercourse in marriage,[70] because, as Libanios says, girls had to serve Artemis before proceeding to the service of Aphrodite.[71] Success at one stage of the maturation process was a prerequisite for a proper relationship with the goddess at the next stage, but females risked the anger of Artemis at any stage. In Thessaly and Macedonia, epigraphical traces of a three-stage ritual of maturation for young girls survive. The girls were apparently divided into three ranked groups: "the young," "those over the young," and "the leaders." Upon completing all or part of the cycle they owed a propitiary sacrifice, called *lytra* (ransom), or *teleiouma* (a dedication to mark completion of physical growth), offered to Artemis Throsia, the goddess who presided over the successful male procreative act. In some cases it was the female who made the dedication; in others, this the responsibility of a male representative, perhaps her husband. The ritual cycle reflected the process of physical development and had to meet the requirements of Artemis, a goddess difficult to please.[72] One commentator describes the girls celebrating the *arkteia* at Brauron

66. Sissa (1990b) 342–43.
67. Chantraine (1946–47) 228–31.
68. Ar. *Lys.* 645.
69. For bears as traditional symbols of maternity, see Perlman (1989) 112–19; Osborne (1985) 163. Lyons (1997) 146–48 explains the theme of ritual substitution in narratives about Artemis and Iphigeneia.
70. *Suda*, s.v. *ἄρκτος ἢ Βραυρωνίοις*.
71. Lib. *Or.* 5.29 (I.313.10 Foerster).
72. Hatzopoulos (1994), for a convincing argument on the linguistic evidence for deriving the participle *nebeusasa* from the Thessalian form of *νέα* rather than constructing a new verb (*νεβρεύσασα* "play the fawn", suggested originally by Hiller von Gaertringen; circulated by Clement [1934]; and followed by almost all who have written on the *arkteia* since). For a fresh appraisal, see Kajava (1999) 15–18; for a good discussion of the issues, see Brulé (1997) 319–30.

as "soothing" or "appeasing" the goddess.[73] Another says that girls had to "placate the goddess for their virginity *(partheneia)* so they would not be objects of her revenge."[74]

The possibility of evoking Artemis's revenge lasted until a young woman had survived childbirth. At Kyrene in the fourth century, the *polis* counted the ritual stages for Artemis among its most important rites, and to prevent the calamities of plague, famine, and death,[75] issued a mandatory series of ritual procedures. The rules that governed these procedures are said to have been delivered as an oracle in Apollo's own voice. Apollo advised attention to three kinds of rituals: 1) a ritual tithe, or "tenth part" *(dekate)* for males on behalf of the city; 2) procedures for protecting suppliants; and 3) female rituals to appease Artemis. Satisfying Artemis and involving her in reproductive ritual was therefore as important to the city as it was to the individual or her family. The inscribed text distinguishes three stages that required sacrifice to Artemis. The first preceded marriage, the second pertained to the bride *(nymphe)* at the time of marriage, and the third took place during pregnancy.[76] Each stage had a ritual obligation, and failure to perform the specified ceremony at the appropriate time required expiatory sacrifices as penalty. The city administered the sanctuary, supervised the sacrifices, and assessed penalties for a female's failure to fulfill her obligations because the city had a stake in the outcome.

Marriage was a time for looking both backward and forward. On the eve of her wedding a girl acknowledged Artemis's protection during her early life by dedicating the symbols of childhood[77] in anticipation of her approaching reproductive responsibility. She also sacrificed to Artemis. Artemis Lysizonos, "she who loosens the belt," presided over the sexual transition associated with marriage because a woman's belt was a visible sign of an invisible boundary. Artemis had to be appeased at the time of marriage and first intercourse to enlist her support in childbirth, when the same physical boundary would be crossed again.[78] In some places, the roles usually assigned to Artemis were distributed among other goddesses. In the

73. Suda, s.v. *ἄρκτος ἢ Βραυρωνίοις· ἀπομειλισσόμεναι τὴν θεάν.*
74. Schol. Theoc. 2.66. For a fuller discussion, see Kearns (1989) 29.
75. The text is damaged at this point.
76. *SEG* 9.72. For a convenient translation and helpful commentary, see Parker (1983) 344–46; for a summary, see Perlman (1989) 128–30.
77. A relief from Tyndaris shows a young girl accompanied by parents making a sacrifice to Artemis Eupraxia; Deubner (1925) 210–12 and pl. 1.
78. Schmitt (1977) 1063; King (1983) 121.

Argive plain, Hera had charge of the stages of the female life cycle, and at Argos itself, the primary divinity who presided over the sexual maturation of young women was Athena. She shared responsibilities with Leto, Chloris, Hera Anthea, Demeter Pelasgis, and Kore. At Kos, young women on the eve of marriage sacrificed to Aphrodite Pandemos with a rite that was required whether they belonged to the citizen class *(politides),* were born of irregular unions *(nothoi),* or were foreigners *(paroikoi, metoikoi).*[79]

Childbirth was the final test because childbirth itself was a crisis.[80] Homer's Artemis was a "lion to women" because she could strike a woman in labor with death.[81] To relieve the pains of labor, women prayed to Artemis,[82] to Artemis Soodina,[83] and to a twin Artemis called Artemides Praiai, "the Tamed Double Artemides."[84] Successful labor required a cooperative Artemis, but she could not ease the crisis unless she was addressed as Artemis Hemere, "Artemis the Tame."[85] After delivery, women recognized the goddess's aid by performing sacrificial rituals called Pausotokeia, "the rituals when childbirth is over."[86] Gratitude for having survived the crisis encouraged women to address Artemis as Lochia, Eulochia, Eileithyia, and Genetaira—epithets stressing her role in aiding birth.[87]

In thanks, new mothers made dedications in sanctuaries of Artemis, like the dedications made in thanks for recovery after disasters such as shipwreck or severe illness.[88] As one commentator says, "When they bear children, they dedicate clothing to Artemis."[89] Artemis could be tamed by gifts of domestic production—the textiles women made with their own hands. So often associated with the wilderness at the outer boundaries of the *po-*

79. Segre, *IKos* ED 178 (*SEG* 43.549); the rite included oath and sacrifice. At Athens, however, after 403 B.C.E., no female or male *nothos* could share in the cults of the family and city; Is. 6.41, 50.

80. Demand (1994) 70–86.

81. *Leonta gunaixi; Il.* 21.483.

82. Eur. *Hipp.* 161–69; Men. *Georg.* 112.

83. *IG* VII 3407, Chaironeia.

84. *IG* VII 3101, Lebadeia.

85. Bacch. 10.39; Callim. *Dian.* 3.236; *IG* V.2 398, Lousoi.

86. Neuter plural, meaning "rituals for ending childbirth"; Pingiatoglou (1983) 112.

87. For a catalogue of inscriptions where Artemis is named as a goddess of childbirth, see Pingiatoglou (1981) 163–69, E65–108; 107–112 (with many examples from Gonnoi). Artemis Eileithyia is more common epigraphically, Artemis Lochia is more common in literary sources.

88. Van Straten (1981) 96–97.

89. Schol. Callim. *Jov.* 77.

lis, Artemis could also be accessed by products from the most intimate spaces of the home.

A recently published relief from a sanctuary of Artemis at Echinos,[90] illustrates the domestication of Artemis yet indicates its instability. The relief shows a new mother bringing an infant to Artemis for the first time.[91] She offers sacrifice in thanks for a safe delivery and presents her daughter to the goddess to enlist divine protection during her upbringing.[92] The infant herself reaches out her tiny hand to the goddess. The entire scene pivots around the baby's hand, the central object in the picture. Artemis holds a torch in her left hand, but her quiver is just barely visible behind her right shoulder, a reminder of the arrows in her arsenal, the arrows potentially fatal to women in childbirth.[93] A female servant carries a tray of offerings: apple, pomegranate, and a bunch of grapes—fruits associated with fertility and sexuality—plus honey cakes and a myrtle branch. A male attendant, below normal size, leads the sacrificial animal. An older woman (perhaps the child's grandmother), whose size (on par with that of the goddess) suggests a donor's status, makes a gesture of prayer with her right hand held up, palm forward. Behind the figures and across the top of the relief a line is strung. Clearly defined objects hang on the line—from left to right: a pair of shoes, a shirt, two fringed garments, and a belted *peplos.*[94] We know such items were included in dedications from inscribed inventories listing the garments dedicated to the goddess, but this is the first recovered example that graphically depicts them. The scene marks the culmination of an important cycle for the mother, and as the baby reaches out to the goddess a new cycle begins.

INSCRIBING CIVIC SUCCESS

Dedications to Artemis, like the dedications to other kourotrophic divinities who nurtured the young, indicate a concern for female reproductive

90. A border town between Malis and Achaia Phthiotis in northern Greece.
91. Dakoronia and Gounaropoulou (1992) 219–23.
92. For praise of women who bear female children, see *TAM* II.1 no. 174.
93. Hom. *Il.* 6.205, 428; 19.59; 21.103, 483; 24;.606.
94. Dakoronia and Gounaropoulou admit that it is difficult to identify these garments with the technical vocabulary of garments in inscriptions. My interpretation of the images differs from theirs in one respect: they identify the fringed garments as bedding; I prefer, from the size, to consider them clothing.

processes and the physical development of infants.[95] Emphasis on the health of the body is also evident in the votives representing female body parts that often appear in Artemis's sanctuaries. One of the earliest items, from the foundation deposit of the original archaic temple of Artemis at Ephesos, is a tiny gold object in the shape of a vulva.[96] Breasts and vulvae appear elsewhere, for instance at Athens, Aivatlar, Menge, and Demetrias, and at Eleutherna on Crete;[97] Delian temple inventories record the dedication of two silver wombs to Artemis.[98] Dedications also include the tools women used in spinning and weaving and the products of their work. Among the tools found at Brauron are spindles, spindle whorls, loom weights, and *epinetra* (thigh guards used for preparing woolen roving for spinning). A child-size *epinetron* found at Brauron may have been a young girl's introduction to spinning. A small relief found in the sanctuary depicts a female figure seated on a rock, with *epinetron* on her right knee and roving in her left hand, reminiscent of Homer's epithet for Artemis herself, χρυσηλάκατος, "goddess with the golden distaff."[99] The textiles and garments donated, however, are long gone, remembered now only because they were listed in the inventories inscribed on stone. As we saw in chapter 6, the exhibition hall at Brauron where woven garments were once displayed on wooden racks has been located by excavation. Identified by the footings for the display racks, the long hall runs behind the dining rooms along the entire central arm of the stoa.[100]

Women dedicated their finest textile products and the tools they used in spinning and weaving to mark the stages of the female life cycle. We can see that the Hippocratic doctor who wrote the essay on the medical problems of virgins had little confidence in the efficacy of such offerings, but the depth of his contempt actually confirms how important freelance diviners and

95. Hadzisteliou Price (1978) 89, 137.

96. Van Straten (1981) 135; late eighth century or early seventh century B.C.E.

97. Collected by van Straten (1981) 111–43. The example from Eleutherna is *ICrete* II XII no. 24, a relief plaque with two breasts inscribed: "Soteria dedicated this relief according to her vow to Artemis Dynatera (all-powerful)." The preceding inscription, no. 23, describes Artemis as having saved a woman's life.

98. *IDélos* 1442 A.55 (145/4 B.C.E.), both were dedicated by a woman named Artemo.

99. *AE* (1961) 24, fig. 23, for a photo; Hom. *Il.* 20.70, for the epithet. Kondis (1967) 189, identifying the female as Artemis herself, adds that the illustration shows only the right half of the otherwise unpublished relief. For Athena represented as a spinning goddess, see Graf (1985) 209–14.

100. Kondis (1967) 173–75 and pl. 106.

rituals of Artemis were to his patients.[101] To deal with reproductive failure, families consulted diviners in the same way that communities consulted oracles to avoid agricultural blight. Girls who recovered dedicated the finest examples of their handiwork because the goddess deserved the very best.

The most detailed evidence for such textiles is the series of inscribed inventories found at Brauron, with duplicates at Athens. The inscriptions catalogue important dedications to Artemis Brauronia. The lists from Athens[102] record inventories of the precious gifts once displayed at the Brauron sanctuary. Lists are arranged according to material: gold, textiles, bronze, and wood.[103] Those found on or near the *akropolis* were probably originally set up in the stoa of Artemis Brauronia near the entrance. A typical inventory lists textiles according to the date of dedication. Individual items were tagged with the names of the women who made them; sometimes the letters of the woman's name were even woven into the fabric. The Athenian inventories are organized according to the year of dedication and, under the year, by the dedicant:

> When Kallimachos was archon (349/8): a little scalloped multicolored *chiton*, Kallippe; this has the letters woven in the pattern. Chairippe, Eukoline, a dotted garment in a wooden display box. Philoumene, a *chiton* made of linen from Amorgos. When Theophilos was archon (348/7): Pythias, a long spotted robe. When Themistokles was archon (342/1): a little variegated purple chiton in a display box; Thyaine and Malthake dedicated it. A variegated purple *chiton* in a display box, [- - - - - - - -] and Eukoline dedicated it. Phile, a belt. Pheidylla, a white woman's *himation* in a display box. Mneso, a frog-green garment. Nausis, a lady's *himation* with broad purple border in wave pattern around the edge. Kleo, a delicate shawl. Phile, bordered textile. Teisikrateia, a multicolored Persian-style shirt with sleeves. Melitta, a white *himation* and a little *chiton* (in rags). Glykera, wife of Xantippos, a little *chiton* with washed-out purple border and two worn garments. Nikolea, *chiton* of linen from Amorgos, around the seated statue. Ivory mirror with handle, on the wall; Aristodamea dedicated it. When Archios was archon (346/5): Archestrate, daughter of Mnesistratos of Paiania, *chiton* with tower pattern, in a display box. Mnesistrate, daughter of

101. Virg. 5–6; see discussion at n. 55, this chapter.

102. From the fragments published as *IG* II^{2} 1514–1531 Linders (1972) reconstructs six *stelai*. These *stelai* were inscribed with inventories of dedications to Artemis Brauronia, made between 355 and 336 B.C.E. For inventories as indications of public administration of a sanctuary, see Aleshire (1989) 14 n.5.

103. Linders (1972) 72. New inscriptions found at Brauron remain unpublished.

> Xenophilos, a white *himation* edged with purple; this covers the stone seated statue. A little smooth *chiton* for a child, without a label; it has a border in tongs pattern. Xenophante, a little scalloped fringed *chiton;* this is on the basket. Nikoboule, a new multicolored coverlet; it has a figured design in the middle: Dionysos pouring a libation and a woman pouring wine. Aristeia, a coverlet in a display box; in the middle it has figures with right hands joined. When Euboulos was archon (345/4): a fine shawl—it is inscribed "sacred to Artemis"—around the old statue; Theano made it.[104]

The inventories record the items handed over when the administrative office was transferred from one board to the next, and because each board was responsible for the items under its jurisdiction, care was taken to describe garments in some detail. The garments remained on display for many years; the same lists (with minor variation) are therefore repeated from year to year. Dated lists survive from the middle of the fourth century. No complete prescript survives, but explicit references to statues of Artemis and her possessions (e.g., "sacred to Artemis") indicate that Artemis was the principal recipient.

Inventories of dedicated clothing are well documented elsewhere, but Artemis seems to be the only divinity to receive so many varieties and so many sizes. Textiles for divinities other than Artemis were usually intended to dress a particular cult statue and were therefore uniform in style and size.[105] Attic inventories do describe items as draped over a statue, but gifts are described in so many sizes that they clearly were not made for the goddess to wear. These garments were personal possessions, property either of the individual who gave the gift or the one on whose behalf the offering was made. Lists similar to those in Attika are found at Tanagra and Miletos. Items inventoried are strikingly diverse. Belts, cloaks, tunics, headgear, veils, and shawls—some made from fine materials, some in exotic styles—indicate that individuals chose their dedications from the best they had to offer. Some items on the list may even have been clothing worn only for a specific ritual, *krokotoi* (yellow dresses) worn by the *arktoi* at Brauron,[106] for instance. A *kalas(e)iris* at Miletos is probably also a ritual garment. The type is known from Andania.[107]

The lists from Tanagra and Miletos are similar in both form and content to the Attic lists. Though lacking the sections that would have specified a

104. *IG* II^2 1514.7–38.
105. Romano (1988) 131–32.
106. Ar. *Lys.* 644–45.
107. Günther (1988) 224.

divinity, they are nevertheless likely to be records of dedications to Artemis.[108] All three dossiers emphasize women's garments but include children's clothing. The Milesian list in addition mentions four garments for ephebes. The variety of sizes suggests that the dedications are connected with life cycle rituals. The Milesian text, organized by condition and type of garment, lists only old, extremely frayed textiles:

> . . . a beautiful, old, useless eastern-style long garment, gray in the middle with gold border; an old useless *himation*, bright in color, with purple border; eight old useless purple garments, frayed; three old useless fine wool mantles, frayed; three purple-dyed *himatia*, useless and frayed; an old Karpasian linen garment; an old useless Sidonian garment; three old useless pieces of fine linen; two other linen napkins, frayed; four old useless ephebic capes; four old useless silken masks (veils?); two other old useless pieces of wool; twelve old useless pieces of linen, an old linen head-dress, two other ones, useless; another one, half worn out, frayed; another useless silken one, frayed; another silken one, half worn to pieces, frayed; two light-green cut woolen ribbons, frayed; another old scarlet one, frayed; two old belts overlaid with gold, another old bright red one with gold embroidered wave pattern; a woolen belt with gold overlaid, old and frayed; another of linen with a little clasp below, half worn out; [- - - - - - - -] Aianaios (?) dedicated (it?); two old belts; two other old ones, larger; a small purple woolen mantle and one with a fine purple border, both for children, frayed; and other children's clothing, frayed.[109]

The beginning and the end of the text are lost, but this is most likely a catalogue of garments dedicated to Artemis. Artemis Kithone (Artemis Clothed in a Tunic)[110] was well known at Miletos.[111] She is associated with clothing because clothing and its fabrication were economically important to the city and culturally significant in the lives of its women. Moreover, the high proportion of belts on the Milesian list is congruent with the worship of Artemis. The symbolic value attached to women's belts is a reflection of the goddess's close involvement in the transitional stages of a wom-

108. For a revised text, based on that of P. Roesch, see Casevitz (1993) 3–9 (*SEG* 43.212).

109. Found in 1912, the text has only recently been published; Günther (1988) 221.

110. Artemis Clothed-in-a-Tunic may be similar to Artemis Katagogis, which Perlman (1989) 127 translates as Artemis the Clothed.

111. Günther (1988) 234–35, for evidence (including a new inscription from the late Archaic period) for Artemis Kithone at Miletos. For the traditions associated with her myths, see Burkert (1979) 131–32 and, more recently, Herda (1998).

an's life.[112] The four ephebic cloaks *(chlamyes ephebikai)* were probably given by young men (or their mothers?) after service as ephebes. The only explicitly male item not easily associable with a life cycle ritual is the "man's cloak" *(himation andreion)* with no name attached; perhaps it was a sample of a woman's work.[113]

The clothing at Miletos was ravaged by age, not by use,[114] but not even age could obliterate its value. Once presented to the goddess, the garments could not be destroyed or thrown away. Made sacred by the act of dedication itself, such gifts had to remain in the sanctuary until they were eventually disposed of by burial within the sacred area. These were valuable items, representing the best clothing their donors possessed and given to the divinity to mark very special occasions. The value for the city was reckoned not only by the value of the garment but also by the meaning of those occasions. In the case of the Milesian ephebes, the dedication marked their change of status to full-fledged male citizens. In the case of the women who dedicated their belts, headgear, fancy dresses, and the clothing of their children, the dedication marked not a single occasion but was part of a full cycle of rituals to produce an adult woman. The textiles dedicated by women on behalf of young daughters who had recovered from the traumas of menarche were measures of the women those daughters would become.[115]

THE NAKED AND THE CLOTHED

Reproduction of the family was a concern of the *polis* because the family was the basic unit of the city. A barren woman was a liability, but a woman who died in pregnancy, miscarriage, or childbirth, whether *parthenos* or *nymphe*, could be a greater threat. Females who died too soon, and females who lost their children, were doomed to roam as *aoroi*, the untimely dead. A woman who died from a reproductive crisis threatened the well-being of infants and other mothers, as did the well-known spirits Mormo, Gello, and Lamia, who were responsible for the sudden death of new babies, little

112. The diffusion of belts as dedications for Artemis is well summarized by Simon (1986) 204–5.

113. *IG* II^2 1514.47.

114. The Greek word I have translated by the English word "frayed" is used by Aristophanes (describing Milesian wool) to mean "gnawed" by moths; Ar. *Lys.* 728–30.

115. For cross-cultural examples of textiles as indicators of life cycle stages, see Barber (1991) 374.

children, and new mothers.[116] Women who died in childbirth had to be remembered, even compensated, for the life they had lost.

As priestess and heroine, Iphigeneia, who also died too soon, would demand compensation for the early deaths of others. The textiles promised to her at the close of Euripides' play could not have been dedicated by the women who had made them. The dead do not give gifts. Rather the textiles had to be offerings from a surviving member of the family, someone who had good reason to fear an angry Artemis, a vindictive Iphigeneia, or even the dead victim herself. The obvious candidate was a surviving husband without children, because a childless widower who still hoped to become a father had to avoid the anger of the goddess, the revenge of her attendant, and above all, the anger of his dead wife.

Artemis was the recipient when all went well. Iphigeneia, it seems, received gifts only after disaster. The first type of gift is an offering of thanks, given in return for an object of prayer.[117] The second is a symbolic offering of propitiation, given as compensation for a loss.[118] An offering to Iphigeneia would be appropriate only after her death, which explains why the Athenians wanted her grave. As a permanent virgin in service to Artemis, Iphigeneia could never reach adulthood. She achieved ritual consequence only by her death. As a mortal deprived of physical fulfillment *(teleiosis)*, she could not preside over the ritual cycle that recognized it. She could never make the offering the Thessalians called *teleiouma*, the offering to Artemis that marked completion of the maturation process and the ritual stages that celebrated it.[119]

A distinctive feature of the Athenian inventories may help us to understand Iphigeneia's status.[120] The lists carefully distinguish between finished garments, unfinished weaving projects, baskets of spun but unworked wool, and rags.[121] One unfinished garment is even still on its frame: "a half-woven little *chiton (chitoniskon)* on a frame with both woof and

116. Johnston (1995) 366–70; worked out in more detail in (1999) 166–99.

117. Schol. Callim. *Jov.* 77.

118. "The phrase εὐπήνους ὑφάς, 'finely woven fabrics' (1465) is distinctive—the epithet is attested only in this play—and occurs here for the third time"; Wolff (1992) 319 n. 30.

119. *IG* IX.2 1235.

120. Kondis (1967) 161, noticing the distinction between labeled and unlabeled textiles, suggests that those with labels were directed to Artemis by live women and those without labels were for Iphigeneia.

121. Mommsen (1899), without evidence, supposed the rags were menstrual rags, dedicated by young girls at the time of menarche.

wool."[122] This half-woven little shirt, like the garments left unfinished or the wool prepared for clothing never made, would have been an appropriate token of a life unfinished, of a woman dead before her time.[123] These unfinished items differ from the ones described by the Hippocratic doctor who treated the suicidal depression of adolescents. He characterizes the textiles dedicated upon a girl's recovery as *eutelestata,* "expensive." The original meaning of this fairly rare, colloquial word, however, would have been "well finished," or "absolutely complete,"—a meaning with consequences for the girl as well as for her projects.

Dedication of woven garments was not a casual act. A young girl's weaving project with figures worked into the fabric was a sign of her accomplishments and a token of her identity. Her family recognized her by the images she wove. Euripides' Orestes confirms his identity to his sister by recalling the content of her adolescent project—a garment with a picture of the sun so horrified at the quarrel of the Tantalids that he changes his course.[124] An infant when Iphigeneia left home, Orestes had learned about the design from their sister, Elektra. Emblematic of their family's suffering, this image could be a test of Orestes' identity because a girl's early projects would have been seen only by close family members.

A young girl's weaving was also a sign of her status in the community. Iphigeneia in exile laments the loss of the opportunity to garner honor by participating in the collective ritual weaving for Hera at Argos or for Athena at home. An Athenian audience would have understood the disappointment of a young girl deprived of the opportunity to display her skill in weaving the images of the battle of the gods with the giants into Athena's robe for the Panathenaia.[125] Display of expertise in textile design was a common feature in public rituals for females of marriageable age. A woman's skill reflected the success and standing of her family. Select local women wove clothing for wooden statues *(xoana)* of Hera at Olympia and Samos, Athena Polias at Athens, Artemis at Brauron and Ephesos, Orthia at Sparta, Leto on Delos, and Apollo at Amyklai.[126] Statues, both wooden

122. *IG* II^2 1514.53–54, 1516.30, 1517.160–61; Linders (1972) 17. Garments were woven to size and the pattern was laid in on the loom; the delicacy of a fine-textured cloth with any design would have been obvious even in a partially finished article.

123. "Gray wool in a basket," *IG* II^2 1518.71–72; "soft wool in a bag, uninscribed," *IG* II^2 1522.26–27.

124. Eur. *IT* 811–17.

125. Eur. *IT* 222–24. Iphigeneia here identifies Athena's foes as the Titans.

126. The evidence is collected by Romano (1986), especially 130–131.

and stone, were dressed in layers of garments; the cleaning and dressing of such images was the focus of several major festivals.[127] At Corinth, young females carrying spindle and distaff performed circle dances.[128] At Lokroi, adolescent girls presented to Persephone the figured fabrics they had woven, and in the act of submitting their work for the god's approval also revealed to the community their own accomplishments and advertized their eligibility for marriage.[129] Alkman's *Partheneion* was a hymn performed on just such an occasion at Sparta—a festival where young girls bestowed a new robe on the statue of Orthia.

Unfinished weaving projects were a sign of interrupted life cycle rituals—and, indeed, of an interrupted life. Euripides' Kreousa recognizes Ion, the son she once abandoned, by the scrap of her own figured fabric used to wrap her infant.[130] She describes her work as a maiden's sampler left unfinished, as incomplete as she was herself. The Gorgon and snakes—symbols of her family and woven into the fabric of her own design—had protected her infant but could not protect her. When Apollo raped her, he brutally interrupted the natural course of her social development and obliterated the ritual steps leading to the early marriage that should have been her right.[131]

The inventory from Miletos lists garments like the ones described in Euripides' plays. They are handwoven, complexly decorated fabrics, preserved until they fell apart because they belonged to the goddess. The evidence for Artemis at Miletos is both diachronic and broad. Kallimachos associates Artemis Chitone (Doric spelling) with Miletos, and the fragment of an Archaic *perirrhanterion* inscribed for Artemis Kithone (Ionic spelling) found at Miletos confirms the long life of the epithet and her interest in clothing.[132] The find spot of the stone, on an upper terrace of the low hill just outside the later city wall, marks a familiar location for Artemis. A scholiast commenting on Kallimachos says that Neleus was the one who

127. Eileithyia at Aigion; Hera on Delos (two statues); Demeter and Kore on Delos; Romano (1988) 130 n. 31.

128. Represented on figured pottery; Jucker (1963) 47–61; Pemberton (2000) 94.

129. Sourvinou-Inwood (1991) 166–69, distinguishing the images of girls carrying their own robes from those of girls taking part in the *peplophoria*, the presentation of a new robe to Persephone.

130. Eur. *IT* 809–17; .

131. Eur. *Ion* 1417–23.

132. Günther (1988) 236–37, fig. 2; letter forms dated 525–500 B.C.E.: "I belong to Kithone." Hesychius identifies "Kithonea" as an epithet of Artemis.

brought her statue *(xoanon)* to Miletos. It was a marvelous statue, made from the wood of a oak tree found heavy with all sorts of fruit.[133] The purity regulations for the sanctuary of Artemis Kithone survive. Three conditions restrict entry: recent contact with the dead, recent contact with a woman in childbirth, and recent contact with a dog that has just given birth.[134] These conditions were dissipated by either waiting two full days or bathing. In Euripides' play, Iphigeneia adds murder to the list when she describes the altar of Artemis at Tauris:

> If anyone touches murder, or childbirth, too, or puts a hand on a
> corpse, believing him defiled, she keeps him from her altars.[135]

The pollution resulting from murder is emphasized here because the play deals with the crime of Orestes. At Miletos, the parturient dog is an issue because families could be polluted by any animal with which they lived in close conjunction.[136]

When Iphigeneia abducts the statue of Artemis from the Taurian temple, she deludes her enemies by claiming the statue's need for a purification *(katharmos)* so hallowed that no one else is allowed to observe it. She is careful to describe the procedures that cleanse a god's image from the touch of a murderer's hand. There are three parts: procession, sacrifice, and cleansing with innocent blood. As she prepares to carry the image of Artemis to the sea, she reminds the Taurians to remain indoors so they will not see it. She describes how she will wash away the taint of blood with the blood of newborn lambs and cleanse the statue with sea water. Although Iphigeneia is directing a mock ceremony, the ritual content she imputes to the situation is deadly serious. She warns all citizens to keep away from the polluted object *(miasma,* 1226; *mysos,* 1229), but warns especially

> anyone who as guardian of the temples keeps hands pure for the gods,
> anyone who marches in procession for joining together in marriage,
> or anyone who is heavy with child.[137]

133. Schol. Callim. *Jov.* 77.
134. *IMiletos* I 202.
135. Eur. *IT* 381–83.
136. Herda (1998) 30 takes the regulation about dogs as a reference to Artemis's association with hunting and the world of nature; Parker (1983) 357–58 points out that dogs are offered to problematic divinities—Ares, Hekate, and Eileithyia. They are included, however, on a list in another sanctuary regulation (for Athena at Lindos) that has nothing to do with these divinities; see *LSS* 91.11: "from the miscarriage of a woman, dog, or donkey."
137. Eur. *IT* 1227–10.

A public thoroughfare is restricted from public use for a temporary ritual activity, the procession to the sea. The proclamation emphasizes three kinds of transition especially sensitive to a statue polluted by murder: the transition between human and divine realms at the entrance to a sanctuary; the transition implied in the sexual joining of two bodies in marriage, represented in the public wedding procession; and the transition implied in pregnancy, when one body temporarily resides in another. Orestes was warned earlier that even to touch the clothing of the goddess's servant could pollute the goddess.[138] The image said to have been defiled by his hand has now itself become a threat. Iphigeneia has already advised the Taurians to remain indoors for safety; her proclamation makes clear those who are most at risk.

Artemis Kithone was associated with similar ominous and risk-laden transitions at Miletos. Her epithet associates her with clothing, a marker of change of status. At Miletos, the local story is one of adolescent crisis: when an entire cohort of adolescent girls was struck with a mad desire to secretly suffocate themselves by hanging, they could be stopped only when citizens threatened to parade their corpses naked through the streets.[139] This story represents adolescent problems in terms of social crisis and joins familiar concerns (risk of early death, failure of reproductive resources, females in a life cycle crisis) with elements of ritual practice (procession, temporary nudity, mimetic performance, reversal of normal behavior). The solution makes sense only if the hanging victims were displayed without their clothes. The contrast between clothed and unclothed suggests a ritual change of clothing, defined by a transitional state of nudity. The young girls who danced for Artemis at Brauron disrobed before putting on the *krokotos*, the special yellow dress for that rite.[140] Vase paintings associated with Brauron depict young girls running or dancing unclothed without shame because their nakedness is protected by seclusion.[141] The Milesian story is not necessarily a report of mass suicide; it is more likely a myth of aborted ritual, a cautionary tale that served to explain a fairly widespread custom. The custom was not the mass suicide of teenage girls but, more

138. Eur. *IT* 798–99.

139. Plut. *Mul. Virt.* 249b-d, discussed by King (1998) 81–82; on the story pattern, see Johnston (1999) 233–37, with a slightly different emphasis than that developed here.

140. Ar. *Lys.* 641–47.

141. Ritual nudity in this context is discussed by Johnston (1999) 234. For evidence at Brauron, see Cole (1984).

likely, the hanging of ceramic female torsos in trees as evidence of ritual. A similar sequence about a hanging victim who was discovered by Artemis at Ephesos preserves what looks like part of the same problematic transitional ritual. This woman must have been naked, too, because the goddess had to dress her in her own costume. When clothed in the robes of Artemis, the dead woman became Hekate.[142] Like Iphigeneia at Brauron, she would never reach maturity and would always need the clothing of others.[143]

At Ephesos, women and children were normally permitted to enter the temple of Artemis only at specific times and for designated festivals,[144] a restriction that suggests strict supervision of the image of Artemis. Ephesos claimed to possess the prototypical portable image of Artemis—a wooden form like the statue carved of special wood at Miletos. Similar portable statues displayed in other Ionian sanctuaries of Artemis were sometimes shown hanging in trees, or draped with fruits, jewelry, and clothing.[145]

Clothing was a special concern for Artemis. She was called Kithone at Miletos after the *kithon,* a tunic with sleeves, identified by Herodotos as Ionian.[146] At her festival in Miletos, called the Neleis, young women wore this garment.[147] Named for Neleus, founder of the city, the festival was structured around public choral dancing that displayed to the entire community the cohort of young females ready and eligible to be exchanged in marriage. The foundation myth described how Neleus settled a war between Miletos and neighboring Myus by marrying his son Pythes to Pieria,

142. Larson (1995) 118 suggests that the female dressed in Artemis's clothing was an object of cult, but the situation is more complex; see Johnston (1999) 233–49 for discussion of this story's variants. Tools for spinning, often found in women's graves, may have had a special meaning. For a spindle and distaff made of bone, found in a sarcophagus with a young pregnant woman and a child just outside of Ephesos (third century B.C.E.), see Trinkl (1994) 79–86.

143. The need to possess something that belongs to other women seems characteristic of the rapacious female deprived of her normal role. Melissa of Corinth, killed by her husband and sexually abused by him after her death, demands compensation because her clothes were not burned with her at the grave. Her ghost cannot be satisfied until her husband gathers the best set of clothes from each woman in Corinth and burns all of them at Hera's sanctuary (Hdt. 5.92).

144. Dion. Hal. *Ant. Rom.* 4.25.4. Artemidoros (4.4) reports a dream about a woman who died after entering the temple of Artemis at Ephesos at the wrong time.

145. Fleischer (1973).

146. The account of the conversion of Athenian dress from Doric to Ionian as preserved by Herodotus, 5.86–87, raises problems of content as well as chronology.

147. Robertson (1988) develops the Ionian context.

daughter of the king of Myus.[148] The festival of Artemis, celebrated in spite of the hostilities, united the women of the two towns. Pythes' love for his wife, kindled for the first time when he saw her dancing at the festival, became a model union for Milesian couples.[149] The festival brought together participants from neighboring communities, integrated marriage into the series of life cycle rituals, and presented the union of husband and wife as a model for resolving conflict.

As a costume for dancing, the *kithon* was associated with Artemis elsewhere, even in Doric areas, where it was called *chiton.* At Syracuse, Artemis Chitonea was honored with a dance and flute song,[150] and a scholiast reports an incident, hard to place, where Dorian teenagers dressed only in a *chiton* danced themselves to a frenzy at a temple of Artemis.[151]

The inventories of garments at Miletos suggest a full complement of life cycle rituals for Artemis. Other elements that fill out the pattern include the portable statue made of a powerful wood, the story about a procession that solves an adolescent reproductive crisis, a meaning for ritual nudity, a tradition of ritual dancing, articulated distinctions between purity and pollution, and expressions of concern for childbirth. The display of finished garments and the detailed records that preserved their memory represented the stability achieved by satisfying Artemis.

PERMANENT PRESS

In the period after the Peace of Nikias (421 B.C.E.), the major political factions at Athens competed by claiming connections to ancient heroes. Innovations in ritual genealogy had wide-ranging political implications. Influenced by elite families who claimed descent from Kodros and Neleus, some Athenians even maintained that the *xoanon* of Artemis Kithone had originally come from Athenian territory. The legislation of 418/7 about clearing the sanctuary of Kodros, Neleus, and Basile and protecting its boundaries suggests concern to acknowledge the connection between Neleus of Miletos and Athens. Clothing is a problem. Herodotus reports that the Athenians had adopted the *kithon* from Ionia, but there is no indication

148. Aristainetos *Ep. Erot.* 1.15.
149. Plut. *Mul. Virt.* 253f–254b. See Herda (1998) 26 n. 191 for what Aristainetos omits.
150. Ath. 14.629e; Herda (1998) 30 n. 230, for confirmation by other sources.
151. Schol. Eur. *Hec.* 934.

that Artemis Kithone traveled with her garments, and Neleus himself has no obvious ritual connection to Attika until his name appears in the decree that redefined the boundaries of his sanctuary in 418/7.

At stake is a divergence of opinion on the issue of Athenian identity. Compromised by long periods of separation from the Attic hinterland in the 420s, the Athenian population could not have been indifferent to the needs of their rural sanctuaries at places like Brauron and Halai, largely left untended during the Peloponnesian War. The revival of a Milesian connection and the emphasis on ritual ties to Ionia, whether real or imagined, provided reassurance after a period of spatial disruption. But what about the compelling Athenian claim that they were born from their own earth? Could the Athenians be autochthonous and Ionian, too? If male identity was really to be divided into a hierarchy of nested identities, which was dominant, which was deeper? In the same decade as the campaign to renovate the sanctuary of Kodros, Neleus, and Basile, Euripides opened up the *matriuschka* doll and directed his audience to examine themselves. His presentation of Kreusa and Xouthos in reproductive crisis challenges assumptions about Athenian identity and Attic history.

A few years later, in his own version of Iphigeneia's story, Euripides presented the Athenian appropriation of a Peloponnesian heroine and a Spartan image of Artemis as elements of local Attic ritual mandated by Athena herself. The irony of Athena's concluding speech to *Iphigeneia among the Taurians,* delivered at a time when Spartan occupation of Dekaleia prevented contact with sanctuaries in the hinterland, would not have gone unnoticed by an audience who assumed that Athenian ritual should extend to the farthest reaches of Attika.[152]

The detailed texts carved in stone and exhibited on the Athenian *akropolis* listing the elaborate clothing made by women's hands testify to the city's continuing concern for the rituals of Artemis. In the fifth century, maybe even during the years of the Peloponnesian War,[153] the Athenians

152. She describes Halai as "a place near the outer borders of Attika"; Eur. *IT* 1450.

153. Little remains but the cuttings for the foundations. There were clearly at least two building periods on the site, and Rhodes and Dobbins (1979) 326–41 are able to distinguish three building phases. The layout of the Brauronion on the *akropolis*—an asymmetrical *pi*-shape—with right wing longer than left, mirrors that of the stoa at Brauron, which remained unfinished after a flood in the fourth-century B.C.E. Tréheux (1988) 354 n. 31, argues that use of the singular (ἱερόν, *IG* II^2 1518, B col. II. 63–64) to refer to both the sanctuary at Brauron and the one on the Athenian *akropolis,* indicates that they were considered a single sanctuary.

expanded their Brauronion, which was a satellite of the sanctuary at Brauron. Athenians had a political and economic interest in Brauron,[154] and they were also committed to Artemis because she nurtured the children of the community.

The little girls who took part in rituals like the *arkteia* were protecting their own productive lives;[155] but the ones chosen to participate in the *arkteia* of the Athenian penteteric Brauronia[156]—a select few chosen from the best families[157]—also represented the young female cohort of the entire city. Just as the entire population could suffer from one person's disregard for ritual, so too could the entire community benefit from responsible and correct performance of ritual by a representative and delegated few. Harpokration implies that "to play the bear" (ἄρκτειν) and "to serve as a tenth" (δεκατεύειν) were one and the same thing.[158] "To be a tenth," or "to serve as a tithe," refers to ritual service undertaken by a few on behalf of the many. Harpocration"s conflation of performing the bear role and undertaking the obligation of special ritual service on behalf of the city indicates a special assignment for the Athenian girls who participated in the city *arkteia* during the Brauronia. Under the jurisdiction of the board of the supervisors of public ritual (the *hieropoioi*), the quadrennial Brauronia represented the interests of the entire community. In the democratic city-state, where certain ritual obligations of the whole were delegated to the few, the girls who performed the *arkteia* at the Brauronia, selected by deme

154. Not least because the harbor gave protected access to Delos from the east coast of Attika; the implications are worked out by Peppas-Delmousou (1988) 324–44, commenting on the unpublished inscription that mentions sacred funds of Apollo.

155. For references regarding the diffusion of *krateriskoi*—the characteristic ritual vessel of the *arkteia*—in sanctuaries of Artemis throughout Attica, see Cole (1984) 240 n. 40. The distribution indicates that some form of the *arkteia* was celebrated in the local demes.

156. Like Aristophanes' Lysistrata, who was proud of her service as "bear," these girls would have represented socially prominent families; Ar. *Lys.* 642–47. Lysistrata's boast about her ritual service as a growing child implies a complete penteteric cycle of ritual responsibilities for daughters of the elite. Sourvinou-Inwood (1988b) 113 argues persuasively that for the penteteric *arkteia*, girls represented their deme and tribe. For *ergastinai* (women who wove the sacred *peplos* for Athena) chosen by tribe, she compares *IG* II^2 1034, 1036 (including *parthenoi* who assisted), 1060, 1942, 1943.

157. Of 125 names on the Athenian lists, sixteen include a term indicating deme of origin (demotic). Seven of the sixteen husbands are known from other texts; Osborne (1985) 158–59.

158. Harp. s.v. δεκατεύειν, with citation from Lysias and Didymus. Hsch. s.v. δεκατεύειν; Bekker, s.v. δεκατεύοντος.

and tribe, offered their service to appease the goddess on behalf of all girls in their age cohort and consequently, for all of Attika. In Euripides' *Erechtheus,* when Praxithea offers her daughter to die on behalf of the city, she says,

> The city as a whole has but one name; its inhabitants, however, are many. How could I destroy these people if it is possible for me to give one girl to die for the sake of all?[159]

Ritual provides a similar opportunity for a small proportion of the population to represent the whole and accomplish something that benefits all. At Kyrene, rituals that marked a female's personal experience came under the purview of the civic administration, because reproduction was a concern of the city as a whole. The regulations from Kyrene place female service to Artemis in the same category as the service of the ritual fractions of the male population obligated to a divinity on behalf of the city.

The females who danced for Artemis at the borders of the *polis* danced for the entire community. Successful performance of such female rituals reaffirmed the community's ability to protect its women and to maintain itself. In rituals concerned with the preservation of the city, groups that appeared most marginal actually played a central role.[160] The characteristics that made females the most vulnerable also emphasized their value and significance. The females who walked unmolested from Athens to Brauron at the time of the Brauronia tested with their own bodies the security of the whole population.[161] Processions and festivals that linked border territories with the heart of the city expressed the confidence and security of a community safe from incursion and confident in its own future. The traditional stories about intrusion upon women's rites at remote sanctuaries, told not so much to record actual events as to rationalize policy, emphasize the unreliability of females and also demonstrate the importance of female ritual. Stories about Theseus's abduction of Helen from the sanctuary of Artemis Orthia near Sparta set the stage for divine disapproval (mythographers stress that Theseus abducted the girl before she reached the right age for marriage) and later provided justification for the Spartan invasion of Attika. Herodotus's story about the Lemnian abduction of Athenian women from Brauron is told in the context of Athenian military control of Lemnos

159. Eur. *Erechtheus, TGF* F 360.16–18 Nauck^2 (F 1.16–18 Diggle).
160. Kearns (1990) 336–37.
161. Ar. *Pax* 872–76 (and schol. at line 874), for male expectation of sexual play associated with the procession to Brauron. Attacks on female rituals fit several patterns; for a summary, see Leitao (1999).

in the fifth century.[162] Acknowledgment of the gods, appeals to precedents for divine support, and political realities were always intertwined.

A series of partially published inscriptions from Brauron now give us some idea of the importance of Artemis during a real war. Brauron was still a strategic harbor in the mid-fifth century. The first inscription indicates that sometime during that period, the Athenians erected at the sanctuary a stele recording the accounts for the sacred funds of Artemis and Apollo.[163] During the Peloponnesian War—when the rural population of Attika withdrew behind the walls of Athens—the safety of the sanctuary at Brauron was an important concern. Another inscription at Brauron, dated 416/5, lists the dedications moved at that time to Athens, where they were placed under the jurisdiction of the Treasurers of the Other Gods.[164] This decree includes a record of the loans repaid by the Athenians to Artemis Brauronia. The goddess appears to have been deeply involved in the Athenian war effort, and after the Peace of Nikias her support was duly recognized. The fact that the text was set up at Brauron indicates that the Athenians were able to use the sanctuary during the temporary peace.[165] By 416/5 the Athenians found it necessary to move valuable dedications to Athens, so they were obviously expecting hostilities to be renewed. They could not have anticipated maintaining the quadrennial festival of the Brauronia in its complete form because the festival required a procession of young females from Athens to Brauron.[166] The fourth-century inventories indicate that regular celebrations of the Brauronia were resumed after the war. One of the latest inscriptions, dated to the third century, describes how the Athenians appointed a special committee concerned with the maintenance of buildings and equipment in the sanctuary at Brauron.[167] The catalogues of sacred offerings and the offerings themselves fell under this committee's purview. Artemis is recognized here as a divinity with a special responsibility for the population of the city. The Athenians who directed the committee to evaluate and preserve her treasures described those items as "all the other things that the city dedicated to the goddess for the sake of the

162. Hdt. 6.137–40.

163. *SEG* 37.31.

164. *SEG* 37.30; Peppas-Delmousou (1988) 324–44.

165. This is the period to which Bouras (1967) dates the construction of the stoa at Brauron.

166. This festival was grouped with all other quadrennial festivals, all of which (except the Panathenaia) were under the jurisdiction of the ten *hieropoioi; Ath. Pol.* 54.6–7.

167. *SEG* 37.89. The inscription itself gives instructions for repair to sanctuary's buildings, which had been neglected during the third century.

health and security *(soteria)* of the *demos* of the Athenians." The formula recognizes the support of the goddess and acknowledges the gifts made to encourage that support.

The sacred inventories were more than records of administrative procedure. The textiles displayed in the sanctuary reminded the city of acts of individual piety, but when the garments for Artemis were inventoried and listed on public documents, the meaning of the display became greater than the accumulation of detail about individual objects. As records of gratitude for the protection of the goddess, the inventories reminded the community of the successful performance of public ritual. The stones on which the texts were inscribed were themselves gifts to the gods and stood to recall a history of collective ritual. Displayed by the city at both sanctuaries, these inventories symbolized the city's achievement in promoting its rituals, supervising its women, and producing its crop of healthy children.

Glossary of Greek Terms

abaton sacred area, where only those who are qualified may set foot

Acheloös river in northern Greece considered the source of all flowing water

adyton like *abaton;* an enclosed area in a sanctuary where only those qualified may enter

agora public space for political and economic activities in a Greek city or town

agoranomoi officials who regulate the market

agos state of pollution due to a curse (cf. adjective, *enages*)

ainigma obscure statement designed to confuse; riddle

Aiolos god of the winds

akathartos unpurified; used to describe a woman not cleansed by menstruation

akousios phonos involuntary homicide

akropolis highest place in a Greek city, often fortified to provide a place of defense in time of siege

alalage war cry, used by males in battle at the moment of attack

Altis sacred area at Olympia

amphictyony league of cities or tribal groups organized around a regional sanctuary

anakalupteria a ritual of uncovering during a wedding ceremony, when the bride lifts her veil to reveal her face to her husband for the first time

andreia oikeia building reserved for males during rituals where men and women are segregated

andron dining room where males of the family entertain male guests

archoi (pl.) at Thasos, a board of magistrates

archon at Athens, the eponymous magistrate

argyramoibeïon at Thasos, a mint where silver coins were struck *arkteia* at Brauron, ritual service as an *arktos* (bear), in honor of Artemis; at Kyrene, the priestess of Artemis was called *arktos*

Artemisia festival of Artemis, held in many Greek cities

asebeia impiety; failure to display required reverence and observe obligatory rituals for the gods

astos (pl. *astoi*) belonging to the community or city (referring to those belonging to the citizen class)

asty central town of a *polis*

asylon of persons or things: protected from violence or being seized; of places: offering sanctuary

athanatos (pl. *athanatoi*) deathless, immortal

basileus king; at Athens, the magistrate in charge of traditional rituals and festivals

Bendis Thracian goddess similar to Artemis

boule council that presides over legislative procedures

bouleuterion building where a council holds its meetings

Bouphonia ritual slaughter of an ox followed by a judicial procedure; at Athens, part of the Dipolieia

Cerberus three-headed dog who guards the entrance to the realm of the dead

charis reciprocal generosity between two individuals, or between a human and a god

chernips washing of hands with pure water before eating a meal or participating in a ritual

chora territory of the *polis;* in contrast to the *asty,* or central town

chresteria rituals for obtaining a god's response via an oracle

chytra earthenware pot

damiourgos (Doric dialect) skilled workman or technical practitioner

deisidaimon god-fearing; often used pejoratively for someone excessive in attention to protective rituals

Delphinion temple of Apollo Delphinios; in classical Athens, location of a law court

demos a geographic division of the *polis;* in Attika, used as a template for dividing the male population into political and military units; hence, the "people"—the male population eligible for political participation

Despoina mistress; title used of female deities, especially Persephone

dike "right judgment"; the legal procedure used to achieve a fair judicial decision

Dipolieia series of rituals (including the Bouphonia) performed at Athens for Zeus Polieus, god of the fortified heights

Eileithyia goddess of childbirth

ekklesia the assembly; in a Greek city, the legislative body comprising all males eligible to vote

Eleusinion temple or sanctuary named for Eleusinian Demeter; at Athens, the Eleusinion is located on the slope between the *agora* and the *akropolis*

enages in a state of pollution due to a curse (cf. noun, *agos*)

engyesis ritual of betrothal; specifically, the father of the bride's pledge "into the hand" of the potential groom to give his daughter and a dowry in marriage

enkoimeterion dormitory; in a temple, the place reserved for ritual sleeping in anticipation of a visit from a god

enkrateia self-control

epikleros a female with no living brothers, obliged to marry her dead father's nearest male relative to produce an heir to the family's *kleros*

epistatai public officials

eranos a festival meal or banquet to which each participant has contributed

Erechtheus ancient hero claimed as progenitor of the citizens of Athens

eros teknopoiias desire to produce children

eschatia (pl. *eschatiai*) edge zone at a frontier or on the coast; border area of the territory of a *polis*

Eteoboutadai Attic family (descended from the hero Boutes) that controlled the hereditary priesthood of Athena Polias

ethnos a population organized in tribal or ethnic units with stronger ties to the wider agricultural territory than to a central town

Eunostos "the one who gives a good return"; a minor deity associated with grain mills

Gaia, Ge the earth, sometimes partially personified, particularly as source of food and nurturance

gamelia rituals associated with the feast a man provides for his phratry (association of male kin) at the formal announcement of his marriage

Genetyllides goddesses who preside over the moment of birth

genos kin structure organized around claim of descent from the founder of a cult and thus asserting hereditary control over an important priesthood

gerarai revered priestesses of Dionysos at Athens, required to refrain from contact with any male

Geryon three-bodied giant, contestant of Herakles

Gorgons three fierce female monsters dwelling in the borderland between life and death; one of them, Medusa, could turn a man to stone if she caught his gaze

hagisterion see *perirrhanterion*

hagnos naturally pure and undefiled

Haloa dual winter festival of Demeter, celebrated by adult females, and Dionysos, celebrated by adult males

Hekatombaion at Athens, the month following the summer solstice

Helios the sun, sometimes personified as male

Hellanodikai judges at the Olympic games

Hephaistia rituals performed for Hephaisotos

Herakleion temple or sanctuary of Herakles

heroön sanctuary dedicated to a hero

hestiatorion building with rooms designed for dining, specifically, with couches on which diners reclined while eating

hiera hodos road connecting a major sanctuary with its home city, made sacred for a festival procession; in Attika, the road between the Athenian *akropolis* and Eleusis, route of the procession for the mysteries

hiera orgas piece of sacred, fertile land; specifically, the tract of land between Megara and Attika, under the protection of Demeter and Kore and thus never cultivated

Hierophant priest in the mysteries (specifically, at Eleusis) who revealed the sacred objects at the high moment of the ceremony

hodos road, pathway

horos (pl. *horoi*) boundary marker, usually a small stone pillar or rectangular *stele*

hosion sanctioned by divine law; describes actions and behavior in the nonsacred realm performed according to the gods' requirements

hydrophoros (pl. *hydrophoroi*) ritual water-carrier, usually female; prominent in rituals of Demeter and Artemis

Hyperboreans those dwelling beyond the North Wind

kanephoros (pl. *kanephoroi*) basket-carrier, usually female, who carries the *kanoun* in procession to a sacrifice

kanoun basket for bread or grain, used in ritual to carry barley and implements for sacrifice

katharma items or matter polluted during a purification ritual and therefore discarded

katharos cleansed, purified

katharsion (pl. *katharsia*) rite of purification and object or animal used to cleanse an area from pollution

katharsis cleansing, purging

Kekrops early mythical king of Athens, represented as having the tail of a serpent *kleros* allotment; the piece of land controlled by a family

kopros excrement, manure, dung

kore (pl. *korai*) young girl

kosmos order; ornament; world or universe

Kourotrophos divinity who "nourishes" (i.e., "nurses") children

Kronos Titan, father of Zeus

kyrios male head of the family, guardian of its women and children

limos hunger; famine

lite (pl. *litai*) prayer of entreaty, usually reserved for desperate circumstances

loimos plague or pestilence

louterion basin on stand, used for bathing

loutrophoros long-necked ceramic vessel used to carry pure water for the bride's bath before marriage

makarismos blessing for wealth, success, and good fortune, pronounced for one who has demonstrably earned it

megaron in Homeric epic, a special central room or hall in a leader's house; later, a sacred building, chamber, or cavity in the ground

Menelaion *heroön* for the Spartan hero Menelaios

miaros (pl. *miaroi*) polluted, filthy

moira portion or allotment; can refer to a span of life, an allotment of land, or a share of possessions

naiskos miniature shrine sometimes used to display sacred objects

naos temple, referring to the physical building

neokoros custodian of a temple

neopoios official in charge of temple construction

obol small coin; in late fifth-century Athens, three obols per day was considered minimum wage

oikema small building, room, or stall

oikos household, family

olbiotatos richest, happiest, most blessed

ololyge high-pitched wavering sound of women's voices, produced by crying out while letting the glottis vibrate; sounded by females at moments of stress or crisis

omphalos technically, navel or umbilical cord; metaphorically, the midpoint, or "navel," of the earth, believed to be at Delphi

opis a word used in poetry to refer to the power of the gods for vengeance and the resulting awe and veneration felt by humans in response to such power

orgeon (pl. *orgeones*) member of a private religious association organized outside the administrative apparatus of the *polis*

Palladion small portable wooden statue of Pallas (later, Athena), symbol of the goddess's attention and protection

Panathenaia principal festival of the Athenian year, in honor of Athena; included athletic events, boat races, contests in reciting Homer, and sacrifices that produced enough meat to feed almost the entire male citizen population of Attika

parthenos (pl. *parthenoi*) unmarried female without sexual experience

pelanos thick mixture of honey, oil, and barley meal offered to the dead, or cooked cakes offered to the gods in ritual

Pelargikon also Pelasgikon; a sacred area on the north slope of the *akropolis* at Athens, left unoccupied out of reverence for the gods

peribolos (pl. *periboloi*) encircling wall or boundary; also the enclosure or precinct itself

perirrhainesthai to sprinkle all around oneself; part of purification before engaging in a ritual

perirrhanterion (pl. *perirrhanteria*) vessel (usually a basin on a columnar stand) at a sanctuary entrance holding pure water for preliminary ritual sprinkling

peristia lustration to invoke the gods' attention in anticipation of a meeting of the assembly

peristiarchos at Athens, the official who performed the *peristia,* marking with the blood of a suckling pig the perimeter of the area where the assembly was about to meet

pinax wooden, ceramic, or stone plaque exhibited in a sanctuary to recall visually a gift or ritual honoring a god

Pnyx at Athens, the place where the Ekklesia met, on a hill west of the *akropolis* and south of the *agora*

polis (pl. *poleis*) Greek city, referring to the autonomous political unit with its town center and rural territory, or the total population and the land they occupied, or occasionally, the community of citizens independent of its land

popanon round cake that accompanied sacrifices

prytaneion public building in the center of the *polis* where the city honored magistrates, foreign ambassadors, and public figures with banquets

prytanis (pl. *prytaneis*) in many Carian and Ionian cities (other than Athens), chief magistrate of the *polis*

Pythaïs sacred embassy *(theoria)* to Delphi from Athens, sent annually from at least the fourth century B.C.E. on

Pythia priestess of Apollo Pythios at Delphi who delivered the god's oracular responses

Pythioi Spartan officials empowered to consult the Apollo at Delphi on behalf of the *polis*

sekos unroofed sacred enclosure or precinct

Selene the moon, personified as female

Semele mother of Dionysos; in the Attic deme Erchia, she was offered sacrifice on the same day as her son

Semnai Theai at Athens, the unnamed goddesses representing the blessings earned through reverence, as opposed to the Erinyes, three goddesses who represented curses

Siren female figure with features of a bird, associated with enchantment, deceit, and death; sometimes represented in gravesite sculpture

sitodeia food shortage, famine

sitodoteia voluntary (but usually mandated) donation to fund the purchase of grain for public distribution in times of scarcity

Skirophorion last month of the Attic year

sophrosyne discretion and self-control

sphagia ritual slaughters (sometimes performed before battle) with emphasis on the blood of the victims (not their consumption); the carcasses were examined to ascertain the god's opinion of a current event

Stenia a women's festival in early autumn

stephanephoros a magistrate having the privilege of wearing a wreath; the eponymous magistrate in some Ionian cities

symposion ceremony for males associated with drinking of wine, dining, and entertainment, performed in private homes; at Thasos, the building used for public banquets and ceremonial wine drinking

Telesterion name used by scholars for the building at Eleusis where the mysteries *(teletai)* were celebrated

temenos piece of land marked as separate from the land of the community; in Homeric epic, the domain of a king or leader; after the ninth century B.C.E., a piece of land considered sacred to a god or hero

themis that which is fixed by either custom or divine ordinance

thesauros treasury

theoria ritual pilgrimage by delegates of a *polis* to a distant sanctuary to observe an important festival or witness an important sacrifice on behalf of the *polis*

thyein to render into smoke the parts of an animal victim slain in sacrifice to a god

Thesmophoria series of nocturnal rituals, offbounds for males, celebrated by the women of the *polis* on behalf of Demeter and her daughter, Kore

Thesmophorion building or precinct where the Thesmophoria were held

Thesmophoroi the two goddesses of the Thesmophoria, Demeter and Kore

tomia cut pieces of the flesh of a sacrificial victim

triodos place where three roads meet, forming a space where no one should step

tropaion marker recording the spot where an enemy turned around in retreat

tyrannis a non-Greek word (probably Lydian) used in Greek to refer to a ruler whose authority is without hereditary entitlement

xenia ritual hospitality extended to visitors, foreigners, strangers, and gods, with the expectation that those entertained owed the same in return

xenismos fulfillment of the obligation of *xenia,* in other words, the feasting of a god or stranger

Bibliography

Ainian, A. M. 1997. *From Rulers' Dwellings to Temples: Architecture, Religion and Society in Early Iron Age Greece (1199–700 B.C.)*. Studies in Mediterranean Archaeology 121. Jonsered, Sweden.

Alcock S. E. 1993. *Graecia Capta: The Landscapes of Roman Greece.* Cambridge, U.K.

Alcock, S. E., J. F. Cherry, and J. L. Davis. 1994. Intensive Survey, Agricultural Practice and the Classical Landscape of Greece. In *Classical Greece: Ancient Histories and Modern Archaeologies,* edited by I. Morris, 137–70. Cambridge, U.K.

Aleshire, S. B. 1989. *The Athenian Asklepieion: The People, Their Dedications, and the Inventories.* Amsterdam.

———. 1994. The Demos and the Priestess: The Selection of Sacred Officials at Athens from Cleisthenes to Augustus. In *Ritual, Finance, Politics,* edited by R. Osborne and S. Hornblower, 325–37. Oxford.

Alroth, B. 1987. Visiting Gods—Who and Why. In *Gifts to the Gods,* edited by T. Linders and G. Nordquist, 9–19. Boreas 15. Uppsala.

———. 1992. Changing Modes in the Representation of Cult Images. In *The Iconography of Greek Cult in the Archaic and Classical Periods,* edited by R. Hägg, 9–46. *Kernos* Supplément 1. Athens and Liege.

Amandry, P. 1993. Notes de topographie et d'architecture delphique. *BCH* 117: 263–76.

Armstrong, D., and A. E. Hanson. 1986. The Virgin's Voice and Neck: Aeschylus' *Agamemnon* 245 and Other Texts. *BICS* 33: 97–100.

Arnould, D. 1994. L'eau chez Homère et dans la poèsie archaïque: Épithètes et images. In *L'eau, la santé et la maladie dans le monde grec,* edited by R. Ginouvès, A.-M. Guimier-Sorbets, J. Jouanna, and L. Villard, 19–24. *BCH* Supplément 28, Paris.

Arrigoni, G., and B. Gentili, eds. 1985. *Le Donne in Grecia.* Rome.

Aubert, J.-J. 1989. Aspects of Uterine Magic. *GRBS* 30: 421–49.

Aubriot, D. 1992. *Prière et conceptions religieuses: en Grèce ancienne jusqu'à la fin du Ve siècle av. J.-C.* Lyon.

Auffarth, C. 1999. Constructing the Identity of the *Polis:* The Danaids as "Ancestors." In *Ancient Greek Hero Cult,* edited by R. Hägg, 39–48. Acta Instituti Atheniensis Regni Sueciae 8.16. Stockholm.

Ault, B. 2000. Living in the Classical Polis: The Greek House as Microcosm. *The Organization of Space in Antiquity,* special issue, *CW* 93: 483–96.

Bain, D. 1991. Six Greek Verbs of Sexual Congress. *CQ* 41: 51–77.

Bammer, A. Les sanctuaires archaïques de l'Artémision d'Éphèse. In *L'espace sacrificiel,* edited by R. Etienne and M.-T. Le Dinahet, 127–30. Publications de la Bibliothèque Salomon-Reinach 5. Paris.

Barber, E. J. W. 1991. *Prehistoric Textiles: The Development of Cloth in the Neolithic and Bronze Ages with Special Reference to the Aegean.* Princeton.

Barton, S. C., and G. H. R. Horsley. 1981. A Hellenistic Cult Group and the New Testament Churches. *JAC* 24: 7–41.

Beattie, A. J. 1951. An Early Laconian Lex Sacra. *CQ* 45: 46–58.

Bergquist, B. 1967. *The Archaic Greek Temenos: A Study of Structure and Function.* Lund, Sweden.

———. 1992. The Archaic Temenos in Western Greece. In *Le sanctuaire grec,* edited by A. Schachter, 109–52. Entretiens sur l'Antiquité Classique 37. Geneva.

Betz, H. D. 1986. *The Greek Magical Papyri in Translation.* Chicago.

Billot, M.-F. 1997. Recherches archéologiques récentes à l'Héraion d'Argos. In *Héra: Images, espaces, cultes,* edited by J. de La Genière, 11–56. Naples.

Bingen, J. 1993. La *lex sacra* SB I 3451 = *LSCG* Suppl. 119. *Chronique d'Égypte* 135–36: 219–28.

Birge, D. 1982. Sacred Groves in the Ancient Greek World. Ph.D. diss., University of California, Berkeley.

Birge, D. E., L. H. Kraynak, and S. G. Miller. 1991. *Excavations at Nemea.* Vol. 1, *Topographical and Architectural Studies: The Sacred Square, the Xenon, and the Bath.* Berkeley.

Blegen, C. 1964. *Corinth.* Vol. 13, *The North Cemetery.* Princeton.

Blok, J., and P. Mason. 1987. *Sexual Asymmetry: Studies in Ancient Society.* Amsterdam.

Bodson, L. 1978. *Hiera Zoia.* Brussels.

Bonnechere, P. 1994. *Le sacrifice humain en Grèce ancienne. Kernos* Supplément 3. Athens and Liège.

Bonner, C. 1950. *Studies in Magical Amulets.* Ann Arbor.

Borgeaud, Philippe. 1988. *The Cult of Pan in Ancient Greece.* Chicago.

Bothwick, E. K. 1991. Bee Imagery in Plutarch. *CQ* 41: 560–62.

Bouras, C. 1967. He anastelosis tes stoas tes Vrauronos: ta architektonia tes provlemata. Athens.

Brackertz, U. 1976. *Zum Problem der Schutzgottheiten griechischer Städte.* Berlin.

Brelich, A. 1969. *Paides e parthenoi.* Rome.

Bremer, J. M. 1981. Greek Hymns. In *Faith, Hope and Worship: Aspects of Religious Mentality in the Ancient World,* edited by H. S. Versnel, 193–215. Leiden.

Bremmer, J. N. 1983. Scapegoat Rituals in Ancient Greece. *HSCP* 87: 299–320. Reprinted 2002 in *Oxford Readings in Greek Religion,* edited by R. Buxton, 271–93. Oxford.

———. 1987. The Old Women of Ancient Greece. In *Sexual Asymmetry: Studies in Ancient Society,* edited by J. Blok and P. Mason, 191–215. Amsterdam.

———. 1994. *Greek Religion.* G&R New Surveys in the Classics 24. Oxford.

———. 1999. Transvestite Dionysos. In *Rites of Passage in Ancient Greece,* edited by M. Padilla, 230–46. Lewisburg.

Brewster, H. 1997. *The River Gods of Greece: Myths and Mountain Waters in the Hellenic World.* London and New York.

Broadbent, M. 1968. *Studies in Greek Genealogy.* Leiden.

Broneer, O. 1942. The Thesmophorion in Athens. *Hesperia* 11: 250–74.

Brown, P. 1988. *The Body and Society: Men, Women, and Sexual Renunciation in Early Christianity.* New York.

Brulé, P. 1988. *La fille d'Athènes: La religion des filles à Athènes à l'époque classique, mythes, cultes, et société.* Paris.

———. 1993. Artémis Amarysia. Des ports préférés d'Artémis: l'Euripe. *Kernos* 6: 57–65.

———. 1997. La Macédoine et les rites d'initiation. *Kernos* 10: 319–30.

———. 1998. Le langage des épiclèses dans le polythéisme hellénique. *Kernos* 11: 13–34.

Brulotte, E. L. 1994. The Placement of Votive Offerings and Dedications in the Peloponnesian Sanctuaries of Artemis. Ph.D. diss: University of Minnesota.

Brumfield, A. C. 1981. *The Attic Festivals of Demeter and Their Relation to the Agricultural Year.* New York.

Bruneau, P. 1970. *Recherches sur les cultes de Délos à l'époque hellénistique et à l'époque impériale.* Paris.

Burford, A. 1969. *Greek Temple Builders at Epidauros; A Social and Economic Study of Building in the Asklepian Sanctuary during the Fourth and Early Third Centuries* B.C. Toronto.

Burkert, W. 1979. *Structure and History in Greek Mythology and Ritual.* Berkeley.

———. 1983. *Homo Necans.* Berkeley.

———. 1985. *Greek Religion.* Cambridge, Mass.

———. 1989. Weibliche und männliche Gottheitten in antiken Kulturen: Mythische Geschlechterrolen zwischen Biologie, Phantasie und Arbeitswelt. In *Aufgaben, Rollen und Räume von Frau und Mann,* edited by J. Martin and R. Zoepffel, 157–79. Munich.

———. 1992. *The Orientalizing Revolution: Near Eastern Influence on Greek Culture in the Early Archaic Age.* Cambridge, Mass.

———. 1996. Greek Temple-builders: Who, Where, and Why? In *The Role of*

Religion in the Early Polis, edited by R. Hägg, 21–29. Acta Instituti Atheniensis Regni Sueciae 8.14. Stockholm.

Butz, P. A. 1996. Prohibitionary Inscriptions and the Influence of the Early Greek Polis. In *The Role of Religion in the Early Greek Polis,* edited by R. Hägg, 75–95. Acta Instituti Atheniensis Regni Sueciae 8.14. Stockholm.

Buxton, R. 1987. Wolves and Werewolves in Greek Thought. In *Interpretations of Greek Mythology,* edited by J. Bremmer, 60–79. London.

———. 1994. *Imaginary Greece: The Contexts of Society.* Cambridge, U.K.

Cahill, N. 2000. Olynthus and Greek Town Planning. *The Organization of Space in Antiquity,* special issue, *CW* 93: 497–515.

Calame, C. 1987. Spartan Genealogies: The Mythological Representation of a Spatial Organization. In *Interpretations of Greek Mythology,* edited by J. Bremmer, 153–86. London and Sydney.

———. 1997. *Choruses of Young Women in Ancient Greece.* Lanham, Md. (Translation of 1977 French edition.)

Cambitoglou, A. 1981. *Archaeological Museum of Andros.* Athens.

Camp, J. M. 1977. The Water Supply of Ancient Athens. Ph.D. diss., Princeton University.

Cantarella, E. 1986. Dangling Virgins: Myth, Ritual, and the Place of Women in Ancient Greece. In *The Female Body in Western Culture,* edited by S. R. Suleiman, 57–67. Cambridge, Mass.

Carson, A. 1990. "Women, Dirt, and Desire." In *Before Sexuality: The Construction of Erotic Experience in the Ancient Greek World,* edited by D. M. Halperin, J. J. Winkler, and F. Zeitlin, 135–69. Princeton.

———. 1999. Dirt and Desire. In *Constructions of the Classical Body,* edited by J. Porter, 77–100. Ann Arbor.

Carter, J. C. 1998. *The Chora of Metaponto: The Necropoleis.* Austin.

Cartledge, P. 1979. *Sparta and Lakonia: A Regional History, 1300–363* B.C.E. London.

Casevitz, M. 1993. Remarques sur la langue des inventaires de Tanagra. In *Boeotia Antiqua III: Papers in Boeotian History, Institutions and Epigraphy,* edited by J. M. Fossey and J. Morin, 3–9. Amsterdam.

Cavanagh, W. G. 1991. Surveys, Cities, and Synoecism. In *City and Country in the Ancient World,* edited by J. Rich and A. Wallace-Hadrill, 97–118. London and New York.

Cavanagh, W. G., and P. Armstrong. 1996. *The Laconia Survey: Continuity and Change in a Greek Rural Landscape. ABSA* Supplement 26–27. London.

Cavanaugh, M. B. 1996. *Eleusis and Athens: Documents in Finance, Religion and Politics in the Fifth Century* B.C. Atlanta.

Chamoux, François. 1953. *Cyrène sous la monarchie des Battiades.* Paris.

Chaniotis, A. 1988a. Habgierige Götter, habgierige Städte: Heiligtumsbesitz und Gebietsanspruch in den kretischen Staatsverträgen. *Ktema* 13:21–38.

———. 1988b. *Historie und Historiker in den griechischen Inschriften:*

Epigraphische Beiträge zur griechischen Historiographie. Heidelberger althistorische Beiträge und epigraphische Studien 4. Stuttgart.

———. 1996. *Die Verträge zwischen kretischen Poleis in der hellenistischen Zeit.* Stuttgart.

———. 1997. Reinheit des Körpers—Reinheit des Sinnes in den griechischen Kultgesetzen. In *Schuld, Gewissen und Person,* edited by J. Assmann, 142–79. Gütersloh, Germany.

Chantraine, P. 1946–47. Les noms du mari et de la femme, du père et de la mère. *REG* 59–60: 228–31.

———. 1974. *Dictionnaire étymologique de la langue grecque.* Paris.

Chirassi, I. 1964. Miti e culti arcaici di Artemis nel Peloponneso e Grecia Centrale. *Istituto Di Storia Antica* no. 3.

Chirassi-Colombo, I. 1979. Paides e gynaikes: Note per una tassonomia del comportamento rituale nella cultura attica. *QUCC* 1: 25–58.

Christidis, A.-P., S. Dakaris, and I. Votokopoulou. 1997. Oracular Tablets from Dodona. In *Poikila Epigraphika,* edited by C. Brixhe, 103–10. Nancy and Paris.

Clay, J. S. 1989. *The Politics of Olympus: Form and Meaning in the Major Homeric Hymns.* Princeton.

Clement, P. 1934. New Evidence for the Origin of the Iphigeneia Legend. *AC* 3: 393–409.

Clinton, K. 1974. *The Sacred Officials of the Eleusinian Mysteries.* Philadelphia.

Coldstream, J. N. 1977. *Geometric Greece.* London.

Cole, S. G. 1980. New Evidence for the Mysteries of Dionysos. *GRBS* 21.

———. 1984. The Social Function of Rituals of Maturation. *ZPE* 55: 233–44.

———. 1992. *Gunaiki ou themis:* Gender Difference in the Greek *Leges Sacrae. Helios* 19: 104–22.

———. 1995. Women, Dogs, and Flies. *AncW* 26: 182–91.

———. 1998. Domesticating Artemis. In *The Sacred and the Feminine in Ancient Greece,* edited by S. Blundell and M. Williamson, 27–43. London and New York.

———. 2000. Landscapes of Artemis. *The Organization of Space in Antiquity,* special issue, *CW* 93: 470–81.

Connor, W. R. 1987. Sacred and Secular: Ἱερὰ καὶ ὅσια and the Classical Athenian Concept of the State. *AncSoc:* 161–88.

Cooper. 1987. Metaphysics in Aristotle's Embryology. In *Philosophical Issues in Aristotle's Biology,* edited by A. Gotthelf and J. G. Lennox. Cambridge, U.K.

Corbett, P. E. 1970. Greek Temples and Greek Worshippers: The Literary and Archaeological Evidence. *BICS* 17: 149–58.

Cornell, T., and K. Lomas. 1997. *Gender and Ethnicity in Ancient Italy.* Accordia Specialist Studies on Italy 6. London.

Crouch, D. 1993. *Water Management in Ancient Greek Cities.* New York and Oxford.

Culley, G. R. 1975. The Restoration of Sanctuaries in Attica: *IG* II^2 1035. *Hesperia* 44: 207–23.

———. 1977. The Restoration of Sanctuaries in Attica II. *Hesperia* 46: 282–98.

Dakoronia, F., and L. Gounaropoulou. 1992. Artemiskult auf einem neuen Weihrelief aus Achinos bei Lamia. *MDAI(A)* 107: 217–27.

Daverio Rocchi, G. 1988. *Frontiera e confini nella Grecia antica*. Rome.

Davies, J. K. 1984. The Reliability of the Oral Tradition. In *The Trojan War*, edited by J. K. Davies and L. Foxhall, 87–110. Bristol.

———. 1997. The "Origins of the Greek *Polis*": Where Should We Be Looking? In *The Development of the Polis in Archaic Greece*, edited by L. G. Mitchell and P. J. Rhodes, 24–38. London and New York.

Dawkins, R. M. 1909. Laconia, I. Excavations at Sparta: Artemis Orthia; The History of the Sanctuary. *ABSA* 16: 18–53.

———. 1929. *The Sanctuary of Artemis Orthia*. London.

de Polignac, F. 1994. Mediation, Competition, and Sovereignty: The Evolution of Rural Sanctuaries in Geometric Greece. In *Placing the Gods: Sanctuaries and Sacred Space in Ancient Greece*, edited by S. E. Alcock and R. Osborne, 3–18. Oxford.

———. 1995a. *Cults, Territory, and the Origins of the Greek City-State*. Chicago. Originally published as *La naissance de la cité grecque: Cultes, espace et société VIIIe–VIIe siècles avant J.-C.* (Paris, 1984.)

———. 1995b. Sanctuaires et société en Attique géometrique. In *Culture et cité: L'Avènement d'Athènes à l'époque archaïque*. Brussels.

Dean-Jones, L. A. 1992. The Politics of Pleasure. *Helios* 19: 72–91.

———. 1994. *Women's Bodies in Classical Greek Science*. Oxford.

Delaney, C. L. . 1987. Seeds of Honor, Fields of Shame. In *Honor and Shame and the Unity of the Mediterranean*, edited by D. D. Gilmore, 35–48. Washington, D.C.

———. 1991. *The Seed and the Soil: Gender and Cosmology in Turkish Village Society*. Berkeley.

Delcourt, M. 1938. *Stérilités mystérieuses et naissances maléfiques dans l'antiquité classique*. Bibliothèque de la Faculté de Philosophie et Lettres de l'Université de Liège 83. Paris.

Demand, N. H. 1990. *Urban Relocation in Archaic and Classical Greece*. Norman, Okla.

———. 1994. *Birth, Death, and Motherhood in Classical Greece*. Baltimore.

Detienne, M. 1985. La cité en son autonomie autour d'Hestia. *Quaderni Di Storia* 22: 59–78.

Detienne, M., and J.-P. Vernant. 1989. *The Cuisine of Sacrifice among the Greeks*. Chicago.

Deubner, L. 1925. Hochzeit und Opferkorb. *JDAI* 40: 210–12.

———. 1932. *Attische Feste*. Berlin.

Dewald, C. 1981. Women and Culture in Herodotus' Histories. In *Representa-*

tions of Women in Antiquity, edited by H. Foley, 91–125. London and New York.

Diehl, E. 1964. *Die Hydria: Formgeschichte und Verwendung im Kult des Altertums*. Mainz.

Dirichlet, G. L. 1914. *De veterum macarismis*. Giessen.

Dontas, G. S. 1983. The True Aglaurion. *Hesperia* 52: 48–63.

Dougherty, C. 1993. *The Poetics of Colonization: From City to Text in Archaic Greece*. New York and Oxford.

———. 1996. Democratic Contradictions and the Synoptic Illusion of Euripides' *Ion*. In *Demokratia: A Conversation on Democracies, Ancient and Modern*, edited J. Ober and C. Hedrick, 271–88. Princeton.

Douglas, M. 1966. *Purity and Danger*. London.

———. 1973. *Natural Symbols; Explorations in Cosmology*. London.

———. 1975. *Implicit Meanings: Essays in Anthropology*. London and Boston.

Dowden, K. 1989. *Death and the Maiden: Girls' Initiation Rites in Greek Mythology*. London.

Drew-Bear, T., and W. D. Lebek. 1973. An Oracle of Apollo at Miletus. *GRBS* 14: 65–73.

Dubois, L. 1980. Un nouveau nom de magistrat à Tirynthe. *REG* 93: 250–56.

DuBois, P. 1988. *Sowing the Body: Psychoanalysis and Ancient Representations of Women*. Chicago.

Ducat, J. 1964. Périrrhantèria. *BCH* 88: 577–606.

Duchêne, H. 1992. *La stèle du port. Fouilles du Port 1: Recherches sur une nouvelle inscription thasienne*. Études Thasiennes 14. Paris.

Ducrey, P. 1995. La muraille est-elle un élément constitutif d'une cité? In *Sources for the Ancient Greek City-State*, edited by M. H. Hansen, 245–56. Historisk-Filosofiske Meddelelser 72. Copenhagen.

Durand, J.-L. 1986. *Sacrifice et labour en Grèce ancienne*. Paris and Rome.

Dyggve, Ejnar. 1948. *Das Laphrion, Der Tempelbezirk von Kalydon*. Det Kongelige Danske Videnskabernes Selskab: Arkaeologisk-Kunsthistoriske Skrifter 1.2. Copenhagen.

Edmunds, L. 1981. The Cults and Legend of Oedipus. *HSCP* 85: 221–38.

Eitrem, S. 1915. *Opferritus und Voropfer der Griechen und Römer*. Kristiania.

Ellinger, P. 1987. Hymapolis et le sanctuaire d'Artemis Elaphébolos dans l'histoire, la la légende et l'espace de la Phocide. *AA* 102: 88–99.

———. 1993. *La légende nationale phocidienne. Artémis, les situations extrêmes et les récits de guerre d'anéantissement*. *BCH* Supplément 27, Paris.

Engelmann, H., and R. Merkelbach. 1971. Ouros, horos. *Οὖρος, ὅρος*. *ZPE* 8: 97–103.

Etienne, R. 1991. Espaces sacrificiels et autels déliens. In *L'espace sacrificiel*, edited by R. Étienne and M.-T. Le Dinahet, 75–84. Publications de la Bibliothèque Salomon-Reinach 5. Paris.

Faraone, C. A. 1990. Aphrodite's *Kestos* and Apples for Atalanta: Aphrodisiacs in Early Greek Myth and Ritual. *Phoenix* 44: 219–43.

———. 1992. *Talismans and Trojan Horses.* New York and Oxford.

Farnell, L. R. 1904. Sociological Hypotheses concerning the Position of Women in Ancient Religion. *ARW* 7: 70–94.

Fehrle, E. 1910. *Die kultische Keuschheit im Altertum.* Gießen.

Feldman-Savelsberg, P. 1999. *Plundered Kitchens, Empty Wombs: Threatened Reproduction and Identity in the Cameroon Grassfields.* Ann Arbor.

Felsch, R. C. S., et al. 1980. Apollon und Artemis oder Artemis und Apollon? Bericht über die Grabungen im neu entdeckten Heiligtum bei Kalapodi 1973–77. *AA* 95: 38–123.

———. 1987. Kalapodi. Bericht über die Grabungen im Heiligtum der Artemis Elaphebolos und des Apollon von Hyampolis 1978–82. *AA* 102: 1–26.

Fleischer, R. 1973. *Artemis von Ephesos und verwandte Kultstatuen aus Anatolien und Syrien.* Leiden.

Foley, H. P. 1994. *The Homeric Hymn to Demeter: Translation, Commentary, and Interpretive Essays.* Princeton.

———. 2001. *Female Acts in Greek Tragedy.* Princeton.

Fontenrose, J. 1978. *The Delphic Oracle: Its Responses and Operations.* Berkeley.

———. 1988. *Didyma: Apollo's Oracle, Cult, and Companions.* Berkeley.

Fornara, C. W. 1983. *The Nature of History in Ancient Greece and Rome.* Berkeley.

Forrest, W. G. 2000. The Pre-Polis Polis. In *Alternatives to Athens: Varieties of Political Organization and Community in Ancient Greece,* 280–92. Oxford.

Forsén, B. 1996. *Griechische Gliederweihungen: Eine Untersuchung zu ihrer Typologie und ihrer religions-und sozialgeschichtlichen Bedeutung.* Helsinki.

Fossey, J. 1987. The Cults of Artemis in Argolis. *Euphrosyne* 15: 71–88.

Foucault, M. 1986. *The Use of Pleasure.* NewYork.

Fowler, R. L. 1998. Genealogical Thinking, Hesiod's Catalogue, and the Creation of the Hellenes. *PCPS* 44: 1–20.

Foxhall, L. 1995a. Monumental Ambitions. In *Time, Tradition and Society in Greek Archaeology,* edited by N. Spencer, 132–49. London and New York.

———. 1995b. Women's Ritual and Men's Work in Ancient Athens. In *Women in Antiquity, New Assessments,* edited by R. Hawley and B. Levick, 97–110. London and New York.

Foxhall, L., and F. A. Forbes. 1982. *Σιτομετρεία*: The Role of Grain as a Staple Food in Classical Antiquity. *Chiron* 12: 41–90.

Fraser, P. M. 1953. An Inscription from Kos. *BSAA* 40: 35–62.

———. 1960. *Samothrace.* Vol. 2, pt. 1, *The Inscriptions on Stone.* Princeton.

Freeland, C. 1987. Aristotle on Bodies, Matter, and Potentiality. In *Philosophical Issues in Aristotle's Biology,* edited by A. Gotthelf and J. G. Lennox, 392–407. Cambridge and New York.

Frontisi, F. 1997. *Dans l'oeil du miroir.* Paris.

Frontisi-Ducroux, F. 1981. Artémis bucolique. *RHR* 198: 25–56.

Gager, J. G. 1992. *Curse Tablets and Binding Spells from the Ancient World.* New York.

Gallant, T. W. 1991. *Risk and Survival in Ancient Greece: Restructuring the Rural Domestic Economy.* Cambridge, U.K.

Gallop, D. 1996. *Aristotle on Sleep and Dreams.* Peterborough, Ont.

Gardner, J. 1989. Aristophanes and Male Anxiety—The Defense of the *Oikos. G&R* 36: 51–62.

Garland, R. 1981. The Causation of Death in the *Iliad:* A Theological and Biological Investigation. *BICS* 28: 43–60.

———. 1984. Religious Authority in Archaic and Classical Athens. *ABSA* 4: 75–123.

———. 1985. *The Greek Way of Death.* Ithaca, N.Y.

———. 1989. The Well-Ordered Corpse: An Investigation into the Motives behind Greek Funerary Legislation. *BICS* 36: 1–15.

———. 1990. Priests and Power in Classical Athens. In *Pagan Priests: Religion and Power in the Ancient World,* edited by M. Beard and J. North, 73–91. Ithaca, N.Y.

Garnsey, P. 1988. *Famine and Food-Supply in the Graeco-Roman World: Responses to Risk and Crisis.* Cambridge, U.K.

Gauthier, P. 1972. *Symbola: Les étrangers et la justice dans les cités grecques.* Paris.

Gehrke, H.-J. 1988. Eretria und sein Territorium. Boreas 11: 15–42.

———. 1993. Gesetz und Konflict: Überlegungen zur frühen Polis. In *Colloquium aus Anlass des 80.Geburtstages von Alfred Heuss,* edited by J. Bleicken, 49–67. Kallmünz.

Gernet, L. 1981a. Law and Pre-Law in Ancient Greece. In *The Anthropology of Ancient Greece,* 143–215. Baltimore.

———. 1981b. The Mythical Idea of Value. In *The Anthropology of Ancient Greece,* 73–111. Baltimore.

———. 1981c. Political Symbolism: The Public Hearth. In *The Anthropology of Ancient Greece,* 322–39. Baltimore.

Geschnitzer, F. 1973. Prytaneion. *RE* Supplement 13: 730–815.

Giannakoupoulos, N. A. 1953. Three New Boundary Markers of the Boundary between Ancient Messenia and Lakonia. *Platon* 5: 147–58.

Gilleland, M. E. 1980. Female Speech in Greek and Latin. *AJP* 101: 180–83.

Ginouvés, R. 1962. *Balineutiké: Recherches sur le bain dans l'antiquité grecque.* Bibliothèque des Écoles Françaises d'Athènes et de Rome 200. Paris.

Giuman, M. 1999. *La Dea, la virgine, il sangue.* Milan.

Golden, M. 1988. Did the Ancients Care When Their Children Died? *G&R* 35: 152–63.

———. 1990. *Children and Childhood in Classical Athens.* Baltimore.

Goldhill, S. 1994. Representing Democracy: Women at the Great Dionysia. In *Ritual, Finance, Politics,* edited by R. Osborne and S. Hornblower, 347–69. Oxford.

Goldstein, M. S. 1978. The Setting of the Ritual Meal in Greek Sanctuaries: 600–300 B.C. Ph.D. diss., University of California, Berkeley.

Gould, J. 1994. Herodotus and Religion. In *Greek Historiography,* edited by S. Hornblower, 90–106. Oxford.

Graf, F. 1979. Das Götterbild aus dem Taurerland. *Antike Welt* 10: 33–41.

———. 1984. Women, War, and Warlike Divinities. *ZPE* 55: 245–54.

———. 1985. *Nordionische Kulte.* Rome.

———. 1992. An Oracle against Pestilence from a Western Anatolian Town. *ZPE* 92: 267–79.

———. 1996. *Pompai* in Greece: Some Considerations about Space and Ritual in the Greek *Polis.* In *The Role of Religion in the Early Greek Polis,* edited by R. Hägg. Acta Instituti Atheniensis Regni Sueciae 8.14. Stockholm.

Graham, A. J. 1971. *Colony and Mother-City in Ancient Greece.* Manchester.

———. 1998. The Woman at the Window: Observations on the 'Stele from the Harbour' of Thasos. *JHS* 118: 22–40.

———. 2000. Thasos: The Topography of the Ancient City. *ABSA* 95: 301–27.

Grandjean, Y. 1988. *Recherches sur l'habitat thasien à l'époque grecque.* Études Thasiennes 12. Paris.

Günter, G. 1994. *Göttervereine und Götterversammlungen auf attischen Weihreliefs:Untersuchungen zur Typologie und Bedeutung.* Beiträge zur Archäologie 21. Würzburg.

Günther, W. 1988. 'Vieux et inutilisable' dans un inventaire inédit de Milet. In *Comptes et inventaires dans la cité grecque,* edited by D. Knoepfler and N. Quellet, 215–37. Geneva.

Hadzisteliou Price, T. 1978. *Kourotrophos, Cults and Representations of the Greek Nursing Deities.* Leiden.

Haldane, J. A. 1965. Musical Themes and Imagery in Aeschylus. *JHS* 75: 37–38.

Hall, E. 1987. The Geography of Euripides' *Iphigeneia among the Taurians. AJP* 108: 427–33.

———. 1989. *Inventing the Barbarian: Greek Self-Definition through Tragedy.* Oxford.

Hall, J. M. 1995. Approaches to Ethnicity in Iron Age Greece. In *Time, Tradition, and Society in Greek Archaeology,* edited by N. Spencer, 6–17. London and New York.

———. 1997. *Ethnic Identity in Greek Antiquity.* Cambridge.

Hammond, N. G. L. 1956. The Battle of Salamis. *JHS* 76: 32–54.

Handorf, W. F. 1974. Lakonische Perirrhanterien. *MDAI(A)* 89: 47–64.

Hansen, M. H., and T. Fischer-Hansen. 1994. Monumental Political Architecture in Archaic and Classical Greek *Poleis,* Evidence and Historical Significance. In *From Political Architecture to Stephanus Byzantius,* edited by D. Whitehead, 23–90. *Historia* Einzelschrift 87. Stuttgart.

Hanson, A. E. 1987. The Eight Months' Child and the Etiquette of Birth: *Obsit Omen! Bulletin of the History of Medicine* 61: 509–602.

———. 1989. Diseases of Women in the *Epidemics.* In *Die Hippokratischen*

Epidemien: Theorie — Praxis — Tradition, edited by G. Baader and R. Winau, 38–51. *Sudhoffs Archiv* Beiheft 27. Stuttgart.

———. 1990. The Medical Writers' Woman. In *Before Sexuality: The Construction of Erotic Experience in the Ancient Greek World,* edited by D. M. Halperin, J. J. Winkler, and F. Zeitlin, 309–37. Princeton.

———. 1991. The Restructuring of Female Physiology at Rome. In *Les écoles médicales à Rome,* edited by P. Mudry and J. Pigeaud, 253–68. Actes du 2ème Colloque International sur les Textes Médicaux Latins Antiques, Lausanne, September 1986. Geneva.

———. 1992a. Conception, Gestation, and the Origin of Female Nature in the *Corpus Hippocraticum. Helios* 19: 31–71.

———. 1992b. The Logic of Gynecological Prescriptions. In *Tratados Hipocráticos (Actas del VIIe Colloque International Hippocratique),* edited by J. A. López Férez. Madrid.

———. 1995a. *Paidopoiïa:* Metaphors for Conception, Abortion, and Gestation in the *Hippocratic Corpus.* In *Ancient Medicine in its Socio-Cultural Context,* edited by P. van der Eijk, H. F. J. Horstmanshoff, and P. H. Schrijvers, 291–307. Amsterdam.

———. 1995b. Uterine Amulets and Greek Uterine Medicine. *Medicina Nei Secoli Arte e Scienza* 7: 281–99.

———. 1998. Talking Recipes in the Gynaecological Texts of the *Hippocratic Corpus.* In *Parchments of Gender: Deciphering the Bodies of Antiquity,* edited by M. Wyke, 71–94. Oxford.

Harrison, A. R. W. 1968. *The Law of Athens.* Oxford.

Hatzopoulos, M. B. 1994. *Cultes et rites de passage en Macedoine.* Athens.

Henderson, J. 1987a. *Aristophanes: Lysistrata.* Oxford.

———. 1987b. Older Women in Attic Comedy. *TAPA* 117: 104–29.

Henrichs, A. 1987. Three Approaches to Greek Mythography. In *Interpretations of Greek Mythology,* edited by J. Bremmer. London.

———. 1994. Anonymity and Polarity: Unknown Gods and Nameless Altars at the Areopagos. *ICS* 19: 27–57.

Herda, A. 1998. Der Kult des Gründerheroen Neileos und die Artemis Kithone in Milet. *JÖAI* 67: 1–48.

Herrmann, J. 1985. Zum Wechselverhältnis von naturräumlicher Siedlung, sozialökonomischer Entwicklung und Staatsbildung in Mitteleuropa vom 7.–11. JH. In *Rapports I, Grands themes, methodologie, sections chronologiques.,* 337–39. Comité International des Sciences Historiques, XVIe Congrès international des sciences historiques. Stuttgart.

Herrmann, P. 1965. Antiochos der Grosse und Teos. *Anadolu* 9: 29–159.

Hertz, R. 1960. *Death and the Right Hand.* Glencoe, Ill. Originally published as *La preeminence de la main droite* (Paris, 1909).

Herzfeld, M. 1987. *Anthropology through the Looking-Glass: Critical Ethnography on the Margins of Europe.* Cambridge.

Herzog, R. 1907. Aus dem Asklepieion von Kos. *ARW* 10: 400–415.

———. 1928. *Heilige Gesetze von Kos.* Abh. Akad. Wiss. 6. Berlin.

Hewitt, J. W. 1909. The Major Restrictions of Access to Greek Temples. *TAPA* 40: 83–91.

Higbie, C. 1997. The Bones of a Hero, the Ashes of a Politician: Athens, Salamis, and the Usable Past. *ClAnt* 278–307.

Higgins, M. D., and R. Higgins. 1996. *A Geological Companion to Greece and the Aegean.* Ithaca, N.Y.

Hirzel, R. 1902. *Der Eid: Ein Beitrag zu seiner Geschichte.* Leipzig.

Hodkinson, S. 1988. Animal Husbandry in the Greek Polis. In *Pastoral Economies in Classical Antiquity,* edited by C. R. Wittaker, 35–74. *PCPS* Supplement 14. Cambridge, U.K.

———. 1997. The Development of Spartan Society and Institutions in the Archaic Period. In *The Development of the Polis in Archaic* Greece, edited by L. G. Mitchell, and P. J. Rhodes, 83–102. London and New York.

———. 1998. Patterns of Bronze Dedications in Spartan Sanctuaries, *c.* 650–350 B.C.: Towards a Quantified Database of Material and Religious Investment. In *Sparta in Lakonia,* edited by W. G. Cavanagh, and S. Walker. London.

Hoepfner, W., and E.-L. Schwandner. 1994^2. *Haus und Stadt im klassischen Griechenland.* Munich.

Holderman, E. S. 1913. *A Study of the Greek Priestess.* Ann Arbor.

Hölkeskamp, K.-J. 1992. Written Law in Archaic Greece. *PCPS* 38: 87–117.

———. 1994. Tempel, Agora und Alphabet. In *Rechtskodifizierung und soziale Normen im interkulturellen Vergleich,* edited by H.-J. Gehrke, 135–64. Tübingen.

Hollinshead, M. B. 1979. *Legend, Cult, and Architecture at Three Sanctuaries of Artemis.* Ph.D. diss., Bryn Mawr.

———. 1985. Against Iphigeneia's Adyton in Three Mainland Temples. *AJA* 89: 419–40.

———. 1999. 'Adyton,' 'Opisthodomos,' and the Inner Room of the Greek Temple. *Hesperia* 68: 189–218.

Holst-Warhaft, G. 1992. *Dangerous Voices: Women's Laments and Greek Literature.* London and New York.

Humphreys, S. C. 1983. *The Family, Women and Death.* London.

———. 1986. Kinship Patterns in the Athenian Courts. *GRBS* 27: 57–91.

Hutchinson, G. O. 1985. *Aeschylus: Septem contra Thebas.* Oxford.

Ilberg, J. 1910. Zur gynäkologischen Ethik der Griechen. *ARW* 13: 1–19.

Immerwahr, H. W. 1971. A Purity Regulation from Therasia Purified. *Hesperia* 40: 235–38.

Isager, S., and J. E. Skydsgaard. 1992. *Ancient Greek Agriculture: An Introduction.* London and New York.

Isler, H. P. 1970. *Acheloös: Eine Monographie.* Bern.

Jameson, M. H. 1951. The Hero Echetlaeus. *TAPA* 82: 49–61.

———. 1969. Excavations at Porto Cheli and Vicinity. *Hesperia* 38: 311–42.

———. 1980. Apollo Lykeios in Athens. *Archaiognosia* 1.

———. 1983. Famine in the Greek World. In *Trade and Famine in Classical*

Antiquity, edited by P. Garnsey, and C. R. Whittaker. *PCPS* Supplement 8. Cambridge, U.K.

———. 1989. Mountains and the Greek City-States. In *Montagnes, fleuves, forets dans l'histoire,* edited by J.-F. Bergier, 7–17. St. Katharinen, Switzerland.

———. 1990. Private Space and the Greek City. In *The Greek City: From Homer to Alexander,* edited by O. Murray and S. R. F. Price, 171–95. Oxford.

———. 1991. Sacrifice before Battle. In *Hoplites: The Classical Greek Battle Experience,* edited by V. D. Hanson, 197–227. London and New York.

Jameson, M. H., D. R. Jordan, and R. Kotansky. 1993. *A Lex Sacra from Selinous.* Durham.

Janko, Richard. 1982. *Homer, Hesiod, and the Hymns: Diachronic Development in Epic Diction.* Cambridge, U.K.

Johnston, S. I. 1991. Crossroads. *ZPE* 88: 217–24.

———. 1995. Defining the Dreadful: Remarks on the Greek Child-Killing Demon. In *Ancient Magic and Ritual Power,* edited by M. Meyer and P. Mirecki, 361–87. Leiden.

———. 1999. *Restless Dead: Encounters between the Living and the Dead in Ancient Greece.* Berkeley.

Jones, C. P. 1999. *Kinship Diplomacy in the Ancient World.* Cambridge, Mass.

Jones, L. A. 1987. *Morbidity and Vitality: The Interpretation of Menstrual Blood in Greek Science.*

Jordan, B. 1979. *Servants of the Gods: A Study in the Religion, History and Literature of Fifth Century Athens.* Hypomnemata 55. Göttingen.

Jost, M. 1985. *Sanctuaires et cultes d'Arcadie.* Paris.

———. 1992. Sanctuaires ruraux et urbains. In *Le sanctuaire grec,* edited by A. Schachter, 205–45. Entretiens sur l'Antiquité Classique 37. Geneva.

———. 1994. The Distribution of Sanctuaries in Civic Space in Arkadia. In *Placing the Gods: Sanctuaries and Sacred Space in Ancient Greece,* edited by S. Alcock and R. Osborne, 217–30. Oxford.

Jouanna, J. 1992. *Hippocrate.* Paris.

———. 1994. L'eau, la santé et la maladie dans *Airs, Eaux, Lieux.* In *L'eau, la santé et la maladie dans le monde grec,* edited by R. Ginouvès, A.-M. Guimier-Sorbets, J. Jouanna, and L. Villard, 25–40. *BCH* Supplément 28. Paris.

———. 1995. Espaces sacrés, rites et oracles dans l'*Oedipe à Colone* de Sophocle. *REG* 108: 38–58.

Jucker, I. 1962. Frauenfest in Korinth. *AntK* 5: 47–61.

Just, R. 1985. Freedom, Slavery and the Female Psyche. *History of Political Thought* 6: 177–84.

Kajava, M. 1999. Arktos: *Ἀρκτεύω* and the Like. *Arctos* 33: 15–65.

Katz, M. A. 1992a. Buphonia and Goring Ox: Homicide, Animal Sacrifice and Judicial Process. In *Nomodeiktes: Greek Studies in Honor of Martin Ostwald,* edited by R. M. Rosen and J. Farrell, 155–78. Ann Arbor.

———. 1992b. Ideology and the "Status of Women" in Ancient Greece. *History and Theory* Beiheft 31: 70–97.

Kearns, E. 1989. *The Heroes of Attica. BICS* Supplement 57. London.

———. 1990. Saving the City. In *The Greek City from Homer to Alexander,* edited by O. Murray and S. R. F. Price, 323–44. Oxford.

Kilian, I. 1978. Weihungen an Eileithyia und Artemis Orthia. *ZPE* 31: 219–22.

King, H. 1983. Bound to Bleed: Artemis and Greek Women. In *Images of Women in Antiquity,* edited by A. Cameron and A. Kuhrt, 109–27. Detroit.

———. 1987. Sacrificial Blood: The Role of *Amnion* in Ancient Gynaecology. In *Rescuing Creusa: New Methodological Approaches to Women in Antiquity,* edited by M. Skinner, 117–26, special issue, *Helios* 13: 117–26.

———. 1998. *Hippocrates' Woman: Reading the Female Body in Ancient Greece.* London and New York.

Knoepfler, D. 1977. Zur Datierung der grossen Inschrift aus Tanagra im Louvre. *Chiron* 7: 67–87.

———. 1988. Sur les traces de l'Artemésion d'Amarynthos près d' Érétrie. *CRAI,* 382–421.

Koerner, R. 1973. Zu Recht und Verwaltung der griechischen Wasserversorgung nach den Inschrifen. *APF* 22: 155–202.

Kondis, I. D. 1967. Artemis Brauronia. *AD* 22: 156–206.

Konstan, D. 1994. Premarital Sex, Illegitimacy, and Male Anxiety in Menander and Athens. In *Athenian Identity and Civic Ideology,* edited by A. L. Boegehold and A. C. Scafuro, 217–35. Baltimore.

———. 2001. *To Hellenikon ethnos:* Ethnicity and the Construction of Greek Identity. In *Ancient Perceptions of Greek Ethnicity,* edited by I. Malkin, 29–50. Washington, D.C.

Kosak, J. 2000. *Polis nosousa:* Greek Ideas about the City and Disease in the Fifth Century B.C. In *Death and Disease in the Ancient City,* edited by V. M. Hope and E. Marshall, 35–54. London and New York.

Kotansky, Roy. 1994. *Greek Magical Amulets: The Inscribed Gold, Silver, Copper, and Bronze Lamellae.* Papyrologica Coloniensia 22.1. Opladen, Germany.

Kraay, C. 1976. *Archaic and Classical Greek Coins.* Berkeley .

Krob, E. 1997. Serments et institutions civiques à Cos à l'époque hellénistique. *REG* 110: 434–53.

Kron, U. 1988. Kultmahle im Heraion von Samos archaischer Zeit. In *Early Greek Cult Practice,* edited by R. Hägg, N. Marinatos, and G. C. Nordquist, 135–48. Acta Instituti Atheniensis Regni Sueciae 4.38. Stockholm.

———. 1996. Priesthoods, Dedications, and Euergetism: What Part Did Religion Play in the Political and Social Status of Greek Women? In *Religion and Power in the Ancient Greek World,* edited by P. Hellström and B. Alroth, 139–82. Boreas 24. Uppsala.

Kuhn, G. 1993. Bau B und Tempel C in Thermos. *MDAI(A)* 108: 29–48.

Kurtz, D., and J. Boardman. 1971. *Greek Burial Customs.* Ithaca, N.Y.

L'Homme-Wéry, L.-M. 2000. La notion de patrie dans la pensée politique de Solon. *AC* 69: 21–41.

Labarre, G. 1994. Koinon Lesbion. *REA* 96: 415–46.

———. 1996. *Les cités de Lesbos aux époques hellénistique et impériale.* Lyon and Paris.

Lacey, W. K. 1968. *The Family in Classical Greece.* Ithaca, N.Y.

Lafond, Y. 1991. Artémis en Achaïe. *REG* 104: 410–33.

Lalonde, G. V., M. L. Langdon, and M. B. Walbank. 1991. *The Athenian Agora.* Vol. 19, *Inscriptions: Horoi, Poletai Records, Leases of Public Lands.* Princeton.

Langdon, M. 1976. *A Sanctuary of Zeus on Mount Hymettos.* Princeton.

———. 2000. Mountains in Greek Religion. *CW* 93: 461–70.

Laqueur, T. 1990. *Making Sex: Body and Gender from the Greeks to Freud.* Cambridge, Mass.

Larson, J. 1995. *Greek Heroine Cults.* Madison.

———. 2001. *Greek Nymphs: Myth, Cult, Lore.* Oxford.

Le Dinahet-Couilloud, M.-T. 1996. Femmes dans le paysage délien. In *Silence et fureur: La femme et le mariage en Grèce; Les antiquités grecques du Musée Calvet,* edited by O. Cavalier, 387–413. Avignon.

Leisi, E. 1908. *Der Zeuge im Attischen Recht.* Frauenfeld.

Leitao, D. 1995. The Perils of Leukippos: Initiatory Transvestism and Male Gender Ideology in the Ekdusia at Phaistos. *ClAnt* 14: 130–63.

———. 1999. Solon on the Beach: Some Pragmatic Functions of the *Limen* in Initiatory Myth and Ritual. In *Rites of Passage in Ancient Greece: Literature, Religion, Society,* edited by M. Padilla, 247–77. Lewisburg, Penn.

Lenfant, D. 1999. Monsters in Greek Ethnography and Society. In *From Myth to Reason? Studies in the Development of Greek Thought,* edited by R. Buxton, 197–214. Oxford.

Lepore, E. 1977. Fiumie città nella colonizzazione greca di Occidente, con speciale riguarda alla Magna Grecia. In *Thèmes de recherches sur les villes antiques d'occident,* edited by P.-M. Duval and E. Frézouls, 267–72. Paris.

Lesky, E. 1951. *Die Zeugungs- und Vererbungslehren der Antike und ihr Nachwirken.* Akademie der Wissenschaften und der Literatur in Mainz, Abhundlungen Der Geistes- und Sozialwissenschaftlichen Klasse 19. Wiesbaden.

Leutsch, E. L., and F. W. Schneidewin. 1958. *Corpus Paroemiographorum Graecorum.* Hildesheim.

Lewis, D. 1955. Notes on Attic Inscriptions. *ABSA* 50: 1–12.

LiDonnici, L. R. 1995. *The Epidaurian Miracle Inscriptions: Text, Translation, Commentary.* Atlanta.

Linders, T. 1972. *Studies in the Treasure Records of Artemis Brauronia Found in Athens.* Acta Instituti Atheniensis Regni Sueciae 4.19. Stockholm.

———. 1994. Sacred Menus on Delos. In *Ancient Greek Cult Practice from the*

Epigraphical Evidence, edited by R. Hägg, 59–64. Acta Instituti Atheniensis Regni Sueciae 8.13. Stockholm.

Lloyd, G. E. R. 1983. *Science, Folklore and Ideology: Studies in the Life Sciences in Ancient Greece.* Cambridge.

Lohmann, H. 1992. Agriculture and Country Life in Classical Attica. In *Agriculture in Ancient* Greece, edited by B. Wells, 29–57. Acta Instituti Atheniensis Regni Sueciae 4.42. Stockholm.

Lonie, I. M. 1969. On the Botanical Excursus in *De Natura Pueri* 22–27. *Hermes* 97: 391–411.

———. 1981. *The Hippocratic Treatises "On Generation" "On the Nature of the Child" "Diseases IV": A Commentary.* Berlin and New York.

Lonis, R. 1979. *Guerre et religion en Grèce à l'époque classique: Recherches sur les rites, les dieux, l'idéologie de la victoire.* Paris.

Loraux, N. 1987. *Tragic Ways of Killing a Woman.* Cambridge, Mass.

———. 1990. Herakles: The Super-Male and the Feminine. In *Before Sexuality: The Construction of Erotic Experience in the Ancient Greek World,* edited by D. M. Halperin, J. J. Winkler, and F. Zeitlin, 21–52. Princeton.

———. 1993. *The Children of Athena: Athenian Ideas about Citizenship and the Division between the Sexes.* Princeton.

Lyons, D. 1997. *Gender and Immortality: Heroines in Ancient Greek Myth and Cult.* Princeton.

MacDowell, D. M. 1963. *Athenian Homicide Law in the Age of the Orators.* Manchester.

Malkin, I. 1987. *Religion and Colonization in Ancient Greece.* Leiden.

———. 1994. Inside and Outside: Colonization and the Formation of the Mother City. *ASAA* n.s. 1: 1–9.

———. 1996. Territorial Domination and the Greek Sanctuary. In *Religion and Power in the Ancient Greek World,* edited by P. Hellström and B. Alroth, 75–82. Boreas 24. Uppsala.

———. 2001. *Ancient Perceptions of Greek Ethnicity.* Cambridge, Mass.

Mallwitz, A. 1988. Cult and Competition Locations at Olympia. In *The Archaeology of the Olympics: The Olympics and Other Festivals in Antiquity,* edited by Wendy J. Raschke, 79–109. Wisconsin.

Mantes, A. G. 1990. *Provlemata tes eikonographias ton hiereion kai ton hiereon sten archaia Hellenike techne.* Demosieumata tou Archaiologikou Deltiou 42. Athens.

Martha, J. 1882. *Les sacerdoces athéniens.* Paris.

Martin, R. 1983. L'espace civique, religieux et profane dans les cités grecques de l'archaïsme à l'époque hellénistique. In *Architecture et Société,* 9–41. Paris and Rome.

Maurizio, L. 1995. Anthropology and Spirit Possession: A Reconsideration of the Pythia's Role at Delphi. *JHS* 115: 69–86.

McClees, H. 1920. *A Study of Women in Attic Inscriptions.* New York.

McClure, L. K. 1999. *Spoken Like a Woman: Speech and Gender in Athenian Drama.* Princeton.

McDonough, C. M. 1999. Forbidden to Enter the Ara Maxima: Dogs and Flies, or Dogflies? *Mnemosyne* 52: 454–77.

Métral, J., and P. Sanlaville, eds. 1981. *L'homme et l'eau en Méditerranée et au Proch Orient.* Lyon.

Meyer, M. 1989. *Die griechischen Urkundenreliefs.* Berlin.

Migeotte, L. 1992. *Les souscriptions publiques dans les cités grecques.* Geneva.

Mikalson, J. 1982. The *Heorte* of Heortology. *GRBS* 28: 214–21.

———. 1983. *Athenian Popular Religion.* Chapel Hill and London.

Miller, S. G. 1978. *The Prytaneion: Its Function and Architectural Form.* Berkeley.

———. 1995. Architecture as Evidence for the Identity of the Early *Polis.* In *Sources for the Ancient Greek City-State,* edited by M. H. Hansen. Acts of the Copenhagen Polis Centre 2. Copenhagen.

Mirhady, D. 1991. Oath-Challenge in Athens. *CQ* 41: 78–83.

Mitsopoulos-Leon, V. 1992. Artémis de Lousoi: les fouilles autrichiennes. *Kernos* 5: 97–105.

Mitsos, M. T. 1949. Inscriptions of the Eastern Peloponnesus. *Hesperia* 18: 73–77.

Mommsen, A. 1899. *Ῥάκος* auf attischen Inschriften. *Philologus* 58: 343–47.

Morgan, C. 1989. Divination and Society at Delphi and Didyma. *Hermathena* 147: 17–42.

———. 1990. *Athletes and Oracles.* Cambridge, U.K.

———. 1991. Ethnicity and Early Greek States: Historical and Material Perspectives. *PCPS* 37: 131–63.

———. 1993. The Origins of Pan-Hellenism. In *Greek Sanctuaries: New Approaches,* edited by N. Marinatos and R. Hägg, 18–44. London.

———. 1994. The Evolution of a "Sacral Landscape". In *Placing the Gods,* edited by S. E. Alcock and R. Osborne, 105–42. Oxford.

———. 1996. From Palace to *Polis?* Religious Developments on the Greek Mainland during the Bronze Age/Iron Age Transition. In *Religion and Power in the Ancient Greek World,* edited by P. Hellström and B. Alroth, 42–57. Boreas 24. Uppsala.

———. 1997. The Archaeology of Sanctuaries in Early Iron Age and Archaic *Ethne:* A Preliminary View. In *The Development of the Polis in Archaic Greece,* edited by L. G. Mitchell and P. J. Rhodes, 168–99. London and New York.

Morgan, C., and J. J. Coulton. 1997. The *Polis* as a Physical Entity. In *The Polis as an Urban Centre and as a Political Community,* edited by M. H. Hansen, 87–144. Acts of the Copenhagen Polis Centre 4. Copenhagen.

Morgan, C., and J. Hall. 1996. Achaian *Poleis* and Achaian Colonisation. In *Introduction to an Inventory of Poleis,* edited by M. H. Hansen, 164–231. Copenhagen.

Morizot, Y. 1994. Artémis, l'eau et la vie humaine. In *L'eau, la santé et la maladie dans le monde grec,* edited by R. Ginouvès et al., 201–16. *BCH* Supplément 28. Paris.

Morris, I. 1986. The Use and Abuse of Homer. *ClAnt* 5: 81–138.

Moulinier, L. 1952. *Le pur et l'impur dans la pensée des Grecs d'Homère à Aristote*. Paris.

Muthmann, F. 1975. *Mutter und Quelle: Studien zur Quellenverehrung im Altertum und im Mittelalter*. Mainz.

Mylonas, G. E. 1961. *Eleusis and the Eleusinian Mysteries*. Princeton.

Németh, G. 1994. *Μεδ' ὄνθον ἐγβαλε̂ν*. Regulations Concerning Everyday Life in a Greek Temenos. In *Ancient Greek Cult Practice from the Epigraphical Evidence*, edited by R. Hägg, 59–64. Acta Instituti Atheniensis Regni Sueciae 8.13. Stockholm.

Neumann, G. 1965. *Gesten und Gebärden in der griechischen Kunst*. Berlin.

———. 1992. Katharos, rein und seine Sippe in den ältesten griechischen Texten. In *Kotinos: Festschrift E. Simon*, edited by H. Froning et al., 71–75. Mainz, Germany.

Nilsson, M. P. 1906. *Griechische Feste von religiöser Bedeutung*. Leipzig.

———. 1961^2. *Geschichte der griechischen Religion*. Vol. 2. Munich.

———. 1967^3. *Geschichte der griechischen Religion*. Vol. 1. Munich.

Ninck, M. 1921. Die Bedeutung des Wassers im Kult und Leben der Alten. Eine symbolgeschichtliche Untersuchung. *Philologus* Supplementband 14, Heft 2. Leipzig.

Nollé, J. 1985. Grabepigramme und Reliefdarstellungen aus Kleinasien. *ZPE* 60: 117–21.

Ober, J. 1995. Greek Horoi: Artifactual Texts and the Contingency of Meaning. In *Methods in the Mediterranean: Historical and Archaeological Views on Texts and Archaeology*, edited by D. B. Small, 91–123. Leiden.

Oberhelman, S. M. 1990. The Hippocratic Corpus and Greek Religion. In *The Body and Text: Comparative Essays in Literature and Medicine*, edited by B. Clarke and W. Aycock, 141–60. Lubbock, Tex.

———. 1993. Dreams in Graeco-Roman Medicine. In *Aufstieg und Niedergang der römischen Welt*, edited by W. Haase and H. Temporini, 121–56. Berlin and New York.

Olender, M. 1985. Aspects de Baubo. *RHR* 202: 3–55.

Ortner, S. 1984. Pollution. *Encyclopaedia Britannica*, 298–304. London.

Osborne, R. 1985. *Demos: The Discovery of Classical Attika*. Cambridge, U.K.

———. 1987. *Classical Landscape with Figures: The Ancient Greek City and Its Countryside*. London and New York.

———. 1993. Women and Sacrifice in Classical Greece. *CQ* 43: 392–405.

———. 1996. Funerary Monuments, the Democratic Citizen and the Representation of Women. In *Démocratie athénienne et culture*, edited by M. Sakellariou, 229–42. Athens.

———. 1997. Law and Laws: How Do We Join Up the Dots? In *The Development of the Polis in Archaic Greece*, edited by L. G. Mitchell and P. J. Rhodes, 74–82. London and New York.

Owens, E. J. 1983. The *Koprologoi* at Athens in the Fifth and Fourth Centuries B.C. *CQ* 33: 44–50.

Page, D. L. 1962. *Select Papyri 3: Literary Papyri.* Cambridge, Mass.

Palaiokrassa, L. 1991. *To hiero tes Artemidos Mounichias.* Vivliotheke tes en Athenais Archaiologikes Hetaireias, 115. Athens.

Papahatzis, N. D. 1978. Deities of Childbirth and Childrearing. *AD* 33: 1–23.

Parke, H. W. 1967. *The Oracles of Zeus.* Cambridge, Mass.

———. 1977. *Festivals of the Athenians.* Ithaca, N.Y.

———. 1988. *Sibyls and Sibylline Prophecy in Classical Antiquity.* London and New York.

Parke, H. W., and D. E. W. Wormell. 1956. *The Delphic Oracle.* Oxford.

Parker, H. N. 1999. Greek Embryological Calendars and a Fragment from the Lost Work of Damastes, *On the Care of Pregnant Women and Infants. CQ* 49: 515–34.

Parker, R. 1983. *Miasma: Pollution and Purification in Early Greek Religion.* Oxford.

———. 1985. Greek States and Greek Oracles. *History of Political Thought* 6.1–2: 298–326.

———. 1996. *Athenian Religion, A History.* Oxford.

Patterson, C. B. 1987. *Hai Attikai:* The Other Athenians. In *Rescuing Creusa: New Methodological Approaches to Women in Antiquity,* edited by M. Skinner, 117–26, special issue, *Helios* 13: 117–26.

———. 1990. Those Athenian Bastards. *ClAnt* 9: 40–73.

Pemberton, E. G. 2000. Wine, Women and Song: Gender Roles in Corinthian Cult. *Kernos* 12: 85–106.

Peppas-Delmousou, D. 1986. The *Theoria* of Brauron. In *Early Greek Cult Practice,* edited by R. Hägg, N. Marinatos, and G. C. Nordquist, 135–48. Acta Instituti Atheniensis Regni Sueciae 4.38. Stockholm.

———. 1988. Autour des inventaires de Brauron. In *Comptes et inventaires dans la cité grecque,* edited by D. Knoepfler and N. Quellet. Université de Neuchâtel, Recueil de Travaux Publiès par la Faculté des Lettres 40. Geneva.

Perlman, P. 1983. Plato *Laws* 833 and the Bears of Brauron. *GRBS* 24: 115–30.

———. 1989. Acting the She-Bear for Artemis. *Arethusa* 22: 111–33.

Pernier, Luigi. 1931. L'Artemesion di Cyrene. *Africa Italiana* 4: 173–228.

Pertusi, A. 1955. *Scholia Vetera in Hesiodi Opera et Dies.* Milan.

Petropoulou, A. 1981. The *Eparche* Documents and the Early Oracle at Oropus. *GRBS* 22: 39–63.

Pfister. 1935. Katharsis. *RE* Supplement 6: 149–52.

Philipp, H. 1992. Le caratteristiche delle relazioni fra il santuario di Olimpia e la Magna Grecia. *La Magna Grecia e i grandi santuari della madrepatria,* 29–51. Atti del Convegno di Studi Sulla Magna Grecia 31. Taranto.

Philippson, P. 1939. *Griechische Gottheiten in ihren Landschaften. Symbolae Osloenses* Supplement 9. Oslo.

Picard, C. 1962. *Études Thasiennes.* Vol. 8 *Les murailles: les portes sculptée à images divines.* Paris.

Pimpl, H. 1997. *Perirrhanteria und Louteria: Entwicklung und Verwendung*

grossor Marmor- und Kalksteinbecken auf figürlichem und säulenartigem Untersatz in Griechenland. Berlin.
Pingiatoglou, S. 1981. *Eileithyia.* Königshausen, Germany.
Pleket, H. W. 1969. *Texts on the Social History of the Greek World.* Epigraphica 2. Amsterdam.
Price, T. H. 1978. *Kourotrophos: Cults and Representations of the Greek Nursing Deities.* Leiden.
Pritchett, W. K. 1979. *The Greek State at War.* Vol. 3, *Religion.* Berkeley.
———. 1980. *Studies in Ancient Greek Topography: Part 3 (Roads).* University of California Publications in Classical Studies 22. Berkeley.
———. 1998. *Pausanias Periegetes.* Amsterdam.
Pulleyn, S. 1997. *Prayer in Greek Religion.* Oxford.
Purcell, N. 1996. Rome and the Management of Water: Environment, Culture and Power. In *Human Landscapes in Classical Antiquity,* edited by G. Shipley, and J. B. Salmon, 180–212. London and New York.
Rackham, O. 1990. Ancient Landscapes. In *The Greek City: From Homer to Alexander,* edited by O. Murray and S. F. R. Price, 85–111. Oxford.
———. 1996. Ecology and Pseudo-Ecology: The Example of Ancient Greece. In *Human Landscapes in Classical Antiquity,* edited by G. Shipley and B. Salmon, 16–43. London and New York.
Raepsaet, G. 1971. Les motivations de la natalité à Athènes. *AC* 40: 80–110.
Raubitschek, A. E. 1974. Kolieis. In *Phoros, Tribute to Benjamin Meritt,* 137–38. Locust Valley, N.Y.
Redfield, J. 1982. Notes on the Greek Wedding. *Arethusa* 15: 181–201.
Reichel, W., and A. Wilhelm. 1901. Das Heiligtum der Artemis zu Lousoi. *JÖAI* 4: 1–89.
Reilly, J. 1997. Naked and Limbless. In *Naked Truths. Women, Sexuality and Gender in Classical Art and Archaeology,* edited by A. O. Koloski-Ostrow and C. Lyons, 154–73. London.
Rhodes, P. J. 1981. *A Commentary on the Aristotelian Athenaion Politeia.* Oxford.
Rhodes, P. J., and D. M. Lewis. 1997. *The Decrees of the Greek States.* Oxford.
Rhodes, R. F., and J. J. Dobbins. 1979. The Santuary of Artemis Brauronia on the Athenian Acropolis. *Hesperia* 48: 325–41.
Richardson, N. J. 1974. *The Homeric Hymn to Demeter.* Oxford.
Ridgway, D. 1992. *The First Western Greeks.* Cambridge, U.K.
Rigsby, K. J. 1996. *Asylia: Territorial Inviolability in the Hellenistic World.* Berkeley.
Robert, L. 1937. *Études anatoliennes.* Paris.
———. 1960. Oropos. *Hellenica* 11–12: 194–203.
———. 1962. *Villes d'Asia mineure: Études de géographie ancienne.* Paris.
———. 1967. Sur des inscriptions d'Ephèse. *RPh* 41: 7–84.
———. 1969. Recherches épigraphiques. *Opera Minora Selecta* 2: 300–315. Paris.
———. 1974. Les femmes théores à Éphèse. *CRAI:* 176–81.

———. 1980. *À traverse l'Asie mineure, poets et prosateurs, monnaies grecques, voyageurs et géographie.* Paris.

Robertson, N. D. 1984. Poseidon's Festival at the Winter Solstice. *CQ* 34: 1–16.

———. 1986. Solon's Axones and Kyrbeis, and the Sixth-Century Background. *Historia* 35: 147–76.

———. 1988. Melanthus, Codrus, Neleus, Caucon: Ritual Myth as Athenian History. *GRBS* 29: 201–61.

———. 1998. The City Center of Archaic Athens. *Hesperia* 67: 282–302.

Roebuck, C. 1951. *Corinth.* Vol. 14, *The Asklepieion and Lerna.* Princeton.

Rolley, C. 1965. Le Sanctuaire des Dieux Patrooi et le Thesmophorion de Thasos. *BCH* 89: 441–83.

———. 1983. Les grandes sanctuaires panhelléniques. In *The Greek Renaissance of the Eighth Century* B.C.*: Tradition and Innovation,* edited by R. Hägg, 109–14. Acta Instituti Atheniensis Regni Sueciae 4.30. Stockholm.

Romano, I. B. 1988. Early Greek Cult Images and Cult Practices. In *Early Greek Cult Practice,* edited by R. Hägg, N. Marinatos, and G. C. Nordquist, 127–34. Acta Instituti Atheniensis Regni Sueciae 4.38. Stockholm.

Romm, J. S. 1992. *The Edges of the Earth in Ancient Thought: Geography, Exploration, and Fiction.* Princeton.

Roscher, W. H. 1909. Die Tessarakontaden und Tessarakontadenlehren der Griechen und anderer Völker. Leipzig.

Rosivach, V. 1987. Autochthony and the Athenians. *CQ* 37: 294–306.

Rougemont, G. 1995. Delphes et les cités grecques d'Italie du sud et de la Sicilie. In *Le Magna Grecia e i grandi santuari della Madrepatria,* 157–92. Atti Di Studi Sulla Magna Grecia 31. Naples.

Rouse, W. H. D. 1902. *Greek Votive Offerings: An Essay in the History of Greek Religion.* Cambridge, U.K.

Rousselle, A. 1980. Observation féminine et idéologie masculine: Le corps de la femme d'après les médicins grecs. *Annales (ESC)* 35: 1089–115.

Rousset, D., and P. Katzouros. 1992. Une délimitation de frontière en Phocide. *BCH* 116: 197–215.

Roux, G. 1974. Quatre récits de la bataille de Salamine. *BCH* 98: 51–94.

Rudhardt, J. 1958. *Notions fondamentales de la pensée religieuse et actes constitutifs du culte dans la Grèce classique.* Geneva.

———. 1971. *Le théme de l'eau primordiale dans la mythologie grecque.* Fribourg, Switzerland

Şahin, S. 1994. Piratanüerfall auf Teos: Volksbeschluss über die Finanzierung der Erpressungsgelder. *EA* 23: 1–36.

Sale, W. 1965. Callisto and the Virginity of Artemis. *RhM* 108: 11–35.

———. 1975. The Temple-Legends of the Arkteia. *RhM* 118: 265–84.

Sallares, R. 1991. *The Ecology of the Ancient Greek World.* London.

Salmon, J. B. 1984. *Wealthy Corinth: A History of the City to 338* B.C. Oxford.

Sansalvador, A. V. 1992. Chamyne, ein Beiname der Demeter in Olympia. *Glotta* 70: 166–80.

Sansone, D. 1988. *Greek Athletics and the Genesis of Sport.* Berkeley.

Sapouna-Sakellaraki, E. 1992. Un dépot de temple et le sanctuaire d'Artémis Amarysia en Eubée. *Kernos* 5: 235–62.

Sartre, M. 1979. Aspects économiques et aspects religieux de la frontiére dans les cités grecques. *Ktema* 4: 213–24.

Sassi, M. M. 2001. *The Science of Man in Ancient Greece.* Chicago.

Saxenhouse, A. 1986. Reflections on Autochthony in Euripides' *Ion.* In *Greek Tragedy and Political Theory,* edited by J. P. Euben, 252–73. Berkeley.

Scafuro, A. C. 1994. Witnessing and False Witnessing: Proving Citizenship and Kin Identity in Fourth Century Athens. In *Athenian Identity and Civic Ideology,* edited by A. L. Boegehold and A. C. Scafuro, 156–98. Baltimore.

Scanlon, T. F. 1984. The Footrace of the Heraia at Olympia. *AncW* 9: 77–90.

Scarborough, J. 1991. The Pharmacy of Methodist Medicine. In *Les Écoles medicales à Rome,* edited by P. Mudry and J. Pigeaud, 203–16. Actes du 2ème Colloque International sur les Textes Médicaux Latins Antiques, Lausanne, September 1986. Geneva.

Schachter, A. 1992. Policy, Cult, and the Placing of Greek Sanctuaries. In *Le sanctuaire grec,* edited by A. Schachter and J. Bingen, 1–57. Entretiens sur l'Antiquité Classique 37. Geneva.

Schaps, D. 1982. The Women of Greece in Wartime. *CP* 77: 154–73.

Scheidel, W. 1999. Emperors, Aristocrats, and the Grim Reaper. *CQ* 49: 254–81.

Schilardi, D. U. 1988. The Temple of Athena at Koukounaries: Observations on the Cult of Athena on Paros. In *Early Greek Cult Practice,* edited by R. Hägg, N. Marinatos, and G. C. Nordquist, 41–50. Acta Instituti Atheniensis Regni Sueciae 4.38. Stockholm.

Schmitt, P. 1977. Athéna Apatouria et la ceinture: Les aspects féminins des Apatouries à Athènes. *Annales (ESC)* 32: 1059–73.

Schmitt Pantel, P. 1992. *La cité au banquet: Histoire des repas publics dans les cités grecques.* Collection de l'École Française de Rome 157. Rome.

Schuller, M. 1982. Der Artemistempel im Delion auf Paros. *AA* 97: 2.231–33.

———. 1984. *Der Artemis-Tempel im Delion auf Paros.* Munich.

Schumacher, R. 1993. Three Related Sanctuaries of Poseidon: Geraistos, Kalaureia and Tainaron. In *Greek Sanctuaries: New Approaches,* edited by N. Marinatos and R. Hägg, 62–87. London.

Schwabl. H. 1972. Zeus. *RE* Supplementband 15: 354.

Scullion, S. 1994. Olympian and Chthonian. *ClAnt* 13: 75–119.

Seiler, F. 1986. *Die griechische Tholos: Untersuchungen zur Entwicklung, Typologie und Funktion kunstmässiger Rundbauten.* Mainz.

Seremetakis, C. N. 1991. *The Last Word: Women, Death, and Divination in Inner Mani.* Chicago.

Shanzer, D. 1985. Merely a Cynic Gesture? *RFIC* 113: 61–66.

Shapiro, H. A. 1993. *Personifications in Greek Art: The Representation of Abstract Concepts.* Zurich.

Shaw, B. 1982–83. Eaters of Flesh and Drinkers of Milk. *AncSoc* 13–14: 5–31.

Siewert, P. 1977. The Ephebic Oath in Fifth-Century Athens. *JHS* 97: 102–11.

Simon, C. G. 1986. The Archaic Votive Offerings and Cults of Ionia. Ph.D. diss., University of California, Berkeley.

Simon, E. 1987. Griechische Muttergottheiten. In *Matronen und verwandte Gottheiten, BJ* Beiheft 44: 157–69, edited by G. Bauchhenss and G. Neumann. Bonn.

Sinn, U. 1978. Das Heiligtum der Artemis Limnatis bei Kombothekra. *AA* 93: 45–82.

———. 1981. Das Heiligtum der Artemis Limnatis bei Kombothekra II: Der Kult. *AA* 96: 25–71.

———. 1988. Der Kult der Aphaia auf Aegina. In *Early Greek Cult Practice,* edited by R. Hägg, N. Marinatos, and G. C. Nordquist, 149–59. Acta Instituti Atheniensis Regni Sueciae 4.38. Stockholm.

———. 1990. Das Heraion von Perachora. *MDAI(A)* 105: 53–116.

———. 1993. Greek Sanctuaries as Places of Refuge. In *Greek Sanctuaries, New Approaches,* edited by N. Marinatos and R. Hägg, 88–109. London.

Sissa, G. 1990a. *Greek Virginity.* Cambridge, Mass.

———. 1990b. Maidenhood without Maidenhead. In *Before Sexuality: The Construction of Erotic Experience in the Ancient Greek World,* edited by D. M. Halperin, J. J. Winkler, and F. Zeitlin, 339–64. Princeton.

Skydsgaard, J. E. 1992. Agriculture in Ancient Greece: On the Nature of the Sources and the Problems of Interpretation. In *Agriculture in Ancient Greece,* edited by B. Wells, 9–12. Acta Instituti Atheniensis Regni Sueciae 4.42. Stockholm.

Snodgrass, A. 1990. Survey Archaeology and the Rural Landscape of the Greek City. In *The Greek City: From Homer to Alexander,* edited by O. Murray and S. R. F. Price, 113–36. Oxford.

———. 1991. Archaeology and the Study of the Greek City. In *City and Country in the Ancient World,* edited by J. Rich and A. Wallace-Hadrill, 1–23. London.

Sokolowski, F. 1935. Note sur les *Νυκτοφυλάξια* à Délos. *BCH* 59: 382–90.

Sommerstein, A. 1995. The Language of Athenian Women. In *Lo spettacolo delle voci,* edited by F. de Martino and A. Sommerstein, 61–85. Bari, Italy.

Sourvinou-Inwood, C. 1988a. Further Aspects of Polis Religion. *AASA* 10: 259–73.

———. 1988b. *Studies in Girls' Transitions: Aspects of the Arkteia and Age Representations in Attic Iconography.* Athens.

———. 1990. What is *Polis* Religion? In *The Greek City: From Homer to Alexander,* edited by O. Murray and S. R. F. Price, 295–322. Oxford.

———. 1991. Persephone and Aphrodite at Locri: A Model for Personality Divisions in Greek Religion. In *Reading Greek Culture,* 147–88. Oxford.

———. 1995. *Reading Greek Death.* Oxford.

Spencer, N. 2000. Exchange and Stasis in Archaic Mytilene. In *Alternatives to Athens: Varieties of Political Organization and Community in Ancient Greece,* edited by R. Brock and S. Hodkinson, 69–81. Oxford.

Stafford, E. J. 1997. Themis: Religion and Order. In *The Development of the Polis in Archaic Greece*, edited by L. G. Mitchell and P. J. Rhodes, 158–67. London and New York.

Starr, C. G. 1978. An Evening with the Flute-Girls. *PP* 33: 401–10.

Strubbe, J. H. M. 1991. "Cursed Be He That Moves My Bones." In *Magika Hiera: Ancient Greek Magic and Religion*, edited by C. A. Faraone, and D. Obbink, 33–59. New York and Oxford.

Taaffe, L. K. 1993. *Aristophanes and Women*. London and New York.

Tausend, K. 1995. Von Artemis zu Artemis? Der antike Weg von Lousoi nach Pheneos. *JÖAI* 64 Beiblatt: 1–20.

———. 1998. Der antike Weg von Pheneos nach Orchomenos. *JÖAI* 67: 109–16.

Te Riele, G.-J. M. J. 1978. Une nouvelle loi sacrée en Arcadie. *BCH* 102: 325–31.

Themelis, P. G. 1996. Artemis Ortheia at Messene. In *Ancient Greek Cult Practice from the Epigraphical Evidence*, edited by R. Hägg, 101–22. Acta Instituti Atheniensis Regni Sueciae 8.14. Stockholm.

Thomas, R. 1989. *Oral Tradition and Written Record in Classical Athens*. Cambridge and New York.

———. 1995. Written in Stone? Liberty, Equality, Orality and the Codification of Law. *BICS* 40: 59–74.

Threpsiades, J., and E. Vanderpool. 1964. Themistokles' Sanctuary of Artemis Aristoboule. *AD* 19A: 26–36.

Tomin, J. 1987. Socratic Midwifery. *CQ* 37: 97–102.

Tomlinson, R. A., and J. M. Fossey. 1970. Ancient Remains on Mt. Mavrovouni, S. Boeotia. *ABSA* 65: 245–52.

Tonkin, E. 1992. *Narrating Our Pasts: Social Construction of Oral History*. Cambridge, U.K.

Travlos, I. 1971. *Pictorial Dictionary of Ancient Athens*. London.

———. 1976. Treis Naoi tes Artemidos Aulidias Tauropolou kai Vrauronias. In *Neue Forschungen in griechischen Heiligtümern*, edited by U. Jantzen, 197–205. Tübingen.

———. 1988. *Bildlexikon zur Topographie des antiken Attika*. Tübingen.

Tréheux, J. 1988. Observations sur les inventaires du *Brauronion* de l'acropole d'Athènes. In *Comptes et inventaires dans la cité grecque*, edited by D. Knoepfler, 345–55. Geneva.

Trinkl, E. 1994. Ein Set aus Spindel, Spinnwirtel und Rocken aus einem Sarkophag in Ephesos. *JÖAI* 63 Beiblatt: 81–84.

Tritle, L. A. 1995. Strabon, Amarynthos, and the Temple of Artemis Amarysia. *Boeotia Antiqua* 5: 59–69.

Turcan, R. 1958. Dionysos dimorphos. *Mélanges d'Archéologie et d'Histoire* 70: 243–93.

Turner, J. 1983. Hiereiai: Acquisition of Feminine Priesthoods in Ancient Greece. Ph.D. diss., University of California, Santa Barbara.

van Andel, T. H., and C. Runnels. 1987. *Beyond the Acropolis: A Rural Greek Past.* Stanford.

van Bremen, R. 1996. *The Limits of Participation, Women and Civic Life in the Greek East in the Hellenistic and Roman Periods.* Amsterdam.

van der Horst, P. W. 1994. Silent Prayer in Antiquity. *Numen* 41: 1–25.

van der Eijk, P. J. 1990. The "Theology" of the Hippocratic Treatise *On the Sacred Disease. Apeiron* 23: 77–119.

———. 1991. "Airs, Waters, Places" and "On the Sacred Disease": Two Different Religiosities? *Hermes* 119: 167–76.

———. 1999. *On Sterility,* a Medical Work by Aristotle? *CQ* 49: 490–502.

van Effenterre, H., and F. Ruzé. 1994. *Nomima: Recueil d'inscriptions politiques et juridiques de l'archaïsme grec.* Collection de l'École Française de Rome 188. Rome.

van Straten, F. T. 1974. Did the Greeks Kneel before their Gods? *BVAB* 49: 159–89.

———. 1981. Gifts for the Gods. In *Faith, Hope and Worship: Aspects of Religious Mentality in the Ancient World,* edited by H. S. Versnel, 65–151. Leiden.

———. 1987. Greek Sacrificial Reprsentations: Livestock Prices and Religous Mentality. In *Gifts to the Gods,* edited by T. Linders and G. Nordquist, 159–70. Acta Universitatis Upsaliensis, Boreas 15. Uppsala.

———. 1992. Votives and Votaries in Greek Sanctuaries. In *Le sanctuaire grec,* edited by A. Schachter, 247–90. Entretiens sur l'Antiquité Classique 37. Geneva.

———. 1995. *Hiera Kala.* Leiden.

Vedder, U. 1988. Frauentod-Kriegertod im Spiegel der attischen Grabkunst des 4.Jhs.v.Chr. *MDAI(A)* 103: 161–91.

Verdeles, N., M. Jameson, and I. Papachristodoulou. 1975. Archaikai epigraphai ek Tirynthos. *AE* 150–205.

Vernant, J.-P. 1983. Hestia-Hermes: The Religious Expression of Space and Movement in Ancient Greece. In *Myth and Thought among the Greeks,* 127–75. London and Boston.

———. 1991. The Figure and Functions of Artemis in Myth and Cult, Sacrifice, Initiation, Marriage. In *Mortals and Immortals: Collected Essays,* 195–219. Princeton.

Versnel, H. S. 1981. Religious Mentality in Ancient Prayer. In *Faith, Hope and Worship: Aspects of Religious Mentality in the Ancient World,* edited by H. S. Versnel, 1–64. Leiden.

———. 1994. Pepremenos: The Cnidian Curse Tablets and Ordeal by Fire. In *Ancient Greek Cult Practice from the Epigraphic Evidence,* edited by R. Hägg, 145–54. Acta Instituti Atheniensis Regni Sueciae 8.13. Stockholm.

Vestergaard, T., et al. 1985. A Typology of the Women Recorded on Gravestones from Attica. *AJAH* 10: 178–90.

Vikela, E. 1994. *Die Weihreliefs aus dem Athener Pankrates-Heiligtum am Ilissos: Religionsgeschichtliche Bedeutung und Typologie.* Mitteilungen des Deutschen Archäologischen Instituts, Athenische Abteilung, Beiheft 16. Berlin.

von Schwenn, F. 1922. Der Krieg in der griechischen Religion. *ARW* 21: 58–71.

von Staden, H. 1989. *Herophilus: The Art of Medicine in Early Alexandria.* Cambridge.

———. 1991. Matière et signification: Rituel, sexe, et pharmacologie dans le corpus hippocratique. *AC* 60: 42–61.

———. 1992. Women and Dirt. *Helios* 19: 7–30.

———. 1993. Spiderwoman and the Chaste Tree: The Semantics of Matter. *Configurations* 1: 23–56.

———. 1994. 'Un autre dieu sobre': Théophraste, Érasistrate et les médecins hellénistiques à propos de l'eau. In *L'eau, la santé et la maladie dans le monde grec,* edited by R. Ginouvès, A.-M. Guimier-Sorbets, J. Jouanna, and L. Villard, 77–94. *BCH* Supplément 28. Paris.

Voutiras, E. 1998. *Dionysophontos Gamoi: Marital Life and Magic in Fourth Century Pella.* Amsterdam.

Wächter, T. 1910. *Reinheitsvorschriften im griechischen Kult.* Gießen.

Wallace, P. W. 1969. Psyttaleia and the Trophies of the Battle of Salamis. *AJA* 73: 293–307.

Walter, U. 1993. *An der Polis teilhaben: Bürgerstaat und Zugehörigkeit im archaischen Griechenland. Historia* Einzelschrift 82. Stuttgart.

Weinreich, O. 1919. *Stiftung und Kultsatzungen eines Privatheiligtums in Philadelphia in Lydien.* Sitzb. Heid. Akad. Wiss. 16. Heidelberg.

———. 1928. Zum Zauber des Menstrualblutes. *ARW* 26: 150–51.

Weiss, C. 1984. *Griechische Flussgottheiten in vorhellenistischer Zeit: Ikonographie und Bedeutung.* Würzburg.

West, M. L. 1966. *Hesiod: Theogony.* Oxford.

———. 1978. *Hesiod: Works and Days.* Oxford.

———. 1985. *The Hesiodic Catalogue of Women.* Oxford.

Wilamowitz-Moellendorff, U. von. 1928. *Hesiodos' Erga.* Berlin.

Williams, C. 1969. Excavations at Corinth 1968. *Hesperia* 38: 38–62.

Winkler, J. 1990. *The Constraints of Desire: The Anthropology of Sex and Gender in Ancient Greece.* New York.

Winter, J. E., and F. E. Winter. 1990. Some Disputed Sites and Itineraries of Pausanias. *EMC* 9: 221–61.

Wiseman, J. 1973. Gods, War and Plague in the Time of the Antonines. In *Studies in the Antiquities of Stobi,* 1: 153–55. Belgrade.

Wolff, C. 1992. Euripides' Iphigenia among the Taurians: Aetiology, Ritual, and Myth. *ClAnt* 11: 308–34.

Wright, D. P. 1987. *The Disposal of Impurity: Elimination Rites in the Bible and in Hittite and Mesopotamian Literature.* Atlanta.

Wright, G. R. H. 1957. Cyrene: Survey of Rock-Cut Features of Sanctuary of Apollo. *JHS* 77: 307–10.

Wycherley, R. E. 1960. Nelion. *ABSA* 55: 60–66.

Zeitlin, F. I. 1982. Cultic Models of the Female: Rites of Dionysos and Demeter. *Arethusa* 15: 129–57.

———. 1989. Mysteries of Identity and Designs of the Self in Euripides' *Ion*. *PCPS* 35: 144–97.

———. 1990. Patterns of Gender in Aeschylean Drama: *Seven Against Thebes* and the Danaid Trilogy. In *Cabinet of the Muses: Essays on Classical and Comparative Literature in Honor of Thomas G. Rosenmeyer*, edited by M. Griffith and D. Mastronarde, 103–15. Atlanta.

Ziebarth, E. 1892. *De iureiurando in iure graeco quaestiones*. Göttingen.

Index

Compositor: G&S Typesetters, Inc.
Text: General, 10/13 Aldus; Greek, Porson
Display: Aldus
Printer and binder: Freisens Corporation